S0-BZX-859

Bourdieu: Critical Perspectives

Bourdieu: Critical Perspectives

Edited by
Craig Calhoun, Edward LiPuma and Moishe Postone

The University of Chicago Press

CRAIG CALHOUN teaches sociology at the University of North Carolina at Chapel Hill; EDWARD LI PUMA teaches anthropology at the University of Miami; and MOISHE POSTONE teaches sociology at the University of Chicago.

The University of Chicago Press, Chicago 60637
Polity Press in association with Blackwell Publishers

Copyright © This collection Polity Press 1993
Written in association with the Center for Psychosocial Studies
Each individual chapter © the author
All rights reserved. Published 1993
Printed in Great Britain
02 01 00 99 98 97 96 95 94 93   1 2 3 4 5
ISBN: 0–226–09092–2 (cloth); 0–226–09093–0 (paper)

Cataloging–in–publication data are available from the Library of Congress, Washington, DC 20540.

This book is printed on acid-free paper

Contents

The Authors

Pierre Bourdieu is Professor of Sociology at the Collège de France and Director of the Centre de Sociologie Europénne.

Rogers Brubaker is Associate Professor of Sociology at the University of California, Los Angeles.

Craig Calhoun is Professor of Sociology and History at the University of North Carolina at Chapel Hill.

Aaron V. Cicourel is Professor of Sociology at the University of California, San Diego.

James Collins is Associate Professor of Anthropology and Reading at the State University of New York, Albany.

Hubert Dreyfus is Professor of Philosophy at the University of California, Berkeley.

Nicholas Garnham is Professor of Communications at the University of Westminster.

William F. Hanks is Associate Professor of Anthropology at the University of Chicago.

Beate Krais is a Research Scientist at the Max Planck Institute for Human Development and Education, Berlin.

Scott Lash is Senior Lecturer in Sociology at Lancaster University.

Edward LiPuma is Associate Professor of Anthropology at the University of Miami.

Moishe Postone is Associate Professor of Sociology at the University of Chicago.

Paul Rabinow is Professor of Anthropology at the University of California, Berkeley.

Charles Taylor is Professor of Philosophy at McGill University.

Loïc J. D. Wacquant is a Junior Fellow at the Society of Fellows, Harvard University.

Acknowledgments

This book grew out of the work of the Social Theory group formed in 1983 at the Center for Psychosocial Studies in Chicago. The editors were all involved in a series of readings and discussions of Bourdieu's work undertaken by the group during the 1980s. Professor Bourdieu joined in these discussions on two occasions, including the conference held between 31 March and 2 April 1989 which led to this book.

A number of people who are not represented as authors nonetheless contributed to the conference and to this book in significant ways. They include especially Bernard Weissbourd and Benjamin Lee (the Chairman and Director, respectively, of the Center for Psychosocial Studies), John Lucy, Lee Schlesinger, David Stark, David Swartz, and Ivan Szelenyi. Elvia Alvarez made major contributions to the success of the project through her tireless administrative efforts. Leah Florence helped a great deal to edit the manuscripts. The index was compiled by Laura Brousseau. By listing our names in inverse order on the title page and the opening page of the Introduction, we hope to signal that this book has been a fully collaborative effort.

Introduction: Bourdieu and Social Theory

Moishe Postone, Edward LiPuma, and Craig Calhoun

Long a dominant figure in French social science, Pierre Bourdieu is increasingly influential internationally. In a series of research projects and publications starting in the 1950s, Bourdieu has addressed an astonishing range of empirical topics and theoretical themes. He has published important works on education, labor, kinship, economic change, language, philosophy, literature, photography, museums, universities, law, religion, and science. He has been a major figure in the development of "practice" as an organizing concept in social research, has emerged as perhaps the foremost contemporary advocate of "reflexive" social science, and has contributed centrally to the attempt to overcome such ubiquitous theoretical oppositions as subjective/object-ive, culture/society and structure/action (introducing the term "struc-turation" among many others today in common usage). Throughout all this work, Bourdieu has developed and continues to refine a distinctive approach to the production of sociological knowledge, one which among other things unites profound theoretical knowledge and reflection with the constant challenge of empirical research and analysis.

The essays presented in this volume reflect an encounter between the theoretical practice of Pierre Bourdieu and several strands in interdis-ciplinary Anglo-American social theory. They set out the essential contours of Bourdieu's project, locate his analytical concepts within the wider arena of social theory, and suggest some of the issues involved in conceptualizing determinate aspects of social life by means of those concepts.

The individual analyses take up these issues along three intersecting lines. The first is the relationship between social structure and practice.

Of critical importance here is Bourdieu's attempt to transcend the gap between the subjective and objective dimensions of social life, which he understands as a gap between embodied, practical knowledge and apparently objective structures which are amenable to theoretical understanding. The second line of inquiry seeks to delineate and clarify Bourdieu's conception of reflexivity, as well as his central concepts of habitus, capital, and field. The third line of inquiry concerns the interrelationship of social structure, systems of classification, and language. Throughout, the contributors analyze how Bourdieu's attempt to move beyond existing theories and develop a new conceptual apparatus engages central issues of social theory and method.

The essays are self-contained; yet because they are joined by constant references to Bourdieu's work, a brief introduction to his theoretical project and a few of its essential concepts may be helpful.

Born in 1930 in the Béarn, the son of a village postman, Bourdieu completed his studies at the École normale supérieure in Paris. Schooled as an anthropologist within the structuralist tradition then dominant, he conducted field work in Algeria. A good part of his research was done during the Algerian war against French colonial rule – an experience that impressed upon Bourdieu the mutual relationship of science, social reflection, and politics. On returning to France, he received a post at the University of Lille, where he composed his early essays on Algeria and initiated a series of new studies, including research into his own native Béarnoise community and popular French culture. During this same period, he was associated with Erving Goffman as a visiting scholar at the Institute for Advanced Study and the University of Pennsylvania. Following the success of his early studies, Bourdieu was awarded a post at the École des hautes études en sciences sociales in Paris, where he was later appointed director of his own research group at the Center for European Sociology. At that Center he initiated the journal *Actes de la recherche en sciences sociales* which, since 1975, has been a primary forum for the publication of his research and that of his co-workers.

Early in his career, still influenced by structuralism, Bourdieu began a theoretical study in which he tried to develop a "general theory of culture" from a Saussurian standpoint. As he critically rethought Saussure's presuppositions – in particular the notion that culture and *langue* stand in opposition to practice and *parole* – he abandoned that project and began to work toward a new sort of theory, a theory of cultural practice. He came to the conclusion that such a theory could be developed only if the analyst were able to transcend inherited oppositions and dichotomies and the limitations of vision they always entail.

Bourdieu's attempts to formulate such an unorthodox theoretical approach have been paralleled institutionally by his efforts to locate and secure a social space that is not identified exclusively with any particular academic discipline. It is only from such a position that Bourdieu feels he can generate a critique of classical social theory.

For Bourdieu, classical social theory is characterized by an opposition between subjectivist and objectivist approaches. Subjectivist viewpoints have as their center of gravity the beliefs, desires, and judgments of agents and consider these agents endowed and empowered to make the world and act according to their own lights. By contrast, objectivist views explain social thought and action in terms of material and economic conditions, social structures, or cultural logics. These are seen as superordinate to, and more powerful than, agents' symbolic constructions, experiences, and actions.

In two of his most significant books, *Outline of a Theory of Practice* and *The Logic of Practice*,[1] Bourdieu explores the ways in which objectivism (especially structuralism) depends on understandings and orientations it does not make explicit even to itself and how a version of subjectivism (associated with Sartre, but also, more generally, with phenomenological approaches) neglects to explore adequately the objective social conditions that produce subjective orientations to action. Neither of these positions can adequately grasp social life. Social life, Bourdieu argues, must be understood in terms that do justice both to objective material, social, and cultural structures and to the constituting practices and experiences of individuals and groups.

A related opposition which Bourdieu seeks to overcome in many of his writings is that between theoretical knowledge of the social world as constructed by outside observers and the knowledge used by those who possess a practical mastery of their world. He attempts to accord validity to native conceptions without simply taking those conceptions at face value.

Finally, in attempting to transcend the opposition between science and its object, Bourdieu treats science and scientists as part and product of their social universe. The scientific field can lay claim to no special privilege as against other fields; it too is structured by forces in terms of which agents struggle to improve their positions. Science seeks to analyze the contribution of agents' conceptions to the construction of social reality, while recognizing that those conceptions frequently misrecognize that social reality. By the same token, scientists' constructions of their own reality – the scientific field and the motivations for scientific behavior – often misrecognize that reality. Consequently, it is essential to advance and endorse a reflexive science of society.

Bourdieu's project, then, can be described generally as an ongoing attempt to overcome theoretically the oppositions that have characterized social theory and to formulate a reflexive approach to social life. Three fundamental concepts lie at the heart of this project: "habitus," "capital," and "field."

The notion of *habitus* is central to Bourdieu's theory of practice, which seeks to transcend the opposition between theories that grasp practice solely as constitut*ing*, as expressed in methodological and ontological individualism (phenomenology), and those that view practice solely as constitut*ed*, as exemplified by Lévi-Strauss's structuralism and the structural functionalism of the descendants of Durkheim. To this end, Bourdieu treats social life as a mutually constituting interaction of structures, dispositions, and actions whereby social structures and embodied (therefore situated) knowledge of those structures produce enduring orientations to action which, in turn, are constitutive of social structures. Hence, these orientations are at once "structuring structures" and "structured structures"; they shape and are shaped by social practice. Practice, however, does not follow directly from orientations, in the manner of attitude studies, but rather results from a process of improvisation that, in turn, is structured by cultural orientations, personal trajectories, and the ability to play the game of social interaction.

This capacity for structured improvisation is what Bourdieu terms the "habitus" (a term that he, like Norbert Elias, reconstituted from classical scholarship). Bourdieu characterizes the habitus as a system of general generative schemes that are both durable (inscribed in the social construction of the self) and transposable (from one field to another), function on an unconscious plane, and take place within a structured space of possibilities (defined by the intersection of material conditions and fields of operation). The habitus is at once intersubjective and the site of the constitution of the person-in-action; it is a system of dispositions that is both objective and subjective. So conceived, the habitus is the dynamic intersection of structure and action, society and the individual. The notion of the habitus enables Bourdieu to analyze the behavior of agents as objectively coordinated and regular without being the product of rules, on the one hand, or conscious rationality, on the other. It is meant to capture the practical mastery that people have of their social situation, while grounding that mastery itself socially.

Bourdieu's notion of *capital*, which is neither Marxian nor formal economic, entails the capacity to exercise control over one's own future and that of others. As such, it is a form of power. This notion of capital also serves to theoretically mediate individual and society. On one level, society is structured by the differential distribution of capital, according to Bourdieu. On another level, individuals strive to maximize their capital. (This does not mean that they have a transitive preference ordering which they seek to maximize. Rather, unaware of some true possibilities, unable to take full advantage or conceive of other possibilities due to their class habitus, agents nonetheless seek to maximize benefits, given their relational position within a field.) The capital they are able to accumulate defines their social trajectory (that is, their life chances); moreover, it also serves to reproduce class distinctions.

Much of Bourdieu's work focuses on the interplay among what he distinguishes as social, cultural, and economic capital. Economic capital is the most efficient form of capital; a characterizing trait of capitalism, it alone can be conveyed in the guise of general, anonymous, all-purpose, convertible money from one generation to the next. Economic capital can be more easily and efficiently converted into symbolic (that is, social and cultural) capital than vice versa, although symbolic capital can ultimately be transformed into economic capital. In this way, Bourdieu appropriates Marx and places class at the center of his analysis of modern society in a manner that allows for a material determination of culture and history.

Although the economic is crucially determining, it must be symbolically mediated. The undisguised reproduction of economic capital would reveal the arbitrary character of the distribution of power and wealth. Symbolic capital functions to mask the economic domination of the dominant class and socially legitimate hierarchy by essentializing and naturalizing social position. That is, noneconomic fields articulate with, reproduce, and legitimate class relations through misrecognition. Class and status, emphatically separated by Weber, are interrelated according to Bourdieu.

The purpose of Bourdieu's concept of *field* is to provide the frame for a "relational analysis," by which he means an account of the multidimensional space of positions and the position taking of agents. The position of a particular agent is the result of an interplay between that person's habitus and his or her place in a field of positions as defined by the distribution of the appropriate form of capital. The nature and range of possible positions varies socially and historically.

Each field is semi-autonomous, characterized by its own determinate agents (for example, students, novelists, scientists), its own accumulation of history, its own logic of action, and its own forms of capital. The fields are not fully autonomous, however. Capital rewards gained in one field may be transferred to another. Moreover, each field is immersed in an institutional field of power and, even more broadly, in the field of class relations. Each field is the site of struggles. That is, there are struggles within given fields, and there are struggles over the power to define a field. The constitution of different forms of capital and their convertibility in various fields of activity become central themes for research.

Bourdieu interrelates the three central concepts we have outlined. He conceives of social practice in terms of the relationship between class habitus and current capital as realized within the specific logic of a given field. An agent's capital is itself the product of the habitus, just as the specificity of a field is an objectified history that embodies the habitus of agents who have operated in that field. The habitus is self-reflexive in that, each time it is animated in practice, it encounters itself both as embodied and as objectified history.

On the basis of these three concepts, Bourdieu has attempted to formulate a reflexive approach to social life that uncovers the arbitrary conditions of the production of the social structure and of those dispositions and attitudes that are related to it. Such an approach is tied to a notion of emancipation. For Bourdieu, the study of human lives would not be worth the trouble if it did not help agents to grasp the meaning of their actions. His approach seeks to illuminate the social and cultural reproduction of inequality by analyzing processes of misrecognition: that is, by investigating how the habitus of dominated groups can veil the conditions of their subordination. Bourdieu has pursued this theme in his accounts of knowledge and its transmission (via the educational system), in his analyses of the social constitution of distinction, and in his treatments of symbolic violence.

His approach is necessarily reflexive. He is aware that there is no point outside the system from which one can gain a neutral, disinterested perspective. As a theorist of society Bourdieu necessarily operates within what he analyzes; he is both an analyst of science and society, and an actor in these fields. Bourdieu's reflections on his own project and position taking draw attention to various problems involved in the quest for a reflexive perspective. Nevertheless, as he clearly indicates, reflexivity is a condition of any critical social theory that attempts to overcome the dualisms characteristic of modern social thought. It is this, in part, that has led Bourdieu in recent years to undertake a massive study of the conditions of production of academic knowledge, technical expertise, and bureaucratic power in contemporary France.

In the mid–1970s, Bourdieu's major writings began to be translated into English. The timing was not coincidental. At about that time, Bourdieu had achieved a central position in the French academic world and was beginning to broaden his influence through teaching and the creation of the Center for European Sociology at the École des hautes études en sciences sociales in Paris. Also at about the same time, a new generation of scholars in Anglo-American universities were searching generally for new orientations in the aftermath of the ruptures of the late 1960s. In particular, many began to explore the contributions of French social theory beyond the enormously influential writings of Sartre, Lévi-Strauss, and Althusser. Bourdieu, Michel Foucault, and Jacques Derrida were appropriated along with others of their generation as part of a wave of thinkers whose work succeeded structuralism (as structuralism had succeeded existentialism).

One effect of translation, as simply of the passage of time, is to tear works from their original intellectual contexts and insert them in new ones. The negative effects of this process are particularly evident in the case of Bourdieu. In particular, the unity of Bourdieu's work, its development of a distinctive method of intellectual production employed in a series of studies of seemingly diverse empirical topics, was generally lost. This loss was encouraged by the fact that Anglo-American academia did not have an interdisciplinary field comparable to "the human sciences" in France. Books that sat next to each other on the shelves labeled "Sciences humaines" in Paris were dispersed to seemingly self-contained displays of books on anthropology, sociology, philosophy, and education (at a minimum) in the bookstores of Oxford, Berkeley, and Chicago. In the mid–1970s, Bourdieu was known to anthropologists and Middle Eastern scholars for a series of elegant structuralist analyses, perhaps most famously his study of the Kabyle house[2] and his short ethnography, *Algeria 1960*.[3] Bourdieu's collaboration with Jean-Claude Passeron, *Reproduction in Education, Culture and Society*, next established him as a "stratification theorist" in sociology and a "reproduction theorist" in education.[4] This was hardly ever linked to his work on Algeria. When *Outline of a Theory of Practice* appeared in English in 1977, it was widely read by anthropologists, but initially all but ignored by sociologists. As Loïc Wacquant shows in this volume, fragmented readings of this sort have continued to dog the English-language reception of Bourdieu's work.

Equally problematic was that many Anglo-American readers were slow to appreciate the organization of French intellectual discourse that produced the antinomies Bourdieu sought to overcome and gave the resources he employed their specific value. As a result, they did not always appreciate how Bourdieu was positioning himself in the intellectual field. For example, when Bourdieu was a student, French intellectual life was dominated by a seemingly binary choice between the towering figures of Lévi-Strauss and Sartre. Although Bourdieu was initially attracted more to Lévi-Straussian structuralism, which shaped his work immensely, he began relatively early to challenge the neo-Kantian certainties of structuralism (as did Foucault and Derrida in different ways and in other parts of the intellectual field). Bourdieu's challenge drew on both Marxism and phenomenology. Though shaped by the opposition he found between subjectivism/existentialism and objectivism/structuralism, his attempt to develop a theory of practice is intended to overcome such dichotomies rather than claim a position within them.

Bourdieu's use of a largely Anglo-American language of strategies is a case in point. We have noted that he developed the notion of the habitus for the purpose of escaping the dualism of objectivist and subjectivist views. The improvisations of the habitus are not merely responses to environmental stimuli, according to Bourdieu. They are moments in strategies – which do not merely express the subjective intentions of the individual actors but are structurally grounded. They are strategies of what Bourdieu termed the "accumulation of capital". To elaborate this idea, Bourdieu drew on Wittgensteinian and Austinian ideas about language use as social action and the Anglo-American discourse of strategic action, especially the vocabulary of economic maximization. This terminology allowed Bourdieu to develop an approach opposed to existing positions in the French debate. However, it also laid the basis for problematic readings by Anglo-American scholars who were apt to understand Bourdieu's usage of these terms outside its context in French discourse, as though it monologically expressed the strategic rationalism of the Anglo-American – especially economistic – discourse.[5] And since, as Bourdieu himself argued, we can never treat language as an entirely neutral object of our manipulation, he has sometimes been drawn by this language further in the direction of a purely strategic, calculating, or rationalistic analysis than he may himself have wanted. In the last few years he has found it necessary to issue more straightforward rejections of rational choice perspectives.[6]

Several essays in this volume take up the set of themes linked to Bourdieu's notion of the habitus and his account of practical reason. Hubert Dreyfus and Paul Rabinow situate Bourdieu in the tradition of phenomenology and existentialism: with his central concept of habitus, he fruitfully develops and socially specifies general ideas advanced by

Merleau-Ponty and Heidegger about the universal structure of being in the world that characterizes humans. They suggest, however, that by attributing a universal meaning to human action (the maximization of symbolic capital), Bourdieu extends objective description to areas requiring an interpretive approach, in a way that introduces serious tensions into his work. Aaron Cicourel explores the way in which Bourdieu's notion of habitus responds to the opposition between structural and processual theories of knowledge and social practice, arguing that it provides a powerful conceptual tool for overcoming this theoretical opposition and for examining domination as everyday practice. Nevertheless, according to Cicourel, the notion of habitus could be further clarified and expanded by conceptual refinements and empirical studies – particularly with regard to language socialization and the ways in which children acquire their understandings of power. Charles Taylor explores Bourdieu's extension of Wittgenstein and his use of insights from the phenomenological tradition to develop an account of practical understanding which must be seen as embodied and must challenge the division of mind (creator of goals) and body (executor of goals) endemic to so much Western thought. Craig Calhoun asks how specific to Western (or modern) practice is some of Bordieu's critical account, and he argues that the habitus, strategic action, and capital accumulation must work differently where large, internally highly differentiated societies join relatively autonomous social fields into heterogeneous structures. Edward LiPuma argues that, by not articulating a developed notion of the symbolic order, Bourdieu introduces tensions into his effort to create a reflexive social theory. Nevertheless, although Bourdieu's project does not fully do justice to the anthropological concept of culture, it could fruitfully inform, and be informed by, that concept.

It is no accident that Bourdieu's critique of subjectivism and objectivism in *The Logic of Practice* appears under the title "critique of theoretical reason," signifying both a general challenge to theoretical systematization and a specific tension with Sartre. Bourdieu has always resisted what he sees as the rigidifying, repressive side of abstract theorization. He has been sharply critical of "theoretical theorists" who try to build abstract synthetic systems and who do not work through engagement with actual empirical analysis but through abstract arguments with each other. In this sense, despite the impressive redirections of social theory that he has produced, he has resisted being labeled a theorist. Rogers Brubaker suggests in his essay that it may be better to view Bourdieu as exemplifying a certain theoretical habitus as he produces a series of cognate empirical analyses rather than to attempt to

pull concepts and propositions from their analytic (and often oppositional, strategic) contexts of use. At the same time, Calhoun suggests that
the rejection of the label "theorist" is itself a situated, strategic choice and
that from other vantage points Bourdieu has more in common with the
tradition of critical theory than his own public self-identification would
indicate.

From their earliest beginnings, Bourdieu's analyses of social practices
were intended to elucidate the workings of social power and offer a
critical, not just a neutral, understanding of social life. Bourdieu's
analyses are critical in a variety of ways. They range from an account of
exploitative conditions of labor in colonial Algeria (especially in *Travail
et travailleurs en Algérie*[7]) to a critique of the existing categories of
knowledge. One of the major contributions of *Outline* and other works
of the 1960s and 1970s was to develop an account of symbolic violence.
Bourdieu showed the ways in which naming was a matter of force, for
example, and in which the production of certain categories of understanding determined and supported relations of domination. Beate Krais
takes up this thread of Bourdieu's argument in her essay and develops it
in relation to gender, a theme relatively neglected in his own work.

Bourdieu's critique of received categories of analysis has led to
investigations of the way language is used and the role of educational
institutions in reproducing such categories and the social hierarchies they
support. He has developed this critique in a variety of works, including
Reproduction in Education, Culture and Society and *Homo Academicus*.[8]
The latter is an attempt to reveal the ways in which the underlying
structures of intellectual habitus and institutions shape the content as
well as the social organization of academic production. This critique is of
immediate practical relevance for French society, as is that of the
production of expertise in Bourdieu's study of the "grandes écoles," *La
noblesse d'État*.[9]

In the present volume, James Collins considers together Bourdieu's
writings on language and education, which are too often read separately.
He shows in both the workings of reproduction, the theme which has
often dominated, and also discusses the ways in which contradictions
open up possibilities for creative action and social change. William
Hanks, by contrast, identifies a gap in Bourdieu's account of language
and in practice-oriented studies of language usage in general. In such
approaches, semantics, the way in which language produces meaningful
content, is generally bracketed in favor of accounts of its social use.
Hanks argues that the syntax and semantics of a language are intrinsically
related to its practical use; thus an analysis of practical use is not
antithetical to an analysis of "meaning."

Several senses of critique come together in Bourdieu's extraordinary study of French taste cultures, *Distinction*.[10] Here Bourdieu offers a critique of received cultural categories and hierarchies, including an argument that the dynamics governing elite and popular tastes are not fundamentally different. This is in line with his broader effort to reveal the extent to which existing cultural categories are linked to structures of domination and strategies of accumulation. *Distinction* is also a critique of the Kantian approach to aesthetics and the narrowing of academic attention that it implies. As both LiPuma and Wacquant show, however, the work has been read without attention to Bourdieu's broader theory, as a one-sidedly structuralist account of patterns of taste. It has also, to some extent, been squeezed into the genre of sociological studies of popular culture and thereby deprived of its essential critical thrust. Ironically, in the Anglo-American context it is necessary to reaffirm the theoretical side of Bourdieu's work, even while in the French context he lays stress on its empirical basis. Without such a focus on theory (albeit not necessarily in the system-building sense), the critical moment of the empirical works tends to be lost.

One of the most distinctive features of Bourdieu's work, in any case, has always been his insistence on joining theoretical and empirical work in an indissoluble approach to analysis. This is yet another instance of his effort to overcome pernicious dichotomies. It is also part of Bourdieu's emphasis on the need to reconstitute the definition of objects of analysis as a crucial part of each research effort, rather than uncritically accept the common usage of either academic discourse or other constructions of social reality. Nonetheless, Cicourel has questioned whether Bourdieu is always sufficiently self-reflexive regarding the construction of his data and empirical accounts. He also suggests some ways in which addressing important empirical issues could contribute to overcoming the dichotomy between structural and processual approaches by enhancing Bourdieu's ideas of symbolic power and habitus.

In his essay, Nicholas Garnham points to a surprising absence in Bourdieu's work. For all of Bourdieu's studies of the organization and reproduction of culture, he has had remarkably little to say about the media, particularly modern electronic media. Garnham shows, however, that Bourdieu's categories can be useful for developing a critical theory that does not rely on a notion of the essential arbitrariness of cultural content but analyzes the social structural implications of television programming. This theme is continued in Scott Lash's chapter, where attention to the media is one strand in a broader analysis of how Bourdieu's work opens up an account of cultural change that is grounded in an economy of cultural production rather than relying on less theorized assertions about shifting contents.

In his concluding remarks, Bourdieu himself discusses the "intellectual mode of production" that characterizes his work. He addresses some potential sources of misunderstanding related to the international circulation of ideas and illustrates the importance of the specific mode and conditions of his own intellectual production with the example of his work on art. Finally, he offers a defense of his work against what he calls "theoreticist" readings and the claim that he develops a historical ontology.

One of the most difficult tasks in putting together this book has been to establish an order for the chapters. This is in part because Bourdieu's work resists a simple ordering of the priority of concepts or themes. It is, in a sense, necessary to have a relatively broad, multidimensional understanding of his work in order to approach any of its specific parts. We cannot, of course, provide that in this introduction. Nor would we pretend that this volume satisfies this need. We recognize, for example, that aesthetics – an important dimension of Bourdieu's writings, particularly on literature and the visual arts – is underrepresented. Neither have we tried to offer a sustained guide to Bourdieu's work. Such a guide may be found in one of several introductions now available or in press.[11] Bourdieu himself has now, together with Loïc Wacquant, produced a more comprehensive discussion of his work – in *An Invitation to Reflexive Sociology*.[12] What we think this volume does offer is an engagement with Bourdieu's work that is true to its multidimensional, multidisciplinary character and that relates several of Bourdieu's main themes and conceptual contributions to the discourses of social and cultural theory in the Anglo-American world.

NOTES

1 These two books overlap considerably; the second represents a reworking and extension of the first after the space of nearly a decade. Indeed, both are temporary syntheses of an analytic orientation which Bourdieu has been developing since the 1960s. Many of their themes were first introduced in various articles. The relatively late translation of *The Logic of Practice* (1990) makes it appear somewhat more distant from *Outline of a Theory of Practice* (1977) than it is. The title of the translation is also a somewhat unfortunate compromise, losing something of the sense of *Le Sens pratique*.
2 Known in English as "The Kabyle House or the World Reversed," appendix to *The Logic of Practice*. The original appeared in French in 1970.

3 Bourdieu 1979a.

4 Bourdieu and Passeron 1977.

5 It is symptomatic that American rational choice theorists initially read Bourdieu as something of a human capital theorist in the vein of Gary Becker. See James Coleman's Introduction to Pierre Bourdieu and James Coleman (eds), *Theory for a Changing Society* (Boulder, Colo.: Westview Press, 1991).

6 Bourdieu and Wacquant, 1992.

7 Bourdieu, *et al.* 1963.

8 Bourdieu and Passeron 1977, Bourdieu 1988b.

9 Bourdieu 1989c.

10 Bourdieu 1984.

11 See Derek Robbins, *The Work of Pierre Bourdieu* (Boulder, Colo.: Westview, 1991); Richard Harker, Cheleen Mahar, and Chris Wilkes, *An Introduction to the Works of Pierre Bourdieu: the practice of theory* (New York: St Martin's, 1990); and David Swartz, "Culture and Domination: the social theory of Pierre Bourdieu" in preparation.

12 Bourdieu and Wacquant 1992.

1

Culture and the Concept of Culture in a Theory of Practice

Edward LiPuma

THE QUESTION OF CULTURE

The key contribution of anthropology to the human sciences has been its development of a concept of culture. The anthropological understanding is that culture is a socially-historically specific, internally shaped symbolic system. Thus it is impossible to grasp culture by reducing it to praxis, social structure, or "basic human impulses" – like maximizing. The anthropological argument is that without a genuine, nonderivative concept of culture, the analysis of cultural concepts and categories degenerates into the illusion of historicism which thinks it can account for a cultural form simply by linking that form to its antecedent; the insufficiency of functionalism which must presume in advance a symbolic order[1] that it cannot account for and which, on the rebound, it then views as an expression of the social structure; or, worst of all, an economic determinism that invariably perceives culture as the afterthought of economic structures and praxis. Against these positions, much anthropology has tried to develop concepts of culture, class, and social structure that are meaning-focused, nonreductionistic, and adequately grounded – a theory with the power to illuminate their intrinsic relations without sacrificing their distinctive features. Bourdieu is of special importance here because his notions of capital, field, and symbolic power are nothing less than a theory of their interrelationship. In this frame, I use his writings on the production of culture to analyze his concept of culture in the anthropological sense. My aim is to thematize the issue of culture: its status, location, and structuring powers in Bourdieu's theory.

EPISTEMOLOGY AND METHODOLOGY

Bourdieu has said repeatedly that the production of scientific texts is a political act. Like all practices, scientific practice is animated by an economic logic working within the more specific logic of a given field. Within the field, scientific analyses are means of position seeking; beyond the field, they are the means by which an observer imposes an "objective" account of those observed upon them. Given this view, there is an epistemological moment in all his work. This is his attempt to define how a sociologist or ethnographer from a particular society, operating within the logic of the scientific field, uses a specific set of methods to produce a field text, which is then returned in transformed form to the society and scientific field that produced the scientist. In *Outline of a Theory of Practice*, his goal was to demonstrate how the social and epistemological "break" entailed in living in a foreign culture invites methods that overemphasize the observer's role, spawn field texts that cannot help but "totalize" and formalize practice, and finally, and destructively, return to the scientific field studies in which the *modus operandi* generating practices has been transformed into rules and models for behavior. By returning to French culture, Bourdieu all but eliminates this social and epistemological break. He and his research team are, after all, "native" informants. But now a new problem arises, in that the usual ethnographic methods, especially participant observation, cannot possibly encompass the diversity of French culture. Thus his objective becomes to use statistics ethnographically by avoiding and unmasking the reductionisms and ideological traps that undermine statistically based sociological studies.[2] In this light, Bourdieu's analyses of Algeria and French society, in concert with his reviews of the scientific field and academic institutions, are intended to drive home the concept that social position and position taking within science are inseparable from scientific knowledge (Bourdieu 1975). What Bourdieu has to say about culture and social structure is as applicable to science and his own project as it is to law or education or politics.

CULTURE AND SOCIAL STRUCTURE

Given the place, at once central and encompassed, of the notion of "field" in Bourdieu's theory and practice, an analysis of his work begins with his view of social structure. He has refined a three-tiered, hierarchical notion of social structure. The most specific level is that of the distinct fields, each with its own history, logic, and agents. These fields are located within a "field of power" defined with respect to the internal dynamics of a class. The differential distribution of power within a class, based on differential access of different fields to economic and/or symbolic power, maps unequal class fractions. Producers from the cultural field – having access to symbolic, as against economic, power – are the "dominated fraction of the dominant class." Last, the classes are located within the general field of class relations and struggles. Analysis of any specific field must, in Bourdieu's view, take account of its social structural hierarchy. This view of social structure tries to link class and status, relate both to action and practice through the habitus, and provide an account of the reproduction of hierarchy.

Bourdieu holds a particular view of the relationship of the social structure to the cultural order and to individual action. His view, based on his reading of modern society, is that there exists an "almost perfect homology" between the structures of culture and those of social organization (in a broad sense). So he feels free to bypass an analysis of the structure of cultural categories and classification systems and their relationship to the social structure. By a similar logic, he sees no reason to analyze how social structure informs the reproduction of these categories and classifications. The homology surfaces in the way in which cultural categories and social groups, such as artist and groups of artists, are treated as the same entity (Bourdieu 1983a). It surfaces in the way that the social field is equated with the cultural order: thus Bourdieu claims that his notion of the semi-autonomous field endowed with its own logic and history can account for the cultural order (pp. 314–15). Because the homology between cultural and social orders works in both directions, an adequate account of cultural production need not analyze the structure of the state and its role in the social reproduction of categories, classifications, and symbolic schemes.

Between the social structure and agents there is a high degree of correspondence, mediated and generated by the habitus. It is through the dispositions inculcated in the habitus as these unfold in the structured space of possibility that the relationship of individuals to a social structure is objectively coordinated. The theory posits a close fit between cultural constructs, social structures, and agents' actions. The possibility of historical change rests in the limited conjuncture between a social structure and the actions of agents as mediated by the habitus – never between the cultural order and social structure. Social reproduction thus approximates historical change. The "field of struggle" within a relational analysis appears as, and is defined by, the strategies that occupants of distinct positions within a given field create (based on their total knowledge, interests, and experiences, which extend beyond that field) and implement in order to "defend or improve their positions" (1983a: 313). Even more, the force and form of a strategy derives from the position which an agent already occupies in the field of forces (ibid.). Selection and use of a given cultural concept (individualism), symbol (flag), or social category (women) will depend on its perceived instrumental value, and the efficacy of use will depend on the relational position of agents. Change in the cultural order will always be a step behind, but harmonious with, the positions and position taking at the level of social relations. So Bourdieu writes that the invention of cultural categories/genres, like the society novel, was a product of the distribution of capital within the literary field and the way in which writers sought to win income, prestige, and other profits by the strategic act of creating a new form of novel (p. 312).

THE ARBITRARINESS OF CULTURE

To develop his concept of cultural capital and the analysis of how it functions within the social system, Bourdieu must employ an extended notion of the arbitrariness of symbols. Though the notion is not developed or explained in any of his works, it nevertheless appears in three senses. The first is that a particular, specific cultural form or practice, such as the use of figurative art in ritual, is arbitrary from a cross-cultural standpoint. While there may be some cultural universals, this sense of arbitrariness is not controversial: much ethnography shows that there exists no *a priori* cross-cultural linkage between a sign vehicle and its meaning. The theory also rests on a second claim: namely, that there is formal arbitrariness within a culture. For instance, inequality in wealth leads to relations of domination and hierarchy, symbolically expressed and socially reproduced through the high, but arbitrary, valuation of upper-class culture. There is no intrinsic *a priori* reason why a certain accent or aesthetic judgment is upper class and another working class or why agents should consider an upper-class accent and taste indicative of higher culture. Although this view upsets bourgeois art theory, it is a main argument in *Distinction* and is consistent with an anthropological concept of culture. But Bourdieu further holds – and this is the critical point – an absolute substantive theory of arbitrariness. The claim is that cultural contents and practices are *historically* arbitrary. Any accent, aesthetic judgment, or philosophical text could have served the same function within the historical evolution of bourgeois distinctions. This third sense of arbitrariness is methodologically critical: it says that a "relational analysis" of social fields need not analyze the structural history of symbolic valuation or the cultural order. There is no theoretical cause to show why specific cultural forms – an accent, artwork, or philosophy – should be singled out or motivated and why they should always appear with a determinate content, as a Parisian accent, a taste for Goya prints, or Kant's Third Critique. On this point there is a telling difference between *Outline* and Bourdieu's studies on France, insofar as *Outline* gave a structural and cultural account of the categories and oppositions of Kabyle society.[3]

BOURDIEU'S CONCEPT OF CULTURE

The cultural/symbolic order runs parallel to the social structure in the sense that it is an independent domain that is derived from, though not reducible to, its role in expressing, reproducing, and legitimizing social structural relations within specific fields. Because culture is "relational," there exists a "space of symbolic stances"[4] which is independent of, yet homologous to, "the space of social positions." When agents classify talking (as when a speech pattern is said to be bourgeois), they take a position in social space through position taking in symbolic space. In Bourdieu's theory, the symbolic system cannot be reduced to, or viewed as simply reflective of, the social structure, because the symbolic orders are specific to given fields. The symbolic order/logic of the artistic field, for example, is the inversion of that of the economic. The analytical project is to reveal the way in which symbolic oppositions express, and can be mobilized within, a given field.

This view of the symbolic order, and thus the constituting capacity of culture, defines the study of cultural production. What a society considers creative is a product of positioning; simultaneously, the acts and instances of positioning itself, its value in the field of cultural production, are determined by its autonomy or perceived creativity. Position defines creativity, while creativity defines the value of any instance of position taking – whether in the theory it is closer to the autonomous or the heteronomous pole. Creativity is defined dialectically in terms of how culturally ascribed attributes of creativity are valued and valorized in relation to social positions that creativity is partly responsible for creating. The claim is that, because the artistic field of cultural production is inseparable from social structure (that is, practical structure) and the two line up in an "almost perfect homology" (Bourdieu 1983a: 326), it is unnecessary to analyze the cultural concepts of cultural production apart from their relationship to social structure. Of relevance is how one artist uses a claim to creativity to take a position in relation to another; how literary agents, managers, and museums use creativity to sell their product on the economic market which they, of course, help to create; and how creative productions become tools of class domination, not least through their ability to impose a definition of what is creative, a wholly arbitrary definition that appears in misrecognized form as an ahistorical and disinterested definition. So the texts on cultural production analyze creativity solely in terms of the way it functions. The idea of homology and the corollary view that a symbolic system is defined relationally award priority to the social over the symbolic order.

Another way of understanding Bourdieu's view of the character of structures which lie outside social structure is to examine his sociology of the language of art. He notes that the influence of art history and criticism is a function of the way in which its linguistic distinctiveness – the high-sounding words light-years away from ordinary speaking – are linked to the structured system of social differences, or classes. This characterization exemplifies his general linguistic theory, which holds that linguistic norms can be appreciated only as a product of, and a means for reproducing, specific historical and political relations. The language of art history and criticism is part and product of a "linguistic market" which functions to (a) redistribute capital within an artistic field through agents' strategies, (b) continually reestablish an orthodoxy in a field whose logic encourages heterodoxy, and (c) express and reproduce class hierarchy. That the working class finds itself at "a loss for words" when trying to describe abstract art presupposes, in a highly misrecognized way, its recognition of the legitmacy of the dominant way of talking about art. Hence, Bourdieu's thesis that because communication occurs within the framework of linguistic inequality, the structure of speech is determined not by language, but by the social conditions under which agents use language to position themselves in a field. Because langauge is treated like any other field, albiet with its own specific logic, its use is organized by the social structures which encompass it. The result is that reference is conceptualized as a residual category. Like the internal structure of cultural concepts or classification schemes, the structure of a language's grammar is thought to be inconsequential to the social use of language. The question posed by a pragmatic of language and culture is whether it is legitimate for Bourdieu to identify the linguistic norms that characterize a speech community with the institutions and ideology of standardization. I would suggest that social institutions, based on an ideology of language, valorize and elevate certain speech forms and behaviors while demoting others. The majority report from the field of language and culture is that linguistic norms are informed by, but never reducible to, social structural forms. Though it is true that speakers use language to position themselves in a social field and that language, because it is omnipresent and internalized at a nonconscious level, is central to all forms of domination and that language use is inseparable from the field of power, it is equally true that all these social uses are defined, inflected, and delimited by the grammar. In sum, we might characterize Bourdieu's theory of culture as a kind of cultural functionalism.[5]

Because "symbolic production is a microcosm of the struggle between the classes" and using symbols to take a position in space "reproduces in a transfigured form the field of social positions" (1979b: 81), the issue is not the character of cultural symbols and categories, but their use as instruments of power – symbolic power. To insist that culture and language are "instruments of power is to make the point that they are *subordinated* to practical [social structural] functions and that the coherence which characterizes them is that of practical logic"; that they are "quasi-systematizations whose orientation is guided by ethical and political dispositions" (p. 82, my emphasis). The symbolic order "owes its structure" to the social conditions of its production and circulation, and its particular "force" to the fact that the power relations which it expresses are manifest "in the misrecognizable form of relations of meaning" (ibid.). The conclusion is that the essence of symbolic power does not inhere in the symbolic order itself but in the form and relation between levels of social structure.[6] Symbolic power is extrinsically related to the cultural/symbolic order.

The theory wants to treat apparently disinterested practices, such as those of the field of cultural production, as economic practices intended to maximize symbolic profits and power. What is unspecified is why symbols should be able to generate such power and profits. The functional reply, that apparently disinterested practices and symbolic constructs are more efficient in reproducing class hierarchy because their effects are misrecognized, begs the question as to why the symbols or what counts as profit is always historically/culturally specific. What is unspecified is the relationship between what social things mean to people and the power they exert over them. For example, the rising bourgeoisie in Spain collect works by Goya to augment their symbolic power and profits; but structurally and consciously this power and profit are directly tied to the place of Goya in the Spanish imagination (LiPuma and Meltzoff 1989). Works by an American artist, even one as famous as Winslow Homer, would have nowhere near the same effect. Thus, Bourdieu's theory must use efficiency as a cross-cultural, trans-historical category to account for symbolic capital, profit, or power, even as it must assume the reverse to generate any specific analysis, such as that of French culture in *Distinction*.

THE POSSIBILITY OF *DISTINCTION*

Recent social theory has emphasized the social conditions for the production of scientific knowledge and text. Bourdieu's own vision of the academic/intellectual field (1988b) raises the issue of the status and function of *Distinction* and his other works on cultural production as products of that field. If we follow his line of argument, then *Distinction* must be taken as a product of the intelligentsia whose effect is to reproduce the symbolic and material interests of the dominant class. But if *Distinction* is more than an example of class relations, if it creates a genuine critique of the cultural dimension of modern capitalism, how can we account for that? How can *Distinction* or any critique be both a product of capitalist society and transcend its ideological masks? If other sociologists, philosophers, and historians of art have ended up producing accounts which legitimate and reproduce class hierarchy, why and how can Bourdieu (or any reader of his texts) escape? What in the totalizing society that is capitalism are the conditions for the production and reception of a text?

The reply that a given scholar is intelligent and perceptive, however accurate, is inadequate. It displaces a social fact to the level of the individual, indulging in a kind of misrecognition that *Distinction* has warned us against (a warning whose roots go back to Durkheim's critique of individualistic explanations of suicide). To deal with the embeddedness of science in society, Bourdieu says that scientists *can* produce true knowledge if they make themselves aware (avoid the pitfalls of misrecognition) of their position within the field of producers of knowledge (1983a: 317). Writing about the artistic field, he notes that one's only hope of producing scientific knowledge – rather than weapons to advance a particular class of specific interests (for example, class interests) – is to make explicit to oneself one's position in the subfield of the producers of discourse about art and the contribution of this field (for example, science) to the very existence of the object of study (ibid.). Without doubting the virtue of self-awareness, the response leaves open the question of how individual awareness is socially possible. The theory of symbolic production in class-based societies does not seem to account for *Distinction* as a product of those societies. To move beyond this problem and account for itself, *Distinction* would require a theory of the structure of symbolic production and reproduction which takes it beyond the theory of how symbolic power functions in a specific field. *Distinction* would have to explain, rather than merely suggest, that in class-based society there is a dichotomy, or pulling apart, of the form and content of scientific works. It would have to show how the critical space between the form and the content of a work creates a contradiction that allows for internal critique and the inclusion of external knowledge (that is, insights gained from cross-cultural and historical research).

To account for *Distinction* and other works on cultural production and also preserve their critique of capitalism, it is necessary to shape something like the following argument. At the level of form, scientific works are of the commodity form. As such, they cannot help but have the function of defending, in a misrecognized fashion, the cultural and economic interests of the dominant class. Further, scientific works are created by members of the dominant class, and their terminology, style, and complexity are beyond the purview and powers of the working class, let alone the unemployed urban poor and the dispossessed. As products of capitalism, scientific products cannot help but express and reproduce class relations. At the level of content, however, science can offer a critique of the workings of capitalism – *Distinction* being an example of such a critique, its possibility at the content level being to bridge the gap between the appearance of capitalism and its reality. To ground his analysis, Bourdieu could (following Marx) give an account of the contradiction created by the commodity form: the space between form and content that allows *Distinction* to give a genuine critique of capitalism. Such an understanding might be further grounded in the concept that comparative cross-cultural and historical perspectives permit analysis to overcome the limits and limitations of categories imposed by the social and historical circumstances of their own origin as embodied in their class habitus. Taussig (1980:12), among others, notes that "it is not only that the study of other societies reveals the way in which they are influenced by ours, but also that such investigations provide us with some critical leverage with which to assess and understand the sacrosanct and unconscious assumptions that are built into and emerge from our social forms."

Though Bourdieu's comments on the genesis of scientific knowledge and practice support the possibility of genuine critique (for example, Bourdieu 1975; 1985c: 209), it is not apparent how the internal design and dynamics of the theory could handle it. The idea that culture is homologous to social structure and that the contents of the symbolic system are a function of distinction (historically arbitrary) means that there are no forms of knowledge and understanding that are not a product of position and position taking within a social field. For instance, one could argue that the notion of field as a symbolic product was created not because it offers a better way of grasping social systems, but because it allows its author to differentiate himself from other competing theorists or positions within the scientific field. We could argue further that the notion of "field" is being embraced by the scientific community not because of its scientific value, but because of the accumulated capital of its author and his "position in the structure of the distribution of this specific capital" (1983a: 312). As Bourdieu observes, strategies of symbolic production "which occupants of the different positions implement in their struggles to defend or improve their positions (i.e., their position-takings) . . . depend for their *force and form* on the position each agent occupies in the power relations" (ibid., my emphasis). The telling words are that the form of a social act and its force or influence on others are determined by the social structural position of its producer. Further, apprehending another's position turns on one's own position and position taking in that field. There is never the critical leverage to step outside the field of the fields of producers. Knowledge of the social order and the categorical forms for knowledge, like the social order itself, are relational. The theoretical outcome is such a strong claim for the indivisibility of knowledge and human interest, stronger even than that articulated by Habermas (1973), that it leads to a positional epistemology. What we can know of ourselves or our society depends entirely on our "orbit" within a field of forces.

The result is that although Bourdieu's work on culture is a genuine critique of capitalism which gets beyond the categories imposed by capitalism, it does not present a way for us to grasp (1) how capitalism can generate forms of thought which are not in its own interest and which do not reproduce class division (recognition of the misrecognized) and (2) the contents of the categories as sources of social understanding. The theory, in order to motivate a concept of field-internal struggle and position taking, imbues consensus and complicity with so much orchestrating power (recall the metaphor of the orchestra without a conductor) that there seems to be no room for a nonpositional epistemology or for the internal division of a social structure along racial or ethnic lines. So French ethnic groups such as Jews, Algerians, and Moroccans do not appear in *Distinction*. Where recent social theory has focused on the way in which regional identities, race, and ethnicity are critical to the cultural construction of culture, such forms have no voice in the theory of culture based on concepts of field, capital, and habitus. There is a certain irony here in that issues of regional, ethnic, and racial culture and the forces of the internationalization of culture which local entities are both being willingly encompassed by and (at another level) resisting have no place in the theory of cultural production (LiPuma and Meltzoff 1993).

Given the state of the theory, then, there does not appear to be a way to explain how society can produce individuals who, operating in specific fields (especially science and art), produce forms of thought that expose and threaten the reproduction of the class structure. Such thought is possible only when the symbolic order and linked fields have a structure and dynamic which are not reducible to, or a function of, the social system (that is, conserving hierarchy and distinction). The notion of struggle within fields and the observation that those who expose capitalism win cultural capital are the ideas that Bourdieu draws on here. They do not seem to explain, however, why the struggle takes a particular form or why that form is sociohistorically possible. It is unclear how to account for the possibility of the theory of cultural production within the limits of its notion of culture. As social theory would point out, *Distinction* the work is content with respect to the form of French culture and capitalism.

The issue of how individuals can forge critiques of their own society is inseparable from the role of the habitus in installing embodied dispositions and stances towards the world. The idea that Bourdieu draws on here is that the distribution of statistical probabilities of life chances for a given class is internalized via that habitus. The working class internalizes that its life chances are limited; that is, the objective probabilities at the systems level are subjectively internalized. Although the habitus appears at first glance to be a bridge between the social and the psychological, the system and the agents, it cannot make the connection because the relationship of individual agency to social classification is not developed. There is no account of why internalization of the habitus is relative, of why it permits some individuals to transcend their habitus (for example, Bourdieu himself), or of how it is inflected by classification schemes (of why groups having insider/outsider status tend to produce, as Simmel observed in his essay on the stranger, privileged social observers). In posing this question about the habitus, we have returned to the possibility of a critical theory of culture. To account for himself, Bourdieu needs an account of why the internalization of objective probabilities is socially relative, of how the internalization processes are organized along gender, ethnic, racial, and regional lines. A complementary way to address this issue would be to reveal the cultural construction of the individual and subjectivity. Note, however, that after describing individualism as a major element in Kabyle society, as realized in the disputes and negotiations about honor and prestige, *Outline* does not go on to offer an account of Kabyle individualism; rather, it takes this individualism as a cross-cultural constant which may then serve as a point of departure for analysis.

THE CATEGORIES OF CULTURE IN *DISTINCTION*

A pivotal aspect of Bourdieu's argument is that the character of reproduction in capitalist societies is different from that in traditional societies. In a traditional world, kinship maps and mediates the relationship between the system's reproduction and the practices of agents. Under capitalism, it is capital itself that mediates the relationship. In both forms of society, mediation is rooted in the habitus. However, there is a difference between the way in which Bourdieu articulates the issue in *Outline* and the way he does so in *Distinction*. *Outline* and the writings on the Kabyle portray kinship and marriage in cultural terms. They grasp a society's conceptual oppositions and hierarchies as a crucial aspect in the organization of social groups/relations and the structuring of its generative principles. In this view, concepts of kinship and kinship groups stand' between the practical actions of agents and social reproduction, because they are instrumental in producing the generative principles and schemes and are thus responsible for the regularity and coherence of social action. By contrast, *Distinction* describes capital, the mediating form, as resting on the distribution and possession of material assets – fundamentally on economic capital. The difference is that whereas kinship is nothing if not cultural, specific, and rooted in speech events – recall, for example, *Outline*'s powerful analysis of the Kabyle concepts and language of patrilateral parallel cousin marriage, "distance from necessity," the inequitable distribution of total resources (1977c: 30–3) – the material power to carry out "gratuitous" acts and impose arbitrary distinctions and the other notions by which *Distinction* portrays the "economic" (pp. 53–6) are abstract and general to any stratified society. Thus the cultural moment of the analysis and the construction of a symbolic order are much less apparent in *Distinction* than in *Outline*.

One way to frame the question is to ask where the categories found in *Distinction* and the other works on cultural production come from and how their internal order can be explained. Why should a cultural category such as the intelligentsia come into existence or an opposition be drawn between the public and private spheres or between men and women (and in particular, why should these cultural categories and oppositions be historically interwoven)? How did the different fields get to be culturally differentiated? Note that the very idea of an autonomous artistic field is foreign to most societies, as is the sharp divide between the social and economic. Why should symbolic distinctions such as distinguished/vulgar, rare/common, disinterested/interested be used rather than others (honor/dishonor in Kabyle society, saving face/shame in Japan). Why should these categories assume the specific hierarchical ordering that they do? Why is disinterested superior to interested, or rare better than common? Why should the ordering of categories be differentially distributed over distinctive fields? If symbolic systems are arbitrary and determined by material relations having their own economically specific logic, how can we account for the specific logic of the determinate fields? Especially, where do distinct types of capital – economic, social, artistic, and so forth – come from culturally? Are they just analytical categories? Are they cultural categories discovered by Bourdieu the native informant rather than Bourdieu the sociologist? Is this why, though they may be empirically and ethnographically accurate for French society, they are also unanalyzed, *Distinction* taking for granted what natives characteristically take for granted?

Reflection on the genesis of cultural categories also raises the question of the relationship between the categories embodied in the theory and the character of cross-cultural research. At issue is the scope or generality of the central concepts of field, capital, and habitus. The issue is whether these categories can, in their present form, be applied to all societies or whether the categories themselves are culturally specific. What needs to be further specified is where cultural and historical specificity enter the analysis. There seem to be three possibilities. The first is that the category forms are universal, although they vary in content. Every society would have an economic field, for example, though the goods and services produced and consumed are socially specific. The second is that the category forms themselves vary cross-culturally in terms of content and their interrelationship (between fields or between specific fields and capital forms). For example, the link between the political field and that of cultural production (for example, the function of the artist in the political field) would differ from one culture to the next. Third, the category forms could be historically and culturally specific. We could conceptualize a society in which there were no fields, types of capital, or perhaps even habitus. Bourdieu's view of culture leads him towards the first alternative, though in the more ethnographic parts of *Distinction*, where he relies on his own intimate knowledge of French society, he seems to lean towards the second alternative.

The functional account of culture rests on the understanding that a specific cultural product, such as a painting, a regional accent, a literary/scientific text, or an academic standard, is a historically "arbitrary [that is, unmotivated] convention." All that is necessary is that the specific cultural product create distinction as a means of expressing and reproducing relations of class inequality. The notion of arbitrariness essential to this functional notion of distinction mandates that meaning in culture, like reference in language, is a residual category. For what some act or words mean is not intrinsic to the effect they have of producing distinction. This view inflects the way that Bourdieu approaches the issue of legitimization, a major concern in his theory and in social theory generally. What is the mechanism by which the viewpoint of the dominant class is imposed? How does something defined as arbitrary – an accent or a concept of art – become the legitimate and dominant culture? The functional relationship between the social hierarchy and legitimate culture is evident: those atop the social hierarchy seek to impose their view of legitimate culture, and holders of legitimate culture use it to reinforce their perch atop the social hierarchy. What is unanalyzed is how this relationship can be constituted outside a theory of meaning. Its constitution is important, because the relationship of cultural reproduction to economic/political power varies cross-culturally and historically (the relationship between culture and social hierarchy in the old Hawaiian kingdom or Inca state is simply not that of any capitalist society). The notion of class distinction and hierarchy does not, in itself, elucidate why the dominant class can impose its will and interests on other classes or the relative distance between classes. Bourgeoisie and working class, for example, may over time stay distinct, yet move in closer and closer orbit (for example, as a result of universal suffrage and civil rights legislation).

By focusing on an example from the educational field, a field of special interest to Bourdieu, we can better grasp the power and consequences of the perspective. The example is the development of intelligence tests and testing in the United States in the early part of this century. There is now substantial evidence showing that the intelligence tests developed and scored by US educators in the 1920s were designed to prevent Jewish, Italian, Polish, and other "less-desirables" from migrating to the United States. The challenge for the tests' creators was to design intelligence tests that fit the canons of science (appeared neutral and impersonal), thus conferring legitimacy, while excluding prospective immigrants. Through this strategy, the IQ test-designers took a position in the scientific field that augmented both their scientific and their political capital. But designing such a test proved so difficult that though the test and testing procedures evolved in this direction, it was sometimes necessary to doctor the results (Gould 1981: 98). The institutional field of power in which the test-designers were located rewarded them for confirming that the immigrant groups were intellectually inferior to Americans of northern European ancestry. However, one of the debates of the period was whether the low-cost labor provided by immigrants was of sufficient value to offset the genetic contamination of the American population. In the debate, members of the dominant fraction of the dominant class (especially factory-owning industrialists who needed cheap, hardworking labor) lined up on both sides of the issue. Some argued that the need for laborers willing to perform undesirable jobs was sufficiently pressing to justify some immigration; others contended that, whatever the need, the risk of biological contamination was simply too great. Note that while the so-called IQ test is formally arbitrary, there is a great deal of historical motivation in the system. There is a strong argument that the only way to begin to grasp why an IQ test was an effective strategy for the scientists, why the institutional field of power rewarded scientists for producing a certain result, or why the dominant class was internally divided, some of its members knowingly and willingly endorsing a position contrary to their own economic interests, is to analyze cultural concepts of biology and ethnicity and their historical evolution.[7]

Though historical arbitrariness is the logical companion of a functional account of culture, it appears to endanger some of Bourdieu's other concepts, especially misrecognition. The reason is that any theory of cognition and recognition is inseparable from a theory of meaning in practice. Bourdieu might overcome this problem by claiming that motivation can be displaced or expunged, and analysis could determine what makes a cultural product look socially and historically un-motivated. But this, by another name, is what Bourdieu calls "misrecognition." Analysis could show how, under the concept of the objective IQ test, which purported to measure innate mental capacity, the cultural politics of discrimination was concealed. Such an analysis would not only support the notion of misrecognition, it would help to explain this specific mode of reproduction and why, if the distortion can be recognized, it is functionally adequate for reproducing capitalism. However, if Bourdieu accounted for this social and historical motivation, he would also introduce a need to account for the nonarbitrariness and conventional motivation of the symbolic order. In effect, while the theory of fields reveals the form and dynamic of the social order, it cannot – given its concepts of symbolic production, historical arbitrariness, the primacy of the economic, and the homology between social structure and culture and its focus on symbolic power – account for the oppositions (for example, male/female), cultural concepts (from individualism to the specific fields), or classification systems (for example, ethnicity) that transect and penetrate all fields.

CONCEPTS OF CLASS IN RELATION TO CULTURE

Bordieu has often claimed that class relations are founded on the distribution of cultural, social, and, most fundamentally, economic capital. Thus, he argues that all capital is accumulated labor (Bourdieu 1986b), and that the chain of reconversion of distinct forms of capital rests on the fact that symbolic capital is ultimately convertible into economic capital. The distribution of economic capital is played out on the cultural level by creation of a hierarchy of symbolic distinctions. Bourdieu (1985c: 204) sums up this relation by saying that "symbolic capital [is] another name for distinction." Thus the forms of thought characteristic of a specific class are historically arbitrary; all that is necessary and sufficient is that the forms of thought generate distinction *between* classes. So Bourdieu writes that "the space of objective differences finds an expression in a symbolic space of visible distinctions, of distinctive signs which are so many symbols of distinction" (1987f: 11). Culture and capital have no necessary relation other than the fact that cultural distinctions help reproduce and express inequalities of economic capital. Unlike Marx, Bourdieu does not envision capital as a structure that simultaneously orients objectivity and subjectivity so that forms·of thought are coincident with the form of classes of a given historical period (Postone 1986).

For the theory to argue for a system of social classification founded on class divisions and class fractions, it must establish or assume the existence of objectively distinct classes (that is, petite bourgeoisie, upper class, and working class), since they are what is reproduced and legitimated. But though *Distinction* has a theory of the functioning of class according to the accumulation, usage (for example, position-taking), and manipulation (for example, conversion strategies) of types of capital and also a theory about how this functioning is misrecognized as such, it lacks a theory of class structuring. The concept that class rests, first of all, on the objective allocation of material goods, as developed so far, is insufficient to establish or ground the concept of class. A theory of how cultural forms inscribe and reproduce the structure of social domination cannot, by itself, account for either the cultural forms or the structure of domination.

On top of the objective distribution of wealth, there lies the symbolic conception of class – the more or less systematic beliefs that people, including those charged explicitly with this task, be they self-appointed or inescapably thrust into the role, have of class relations. The idea of class as a symbolic product comes through clearly in Bourdieu's analysis of the genesis of groups in social space; he writes: "A class exists insofar – and only insofar – as mandated representatives endowed with *plena potestas agendi* can be and feel authorized to speak in its name" (1985c: 217). Thus, the existence of the working class

> is itself based on the existence of a *working class in representation*, i.e., of political and trade-union apparatuses and professional spokesmen, virtually interested in believing that it exists and in having this believed both by those who identify with it and those who excluded themselves from it, and capable of making the "working class" *speak* and with one voice, of invoking it, as one invokes gods or patron saints, even of symbolically manifesting it through *demonstration*, a sort of theatrical deployment of the class-in-representation. (1985c: 217, emphasis original).

Observe that the duplexity of class – first, as the objective distribution of economic wealth and second, as the symbolic form and forms of that distribution – comes close to reintroducing the division between the material and the symbolic, practice and thought, that Bourdieu seeks to overcome. How else does material or economic distribution take place other than by a practical logic of interests prior to and with greater authority than both the cultures and histories of capitalist societies. Is it the case, given the position, that cultural and historical specificity lie only in the distributions and functioning of symbolic forms? If (as in some brands of Marxist theory) culture bears no intrinsic relationship to capital and class, then the theory is forced to envision capital and class, as well as labor, as trans-historical and cross-cultural categories. To endorse this definition would (as in more than a few Marxist theories) render it unclear how one would ground and account for the historical and cultural specificity of social class or the content of specific classes, like the French bourgeoisie of the late twentieth century. Even more, it would threaten the concept of reproduction itself. Consider that a quest for distinction cannot tell us why what is produced as cultural content (for example, the expansiveness of a Cadillac or the sculpture of Henry Moore) is functionally adequate for the reproduction of a social and political economy. There exists a problem of motivation; for motivation must, of necessity, be something more than distinction. Motivation must be provided with a set of aims and images in order to motivate and direct agents to produce specific goods with specific features. For example, the quest for distinction which stimulates the production of luxury cars cannot explain why "high-end" German car-makers (for example, Mercedes) bankrolled the development of a computerized, anti-lock braking system and why such a system is functionally adequate for reproducing postmodern capitalism. To understand what motivated German car-makers requires knowledge about cultural ideas of technology and performance, the historical place of the automobile in the production of the modern capitalist consciousness, how these ideas are interrelated to capital, plus cultural notions of distinction (that auto-makers could make a nonvisible feature "distinctive" through mass media advertising). Similarly, a realized aim of business economics is to show that development of life-preserving drugs, more powerful computers and computer programs, as well as new financial instruments is a real functional necessity from the standpoint of the reproduction of modern-day capitalism.

The issue of motivation surfaces in *Distinction*'s analysis of the relation between the supply and demand for cultural goods:

> the matching of supply and demand is neither the result of the objective orchestration of two relatively independent logics, that of the fields of production and that of the field of consumption. There is a fairly close homology between the specialized fields of production in which products are developed and the fields . . . in which tastes are determined. This means that the products developed in the competitive struggles . . . meet, without having expressly to seek it, the demand which is shaped in the . . . antagonistic relations between the different classes or class fractions over material or cultural consumer goods, or more exactly, in the competitive struggles between them over these goods, which are the source of the changing of tastes. (p. 230)

On this understanding, it is the distinction of, and struggle between, the classes that furnish the motivation in the fields of production. Nevertheless, as the discussion of specific products indicates (for example, the play "Le Tournant," on pp. 234–5), an account of production must embrace a more specific and, at the same time, more cultural set of motivations. There needs to be some way of speaking about how the cultural order, as inscribed in schemes of consumption, defines goals and trajectories for production, which production, imbued with a structure and momentum of its own, then transforms in such a way as to produce this "homology." In other words, the character of Bourdieu's account of cultural production itself suggests the necessity for an analysis of the relationship between culture and capital.

The form and value that maximization is given, position taking in a structured field of positions via the accumulation of capital, threatens to reintroduce the micro–macro distinction that Bourdieu seeks to transcend. The reason is that historical arbitrariness seems to imply the existence of a strategic individual oriented by a cross-cultural concept of rational maximization. Otherwise, it would appear impossible to motivate the social reproduction of a given social formation (capitalism). The apparent reintroduction of a distinction between the universality of rational maximization at a micro-level and the historical specificity of cultural forms at the macro-level produces a further problem; for it is a canon of long-standing in anthropology that a theory cannot account for cultural/historical variability and specificity in terms of a cross-cultural or a trans-historical mechanism. One answer is that strategizing practices of individuals can generate and reproduce a specific mode of life only if mediated by culture – and in the case of capitalism by capital as well, the system of forms that determines the aims and images of social reproduction, thereby imbuing it with a historical trajectory. However, for Bourdieu's theory to embrace culture and capital in this way would grant them a certain authority over social structure and the positioning of agents within it. Culture and capitalism would, in this respect, ground the analysis of the specific fields. Even more, this would suggest that the very notions of rationality and maximization are culturally and historically defined and need to be so specified.

In the practice of ethnography, Bourdieu is sensitive to the influence of the symbolic order, as any reading of his studies of the working class's views or the Berber house makes clear. At times, he argues that social classifications (surely a product of culture and history) help to shape class relations, thereby becoming part of the structure of domination and class struggles. If this is true, then certainly class is never the objective distribution of economic power and wealth, inasmuch as culture and history are instrumental in mapping what is economic, power, and distribution.

CONCLUSION: FROM CULTURE TO CULTURE

Bourdieu has argued that social position and position taking are inseparable from the production of scientific knowledge and that scientific practice must be self-reflexive in that it grasps its own social effects and can account for itself. The basis for this kind of self-understanding lies in the way a theory defines the relationship between cultural content, social position, and agency. Bourdieu locates this relationship almost exclusively in the linkage between the social structure and the action of agents as mediated by their habitus. This view flows from his notion of distinction, which is founded on the idea that cultural forms are historically arbitrary. This *modus operandi* produces a theory of symbolic functionalism which equates culture with the history and internal dynamic of the various fields. It does not seek – nor can it account for – cultural forms or the power that they exert over agents through their meaningfulness.

The deployment of a theory of symbolic functionalism streamlines Bourdieu's analyses of the uses of power within particular fields. But it is unclear how the theory could account for the cultural critique of capitalist society that it wishes to pursue. The unaccounted aspect stems from the fact that Bourdieu's project presupposes, but does not offer, a theory of the interrelationship between culture and capital. Further, it does not offer an account of the relationship between systems of social classification and agency, though this too is presupposed. It thus leaves certain critical question unanswered. The issue is whether Bourdieu's advanced vision of social structure must embrace a more elaborated and central theory of culture and the symbolic order if it is to account for the cultural and historical specificity of the social phenomena under discussion. Specifically, it is necessary for Bourdieu to revise or replace his theory of culture if he is to preserve his relational theory of social structure and the overall thrust of his project.

NOTES

1 For the purposes of the analysis I will consider "culture" and "symbolic order" as interchangeable terms. By culture/symbolic order is meant the specific symbols (e.g. national flag), the cutural conceptions of social organization (e.g. kinship), and the social classification schemes (e.g. race and enthnicity) that exist wihin a particular society.

2 Bourdieu also advocates the inverse procedure: the use of statistics in the study of small-scale societies, the methodological aim being to ethnographically sensitize sociological statistics and also statistically sensitize ethnographic studies.

3 It should not go unnoticed that Bourdieu has translated, thereby transforming, Saussurian ideas about arbitrariness and distinction into the social field. That is to say, Bourdieu's theory of value is Saussurian (or is a version of Saussurian theory), with social structure being substituted for language structure. Similarly, the value of agents' positions in a field, like phonemes, are relational. From here, however, as *Outline* and other writings make clear, Bourdieu wishes to transcend Saussurian concepts, by introducing the concept of the habitus to relate social structure to agents' practices, thus avoiding the structuralist error of seeing action as mere execution of the structure. Bourdieu also departs from Saussure in that he sees conceptual structures as constituted less by the internal relations among their elements

than by the social structure which encompasses them. Paradigmatically, the categories and oppositions of a specific field are constituted by the field of power in which it is immersed, and more generally by the field of class relations.

4 A rejoinder to some objections. Presentation made to session on Soziologische Theorien uber Klassen und Kulture at the Meeting of the German Sociological Association, Düsseldorf, Germany, 12–14 February 1987. Translated by Loïc Wacquant.

5 This is not, of course, cultural functionalism in the Parsonian sense.

6 Note that Bourdieu sometimes claims that ideologies owe their structure to the functions they fulfill (Bourdieu 1979b), while his specific analyses of French or Algerian society indicate that the functions which these ideologies fulfill owe their specificity to their structure. Recall, for example, that the workless Algerian peasant in his disenchantment with the world does not invoke just any ideology to account for a legitimize his unemployment (e.g. he does not invoke the ideology of long-time urban residents), but a structural permutation of the ideology present in traditional society (Bourdieu 1979a).

7 It is clear that the terms and purposes of the distinction (how well native Americans performed on the tests by contrast with immigrants) were not to express or reproduce class divisions (the immigrants could have been admitted to lower-class America – indeed, some were – and some of them were from the dominant class, particularly the eastern european Jews), but rather to enforce segregation based on cultural concepts of ethnicity and of genetic pollution.

REFERENCES

Gould, S. 1981: *The Mismeasure of Man.* New York: W. W. Norton and Co.

Habermas, J. 1973: *Theory and Practice.* Boston: Beacon.

LiPuma, E. and Meltzoff, S. 1989: Towards a theory of culture and class: an Iberian example. *American Ethnologist,* 16: 313–34.

—— 1993: Economic mediation and the power of associations: towards a theory of encompassment. *American Anthropologist* (forthcoming).

Postone, M. 1986: Towards a reconstruction of the Marxian critique of modernity. Working Papers and Proceedings of the Center for Psychosocial Studies, no. 3. Chicago: Center for Psychosocial Studies.

Taussig, M. 1980: *The Devil and Commodity Fetishism in South America.* Chapel Hill: University of North Carolina Press.

2

Can there be a Science of Existential Structure and Social Meaning?

Hubert Dreyfus and Paul Rabinow

Pierre Bourdieu has developed one of the most analytically powerful and heuristically promising approaches to human reality on the current scene. As opposed to the other two plausible living contenders, Jürgen Habermas and Jacques Derrida, Bourdieu has continued and enriched the line of modern thought that runs from Durkheim and Weber through Heidegger to Merleau-Ponty and Foucault. Unlike Habermas, who is seeking universal, rational, procedural norms based on speech acts which, though empty, would ground evaluations of all human action, and unlike Derrida, who, also prioritizing language, sees all human reality as ungrounded and pushes us towards the recognition and furthering of multiplicity and instability for their own sake, Bourdieu, through an analysis of the prelinguistic, embodied structures that give stability and intelligibility to human action, provides an account both of the universal structures of human being and of the contingent practices that sustain, perpetuate, and modify these structures.

Bourdieu's theory of the *sens pratique* allows him to use phenomenological insights from early Heidegger and Merleau-Ponty to give a highly satisfactory account of the essential social character of human reality. We want, however, to distinguish two components in Bourdieu's work: an ontologically informed research program, which we call "empirical existential analytics", and the scientific theory of social meaning – Bourdieu's theory of symbolic capital – which we argue is a specific and contestable interpretation of who we are and what we are always up to. We think that these two components are analytically separable and that objective description is the appropriate way to approach what human beings *are* and how their social practices cohere. We hold, however, that the *meaning* of human action is not accessible to a scientific theory; to understand the significance of human action requires an interpretive approach (for an elaboration and defense of our view, see Dreyfus and Rabinow 1983).

The apparent coherence of Bourdieu's objective account of the general and specific structures of the habitus and of the struggle for symbolic capital that the habitus seems to embody obscures from both Bourdieu and his critics another distinction. Without arguments to the contrary, it would seem that one has no right to conclude from the universal *ontological structure* of human being that the many ways that this structure gets filled out in the everyday life of societies covers up a specific truth, universal or otherwise, about the *meaning* of human being. Bourdieu would seem to owe us an argument as to why we should not take seriously the distinction between coping skills and their alleged unifying meaning, and, if we do, how the same methodology could be expected to be applicable to both domains. In our view, if one were to address these issues, then the debate over the importance of Bourdieu's work would be clarified and raised out of the current polemical stalemate.

We would like to show here: (1) that Bourdieu implicitly operates with two different methods and two different vocabularies when dealing with one or the other of the domains we have distinguished; (2) that as soon as the distinction of domains is made explicit, we can see the appropriateness of Bourdieu's objective approach to the study of everyday realities, but without further argument there is as yet no reason to believe that the same method can be fruitfully applied to the study of the meaning of human being – if there is any; (3) that the attempt to give a scientific account of the truth of human being leads to what seem to be serious methodological problems; and (4) that methodological caution would suggest we stick to the phenomenological evidence that different societies have had different cultural understandings of what human life is all about, that our culture has had a whole series of such understandings, and that we are situated in the latest one.

AN EMPIRICAL ANALYTICS OF SOCIAL EXISTENCE

Husserl, Heidegger, and Merleau-Ponty, in spite of their disagreement, all held that in order to guide empirical studies, one needs to have an adequate ontology of the domain to be investigated. As we are using the term, ontology gives us the *general* structures of human being. Phenomenological ontology studies the structures of skills (perception and motility) and the way in which they give us access to various modes of being and constitute us as the kinds of being we are.

Bourdieu's notion of habitus, which guides his study of social human being, demonstrates the importance of having a solid ontological basis for one's research. Habitus, as Bourdieu uses the term (1979a: vii), refers to "a system of durable, transposable dispositions which functions as the generative basis of structured, objectively unified practices." Human beings are socialized into this system of dispositions that enables them to produce on the appropriate occasion skillful social activity that embodies, sustains, and reproduces the social field that in turn governs this very activity. Bourdieu remarks: "Merleau-Ponty, and also Heidegger, opened the way for a non-intellectualist, non-mechanistic analysis of the relations between agent and world" (1990d: 10).

The general form of this existential ontology is already fully worked out in *Being and Time*. Everyday coping (primordial understanding as projecting) is taken over by each individual by socialization into the public norms (the one) and thus forms a clearing that "governs" people by determining what possibilities show up as making sense. Heidegger moves beyond Husserl and the Cartesian tradition when he points out that:

> The one (*Das Man*) as that which forms everyday being-with-one-another . . . constitutes what we call *the public* in the strict sense of the word. It implies that the world is always already primarily given as the common world. It is not the case that on the one hand there are first individual subjects which at any given time have their own world; and that the task would then arise of putting together, by virtue of some sort of an arrangement, the various particular worlds of the individuals and of agreeing how one would have a common world. This is how philosophers imagine these things when they ask about the constitution of the intersubjective world. We say instead that the first thing that is given is the common world – the one. (1985: 246)

Bourdieu makes this point forcibly from the side of the human sciences, in introducing his notion of habitus:

> [H]abitus is the product of the work of inculcation and appropriation necessary in order for those products of collective history, the objective structures (e.g., of language, economy, etc.), to succeed in reproducing themselves more or less completely, in the form of durable dispositions, in the organisms (which one can, if one wishes, call individuals) lastingly subjected to the same conditionings. (1977c: 85)

Bourdieu also sees the sense in which, thanks to the habitus, *the* world is prior to *my* world . " Since the history of the individual is never anything other than a certain specification of the collective history of his group or class, *each individual system of dispositions* may be seen as a *structural variant* of all the other group or class habitus" (p. 86).

Heidegger's existential ontology is the best description of human social being that philosophers have yet offered, but it is totally abstract. Heidegger is not interested in how the clearing – the understanding of being – is instantiated and how it is picked up by individuals and passed along from one generation to the next. Wittgenstein (1973), with his emphasis on forms of life, and Merleau-Ponty (1962), with his descriptions of the lived body, help us to see that Heidegger's ontology can be extended to the ontic realm – that is, to the domain of social and historical analysis. To fill in being-in-the-world one must see that what Heidegger is talking about are social *practices* (Wittgenstein) and that these practices are *embodied skills* that have a common style and are transposed to various domains (Merleau-Ponty); that is, that social skills have a unity and form a social field (Bourdieu). This makes possible an account of how durable and transposable bodily dispositions are appropriated and "projected" back into the situation without appeal to conscious or unconscious representations. Such is Merleau-Ponty's account of embodiment, relating action and the perceptual field by way of an intentional arc: "[T]he life of consciousness – cognitive life, the life of desire or perceptual life – is subtended by an 'intentional arc' which projects round about us our past, our future, our human setting, our physical, ideological and moral situation, or rather which results in our being situated in all these respects" (1962:136).

Merleau-Ponty, however, deals only with the general structure of perception and action. It is Bourdieu's notion of habitus that finally makes these ideas concrete. His use of phenomenological ontology allows us to see the way in which the bodily habitus anchors the homologies and analogies of the social field, how the ability to respond appropriately to events in the world arises from skills without recourse to rules and representations, and how what it is to be something in the social world is determined by and reciprocally determines practice. As Bourdieu nicely says (1990d: 194), there is an "ontological complicity between the habitus and the social field." Our socially inculcated dispositions to act make the world solicit action, and our actions are a response to this solicitation. Bourdieu, like Merleau-Ponty, exploits the richness of the word *sens* to capture the directedness of comportment; he also thinks of each practice as getting its significance from its place in the whole.

Such an ontology sets up the possibility of three kinds of research:

1 One can refine, extend, and unify the ontology. (For example, Bourdieu extends phenomenological ontology to the social field.)

2 One can give an objective description of how the general ontological structure works and show ethnographically how it gets worked out in specific societies at specific times (for example, an account of how the Berbers' habitus produces and is produced by the structure of the Berber house), thereby offering a "radical critique of theoretical reason" that accounts for the failure of other theories by showing that they are based on a mistaken ontology that privileges theory (for example, that Lévi-Strauss's structuralist theory of gift exchange cannot account for what it is to be a gift).

3 One can give an account of the meaning of the organized practices that relates comportment to an implicit understanding of what human beings are up to – an understanding that it is the job of the social scientist to make explicit.

These three dimensions of investigation comprise what we mean by an ontologically informed research program whose results – and this is Bourdieu's outstanding achievement – give us the categories in which to see what social reality is, through a specific and general description of how social practices work, and in the process demonstrates the scope and limits of human science.

AN EMPIRICAL METAPHYSICS OF CULTURAL MEANING

In order to launch his *science* of human being, Bourdieu needs an explanatory principle that would account for the significance of *all* practices beyond their local sense. We call "metaphysical" any such account that claims to know objectively what it is to be a human being. For example, the meaning of human being might be that man is created by God to serve and praise him, or that man is the highest manifestation of the will to power, or that human being is "a null basis of a nullity" called to face up to its nothingness. A science of human behavior for Bourdieu cannot just catalog these interpretations but must produce a single account of what human life is all about. In Bourdieu's account, "social life . . . is a race of all against all": "The competition for a social life that will be known and recognized, which will free you from insignificance, is a struggle to the death for symbolic life and death" (1990d: 196).

Bourdieu's originality consists in seeing that this is not a Hobbesian psychological claim. It is not a statement of a "naive finality," but an ontological claim about how "the principle of competition" in the social field is "the principle of all truly social energy" and is "productive of agents who act" (1983b: 2). Or more precisely:

> The motor – what is sometimes called motivation – resides neither in the material or symbolic purpose of action, as naive finalists imagine, nor in the constraints of the field, as the mechanistic thinkers suppose. It resides in the relation between the habitus and the field, which means that the habitus contributes to determining what determines it. (p. 194)

Bourdieu offers a specific account of how the social field works. It is a competition, not just for life and security as in Hobbes, but for advantage, and not just material advantage as in Marx, but more general symbolic advantage.

> [T]he science of economic practices is a particular case of a *general science of the economy of practices* capable of treating all practices, including those purporting to be disinterested or gratuitous, and hence noneconomic, as economic practices directed towards the maximizing of material or symbolic profit (1977c: 183).

We think Bourdieu's project shows that he has correctly understood that for there to be a normal science, there must be specific, falsifiable, universal claims. In a human science, then, such a claim sets up a field of research in which the claim can be tested and in which any anomalies that arise can be seen as puzzles motivating further research. Such a program would establish sociology as a normal science.

Although Bourdieu does not thematize the distinction between *objective description* (point two in the ontological research program mentioned above) and *scientific theory* (which we are arguing goes beyond that program), his writings contain ample examples of both methods at work. Recognizing such a distinction would pose no serious problems for Bourdieu. For example, his analysis shows that one can describe the working of habitus (the Berber house) without recourse to the notion of symbolic capital. Indeed, Bourdieu's writings show that not only is objective description a convincing method for describing structures such as the Berber house, but that the method can be successfully extended to descriptions of the various social ways of making sense of what Merleau-Ponty calls "facticities", such as the seasons, fertility, death, eating, and so forth.

Bourdieu's attempt to formulate a scientific theory of social meaning has a radically different structure, however, from his objective description of social practices, and it raises many problems. Like the scientific revolution in the physical sciences, Bourdieu's unified science necessarily denies the validity of the manifold significance of the practices to the practitioners. Behind these appearances he finds the explanatory reality – the meaning of human being (maximizing symbolic capital) – which structures the social field embodied in the habitus. But in a theory of human being, unlike a theory of nature, the theory must account for why the practitioners are deluded and why the scientist is not. One way to account for the apparent anomalies, the disparity between appearance and reality, is to claim that the practices only work because their true meaning is repressed, denied, disguised, concealed, and so on. Thus the logic of such a scientific theory of human being leads Bourdieu, as it did Marx and Freud, to postulate a repressed truth and to claim to be able to liberate humanity by revealing it.

Like Heidegger in Division Two of *Being and Time*, one could look for an explanation of this ontological complicity: namely, that the interestedness of everyday life – that is, the illusion that there are intrinsic meaningful differences – is a motivated cover-up of the basic arbitrariness of human purposes, sedimented in the social field, which Heidegger calls "fallenness". Bourdieu opts for the cover-up story. *Illusio* is his name for the self-deception necessary to keep players involved in the game: "*Illusio* in the sense of investment in the game doesn't become illusion, in the originary sense of the art of deceiving myself . . . until the game is apprehended from the outside, from the point of view of the impartial spectator, who invests nothing in the game or in its stakes" (1990d: 195).

Such a structure, which has been called a "hermeneutics of suspicion", may well be inevitable in scientific theories of human being. If there *were* an invariant, contentful human nature underlying and explaining appearances, this Galilean strategy would be the one to follow, but if there is no invariant human nature, then we would expect serious methodological difficulties to emerge. Such a theory must be able to answer objections, such as Popper's, that its redescription of the phenomenon cannot be falsified and, consequently, that it is not a science. The more common sense denies that *all* action is motivated *solely* by the attempt to use the structure of the social field to increase symbolic capital, the more the scientist sees evidence of the necessity of preserving the *illusio* in order for the system to work. But if the theorist, in the name of science, denies the surface meaning of the phenomenon – that is, uses the objections of the actors that they are being misinterpreted as further evidence for the universal principle being affirmed – then either the theory must have independent evidence, such as successful prediction and control, to justify this move, or else its claims to scientificity remain questionable. The theory will be able to take care of all anomalies, but only by making it impossible for there to be true anomalies.

An even stronger objection to Bourdieu's particular version of this demystifying methodology would be that symbolic capital is circularly defined so that whatever one acquires by one's social behavior can be tautologically reencoded in terms of symbolic capital:

> Everyone knows by experience that what gets the senior civil servant going may leave the research scientist cold and that the artist's investments remain unintelligible to the banker. This means that a field can function only if it can find individuals who are socially predisposed to behave as responsible agents, to risk their money, their time, and sometimes their honor or their life, to pursue the objectives and obtain the profits which the field offers and which, seen from another point of view, may appear illusory. (1990d; 194)

Everything from accumulating monetary capital to praise for being burned at the stake automatically counts as symbolic capital. To say that whatever people do they do for social profit does not tell us anything if profit is defined as whatever people pursue in a given society.

These two problems arise because, in order to have a science, Bourdieu needs to claim that there is an analog to human nature and use it as a universal, explanatory principle. If, however, in response to the methodological problems it raises, one gives up this universal claim, as well as the science that it makes possible and that it is in turn supposed to justify, none of Bourdieu's objective descriptive contributions to our understanding of specific societies and society in general need be sacrificed. Bourdieu's powerful analyses have revealed to us a world permeated by strategies and strategists of symbolic capital and a social field that motivates and produces such strategies and strategists. All that needs to be abandoned is the empty claim that the struggle for symbolic capital alone constitutes human beings and the social field. Bourdieu's own metaphysics of meaning can still be retained as a hermeneutic strategy for opening up socially important areas of investigation that have so far been neglected by the human sciences. But the principle that is revealing as a heuristic principle becomes concealing if it is understood as totalizing; for then (1) it conceals what does not fit, or else (2) it requires a repression account of exceptions, and (3) the resulting demystifying methodology can never take actors' self-understanding at face value. (Not that they are always right, but the idea that a specific illusion is required to make the system work demands that the actors can *never* be right about their specific motivations.)

In order to preserve the revealing power of Bourdieu's insight, while avoiding its concealing effects, one must abandon the claim to have a scientific sociology. But all that is abandoned ultimately is the illusion that one is doing real science and all the symbolic (and material) capital that accompanies this privileged position.

The most telling objection, however, comes from the critique of metaphysics built into the ontology of Heidegger and Merleau-Ponty, which Bourdieu uses to such great advantage in his analyses of social reality. The very phenomenon of the ontological complicity of social space and habitus leads these thinkers to the thesis that one is inevitably situated within one's culture's understanding of reality. This ontology was developed to criticize the will to truth in the Platonic metaphysical tradition. But the Platonic view that truth can be arrived at by a completely detached unsituated thinker is the metaphysics that makes possible modern science.

Bourdieu's attempt to combine these two, antithetical ontologies seems to us a dubious undertaking. The strain shows when Bourdieu, on the one hand, points out the dangers of the unselfconscious projection of our science onto the understanding of reality implicit in the practices of other cultures, as when anthropologists try to understand native navigation as the application of an unconscious theory, and, on the other hand, demystifies the Algerian peasant who "maintain[s] a magical relationship with the land [that] make[s] it impossible for him to see his toil as labour" (1977c: 174). Thus Bourdieu's ontology enables him to avoid the mistake of reading the sociologist's theoretical approach to reality into the practices of other societies, whereas scientific theory requires him to impose our Western demystifying understanding of reality on other societies as the condition for arriving at a scientific understanding of their culture.

It follows from the Heideggerian/Merleau-Pontian understanding of human finitude as our inevitable involvement in a particular understanding of reality that constitutes us, that, as Bourdieu recognizes and demonstrates, you cannot get out of your own *sens pratique* just by recognizing that you have one. But this would seem to leave Bourdieu with a dilemma. If we are stuck in our embodied habitus, as Merleau-Ponty holds, then there is no position from which to do an objective, detached study of one's own sense of reality. If, however, in the interests of liberation, one claims, as Bourdieu does in *Leçon sur la leçon* (1982b), that doing objective social science enables one to stand outside the habitus and its *illusio* and demonstrate the working of social injustice, there is no convincing way of accounting for this new motivation. Bourdieu's answer appears to be that when the scientist gets outside the social habitus, he or she is simply open to a new motivation: namely, to expose social injustice. Heidegger held a similar view: both that anxiety is the experience that human life is ungrounded and that nothing is worth doing and that authentic action unproblematically consists in simply doing what shows up as needing to be done. But Heidegger abandoned this unconvincing solution, as well as the problem, when he abandoned Division Two of *Being and Time* as still too metaphysical. Bourdieu's fruitful research program based on the ontology of Merleau-Ponty would in no way be compromised if he, like Heidegger, abandoned the claim to be speaking from a uniquely authentic position. But he would then be obliged to admit that his *Wissenschaft* belongs not among the natural sciences but among the human ones.

REFERENCES

Dreyfus, Hubert and Rabinow, Paul 1983: *Michel Foucault: beyond structuralism and hermeneutics*, 2nd edn. Chicago: University of Chicago Press.
Heidegger, Martin 1985: *The History of the Concept of Time*, trans. T. Kisiel. Bloomington: Indiana University Press.
Merleau-Ponty, M. 1962: *Phenomenology of Perception*. London: Routledge & Kegan Paul.
Wittgenstein, Ludwig 1973: *Philosophical Investigations*, trans. G. E. M. Anscombe. New York: Macmillan.

3

To Follow a Rule . . .

Charles Taylor

Great puzzlement has arisen about rules and conventions, as we try to understand their place in human life in the light of modern philosophy. One facet of this was pressed most acutely and famously by Wittgenstein in his *Philosophical Investigations*[1] and further elaborated by Saul Kripke in his book on the subject. It concerns what it means to understand a rule. Understanding seems to imply knowledge or awareness; yet Wittgenstein shows that the subject not only isn't but *couldn't* be aware of a whole host of issues which nevertheless have a direct bearing on the correct application of a rule.

Wittgenstein shows this by raising the possibilities of misunderstanding. Some outsider, unfamiliar with the way we do things, might misunderstand what to us are perfectly clear and simple directions. You want to get to town? Just follow the arrows. But suppose that what seemed the natural way of following the arrow to him or her was to go in the direction of the feathers, not of the point? (i: 85). We can imagine a scenario: there are no arrows in the outsider's culture, but there is a kind of ray gun whose discharge fans out like the feathers on our arrows.

Now this kind of example triggers off a certain reaction in our intellectualist philosophical culture. What the stranger fails to understand (you follow arrows towards the point), we must understand. We *know* how to follow arrows. But what does this mean? From the intellectualist perspective, it must be that somewhere in our mind, consciously or unconsciously, a premise has been laid down about how you follow arrows. From another angle, once we see the stranger's mistake, we can explain what he or she ought to do. But if we can give an explanation, we must already *have* an explanation. So the thought must reside somewhere in us that you follow arrows this way.

Or we could come at the same point from another direction. Suppose we didn't have such a thought. Then when the issue arises as to whether we really ought to follow arrows towards the point, we would be in

doubt. How would we know that this was right? And then how would
we follow the directions?

Now this kind of reply runs into insuperable difficulties, because the
number of such potential misunderstandings is endless. Wittgenstein
makes this point over and over again. There are an indefinite number of
points at which, for a given explanation of a rule and a given run of
paradigm cases, someone could nevertheless misunderstand, as our
stranger did the injunction to follow the arrows. For instance (i: 87), I
might say that by "Moses" I mean the man who led the Israelites out of
Egypt, but then my interlocutor might have trouble with the words
"Egypt" and "Israelites". "Nor would these questions come to an end
when we get down to words like 'red', 'dark', 'sweet'." Nor would even
mathematical explanations be proof against this danger. We could
imagine someone to whom we teach a series by giving a sample range,
say: 0, 2, 4, 6, 8. The person might carry on quite well till 1,000, and then
go 1,004, 1,008, 1,012. He or she is indignant when we say that this is
wrong. The person understood our sample range to be illustrating the
rule: "Add 2 up to 1,000, 4 up to 2,000, 6 up to 3,000, and so on" (i: 185).

If in order to understand directions or know how to follow a rule, we
have to know that all these deviant readings are deviant, and if this means
that we have to have formulated thoughts to this effect already, then we
need an infinite number of thoughts in our heads to follow even the
simplest instructions. Plainly this is crazy. The intellectualist is tempted
to treat all these potential issues as though they would have to be
resolved by us already, if we are to understand the directions. ("It may
easily look as if every doubt merely *revealed* an existing gap in the
foundations; so that secure understanding is only possible if we first
doubt everything that *can* be doubted, and then remove all these
doubts"(i: 87). But since any explanation leaves some potential issues
unresolved, it stands in need of further explanations to back it up. And
further explanations would have the same lack and so the job of
explaining to somebody how to do something would be literally endless.
" 'But then how does an explanation help me to understand, if after all it
is not the final one? In that case the explanation is never completed; so I
still don't understand what he means, and never shall!' - As though an
explanation as it were hung in the air unless supported by another one"
(i: 87).

The last remark, the one not in single quotes, is Wittgenstein's reply to
his interlocutor. It hints at the mind-set of the intellectualist. This
outlook seeks securely founded knowledge. We recognize an obsession
of the modern intellectual tradition, from Descartes. It didn't see this as a

problem, because it thought we could find such secure foundations, explanations in terms of features which were self-explanatory or self-authenticating. That's why the imagined interlocutor placed his hopes in words like "red", "dark", "sweet", referring to basic empirical experiences on which we can ground everything else. The force of Wittgenstein's argument lies in its radical undercutting of any such foundationalism.

Why can someone always misunderstand? And why don't we have to resolve all these potential difficulties before we can understand ourselves? The answer to these two questions is the same. Understanding is always against a background of what is taken for granted, just relied on. Someone who lacks this background can always come along and so the plainest things can be misunderstood, particularly if we let our imagination roam and imagine people who have never even heard of arrows. But at the same time, the background, as what is simply relied on, isn't the locus of resolved questions. When the misunderstanding stems from a difference of background, what needs to be said to clear it up articulates a bit of the explainer's background which may never have been articulated before.

Wittgenstein stresses the unarticulated – at some points even unarticulable – nature of this understanding. " '[O]beying a rule' is a practice" (i: 202). Giving reasons for one's practice in following a rule has to come to an end. "My reasons will soon give out. And then I shall act, without reasons" (i: 211). Or later, "If I have exhausted my justifications I have reached bedrock, and my spade is turned. Then I am inclined to say: 'This is simply what I do' " (i: 217). More laconically, "When I obey a rule, I do not choose. I obey the rule *blindly*" (i: 219).

There are two broad schools of interpretation of what Wittgenstein is saying here, which correspond to two ways of understanding the phenomenon of the unarticulated background. The first would interpret the claim that I act without reasons as involving the view that no reasons can be given here, that no demand for reasons can arise. This is because the connections which form our background are just *de facto* links, not susceptible of any justification. For instance, they are simply imposed by our society; we are conditioned to make them. They become "automatic," which is why the question never arises. The view that society imposes these limits is the heart of Kripke's interpretation of Wittgenstein. Or else they can perhaps be considered as "wired in." It's just a fact about us that we react this way, as it is that we blink when something approaches our eyes, and no justification is in order.

The second interpretation takes the background as really incorporating *understanding*; that is, as a grasp on things which, although quite unarticulated, may allow us to formulate reasons and explanations when challenged. In this case, the links are not simply *de facto*, but make a kind of sense, which is precisely what one would be trying to spell out in the articulation.

On the first view, then, the "bedrock" on which our explicit explanations rest is made up of brute connections; on the second, it is a mode of understanding and thus makes a kind of unarticulated sense of things.

What suggest the first interpretation are phrases like "I obey the rule blindly," and perhaps even the image of bedrock itself, whose unyielding nature implies that nothing further *can* be said. What tell against it are other passages in which Wittgenstein says, for example, that following a rule is not like the operations of a machine (i: 193–4), or that "To use a word without justification does not mean to use it without right" (i: 289 – although I can imagine an interpretation of this compatible with the first view). Above all, I want to say that it is his insistence that following rules is a *social* practice. Granted, this also fits, perhaps, with Kripke's version of the first view. But I think that, in reality, this connection of background with society reflects an alternative vision, which has jumped altogether outside the old monological outlook which dominates the epistemological tradition.

Whatever Wittgenstein thought, this second view seems to me to be right. What the first cannot account for is the fact that we do give explanations, that we can often articulate reasons when challenged. Following arrows towards the point is not just an arbitrarily imposed connection; it makes sense, granted the way arrows move. What we need to do is follow a hint from Wittgenstein and attempt to give an account of the background as understanding, which also places it in social space. This is what I would now like to explore.[2]

The exploration that follows runs against the grain of much modern thought and culture; in particular, of our scientific culture and its associated epistemology, which in turn, have molded our contemporary sense of self.

Among the practices which have helped to create this modern sense are those which discipline our thought to disengagement from embodied agency and social embedding. Each of us is called upon to become a responsible, thinking mind, self-reliant for his or her judgments (this, at least, is the standard). But this ideal, however admirable in some respects, has tended to blind us to important facets of the human condition. There is a tendency in our intellectual tradition to read it less as an ideal than as something which is already established in our constitution. This reification of the disengaged first-person-singular self is already evident in the founding figures of the modern epistemological tradition – for instance, Descartes and Locke.

It means that we easily tend to see the human agent as primarily a subject of representations: representations about the world outside and depictions of ends desired or feared. This subject is a monological one. She or he is in contact with an "outside" world, including other agents, the objects she or he and they deal with, her or his own and others' bodies, but this contact is through the representations she or he has "within." The subject is first of all an "inner" space, a "mind" to use the old terminology, or a mechanism capable of processing representations if we follow the more fashionable computer-inspired models of today. The body, other people or objects may form the content of my representations. They may also be causally responsible for some of these representations. But what "I" am, as a being capable of having such representations, the inner space itself, is definable independently of body or other. It is a center of monological consciousness.

It is this stripped-down view of the subject which has made deep inroads into social science, breeding the various forms of methodological individualism, including the most recent and virulent variant, the current vogue of rational choice theory. It stands in the way of a richer, more adequate understanding of what the human sense of self is really like and hence of a proper understanding of the real variety of human culture and so of a knowledge of human beings.

What this kind of consciousness leaves out are: the body and the other. Both have to be brought back in if we are to grasp the kind of background understanding which Wittgenstein seems to be adverting to. And in fact, restoring the first involves retrieving the second. I want to sketch briefly what is involved in this connection.

A number of philosophical currents in the last two centuries have tried to get out of the cul-de-sac of monological consciousness. Prominent in this century are the works of Heidegger (1927), Merleau-Ponty (1945), and of course, Wittgenstein (1953) himself. What all these have in common is that they see the agent not primarily as the locus of representations, but as engaged in practices, as a being who acts in and on a world.

Of course, no one has failed to notice that human beings act. The crucial difference is that these philosophers set the primary locus of the agent's understanding in practice. In the mainline epistemological view, what distinguishes the agent from inanimate entities which can also affect their surroundings is the former's capacity for inner representations, whether these are placed in the "mind" or in the brain understood as a computer. What we have which inanimate beings don't have – understanding – is identified with representations and the operations we effect on them.

To situate our understanding in practices is to see it as implicit in our activity, and hence as going well beyond what we manage to frame representations of. We do frame representations: we explicitly formulate what our world is like, what we aim at, what we are doing. But much of our intelligent action in the world, sensitive as it usually is to our situation and goals, is carried on unformulated. It flows from an understanding which is largely inarticulate.

This understanding is more fundamental in two ways: first, it is always there, whereas sometimes we frame representations and sometimes we do not, and, second, the representations we do make are only comprehensible against the background provided by this inarticulate understanding. It provides the context within which alone they make the sense they do. Rather than representations being the primary locus of understanding, they are similarly islands in the sea of our unformulated practical grasp on the world.

Seeing that our understanding resides first of all in our practices involves attributing an inescapable role to the background. The connection figures, in different ways, in virtually all the philosophies of the contemporary counter-current to epistemology, and famously, for example, in Heidegger and Wittgenstein.

But this puts the role of the body in a new light. Our body is not just the executant of the goals we frame or just the locus of the causal factors which shape our representations. Our understanding itself is embodied. That is, our bodily know-how and the way we act and move can encode components of our understanding of self and world. I know my way around a familiar environment in being able to get from any place to any place with ease and assurance. I may be at a loss when asked to draw a map or even to give explicit directions to a stranger. I know how to manipulate and use the familiar instruments in my world, usually in the same inarticulate fashion.

But it is not only my grasp on the inanimate environment which is thus embodied. My sense of myself and of the footing I am on with others are in large part embodied also. The deference I owe you is carried in the distance I stand from you, in the way I fall silent when you start to speak, in the way I hold myself in your presence. Or alternatively, the sense I have of my own importance is carried in the way I swagger. Indeed, some of the most pervasive features of my attitude to the world and to others are encoded in the way I carry myself and project in public space: whether I am "macho" or timid or eager to please or calm and unflappable.

In all these cases, the person concerned may not even possess the appropriate descriptive term. For instance, when I stand respectfully and defer to you, I may not have the word "deference" in my vocabulary. Very often, words are coined by (more sophisticated) others to describe important features of people's stance in the world. (Needless to say, these others are often social scientists.) This understanding is not, or is only imperfectly, captured in our representations. It is carried in patterns of appropriate action: that is, action which conforms to a sense of what is fitting and right. An agent with this kind of understanding recognizes when he or she or others "have put a foot wrong." His or her actions are responsive throughout to this sense of rightness, but the "norms" may be quite unformulated, or formulated only in fragmentary fashion.

In recent years, Pierre Bourdieu (1977c, 1990e) has coined a term to capture this level of social understanding – the "habitus." This is one of the key terms necessary to give an account of the background understanding invoked in the previous section. I will return to this in a minute. But first I want to make the connection between the retrieval of the body and that of the other.

In fact, one can see right away how the other also figures. Some of these practices which encode understanding are not carried out in acts of a single agent. The above example of my deference is a case in point. Deferent and deferred-to play out their social distance in a conversation, often with heavily ritualized elements. And indeed, conversations in general rely on small, usually focally unnoticed rituals.

But perhaps I should say a word first about this distinction I'm drawing between acts of a single agent – (let's call them "monological" acts) – and those of more than one – ("dialogical" acts. From the standpoint of the old epistemology, all acts were monological, although often the agent coordinated his or her actions with those of others. But this notion of coordination fails to capture the way in which some actions require and sustain an integrated agent. Think of two people sawing a log with a two-handed saw or a couple dancing. A very important feature of human action is rhythmizing, cadence. Every apt, coordinated gesture has a certain flow. When this is lost, as occasionally happens, one falls into confusion; one's actions become inept and uncoordinated. Similarly, the mastery of a new kind of skilled action goes along with the ability to give one's gestures the appropriate rhythm.

Now in cases like the sawing of the log and ballroom dancing, it is crucial to their rhythmizing that it be shared. These activities only come off when we can place ourselves in a common rhythm, in which our component action is taken up. This is a different experience from coordinating my action with yours, as when I run to the spot on the field where I know you are going to pass the ball.

Sawing and dancing are paradigm cases of dialogical actions. But there is frequently a dialogical level to actions that are otherwise merely coordinated. A conversation is a good example. Conversations with some degree of ease and intimacy move beyond mere coordination and have a common rhythm. The interlocutor not only listens, but participates by nodding his or her head and by saying "unh-hunh," and the like, and at a certain point the "semantic turn" passes to him or her by a common movement. The appropriate moment is felt by both partners, in virtue of the common rhythm. The bore and the compulsive talker thin the atmosphere of conviviality because they are impervious to this. There is a continuity between ordinary, convivial conversation and more ritualized exchanges: litanies or alternate chanting, such as one sees in many earlier societies.[3]

I have taken actions with a common rhythmizing as paradigm cases of the dialogical, but they are only one form of these. An action is dialogical, in the sense that I'm using the word here, when it is effected by an integrated, nonindividual agent. This means that for those involved in it, its identity as this kind of action essentially depends on the agency being shared. These actions are constituted as such by a shared understanding among those who make up the common agent. Integration into a common rhythm can be one form that this shared understanding takes. But it can also come into being outside the situation of face-to-face encounter. In a different form it can also constitute, for instance, a political or religious movement whose members may be widely scattered but are animated by a sense of common purpose – such as that which linked the students in Tienanmen Square with their colleagues back on the campuses and, indeed, with a great part of the population of Peking. This kind of action exists in a host of other forms, and on a great many other levels as well.

The importance of dialogical action in human life shows the utter inadequacy of the monological subject of representations which emerges from the epistemological tradition. We can't understand human life merely in terms of individual subjects who frame representations about and respond to others, because a great deal of human action happens only insofar as the agent understands and constitutes him or herself as an integrall part of a "we."

Much of our understanding of self, society, and world is carried in practices which consist in dialogical action. I would like to argue, in fact, that language itself serves to set up spaces of common action, on a number of levels, intimate and public.[4] This means that our identity is never defined simply in terms of our individual properties. It also places us in some social space. We define ourselves partly in terms of what we come to accept as our appropriate place within dialogical actions. In the case that I really identify myself with my deferential attitude towards wiser people like you, then this conversational stance becomes constituent of my identity. This social reference figures even more clearly in the identity of the dedicated revolutionary.

The background understanding invoked in the first section, which underlies our ability to grasp directions and follow rules, is to a large degree embodied. This helps to explain the combination of features it exhibits: that it is a form of *understanding*, a making sense of things and actions, but at the same time is entirely unarticulated, and, thirdly, can be the basis of fresh articulation. As long as we think of understanding in the old intellectualist fashion, as residing in thoughts or representations, it is hard to explain how we can know how to follow a rule or in any way to behave rightly without having the thoughts which would justify this behavior as right. We are driven either to a foundationalist construal, which would allow us to attribute only a finite list of such thoughts justifying an action from scratch, as it were, or else, abandoning this, to conceive of a supporting background in the form of brute, *de facto* connections. This is because intellectualism leaves us with the choice only of an understanding which consists of representations or of no understanding at all. Embodied understanding provides us with the third alternative we need to make sense of ourselves.

At the same time, it allows us to show the connections of this understanding with social practice. My embodied understanding doesn't exist only in me as an individual agent; it also exists in me as the co-agent of common actions. This is the sense we can give to Wittgenstein's claim that "obeying a rule" is a practice (i: 202), by which he means a social practice. Earlier (i: 198) he asks: "What has the expression of a rule – say a sign-post – got to do with my actions? What sort of connection is there?" His answer is: "Well, perhaps this one: I have been trained to react to this sign in a particular way, and now I do so react." This may sound at first like the first interpretation I mentioned above: the training would set up a brute *de facto* tendency to react. The connection would be merely causal. But Wittgenstein moves right away to set aside this reading. His imaginary interlocutor says: "But that is only to give a causal connection"; and the Wittgensteinian voice in the text answers:

"On the contrary; I have further indicated that a person goes by a sign-post only insofar as there exists a regular use of sign-posts, a custom [*einen ständigen Gebrauch, eine Gepflogenheit*]."

This standing social use makes the connection, which is not to be understood as a merely causal connection. This is perhaps because the standing use gives my response its *sense*. It doesn't merely bring it on through a brute causal link. But the sense is embodied, not represented. That is why Wittgenstein can ask in the immediately following passage (i: 199): "Is what is called 'obeying a rule' something it would be possible for only *one* man to do only *once* in his life?" This rhetorical question demanding a negative answer is understood by Wittgenstein to point not just to a factual impossibility, but to something which doesn't even make sense. "This is a note," he adds, "on the grammar of the expression 'to obey a rule'." But if the role of society were just to set up the causal connections underlying my reactions, then it couldn't be senseless to suppose that those connections held only for one person at one time, however bizarrely unlikely. In fact, the social practice is there to give my actions the meaning they have, and that's why there couldn't just be one action with this meaning.

Because the wrong, intellectualistic epistemology has made deep inroads into social science, to ill effect, it is important that the scientific consequences of embodied understanding be developed. This is what makes Bourdieu's notion of "habitus" so important and potentially fruitful.

Anthropology, like any other social science, can't do without some notion of rule. Too much of human social behavior is "regular," in the sense not just of exhibiting repeated patterns but also of responding to demands or norms which have some generalizable form. In certain societies, women defer to men, young to old. There are certain forms of address and marks of respect which are repeatedly required. Not conforming is seen as wrong, as a "breach." So we quite naturally say for example, that women use these forms of address not just haphazardly and not (in the ordinary sense) as a reflex, but "following a rule."

Suppose we are trying to understand this society. We are anthropologists, who have come here precisely to get a picture of what the people's life is like. Then we have to discover and formulate some definition of this rule; we identify certain kinds of predicament – say, a woman meeting her husband or meeting a man who is not her husband in the village or meeting this man in the fields – and define what appears to be required in each of these situations. Perhaps we can even rise to

some more general rule from which these different situational requirements can be deduced. But in one form or another, we are defining a rule
through a *representation* of it. Formulating in this case is creating a
representation.

So far, so necessary. But then intellectualism enters the picture, and we
slide easily into seeing the rule-as-represented as somehow causally
operative. We may attribute formulations of the rule as thoughts to the
agents. But more likely, since this is very implausible in some cases, we
see the rule-as-represented as defining an underlying "structure." We
conceive this as what is really causally operative, behind the backs of the
unsophisticated agents, as it were.

So argues Bourdieu. "Intellectualism is inscribed in the fact of
introducing into the object the intellectual relation to the object, of
substituting the observer's relation to practice for the practical relation to
practice" (1990e: 34).[5] Of course, writing on the French scene, Bourdieu
naturally gives an important place to structuralism, which is his main
target here. It bulks less large in the English-speaking world. But the
reified understanding of rule-as-representation doesn't haunt only the
school of Lévi-Strauss. It obtrudes in a confused and uncertain form
wherever the issue Bourdieu wants to pose has not been faced: just how
do the rules *we* formulate operate in *their* lives? What is their *Sitz im
Leben*? So long as this issue is not resolved, we are in danger of sliding
into the reification that our intellectualist epistemology invites, in one or
other of the two ways mentioned. "To slip from *regularity*, i.e. from
what recurs with a certain statistically measurable frequency and from
the formula which describes it, to a consciously laid down and
consciously respected *ruling* (*règlement*), or to unconscious *regulating*
by a mysterious cerebral or social mechanism, are the two commonest
ways of sliding from the model of reality to the reality of the model"
(p. 39).

There's a mistake here, but is it important? If we have to represent the
rules to grasp them and we define them right, what does it matter how
exactly they operate in the lives of the agents? Bourdieu argues that an
important distortion occurs when we see the rule-as-represented as the
effective factor. The distortion arises from the fact that we are taking a
situated, embodied sense and providing an express depiction of it. We
can illustrate the difference in the gap which separates our inarticulate
familiarity with a certain environment, enabling us to get around in it
without hesitation, on one hand, and a map of this terrain, on the other.
The practical ability exists only in its exercise, which unfolds in time and
space. As you get around a familiar environment, the different locations
in their interrelation don't all impinge at once. Your sense of them is

different, depending on where you are and where you are going. And some relations never impinge at all. The route and the relation of the landmarks look different on the way out and the way back; the way stations on the high road bear no relation to those on the low road. A way is essentially something you go through in time. A map, on the other hand, lays out everything simultaneously and relates every point to every point, without discrimination (pp. 34–5).

Maps or representations, by their very nature, abstract from lived time and space. To make something like this the ultimate causal factor is to make the actual practice in time and space merely derivative, a mere application of a disengaged scheme. It is the ultimate in Platonism. But this is a constant temptation not only because of the intellectualist focus on the representation, but also because of the prestige of the notion of law as it figures in natural science. The inverse square law is such a timeless, aspatial formula which "dictates" the behavior of all bodies everywhere. Shouldn't we be seeking something similar in human affairs? This invitation to imitate the really successful modern sciences also encourages the reification of the rule.

But this reification crucially distorts, and this in three related ways: it blocks out certain features that are essential to action; it does not allow for the difference between a formula and its enactment; nor does it take account of the reciprocal relation between rule and action, that the second doesn't just flow from the first, but also transforms it.

Abstracting from lived time and space means abstracting from action, because the time of action is asymmetrical. It projects a future always under some degree of uncertainty. A map or a diagram of the process imposes symmetry. Take a society, such as those described by Marcel Mauss or the Kabyle communities studied by Bourdieu, where a reciprocal exchange of gifts plays an important role in defining and confirming relationships. One can make an atemporal schema of these exchanges and of the "rules" which they obey. One may then be tempted to claim, as Lévi-Strauss does, that "'the primary, fundamental phenomenon is exchange itself, which gets split up into discrete operations in social life'" (p. 98).[6]

But this leaves out of account the crucial dimension of action in time. Bourdieu points out several ways in which this might matter. Not all of them directly back up his main point. For instance, he points out that there is a proper time (a *kairos*) for reciprocating a favor. If one gives something back right away, it stands as a rebuff, as though one didn't want to be beholden to the original giver. If one delays too long, it's a sign of neglect. But this is an aspect of time which could itself be expressed in some abstract formula. Where the time of action becomes crucial is where we have to act in uncertainty and our action will irreversibly affect the situation. In the rule book of exchanges (which would be an anthropologist's artifact), the relations look perfectly reversible. But on the ground, there is always uncertainty, because there are difficult judgment calls. In Kabylia, the gift relation is a recognition of rough equality of honor between the participants. So you can make a claim on a higher-ranked person by giving him a gift and expose yourself to the danger of a brutal refusal if you have presumed too much (or have your prestige raised if your gamble pays off). At the same time, you dishonor yourself if you initiate a gift to someone too far below you.

What on paper is a set of dictated exchanges under certainty is lived on the ground in suspense and uncertainty. This is partly because of the asymmetrical time of action, but also because of what is involved in actually acting on a rule. A rule doesn't apply itself; it has to be applied, and this may involve difficult, finely tuned judgments. This was the point made by Aristotle and underlay his understanding of the virtue of *phronēsis*. Human situations arise in infinite varieties. Determining what a norm actually amounts to in any given situation can take a high degree of insightful understanding. Just being able to formulate rules will not be enough. The person of real practical wisdom is marked out less by the ability to formulate rules than by knowing how to act in each particular situation. There is, as it were, a crucial "phronetic gap" between the formula and its enactment, and this too is neglected by explanations which give primacy to the rule-as-represented.

These two points together yield the uncertainty, the suspense, the possibility of irreversible change that surrounds all significant action, however "rule-guided." I give you a gift in order to raise myself to your level. You pointedly ignore it, and I am crushed. I have irremediably humiliated myself; my status has declined. But this assumes added importance, when we take into account the way in which the rules are transformed through practice. This latter is not the simple putting into effect of unchangeable formulae. The formula as such exists only in the treatise of the anthropologist. In its operation, the rule exists in the practice it "guides." But we have seen that the practice not only fulfills the rule, but also gives it concrete shape in particular situations. Practice is, as it were, a continual "interpretation" and reinterpretation of what the rule really means. If enough of us give a little "above" ourselves and our gesture is reciprocated, we will have altered the generally understood margins of tolerance for this kind of exchange between equals. The relation between rule and practice is like that between *langue* and *parole* for Saussure: the latter is possible only because of the preexistence of the former, but at the same time the acts of *parole* are what keep the *langue* in being. They renew it and at the same time alter it. Their relation is thus reciprocal. *Parole* requires *langue*, but at the same time, in the long run what the *langue* is, is determined by the multiplicity of acts of *parole*.

It is this reciprocity which the intellectualist theory leaves out. In fact, what this reciprocity shows is that the "rule" lies essentially *in* the practice. The rule is what is animating the practice at any given time, not some formulation behind it, inscribed in our thoughts or our brains or our genes or whatever. That is why the rule is, at any given time, what the practice has made it. But this shows how conceiving the rule as an underlying formula can be scientifically disastrous. We miss the entire interplay between action under uncertainty and varying degrees of phronetic insight, on one hand, and the norms and rules which animate this action, on the other. The map gives only half the story; to make it decisive is to distort the whole process.

A rule which exists only in the practices it animates, which does not require and may not have any express formulation – how can this be? Only through our embodied understanding. This is what Bourdieu is trying to get at with his "habitus." The habitus is a system of "durable, transposable dispositions" (p. 53); that means, dispositions to bodily comportment, say, to act or to hold oneself or to gesture in a certain way. A bodily disposition is a habitus when it encodes a certain cultural understanding. The habitus in this sense always has an expressive dimension. It gives expression to certain meanings that things and people have for us, and it is precisely by giving such expression that it makes these meanings exist for us.

Children are inducted into a culture, are taught the meanings which constitute it, partly through inculcation of the appropriate habitus. We learn how to hold ourselves, how to defer to others, how to be a presence for others, all largely through taking on different styles of bodily comportment. Through these modes of deference and presentation, the subtlest nuances of social position, of the sources of prestige, and hence of what is valuable and good are encoded.

Adapting a phrase of Proust's, one might say that arms and legs are full of numb imperatives. One could endlessly enumerate the values given body, *made* body, by the hidden persuasion of an implicit pedagogy which can instil a whole cosmology, through injunctions as insignificant as "sit up straight" or "don't hold your knife in your left hand", and inscribe the most fundamental principles of the arbitrary content of a culture in seemingly innocuous details of bearing or physical and verbal manners, so putting them beyond the reach of consciousness and explicit statement. (p. 79)

This is one way in which rules can exist in our lives, as "values made flesh." Of course, it is not the only way. Some rules *are* formulated. But these are in close interrelation with our habitus. The two normally dovetail and complement each other. Bourdieu speaks of habitus and institutions as "two modes of objectification of past history" (p. 57). The latter are generally the locus of express rules or norms. But rules aren't self-interpreting; without a sense of what they're about and an affinity with their spirit, they remain dead letters or become a travesty in practice. This sense and this affinity can only exist where they do in our unformulated, embodied understanding. They are in the domain of the habitus, which "is a practical sense which reactivates the sense objectified in institutions" (p. 67).

We return here to the question we started with, the place of rules in human life. We started with the puzzle of how an agent can understand a rule and be guided by it without having even an inkling of a whole host of issues which must (it would appear) be resolved before the rule can "guide" him properly. The intellectualist bent of our philosophical culture made this seem paradoxical. But the answer is to be found in a background understanding which makes these issues irrelevant and so keeps them off our agenda. Rules operate in our lives, as patterns of reasons for action, as against just constituting causal regularities. But express reason-giving has a limit and in the end must repose in another kind of understanding.

What is this understanding? I have been arguing that we should see it as embodied. Bourdieu has explored how this kind of understanding can arise and how it can function in our lives, along with the institutions which define our social existence. So he too recurs to a picture, very much like the one I would like to attribute to Wittgenstein. Express rules can function in our lives only along with an inarticulate sense which is encoded in the body. It is this habitus which "activates" the rules. If Wittgenstein has helped us to break the philosophical thrall of intellectualism, Bourdieu has begun to explore how social science could be remade, once freed from its distorting grip.

NOTES

1 References to this book are included parenthetically in the text, by part and paragraph number (e.g. i: 258).

2 This question of how to understand Wittgenstein's argument is discussed at greater length in Fultner 1989.
3 See, e.g. Urban 1986, from which have drawn much of this analysis.
4 I have tried to argue this in Tayor 1985.
5 Unstipulated page references in the text henceforth are to this work.
6 Bourdieu quotes here from Lévi-Strauss 1987: 47.

REFERENCES

Fultner, Barbara 1989: Rules in context: a critique of Kripke's interpretation of Wittgenstein. M.A. thesis, McGill University.

Heidegger, Martin 1927: *Sein und Zeit*. Tübingen: Niemeyer.

Kripke, Saul 1972: *Wittgenstein on Rules and Private Language*. Cambridge, Mass.: Harvard University Press.

Lévi-Strauss, Claude 1987: *Introduction to the Work of Marcel Mauss*, trans. F. Baker. London: Routledge & Kegan Paul. (First French edn 1950.

Merleau-Ponty, Maurice 1945. *La Phénoménologie de la perception*. Paris: Gallimard.

Taylor, Charles 1985. Theories of meaning. In *Human Agency and Language*, New York: Cambridge University Press.

Urban, Greg 1986: Ceremonial dialogues in South America. *American Anthropologist*, 88, 371–86.

Wittgenstein, Ludwig 1973: *Philosophical Investigations*, trans. G. E. M. Anscombe. Oxford: Basil Blackwell.

4

Habitus, Field, and Capital: The Question of Historical Specificity

Craig Calhoun

The novelist Kurt Vonnegut studied anthropology at the University of Chicago, his studies interrupted by World War II. In one of his novels, he reports that anthropology seems to have had two messages. Before the war, he was taught that all people were different; after the war, that all people were the same.

Anthropology – and the human or social sciences generally – have indeed had these two messages throughout their history. Anthropology has perhaps been the paradigmatic science of otherness, but sameness, ethnocentrism, or explicit universalism has been predominant in sociology, economics, psychology, and most of the other human sciences. Today, the debate continues with particular vociferousness. On the one side stand poststructuralists, postmodernists, some feminists, and others who would base an identity politics on the absoluteness of otherness, the radical incompatibility of different intellectual traditions, and even the impossibility of full communication across lines of cultural or other basic differences. On the other side stand defenders of Enlightenment universalism, modernism, and rationality as a basis for communication, among whom Jürgen Habermas is the most prominent.

The postmodernists push their case sharply enough to run the risk of stepping onto the slippery slope of radical relativism; some, indeed, dive onto that slope head first. Habermas defends the Enlightenment project by means of a rationalism so thoroughgoing that it runs the risk of seeming vulnerable to the charges that Hegel leveled against Kant's moral philosophy. Hegel's four key charges were: excessive formalism, abstract universalism, impotence of the mere ought, and the terrorism of pure conviction.[1] In particular, accounts like Habermas's seem to require a strong separation of form from content and thus to lose touch with the concreteness of actual human social life. Pierre Bourdieu has tried in the strongest terms to distinguish his work from the tradition for which Habermas speaks, seeking to do theory primarily in concrete, empirical analyses and to oppose the antinomy of form and content (among many other antinomies). Yet, he is hard to place among the postmodernists (though like many he might be considered a "poststructuralist"). His quest for another path is valuable and will be supported in this essay. Yet I will also argue that because of a lack of clarity on one issue dividing so-called modernists and postmodernists – universalism versus historical specificity – Bourdieu's position is more ambiguous than at first appears and hence more problematic.

Overall, the debate between self-declared modernists and post-modernists seems to echo the inconclusive debate on rationality and cross-cultural analysis which was sparked off by Winch's (1958) Wittgensteinian argument for a contextualization of knowledge so radical that it seemed to make cross-cultural understanding an impossible goal (see the anthologies by Wilson (1970) and Hollis and Lukes (1982)). That debate generated a variety of interesting arguments but, ultimately, was carried out at such a remove from the empirical work of most social scientists (and the practical concerns of most political activists) that it was unable to effect much reform of our understanding. In the postmodernist/modernist debate as well, sensible third paths seem hard to identify, since the positions are rhetorically overdrawn, in part because they tend to be presented in great abstraction from actual analysis and social practice. The apparent exceptions, like Foucault and Bourdieu, are in fact not protagonists of the debate. Though Foucault's work is now central to it, this was not his main frame of discourse. He offered a critique of modernity, to be sure, but no argument for postmodernism as cultural form or social reality.

In the present essay, which I am afraid is fairly abstract itself, I want to pose the question of whether Pierre Bourdieu's work might offer some suggestions as to such a sensible third path between universalism and particularism, rationalism and relativism, modernism and postmodern-ism – the whole linked series of problematic dichotomies. I do not want to set it up as an argument of the same sort, in part because I think that Bourdieu has admirably stayed away from such absolute claims as are made on both sides of those divides; his call for heterodoxy in social science strikes me as eminently sound (Bourdieu 1988f and, in a similar vein, Bourdieu and Passeron 1967). But Bourdieu's work has substantial similarities to both sides of the current discourse, even while it is sharply distinct. It shares with what on the American side of the Atlantic is often labeled "poststructuralism" or "postmodernism" both structuralist roots and a recognition that structuralists were wrong to reject all critical inquiry into basic categories of knowledge as necessarily based on a philosophy of the subject. Like Derrida and Foucault, Bourdieu has carried out significant critical, epistemological inquiries without embracing traditional philosophy of consciousness or subjectivity. Yet Bourdieu is unlike these other "poststructuralists" in his more agonistic (though still deep) relationship to Heidegger (Bourdieu 1988d), in his determination to develop a genuinely *critical* theory (in a sense that I shall develop more below), and in his emphasis on the material practicality of social concerns, even in the realm of culture. He has also sharply rejected the substitution of quasi-poetic discourse "which becomes its own end [and] opens the door to a form of thinly-veiled nihilistic relativism . . . that stands as the polar opposite to a truly reflexive social science" (in Wacquant 1989: 35).[2]

This sort of argument places Bourdieu somewhat closer to Habermas.[3] Both, I would suggest, are heirs to the tradition of critical theory, not just in the Frankfurt school but extending back to Marx, and both propose projects that substantially reformulate the foundations for critical theory. It may be somewhat surprising to place Bourdieu in the camp of critical theorists, so let me defend that for a moment. It is true that Bourdieu follows the lead of the older generation of Frankfurt school theorists – Adorno, Horkheimer, and Marcuse – much less closely than does Habermas. Moreover, he is greatly indebted to other traditions which have little resonance in Frankfurt school thought – notably the phenomenology of Merleau-Ponty and Lévi-Straussian structuralism. Nonetheless, to restrict the label "critical theory" to followers of the Frankfurt school is to make it, unreasonably, into a kind of proprietorial claim and to lose sight of core features that give it meaning and significance today. We might understand critical theory, I think, as the project of social theory that undertakes simultaneously critique of received categories, critique of theoretical practice, and critical substantive analysis of social life in terms of the possible, not just the actual. All three moments are important, and Bourdieu shares all three with Horkheimer and Adorno, even though his theoretical style and substantive analyses differ.

There are other important similarities between Bourdieu and Habermas. Both strive to maintain an analytic focus on agents or agency, while avoiding the philosophy of the subject.[4] Both are engaged in projects intended to overcome, or enable one to overcome, the traditional opposition of theory to practice. Both derive significant insights from

Weber's account of Western rationalization as well as from Marxism (though they do quite different things with these insights in their respective theories).

The differences from Habermas are many also. They start, perhaps, with Bourdieu's opposition to theoretical system building, to what he has called "theoretical theory" (in Wacquant 1989: 50), the development of conceptual schemes divorced from concrete analytic objects or projects.[5] One may evaluate this negatively, pointing out that Bourdieu engages in a good deal of generalization even while he declines to work out a full theoretical basis for it, or positively, noting how he avoids the charge of arbitrary formalism which has been leveled at Habermas. In any case, the difference is significant. So is that which stems from Bourdieu's focus on the relationships of power that constitute and shape social fields (on fields, see 1990e, 1984: 113–20, 1988b, 1987b). Power is always fundamental to Bourdieu, and it involves domination and/or differential distribution. For Bourdieu, in other words, power is always *used*, if sometimes unconsciously; it is not simply and impersonally systemic.[6] Habermas's theory, like Parsons's, allows both relational and distributive understandings of power to take a back seat to power understood as a steering mechanism and a general social capacity.

In short, there is reason to think that Bourdieu is engaged in a project of critical theory similar to Habermas's, but that his work is much more open to the kind of positive insights that have been offered by the so-called poststructuralists (some of which, like the imbrication of knowledge in relations of power, he put forward at least as early as those poststructuralists who became famously associated with them). His work is essentially contemporary with these others (for example, Foucault and Derrida) and of comparable scope, though it has been less widely read in the English-language world. I want here to explore the idea that it might suggest ways out of what is increasingly becoming a sterile and boring impasse between Habermas and the postmodernists. I will not make any effort to summarize that debate, though it forms my frame (see Calhoun 1989, 1991). And I will take up only one thread of the dispute. This is the issue of difference. Some postmodernists make such a fetish of attention to difference that they are prepared to embrace a thoroughgoing relativism, which Bourdieu has sharply opposed. Habermas, on the other hand, is sufficiently rigid in his universalism (even though he distinguishes his own as lower-case *u*, compared to Kant's capital *U*; see Habermas 1989) and his separation of form from content that he seems unable to offer much more than lip service to the importance of difference, to the idea that social and cultural differences might be positively desirable, not merely tolerable on liberal grounds.

Difference as such is not a central theme of Bourdieu's. I am not sure that it is even a peripheral theme. In at least one way his theory is weakened by inattention to this issue: he offers an inadequate account of how to address the most basic categorial differences among epochs, societies, and cultures and corresponding differences in how his analytic tools fit or work in historically or culturally distinct instances. Despite this, I will argue that Bourdieu's work gives us extremely useful ways of approaching parts of this issue and that it thereby contributes importantly to getting contemporary theoretical discourse out of the rut of postmodernist versus modernist.

The issue of how to understand differences in societal types, epochs, civilizations, or cultures is a central one for social theory. It figures at least implicitly in the modernist/postmodernist debate as the question of whether the contemporary era is, or is about to become, distinct in some basic categorial way from that of the last three hundred or more years. The very idea of modernity, of course, posits a break with the premodern (usually conceived of as the medieval European and/or as a category which collapses and obscures the wide range of variation in non-Western societies). Some such idea of the distinctiveness of the modern West has informed anthropology and sociology from their inception, despite recurrent criticism of various specific formulations: *Gemeinschaft/ Gesellschaft*, traditional/modern, folk/urban, and so forth. The dual messages of anthropology (to which I alluded at the beginning) have in part to do with efforts on the one hand to show that "primitive" people are rational, despite the manifest conflicts between their beliefs and practices and what we "know" to be true, and on the other hand to maintain the otherness of the people studied, either out of respect for their concrete way of life or as a mirror for our own. The post-Winch rationality debates were about just these issues: for example, about how we can determine whether or not the people of a different culture are "rational".

It seems to me that Bourdieu's work both reveals the general ambivalence about this issue and suggests a way of grappling with part of it. I will try to demonstrate the latter by developing an account of the transformation of the workings of the habitus involved in movement from a minimally codified "traditional" social organization towards, on the one hand, more complex civilizations outside the modern Western ambit and, on the other, capitalist states in the modern West. More briefly, and with more attention to problems, I will look at Bourdieu's later argument regarding multiform and convertible capital. At stake is whether we should understand Bourdieu's analytic apparatus – his conceptual tools like habitus, field, and capital – as applying universally, without modification, or as situationally specific. Moreover, in either case, we want to know whether they help us to make sense of differences among situations, not just their commonalities. Bourdieu is concerned with both sides of this:

> There are *general laws of fields*: even such different fields as the field of politics, the field of philosophy, and the field of religion have functionally invariant laws (it's because of this fact that the project of a general theory is not senseless, and that, therefore, one can make use of what one understands of the functioning of each particular field to interrogate and interpret other fields, thereby getting past the mortal antinomy between idiographic monographs and formal and empty theory). (Bourdieu 1984: 113, all emphases in quotations original)

The issue is not, as critics have sometimes charged, whether Bourdieu neglects change or struggle; he does not, but rather pays attention to both.[7] The issue is how to describe a change so basic that it calls for different categories of analysis. In his early work, Bourdieu contrasted Kabylia with France, the traditional with the modern. Starting in the 1960s, he embarked on a long-range trajectory of studies of France which used the categories he had developed in studying Kabylia and argued substantially for the similarity of the basic social issues across cases.[8] Bourdieu does not decide the issue for us. He has described his project as "uncovering some of the universal laws that tendentially regulate the functioning of all fields" (in Wacquant 1989: 36). But in the same interview, he also uses more qualified expressions: "One of the purposes of the analysis is to uncover *transhistorical invariants*, or sets of relations between structures that persist within a clearly circumscribed but relatively long historical period" (ibid.).

Bourdieu is simply unclear as to how historically and comparatively specific his conceptual frameworks and analytic strategies are meant to be. He has not done much systematic comparative or historical analysis that would indicate how – or indeed, whether – he would make critical distinctions among epochs or types of societies or cultures. His conceptual development is generally couched in the context of concrete analysis – part of his opposition to "theoretical theory"; this makes for an element of contextual specificity to his terms. On the other hand, it leaves the historical and comparative frame for such specificity relatively unexamined. Bourdieu's predominant presentation tends towards a trans-historical conceptual framework and analytic approach which partially obscures the specificity of epochs and types of society or culture. At the same time, much of his conceptual apparatus can be employed in an analytic approach which does a better job of achieving historical and cultural and social organizational specificity. In other words, we can use Bourdieu's conceptual apparatus to develop an account of breaks that so distinguish social arrangements and cultures that different issues arise and different analytic categories and strategies become appropriate.

Some of Bourdieu's categories may readily fit all social settings; for example, I would think that no one could be without a habitus. Others are trickier. Is the notion of capital altogether trans-historical? The issue is muddied by divergent readings of Marx and some ambiguity as to how closely related to Marx Bourdieu means his conception to be. This is worth exploring in some detail.

Bourdieu appears to begin his analyses of capital with Marx very much in mind. In one major essay, for example, he introduces this definition in the first paragraph: "Capital is accumulated labor (in its materialized form or its 'incorporated,' embodied form) which, when appropriated on a private, i.e., exclusive, basis by agents or groups of agents, enables them to appropriate social energy in the form of reified or living labor" (1986b: 241). Bourdieu intends to take quite seriously this version of a labor theory of capital, describing the social world as "accumulated history" and going on to argue that we can analyze the various forms of capital in terms of the different means whereby they are accumulated and transmitted to succeeding generations. "The universal equivalent, the measure of all equivalences, is nothing other than labor-time (in the widest sense); and the conservation of social energy through all its conversions is verified if, in each case, one takes into account both the labor-time accumulated in the form of capital and the labor-time needed to transform it from one type into another" (1986b: 253). Bourdieu's qualifier about the widest sense of labor-time is appropriate, for, unlike Marx, Bourdieu does not examine the historically specific conditions under which labor is abstracted into temporal units of measurement. As this passage makes clear, Bourdieu means by "labor-time" simply the amount of work. For a universal equivalent, this is somewhat problematic. We must wonder how the various concrete forms of work involved in the reproduction or production of capital are in fact made equivalent to each other where a process of abstraction (for example, into commodified labor) is lacking. Bourdieu's account works well to show how qualitatively different forms of work may contribute to the putatively common project of achieving or reproducing hierarchical distinction. It does not show us any way in which these qualitatively different forms of work are transformed into a quantitative equivalent. In certain ways, then, Bourdieu adds to the account one can derive from Marx – for example, by arguing that a much wider range of labor is productive of capital than Marx suggested, including the labor of familial reproduction of the embodied sensibilities which distinguish classes. On the other hand, by treating capital as wealth or power, he sacrifices one of the linchpins of Marxist theory and, despite his use of terms like "universal equivalent," loses the capacity to clarify the nature of a social system which produces universal equivalents.

What is of interest in this is not an argument over Bourdieu's choice among the many possible readings of Marx. Rather, it is the implications of this sort of account of capital for the analysis of a range of historical epochs or culturally different contemporary social arrangements. Certainly one could apply the idea of different forms of capital anywhere, so long as one simply meant to point out descriptively the existence of different resources of power, differently reproduced. But if the convertibility of capital is something more than a postulate or a restatement of the definition of capital as power (and hence of cultural or social attributes as capital only to the extent that they yield power), then it would seem to be historically variable. That is, at the very least, the extent and ease of convertibility must be quite different in different contexts. A high level of convertibility is, I think, characteristic especially of relatively complex, market-based, and above all capitalist societies. Capitalism, moreover, seems to have a logic of increasing convertibility. Where capitalist relations enter, traditional barriers to conversion of forms of capital are undermined. Bourdieu (1977c) himself showed this accurately in his accounts of the behavior and relationships of Algerian peasants who had earned substantial amounts of cash outside the traditional village field of production. Their attempts to convert their economic capital into cultural and social capital were thwarted and made difficult by the traditional normative structure and habitus. At the same time, as the introduction of cash gained a foothold, it proved insidious, undermining customary patterns of practice. Paying for services in money rather than accumulated social debt undermined a pattern of more or less stable reproduction and helped to bring about basic changes.

What Bourdieu's newer approach to capital lacks, then, is an idea of capitalism. That is, he is not in a position to give an account of what is distinctive to those societies which operate with a compulsion to expand their reach and whose patterns of practice have a corrosive power over others. Bourdieu uses a number of shorthand expressions for the societies in which fields proliferate and are sharply divided and in which the convertibility among forms of capital is most central to social organization. Like the rest of us, he calls them variously "relatively complex," "differentiated," "highly codified," and so forth. A Marxian understanding of capitalism would be one way to clarify this opposition – or at least aspects of it – theoretically. I will want to suggest that Bourdieu's theoretical framework potentially offers us additional ways to make these sorts of terms much more precise and more useful. First, though, we must examine the significance of the fact that he stays away from describing any of these complex societies as capitalist and from addressing the special role that capital accumulation plays in their constitution.[9] Where Marx stressed that capital was not simply wealth, but a moment in the complex relations of production called "capitalism," that it entailed a compulsion to intensify and expand the processes of exploitation whereby it was produced, and that it turned crucially on the distinction of its constitutive category, abstract labor power, from mere work, Marx was laying the foundations for a historically specific theory of capitalism.[10] Bourdieu, on the other hand, consistently sees capital simply as a resource (that is, a form of wealth) which yields power (1986b: 252; 1987f: 4). The link to Marx suggested by the common emphasis on capital and labor, a suggestion reinforced by aspects of Bourdieu's rhetoric, is thus misleading.

Bourdieu's considerable achievements in his work on cultural capital are linked with this difference from Marx. Bourdieu's key original insights are that there are immaterial forms of capital – cultural, symbolic, and social – as well as a material or economic form and that with varying levels of difficulty it is possible to convert one of these forms into the other. It is this notion of multiform, convertible capital that underpins his richly nuanced account of class relations in France (Bourdieu 1984):

> The social world can be conceived as a multidimensional space that can be constructed empirically by discovering the main factors of differentiation which account for the differences observed in a given social universe, or, in other words, by discovering the powers or *forms of capital* which are or can become efficient, like aces in a game of cards, in this particular universe, that is, in the struggle (or competition) for the appropriation of scarce goods of which this universe is the site. It follows that the structure of this space is given by the distribution of the various forms of capital, that is, by the distribution of the properties which are active within the universe under study – those properties capable of conferring strength, power and consequently profit on their holder. . . . These fundamental

social powers are, according to my empirical investigations, firstly *economic* capital, in its various kinds; secondly *cultural* capital or better, informational capital, again in its different kinds; and thirdly two forms of capital that are very strongly correlated, *social* capital, which consists of resources based on connections and group membership, and *symbolic* capital, which is the form the different types of capital take once they are perceived and recognized as legitimate. (1987f: 3–4)

Economic capital is essentially that which is "immediately and directly convertible into money" (1986b: 243), unlike educational credentials (cultural capital) or social connections (social capital). The most interesting parts of Bourdieu's work in this area are his treatments of cultural capital. He has made particular strides by recognizing how much of cultural capital presupposes embodiment of distinctive and distinguishing sensibilities and characteristic modes of action. Thus it is that he is able to show how the labor of parents is translatable into the "status attainment" of their children in ways not directly dependent on financial inheritance or even on better schools. Such parental labor depends on the availability of time free from paid employment, however, which shows the dependence of the other forms of capital on economic capital (p. 253).[11] The importance of this sort of cultural capital is greatest, moreover, where for some reason it is advantageous to deny or disguise the inheritability of position (p. 246). Bourdieu does not directly explore the social conditions and histories which make such "strategies of reproduction" particularly advantageous.

The issue is an important one. Bourdieu repeatedly urges us to see history and sociology as inseparably linked (for example, 1990d: 42; Wacquant 1989: 37; and Bourdieu and Wacquant 1992; 90–99), but his sociology does not offer much purchase on the transformation of social systems. It is geared towards accounts of their internal operation. The issue is not simply whether Bourdieu offers a "motor of history" in the crude Marxist sense. Rather it is that his accounts of the general system of social and cultural organization always render it as essentially conservative; they suggest no reasons why a logic of reproduction would not work. There is nothing in his theory like the notion of contradictions in Marx's (or Hegel's). Bourdieu's theory does imply dynamism; but, crucially, it does so at the level of the strategic actor (individual or collective or, in those writings where he is more attentive to the problems of rooting his analysis in any positing of actors as fundamental, at the level of the strategy itself). That is, the motive force of social life is the pursuit of distinction, profit, power, wealth, and so on. Bourdieu's account of capital is an account of the resources that people use in such pursuit. In this sense, despite his disclaimers, Bourdieu does indeed share a good deal with Gary Becker and other rational choice theorists. Bourdieu sharply, and probably rightly, rejects the charge of economism; he is not assuming that the "interests" which are fundamental are basically "economic." He deals less with the charge that he fails to consider action which is not consciously or unconsciously strategic. He accepts the notion of interest, albeit as part of a "deliberate and provisional reductionism," in order to be able to show that cultural activity is not "disinterested," as Western thought has often implied since the development of the modern ideology of artistic production.[12] He is quick and forceful in pointing out that

> the concept of interest as I construe it has nothing in common with the naturalistic, transhistorical, and universal interest of utilitarian theory. . . . Far from being an anthropological invariant, interest is a *historical arbitrary*, a historical construction that can be known only through historical analysis, *ex post*, through empirical observation, and not deduced a priori from some fictitious – and so naively Eurocentric – conception of "Man." (Wacquant 1989: 41–2)

Quite so; but then we must ask why this particular concept of interest arose historically and gained special power in both lay and academic analyses of human action in the present epoch. In any case, this recourse to empiricism rather than naturalism is not so problematic for economic or rational choice theorists as Bourdieu believes. "Revealed preference," they can reply. There are certainly important differences between Bourdieu's theory of practice and rational choice theory.[13] But though Bourdieu points out the historical particularity of all interests, he does not deny the universality of interested action. Implicitly, at least, he goes further, beyond treating all action simply as interested – which is little more than saying "motivated". He treats all interests, historically particular though their contents may be, as formally similar in their implication of strategies designed to advance some manner of acquisition of power or wealth. Bourdieu is saying something more trans-historical and anthropologically invariant about human actors than he lets on, especially in his accounts of capital.

Bourdieu's theory is social in a powerful sense in which rational choice theory is not. His conception of strategy in the idea of an intersubjective habitus conditioned by "objective" situations gives a much less reductionistic and more useful sense of human action. Bourdieu's sociology provides for effective accounts of the influences which objective circumstances, historical patterns of distribution of various resources, and the trajectories of different actors through social fields all have on power relations. It relies little on any notion of creativity. Most centrally, it gives an account of the various socially determined interests people may pursue and the ways in which social structures constrain such action, but not of any internal tendencies of those structures to change in particular directions. Bourdieu's theory is at its best, therefore, as a theory of reproduction, and at its weakest as a theory of transformation. In this it shows its structuralist (perhaps even functional-ist) roots.

Bourdieu has rightly protested that his work is by no means bracketable as a theory of reproduction *tout court* (1990d: 46 and Wacquant 1989). But he is centrally concerned with how the various practical projects of different people, the struggles in which they engage, and the relations of power which push and pull them nonetheless reproduce the field of relations of which they are a part. "The source resides in the actions and reactions of agents who, unless they exclude themselves from the game, have no other choice than to struggle to maintain or improve their position in the field, thus helping to bring to bear on all the others the weight of the constraints, often experienced as intolerable, which stem from antagonistic coexistence" (1990d: 193). In *Homo Academicus* and *La noblesse d'État*, Bourdieu reports that he is impressed by the stability of the basic field of relations even while incumbents change and struggles continue. In his work on Kabylia (for example, 1977c), ruptures in traditional practices always appear as the result of exogenous influences.

When Bourdieu approached the idea of reproduction, a key under-lying concern was to overcome the antinomy between structure and action (1990d: 9–17, 34, 46). He wanted to show how patterns of social life could be maintained over time without this either being specifically willed by agents or the result of external factors beyond the reach of agents' wills. That is, he wanted to show that reproduction was the result of what people did, intentionally and rationally, even when reproduction was not itself their intention: "Each agent, wittingly or unwittingly, willy nilly, is a producer and reproducer of objective meaning. Because his actions and works are the product of a *modus operandi* of which he is not the producer and has no conscious mastery, they contain an 'objective intention', as the Scholastics put it, which always outruns his conscious intentions" (Bourdieu 1977c: 79). The practice which the habitus makes possible is not merely a determined result of the antecedent conditions; neither is it the sort of intentional action which many theories conceive of as action following a rule.

Talk of rules, a euphemized form of legalism, is never more fallacious than
when applied to the most homogenous societies (or the least codified areas
of differentiated societies) where most practices, including those seemingly
most ritualized, can be abandoned to the orchestrated improvisation of
common dispositions: the rule is never, in this case, more than a second-
best intended to make good the occasional misfirings of the collective
enterprise of inculcation tending to produce habitus that are capable of
generating practices regulated without express regulation or any institutionalized call to order. (Bourdieu 1977c: 17)

The last part of this quotation poses an essential issue: how is the
coordination of actions to be achieved without either external determination (or, what amounts to almost the same thing, reference to the
unconscious as an equally unwilled internal determination) or the
issuance of some formal rule or communication involving a decision
process (and hence the self-imposition of a rule)? Objectivists either
simply record regularities without explaining them or reify various
analytic notions such as "culture," "structures," or "modes of production" and imagine that they exist as such in the world, external to actors,
constraining them towards regularity. Bourdieu's attack on this objectivism was powerful, but it is worth noting that it did not involve
systematic attention to differences among societies in the extent to which
formal rules are issued or to which action appears to actors as reified
external determination.[14]

In *Outline*, Bourdieu's argument was aimed particularly at French
structuralists, and he adopted the language of economizing strategies
(from a mainly Anglo-Saxon discourse) largely to challenge the
structuralist elimination of agents, of practices. But even here, he was
careful to show that the economizing was not that of individuals
understood discretely, but inhered in the habitus as a social creation.
Bourdieu was careful to distinguish his position also from a subjectivism
which imagined that agents were not overwhelmingly products of their
backgrounds and situations or that their actions simply originated with
their choices among abstractly conceived possibilities. Sartre was the
particular subjectivist he had most in mind, and Bourdieu pointed precisely to the problem that Sartre created for himself by refusing to
recognize anything resembling durable dispositions. He thereby made
each action into "a sort of unprecedented confrontation between the
subject and the world" (Bourdieu 1977c: 73). In so doing, he made social
reality inexplicably voluntary and ultimately, therefore, arbitrary.
Against this view, Bourdieu argued that agents acted within socially

constructed ranges of possibilities durably inscribed within them (even in their bodies) as well as within the social world in which they moved. Moreover, the relation between agent and social world is a relation between two dimensions of the social, not two separate sorts of being.

> The source of historical action, that of the artist, the scientist, or the member of government just as much as that of the worker or the petty civil servant, is not an active subject confronting society as if that society were an object constituted externally. The source resides neither in consciousness nor in things but in the relationship between two stages of the social, that is, between the history objectified in things, in the form of institutions, and the history incarnated in bodies, in the form of that system of enduring dispositions which I call habitus. (1990d: 190)

Against some of the cruder forms of economistic choice theory, Bourdieu held that agents' use of the possibilities available to them, while strategic in a sense, was often not strictly speaking calculation because not discursive. The economizing or calculation was built into the practical play of the game. An analyst might, thus, see how a course of behavior effectively achieved some end, while the actor engaged in the behavior believed that she was merely being a good friend or wife or daughter. It was essential to some strategies that they could only be carried out by people who misrecognized them. Above all else, it was crucial to grasp, Bourdieu argued, that agents did not generally adopt the theoretical attitude of seeing action as a choice among all objective possibilities; they usually saw only one or a few possibilities. "The habitus is the source of these series of moves which are objectively organized as strategies without being the product of a genuine strategic intention – which would presuppose at least that they are perceived as one strategy among other possible strategies" (Bourdieu 1977c: 73).

Bourdieu's concern was (and to a large extent still is) with how the coordination of social activities is achieved. His riposte to both objectivism and subjectivism was to stress practical mastery, a sense of playing the game which was at once active and nondiscursive. "We shall escape from the ritual either/or choice between objectivism and subjectivism in which the social sciences have so far allowed themselves to be trapped only if we are prepared to inquire into the mode of production and functioning of the practical mastery which makes possible both an objectively intelligible practice and also an objectively enchanted experience of that practice" (Bourdieu 1977c: 4). Bourdieu stressed that this was not simply a matter of phenomenologically reconstructing lived experience. It was necessary that a theory of practice give a good account of the limits of awareness involved in lived experience, including both misrecognition and nonrecognition, as well as show the kind of genuine knowledge which was involved, often nondiscursively, in practice. Moreover, there was struggle over knowledge, including the prelinguistic:

The individual or collective classification struggles aimed at transforming the categories of perception and appreciation of the social world and, through this, the social world itself, are indeed a forgotten dimension of the class struggle. But one only has to realize that the classificatory schemes which underlie agents' practical relationship to their condition and the representation they have of it are themselves the product of that condition, in order to see the limits of this autonomy. (1984: 483–4)

Thus critics (for example, Garnham and Williams 1980) have overstated the extent to which Bourdieu's account focused on reproduction at the expense of openings to the possibilities for action to create a new and different world – for example, to revolutionary struggle. Bourdieu's emphasis on reproduction did not foreclose contrary action, though neither did it introduce any notion of systematic pressures for such action. Bourdieu addressed the issue of revolutionary collective actions directly, although very briefly, and argued that they were imbricated within conjunctures and still crucially dependent on the same habitus which had hitherto organized reproduction. In other words, revolution did not mark a break with the habitus, but was based on it, even though it broke the pattern of stable reproduction:

It is just as true and just as untrue to say that collective actions produce the event or that they are its product. The conjuncture capable of transforming practices objectively coordinated because subordinated to partially or wholly identical objective necessities into *collective action* (e.g., revolutionary action) is constituted in the dialectical relationship between, on the one hand, a *habitus*, understood as a system of lasting, transposable dispositions which, integrating past experiences, functions at every moment as a *matrix of perceptions, and actions* and makes possible the achievement of infinitely diversified tasks . . . and an *objective event* which exerts its action of conditional stimulation calling for or demanding a determinate response, only on those who are disposed to constitute it as such because they are endowed with a determinate type of dispositions. (1977c: 82–3)

This, Bourdieu suggests, is the source of "the frequently observed incapacity to think historical crises in categories of perception and thought other than those of the past, albeit a revolutionary past" (ibid.).[15] Bourdieu also recognizes the role of the modern market and related economic changes – capitalism, I would say, though at this specific point he does not – in freeing "agents from the endless work of creating or restoring social relations" and providing the occasion for the break with the idea that society is held together by will and the recognition of the more or less impersonal, self-regulating mechanisms which play a central role in social integration (1977c: 189).

In this line of argument, we can see something of an analogue to Habermas's story of the uncoupling of the system and the lifeworld (1984, 1988b). In Bourdieu's account in *Outline*, the creation of self-regulating systematicity marks a crucial epochal break distinguishing kinds of societies and implicitly modes of analysis appropriate to them.

> The greater the extent to which the task of reproducing the relations of domination is taken over by objective mechanisms, which serve the interests of the dominant group without any conscious effort on the latter's part, the more indirect and, in a sense, impersonal, become the strategies objectively oriented towards reproduction: it is not by lavishing generosity, kindness or politeness on his charwoman (or on any other "socially inferior" agent) but by choosing the best investment for his money, or the best school for his son, that the possessor of economic or cultural capital perpetuates the relationship of domination which objectively links him with his charwoman and even her descendants. Once a system of mechanisms has been constituted capable of objectively ensuring the reproduction of the established order by its own motion . . . , the dominant class have only to *let the system they dominate take its own course* in order to exercise their domination; but until such a system exists, they have to work directly, daily, personally, to produce and reproduce conditions of domination which are even then never entirely trustworthy. (1977c: 189–90)

Bourdieu's distinction is very close to that which I would make between direct and indirect social relationships (Calhoun 1992). And at this point, without particularly stressing it or even labeling it, Bourdieu has given us an account not just of a distinctive mode of domination, but of the break between two modes of societal integration. In the first, the coordination of actions in society is achieved primarily through a web of personal relationships, each of which must be played like a highly nuanced game. This game has hardly ended in modern societies, I might add; the key difference is that it is no longer the central, constitutive way of organizing social relationships at large. Rather, the various apparently self-regulating systems perform that function most centrally. It is at this point, moreover, that it becomes particularly necessary for Bourdieu to introduce his concept of field.[16]

Bourdieu gives no particular reason why "less differentiated" societies should not be described in terms of fields, though this is not done in *Outline*, and at points Bourdieu suggests that "complex or differentiated" societies are precisely those which are characterized by having a number of fields. In any case, once attention is turned to "more complex" societies, something like the field concept is needed. Why? The reason has to do, I think, with an uncoupling of fields.[17] This uncoupling manifests itself first of all as a reduction in the extent to which the same agents are linked to each other in a variety of fields – say kinship, religion, and economic production – in other words, a reduction in the "multiplexity" of relationships, to use Max Gluckman's (1962) concept. But the uncoupling also manifests itself in a growing heterogeneity among fields, a reduction in the extent to which each is homologous with the others. This latter – if I am right – presents somewhat more of a problem for Bourdieu, given his general argument (for example, in *Distinction*) that the various fields are homologous. This does not necessarily preclude pursuit of a "general theory of fields," though it may limit it. The extent of homology can readily be made into an empirical variable, but the issue is important.

To see why, let us turn to a schematized notion of macro-historical social change. The change we are interested in lies in the means whereby which coordination of social action is achieved. At one level, what we are doing is adding some needed complexity to the Weberian notion of movement from tradition to modernity.[18]

Weber conceived of tradition simply as respect for "that which has always been" (1922: 36) and of traditional social organization primarily as simple continuity rather than the more complex project of reproduction. But let us think of tradition not in Bagehot's sense of the hard cake of culture, but, truer to its etymology, as an active verb, as *traditio* (cf. Shils 1981), referring to the passing on or handing down of information. Tradition, then, is a mode of transmission of information, particularly, for present purposes, that crucial to the coordination of action. Following Bourdieu's account of the habitus, we may note that the information need not be rendered discursive; it may be tacit knowledge, even knowledge embodied in modes of action which agents are unable to bring to linguistic consciousness, like basketball players their hook shots.

The habitus, on Bourdieu's account, works to shape this process even while it provides the regulated source of improvisations – indeed, precisely because it does. One of the crucial features of Bourdieu's account of the habitus is that it allows for a process of continual correction and adjustment: "The habitus . . . makes possible the achievement of infinitely diversified tasks, thanks to analogical transfers of schemes permitting the solution of similarly shaped problems, and thanks to the unceasing corrections of the results obtained" (Bourdieu 1977c: 83). Most tradition is not passed down in situations – for example, ritual performances or schools – in which that passing down is itself the main manifest project. On the contrary, most passing on and subsequent affirmations of culture take place in the course of interested actions in which people pursue a variety of ends, both conscious and unconscious. As people succeed or fail, meet with approval or disapproval, in trying to carry out their manifold projects of daily life, they may adjust slightly the traditional information that they have received from various others in the course of previous interactions. A basketball player, to return to that example, may imitate – or be explicitly taught – another's shot technique; but he learns to adjust the velocity to compensate for his own height or to add spin because it makes a favorable bounce more likely. The adjustments may be unconscious or conscious and in either case mandated by the recurrent evaluation of each shot as a success or a failure. But the example is imperfect; for the basketball player, we may assume, at least knows that he is playing basketball. Or does he? Might this be a limited perception of what is in fact a more complex strategy; achieving success in one field which seems relatively open while minimizing investment in another – say school – which seems closed, while half-consciously or even unconsciously engaging in strategies for achieving a sense of personal autonomy or perhaps escaping a ghetto and gaining a better standard of living?

Regardless, the basketball player illustrates the possibility of continued correction or adjustment in the passing on of tradition. This may be a crucial element of traditionality, of the extent to which tradition can actually serve to coordinate social activity, in many settings. If tradition were rigid, it would soon meet with disastrous consequences and prove itself an extremely inefficient means of coordinating action. It is precisely because it can be adjusted with (often unconscious) regard to the success or failure of various practical projects that the tradition embodied in the habitus can be supple enough to change with other aspects of a society.

More complex societies never lose this element of tradition, but it comes to organize somewhat less of what goes on and is often compartmentalized within specific spheres or at least at the local level.

Thus, in classical India and China, tradition of this kind took place constantly, resulting in a variety of local adaptations and idiosyncrasies. At the same time, the passing on of information – still tradition and still with an attitude of preservation not innovation – took place through other, especially textual means. These other means introduced a new institutional dimension – the role of authorized arbiters of correctness. This, I take it, is what Bourdieu refers to when he speaks of the "codification" of culture.

> The extent to which the schemes of the *habitus* are objectified in codified knowledge, transmitted as such, varied greatly between one area of practice and another. The relative frequency of sayings, prohibitions, proverbs and strongly regulated rites declines as one moves from practices linked to or directly associated with agricultural activity, such as weaving, pottery and cuisine, towards the divisions of the day or the moments of human life, not to mention areas apparently abandoned to arbitrariness, such as the internal organization of the house, the parts of the body, colours or animals. Although they are among the most codified aspects of the cultural tradition, the precepts of custom which govern the temporal distribution of activities vary greatly from place to place and, in the same place, from one official informant to another. We find here again the opposition between official knowledge . . . and all kinds of unofficial or secret, even clandestine, knowledge and practices which, though they are the product of the same generative schemes, obey a different logic. (1990e: 333–4)

In China, India, much of Islamic civilization, and, indeed, medieval Europe at least for a time, the operation of these more codified modes of transmission did not imperialistically challenge the simultaneous operation of more informal tradition within personal interaction. One of the distinctive features of the modern West may be the extent to which the transmission of "official" information through authoritative channels has in fact been destructive of the transmission of information through direct interpersonal relationships.[19]

Linked to this is the problematization of the informal tradition through differentiation of fields, increasing contact with people of different cultures, and increasing exercise of individual choice. The first, I think, is clear enough to need little comment. As various fields become differentiated, the information which can be passed on informally as part of the ordinary round of daily life becomes segmented. If more general information is called for, it is increasingly likely to be passed on through codified, authoritative means. And it is likely that, at the very least, those in power will find it necessary that some such information – say, about the virtues of their rule – be passed on. Information of this sort may still be traditional in the colloquial and/or Weberian sense that it embodies an attitude of deference for "what has always been" (whether or not it is in fact ancient being a matter quite secondary to whether it is believed to be so). This attitude is more likely to be ruptured when people are brought into routine contact with others quite different from themselves, especially under a common rule (which prevents them from treating their fellow-subject as quite radically other). Bourdieu addresses this point through his notion of a passage from the "doxic" attitude of not considering another form of existence or belief to the "orthodox" attitude of correctness with regard to authoritative standards of belief (1977c, 1990e). The next step is brought about by the increase in apparently independent decision making (either by individuals or by groups) which poses the challenge of heterodoxy. What apparent independence means is not just not following traditional rules, but acting in a habitus which is not highly congruent with those of others in one's fields.[20]

Bourdieu does not address this increase of independent decision making very directly in either *Outline* or *The Logic of Practice*. It is linked to his borrowing of economizing language to describe the strategies built into the play of the habitus. We need, however, to unpack the several dimensions of the notion of rationality. A notion of maximization is in fact only one possible meaning or aspect of rationality. Bourdieu suggests that at least some sort of maximizing is universal, because there is always scarcity. Of course, there may also be scarcity which is specific to various social fields, and maximizing may be in part a historically specific orientation to action. Just as maximizing is variable, so are the other dimensions of rationality. There is, for example, the question of how far a strategizer extends his or her horizons of calculation, how many of the objectively possible courses of action and their potential effects he or she actually analyzes. One of the crucial characteristics of the configuration of habitus and field in "traditional" societies was that they radically limited the range of options considered by rational actors. Whether actors were maximizing or not, this gave a much greater chance to traditionality as a means of coordinating action. For every increase in the range of options that a decision-maker considers not only increases the complexity of his or her own decision making but makes that person less predictable to others. This loss of predictability is apt to become part of a vicious circle, as others in a decision-maker's field are led to plan on shorter and shorter time horizons in order to allow themselves the opportunity to adjust to the unpredictability. This sort of attitude, this vicious circle, is antithetical to maintenance of stable traditional patterns of social relations. When coupled with increasing scale or reach of social relations, it leads to the necessity of adopting statistical measures of the probability of various courses of action, preferably averaged not only over time but across a range of other members of a field. At this point, we have left the coordination of action through tradition and entered the world of at least putatively self-regulating systems.

These self-regulating systems call for a more theoretical kind of understanding; the practical attitude of the habitus is less likely to be able to attain practical mastery of relationships within them. This is not to say that there is no longer any reason to talk of the habitus as governing the generation of improvisational strategies for dealing with such systems. On the contrary, there is no conceivable point at which human beings could be perfect rational actors; since they always operate within various forms of bounded rationality, it will always be necessary to consider the socially produced means of generating strategies which are open to them and which reflect the organization of the fields in which they act and their own trajectories through them. And in this sense a theoretical attitude should not be too sharply opposed to the notion of habitus (as Bourdieu – for example, 1977c – has sometimes implied). Rather, a theoretical attitude should be seen as a variety of habitus, itself reflecting a certain social placement and participation in specific socially con-structed projects. Thus it is not simply that "moderns" adopt theoretical attitudes, but that certain members of modern societies do so with regard to certain of their practices. An economist employed by the Ministry of Finance may rely on a theoretically informed habitus in conceptualizing the stock market and developing his own practical dealings with it (or its consequences). At the same time, a "pit trader" may work on the floor of the stock exchange, executing buy and sell orders with a supreme practical mastery minimally informed by any theoretical understanding of the overall market (though it is true that his or her habitus would be unlikely to resemble the doxic complete investment of a member of a highly homogenous and relatively self-contained society, for the floor trader would almost certainly be aware of the availability of other ways of understanding stock markets).

In a modern society, apparently self-regulating systems like large-scale markets are crucial links in the reproduction of patterns of social relations. Both they and the relatively high levels of distinction among fields encourage an attitude of a high level of rationality (understood as selecting among a wide range of options on the basis of maximal information about likely outcomes in order to efficiently pursue some goal). Therefore, even in the absence of internal contradictions which hamper their capacity to reproduce stably, the self-regulating systems are apt to give rise to social relational patterns which undermine stable reproduction. Of course, such systems – for example, capitalism – may have basic internal contradictions, in which case stability is even more doubtful.

This conclusion need not be seen as problematic for Bourdieu's work (indeed, it is produced through thinking along with parts of Bourdieu's work) *except* insofar as he *assumes*, rather than empirically demonstrates, a high level of homology among fields, an absence of systemic contradictions, and therefore a tendency towards social integration and stable reproduction of the encompassing field of power. I think he tends towards assuming this in *Distinction* (1984), *Homo Academicus* (1988b) and *La noblesse d'État* (1989c). But I do not think that this assumption is necessary to his analysis.

My argument in this essay has led to the conclusion that there are important, basic differences among kinds of societies. I believe that thinking through Bourdieu's own arguments suggests this, although he has not made it entirely clear what sorts of categories should be taken as historically specific and which as trans-historical. There are, of course, many possible kinds of difference and issues about difference which might be raised; I have only introduced, not exhausted, that subject. Indeed, there is a certain ambiguity about just what is to be generalized and what not in Bourdieu's empirical studies of various fields. Obviously the answers turn on further empirical investigations, but there is an implication of greater formal comparability than seems immediately warranted. It is one thing to ask how much the conceptual apparatus and analytic strategy of *Homo Academicus* would have to change to address the American case. It is a deeper matter to ask the reasons (not merely the "amorphous anecdotes of factual history" 1990d: 46) underlying the transformation of the medieval university through various stages into its modern namesake and successor. As Bourdieu recognizes, "it is necessary to write a structural history which finds in each state of the structure both the product of previous struggles to transform or conserve the structure, and, through the contradictions, tensions and power relations that constitute that structure, the source of its subsequent transformations" (1990d: 42).

Be that as it may, the specific sort of difference in transmission of culture addressed above is very important. It establishes, first of all, the basic grounding for addressing the question of what societies or modes of organizing social life are comparable for purposes of comparative research. And not least of all, it brings us back to the modernity/postmodernity debate.

On the one hand, Bourdieu's analyses of the relationship between habitus and field can be seen as adding crucial dimensions to Habermas's argument concerning the centrality of an uncoupling of system and lifeworld to the history of rationalization in the West.[21] At the same time, Bourdieu's analysis shows a weakness in Habermas's which results from Habermas's thoroughgoing rationalism and inattention to both the importance of practical mastery in any account of social action and especially the role of tradition transmitted informally as part of everyday strategic activity in accomplishing the coordination of social action and therefore in some cases societal integration.[22] My examination of Bourdieu's account also suggests that in order to mount more than a superficial claim to a "postmodern condition" (*pace* Lyotard 1984) one would need to show a basic change in the mode of coordinating action and/or in the basic relational organization of fields and the relation of habitus to fields.

This is a dimension that is missing from most postmodernist accounts. That is, they address various changes in media and style and the shift from production-oriented capitalism to an advertising and seduction-based consumerism and so forth, but they do not address the empirical question of whether social relations, most basically relations of power, are in fact changing. I read Bourdieu as arguing that they are remarkably stable, but this is not the key point. Rather, the point is what would have to be shown in order to make a good case for a postmodernist transformation of society.

At the same time that Bourdieu's work points to these gaps in the modernist/postmodernist debate – and thus potentially to a more interesting direction for theoretical and empirical exploration – it can be seen to suffer from a weakness or gap of its own. This is (to condense a cluster of related matters) a very minimal level of attention to the actual workings of the self-regulating systems of modern, large-scale societies and, more generally, what I have called indirect social relations – those mediated by information technology (communications, especially, but also other computer applications and surveillance) and complex administrative organizations as well as by markets and other self-regulating systems. Bourdieu has made profound contributions to our understanding of the relationship of embodied, prelinguistic, or nondiscursive knowledge to social action. His concepts of habitus and field direct our attention to crucial phenomena. But his other most distinctive notion, that of capital as multiform – social, cultural, economic, and symbolic – grasps only an aspect of capitalism. It grasps primarily the aspect which is distributive and/or central to relations of power. It does not grasp equally the sense in which capital itself – on an alternative reading of Marx (such as that of Lukács 1922 or Postone 1993) – is a form of mediation. Bourdieu (for example, 1983a, 1985c, 1986b) tends to reduce capital to power or a complex notion of wealth defined as resources for power, quite in contradiction to Marx's argument. More generally, Bourdieu's work so far shows an insufficient attention to the nature of mediation, the constitution of actors, and the modes of coordinating action in contemporary large, complex societies. This is hardly a severe criticism, for I do not see Bourdieu's theory closed to these considerations in any way; rather, it seems to me to be simply an important direction for our attention to turn. The roles of information technology, very large-scale administrative organizations, and impersonal markets are all important, both in their own right and as factors militating for basic changes in habitus and fields.

NOTES

1 Habermas has recently argued (1989) that discourse ethics is not much damaged by these criticisms.

2 Bourdieu here is specifically criticizing recent trends in anthropology (e.g. Clifford and Marcus (eds.) 1986) and the sociology of science (e.g. Latour 1987).

3 My account of Habermas's theory here relates primarily to his work from the mid–1960s to the present, especially his theory of communicative action and his discourse ethics (Habermas 1984, 1988b).

4 See Habermas (1988a) for a suggestion of how central a goal this is for his project. See also the interviews with Bourdieu in Wacquant 1989: 37.

5 More generally, Bourdieu has sharply rejected the intellectual totalism he associates with the Frankfurt school, with Sartre, and to some extent with Marxism generally. "Never before, perhaps, has there been so complete a manifestation of the logic peculiar to the French intellectual field that requires every intellectual to pronouce himself totally on each and every problem" (Bourdieu and Passeron 1967: 174; see also the preface to 1990e, 1988f, and Wacquant 1989). Bourdieu sees this as a feature not only of Marxism but of an intellectual field in which Marxism occupies a central place, obliging every intellectual to declare and explain his or her adherence or nonadherence.

6 Even capital becomes, for Bourdieu, a matter primarily of power (1986b: 252).

7 "It follows that the form taken by the structure of systems of religious practices and beliefs at a given moment in time (historical religion) can be far from the original content of the message and it can be completely understood

only in reference to the complete structure of the relations of production, reproduction, circulation, and appropriation of the message and to the history of this structure" (1991a: 18). Bourdieu goes on to stress the centrality of struggles for the monopoly of religious capital, including both struggles between clergy and laity and those between priestly authorities and heretical, quasi-religious or other challengers. "Genesis and structure of the religious field" has not been widely enough recognized as Bourdieu's key, seminal text on fields. There he shows clearly what he means by going beyond the "pure" study of meaning and interaction to study the underlying relations of struggle which produce and shape meanings and interactions and constitute their frame. The approach to religion expounded there anticipates that which he has more recently begun to develop towards the state (cf. Bourdieu 1989c).

8 As in his study of kinship and matrimonial strategies in his own village in Béarn (1990e: 249–70), Bourdieu's account revealed many commonalities with what he had seen in Kabylia and in general showed that his approach could yield insights into either setting just as readily. On the other hand, it did not address certain basic issues of difference between the settings – e.g., the fact that kinship is more central to the constitution of Kabyle society than it is to France, where it is central primarily to a compartmentalized local field but not to the state or the economy in general.

9 The issue is somewhat clouded because Bourdieu developed his tools as part of his continuing engagement with concrete analytic problems; so we cannot be sure when to treat a conceptual or analytic shift as having to do with a change in case (from his earlier work in Kabylia to his more recent work in France) and when with an intention to reformulate more generally. Thus, e.g., the concept of field plays little role in the *Outline of a Theory of Practice*, a substantial role in *The Logic of Practice*, and a central role in Bourdieu's more recent writings on French academia and professions (1984, 1987b, 1989c). Is this simply theoretical advance? Or is it a result of reflection on a different sort of society?

10 This is evident not only in *Das Kapital*, but especially in the *Grundrisse*, where the direction of Marx's thinking is sometimes clearer because its processes are more transparently laid out. See the forceful argument for this reading of Marx in Postone 1993.

11 Bourdieu's argument is that children gain from the added nurturance they receive from mothers who stay at home with them, something that only mothers in relatively well-off families can do. This illustrates the point well, though it is both empirically uncertain and arguably based on sexist assumptions.

12 See Wacquant 1989: 41. Bourdieu's arguments on the genesis of this notion of a pure aesthetics and its consequences for the analysis of culture are themselves important; see 1980a, 1987c.

13 Bourdieu suggests, indeed, that "far from being the founding model, economic theory (and rational action theory which is its sociological

derivative) is probably best seen as a particular instance, historically dated and situated, of field theory" (Wacquant 1989: 42). See also discussion in Wacquant and Calhoun 1989.

14 "Genesis and structure of the religious field" (Bourdieu 1991a) is a partial exception to this, making a point of historically different levels of codification or systematization of religion. The promulgation of increasingly codified religious systems is a product of specific groups – generally priests or clergy – struggling to institutionalize their dominance in the religious field. Simultaneously, such systematization furthers the autonomy of the religious field.

15 See Calhoun 1983 for an attempt to develop systematically the role of this grounding of radicalism in an older habitus.

16 And alongside the concept of field, that of multiform (social, symbolic, and cultural, as well as economic) and convertible capital. "The structure of a field is a state of balanced forces [*rapport de force*] between agents and institutions engaged in a war, or, if one prefers, it is a distribution of the specific capital which, accumulated in the course of previous wars, orients future strategies" (1984: 114; see also 1986b).

17 In discussion at the conference at which this essay was first presented, Bourdieu accepted and reiterated the importance of proliferation of fields for describing "complex" societies, by contrast with societies in which the division into fields is minimal.

18 This is the sort of "long-term history" which Bourdieu derides as "one of the privileged places of social philosophy" (1990d: 42). But, in the same paragraph, Bourdieu sets himself "the problem of the modern artist or intellectual," a problem intrinsically framed by reference to long-term history. So it is hard to escape broad historical schemas, like Weber's, even when one correctly notes the weakness of their empirical foundations or their susceptibility to overgeneralization.

19 Bourdieu suggests that codification renders things simple, clear, and communicable (1990d: 101). This seems sound, although he does not consider (at least to my knowledge) the possible counterbalancing aspect, the extent to which codification (alongside writing) allows for a dramatic increase in information flow and accordingly in overall complexity, even if the bits are simple.

20 The notion is much like that of Simmel's account (1903, 1967) of individuality as deriving from distinctiveness in social networks, specific intersections of social circles.

21 I have argued elsewhere (Calhoun 1989 and 1991) that Habermas's is a flawed conceptualization of a fundamentally important change.

22 I think that Bourdieu would also have a good deal of trouble with Habermas's discourse ethics. In the first place, there is Habermas's attempt to work through a notion of communication devoid of interested action. Bourdieu would presumably reject this, even as a regulative ideal. "Every exchange contains a more or less dissimulated challenge, and the logic of challenge and riposte is but the limit towards which every act of

communication tends. . . . To reduce to the function of communication . . . phenomena such as the dialectic of challenge and riposte and, more generally, the exchange of gifts, words, or women, is to ignore the structural ambivalence which predisposes them to fulfill a political function of domination in and through performance of the communication function" (1977c: 14). Even in the realm of "universal norms," Bourdieu wants to ask "who has an interest in the universal" and to see the history of reason as inescapably interested, like all other history (1990d: 31–2). See also discussion in Wacquant 1989, e.g. p. 50.

REFERENCES

Calhoun, C. 1983: The radicalism of tradition: community strength or venerable disguise and borrowed language? *American Journal of Sociology*, 88, no. 5, 886–914.
—— 1989: Social theory and the law: systems theory, normative justification and postmodernism. *Northwestern University Law Review*, 83, 1701–63.
—— 1991: Culture, history and the problem of specificity in social theory. In S. Seidman and D. Wagner (eds.), *Embattled Reason: postmodernism and its critics*. New York and Oxford: Basil Blackwell, 244–88.
—— 1992: The infrastructure of modernity: indirect relationships, information technology, and social integration. In H. Haferkamp and N. J. Smelser (eds.), *Social Change and Modernity*, Berkeley: University of California Press, 205–36.
Clifford, J. and Marcus, G. E. (eds.) 1986: *Writing Culture: The poetics and politics of ethnography*. Berkeley: University of California Press.
Garnham, N. and Williams, R. 1980: Pierre Bourdieu and the sociology of culture. *Media, Culture and Society*, 2–3, 297–312.
Gluckman, M. 1962: Les rites de passage. In M. Gluckman (ed.), *Essays on the Ritual of Social Relations*, Manchester: Manchester University Press.
Habermas, J. 1984: *The Theory of Communicative Action*, Vol. 1: *Reason and the Rationalization of Society*. Boston: Beacon.
—— 1988a: *The Philosophical Discourse of Modernity*. Cambridge, Mass.: MIT Press.
—— 1988b: *The Theory of Communicative Action*, Vol. 2: *Lifeworld and System: A critique of functionalist reason*. Boston: Beacon.
—— 1989: Morality and ethical life: does Hegel's critique of Kant apply to discourse ethics? *Northwestern University Law Review*, 83, 38–53.
Hollis, M. and Lukes, S. (eds.) 1982: *Rationality and Relativism*. Cambridge, Mass.: MIT Press.
Latour, B. 1987: *Science in Action*. Cambridge, Mass.: Harvard University Press.
Lukács, G. 1922: *History and Class Consciousness*. Cambridge, Mass.: MIT Press.
Lyotard, J-F. 1984: *The Postmodern Condition* (with "Answering the question: what is postmodernism?"). Minneapolis: University of Minnesota Press.

Postone, M. 1993. *Time, Labor, and Social Domination: a reinterpretation of Marx's critical theory*. Cambridge: Cambridge University Press.

Shils, E. 1981: *Tradition*. Chicago: University of Chicago Press.

Simmel, G. 1903 [1971]: The metropolis and mental life. In D. N. Levine (ed.), *Georg Simmel on Individuality and Social Forms*, Chicago: University of Chicago Press, 324–39.

—— 1967: *Conflict and the Web of Group Affiliations*, ed. K. Wolff. New York: Free Press.

Wacquant, L. 1989: Toward a reflexive sociology: a workshop with Pierre Bourdieu. *Sociological Theory*, 7, 26–63.

—— and Calhoun, C. 1989: "Interêt, rationalité, et histoire: à propos d'un débat Americain sur la theorie d'action. *Actes de la recherche en sciences sociales*, no. 78 (June), 41–60.

Weber, M. 1922 [1978]: *Economy and Society*. Berkeley: University of California Press.

Wilson, B. (ed.) 1970: *Rationality*. Oxford: Basil Blackwell.

Winch, P. 1958: *The Idea of a Social Science*. London: Routledge.

5

Aspects of Structural and Processual Theories of Knowledge

Aaron V. Cicourel

INTRODUCTION

This chapter has three parts. In the first, I address structural and processual theories of knowledge and social practice, calling attention to the way that each of these perspectives ignores the other, as well as to a number of methodological issues. The second part examines symbolic power and the kinds of empirical difficulties that can arise in the pursuit of a structural view of power. The third part briefly builds on and modifies the notion of habitus by reexamining and extending its conceptual structure and by suggesting empirical materials that can clarify developmental aspects of children's social knowledge, power, and decision making, or what elsewhere (Cicourel 1974) I have glossed as a "sense of social structure."

Throughout, I have depicted Bourdieu as a structuralist who is deeply sensitive to a meta-level conception of social practices. The use here of the term "structuralist" refers to levels of theory and data which are removed from the moment-to-moment interactional implementation of locally instantiated social organization. In this loose view of structuralism, domination or power is inferred by reference to abstract reports about decisions, the distribution of positions and resources in organizations, reports about access to persons in positions of power and reports about their differential use of an office to control the activities of others. Power, therefore, is structural in this view, because its sanctioned, enforced use is not observed in a locally managed environment accessible to the research analyst.

The essay reflects aspects of a long-standing dialogue with Pierre Bourdieu. Thanks to Bernard Conein, Paul Filmer, Hugh Mehan, Elinor Ochs, and Mel Pollner for helpful remarks on earlier drafts and Bernard Laks for useful comments on a later draft.

In order to address several levels of analysis, sometimes in the same paragraph or even in the same sentence, I use a number of meta-theoretical terms. These terms helped me to contrast Bourdieu's basic preoccupation with the structural origins of everyday and scientific knowledge and practice with a view that sees the study of social structure as a systematic examination of locally managed aspects of talk and social interaction. These two approaches sometimes overlap and supplement each other and often neglect cognitive, ethnographic, or organizational and developmental-linguistic elements that can enhance structural and processual perspectives, particularly with respect to socialization practices or the important notion that Bourdieu terms "habitus."

Bourdieu and ethnomethodologists are both preoccupied with the privileged status of the scientific observer, which for the most part goes unrecognized when research analysts study their own culture or even one viewed as foreign or exotic. The recognition that an implicit theory of practice emerges which also ignores the social conditions that make possible a social institution of science is not pursued by these two perspectives in the same way either theoretically or empirically. There are, however, common epistemological traditions that each draws upon.

The contrast between these two perspectives can be characterized as follows. For Bourdieu the origin of symbolic power is an imposition of culturally arbitrary conditions by an arbitrary power under the guise of a legitimate order (Bourdieu and Passeron 1977), and this power derives from a particular type of symbolic environment and aspects of material environment or habitus that consist of "systems of durable, transposable dispositions" that he terms "structured structures" (Bourdieu 1977c: 72). Habitus is something like a self-regulating system of generative principles whose durable existence produces practices that are the outcome of two systems of relations. The first refers to the idea of an objective structure that defines the social conditions in which the production of the habitus that engendered the practices occurs. The second refers to the conditions that represent a particular state of the habitus (Bourdieu 1977c: 78). The notion of habitus is cumulative in the sense that the structuring determinations or experiences which it produces early in life influence later acquisitions of habitus. The experiences acquired in the family influence the structuring of school experiences, and both these have their effect on work experiences.

The ethnomethodological view does not give primacy to these layers of "structured structures" that keep influencing subsequent life experiences and practices, but focuses on the cultural emergence and enforced use of practical reasoning said to be constitutive of daily social interaction and reciprocally necessary for sustaining an unquestioned belief in the idea of an objective reality or social structure. Both perspectives would probably agree however, that the principle structures that are relevant for understanding social action are environmental in nature, in contrast to the idea of mental structures, folk models, or schemata.

Bourdieu is perhaps unique among major theorists for his preoccupation with and knowledge of methodological issues and practice. Not only did his first book, *Travail et travailleurs en Algérie* (Bourdieu *et al.* 1963), describe the conditions under which he had conducted his sociological research, but similar concerns can be found in *La Noblesse d'État* (1989c), in which he describes how he gained access to the materials employed in his research. In *Outline of a Theory of Practice* (1977c) Bourdieu frequently mentions methodological problems associated with ethnographic research. A critique of sampling and the way in which respondents react to the framing of questions appears in the "Culture and Politics" chapter of *Distinction* (1984) in the context of using the same questionnaire across social classes. The selective examples presented from actual interviews are rich in detail. His general point is that it is difficult to ask working- and middle-class respondents the same questions as if they will understand them similarly. Bourdieu raises a number of objections about surveys of personal opinion and, for example, the significance of "don't know" responses to questions about politics. Aspects of the ecological validity of the survey questions might have been clarified if a sociolinguistic analysis of all the responses to the questionnaire had been made by contrasting such an analysis with the inferences made from the aggregated tables of coded responses.

In his penetrating examination of survey and other data gathered about those who were successful in national university examinations around the years 1966, 1967, and 1968, Bourdieu provides extensive data on the organizational structures responsible for making important decisions about the production of educational and occupational elites in French society. General data on the hierarchically classified schools in the sample and a set of files on 154 students assembled by a professor of philosophy are also analyzed, including five to six pages of notes on each student's academic characteristics, as well as data on the student's date of birth, the occupation and address of the student's parents, and the secondary schools attended. The research reported in *La Noblesse d'État* thus includes several important sources of primary and secondary information that are consistent with Bourdieu's structural theory of power and social stratification. His discussion of the manner in which the survey was executed, the kinds of schools involved, including fortuitous contingencies associated with obtaining data, implementing the research, and the limits of the data obtained is presented in considerable detail in an appendix on method, as well as in several brief sections of the text itself. The methodological remarks both challenge and make careful use of traditional types of sociological methods and sources of data.

SELECTIVE ASPECTS OF THEORIES OF STRUCTURE AND PROCESS

A major assumption here is that different levels of analysis are neither self-evident nor self-sustaining theoretically, substantively, and methodologically. Each level constrains and facilitates the existence of the others. Universal aspects of cognitive, cultural, and language structure and use are necessary but not sufficient conditions to predict and/or explain structural effects and locally managed and instantiated social action. Although variable exceptions can be proposed, structural and processual theorists have given insufficient attention to the ethnographic or ecological contexts and organizational constraints that give rise to data presumed to lend support to theoretical propositions. The data used in both perspectives are seldom addressed as problematic conditions for theory building. Contextual conditions of data gathering are usually ignored, as are pertinent biographical information on the research analysts and their relationship to those persons from whom data are obtained. In addition, theorists do not address the ways in which materials or data are assembled or constructed differentially because of the authority and power wielded by or attributed to members of institutionalized settings.

We know little about the organizational conditions under which private and public agencies produce official or semi-official or informal verbal and numerical accounts or summaries of an organization's activities that are subsequentiy cited as "facts" or reorganized by social scientists as data. The epistemological foundations of a discipline cannot afford to ignore the evidential base of substantive claims to knowledge. For example, the contexts or occasions when respondents are inter- viewed under contrived conditions are not contrasted with their behavior in natural settings. We know little about organizational and interpersonal differences in the way accounts, conversations, assess- ments, or decisions are produced. Theorists pay little attention to the fact that when research analysts contact respondents and prompt them to produce desirable responses, they reproduce the conditions that reflect the power relations that are often the object of the research. The way the research analyst poses questions and codes them contributes to the potential and realizable domination that can occur. Research analysts often neglect to examine the folk notions of power and the conversational or interactional dominance they bring to their research activities and how these conditions can influence the data generated and the theoretical explanations produced. Research and theory that builds on social processes, therefore, inevitably involve local sociology of knowledge conditions that are often ignored by the research analyst.

Processual and structural theorists not only neglect the construction processes that create the data employed by research analysts, they also underrepresent or disregard the cognitive mechanisms or processes whereby respondents or the personnel of private and public agencies organize their experiences and produce the data or products consumed by social scientists (for example, technical reports, surveys or interviews, legal briefs, memoranda, death certificates, census data). Cognitive activities are embedded in interactional exchanges about what counts as data, coding procedures, and organizational policies and constraints. These activities rely on forms of language use as if they were self-evident resources.

In more general terms, structural and processual theorists and research analysts tend to neglect the sources needed to sustain independent structural and processual approaches in the social sciences. Each approach uses the other as a resource, not as a topic of equal relevance. Each approach views its own conceptual level of analysis and data as self-evidently applicable to the theoretical issues addressed and the methodological strategies employed.

In *Outline of a Theory of Practice* (1977c: 2), Bourdieu avoids some of the above criticisms by taking account of the conditions necessary for adequate scientific practice in the social sciences. He notes that anthropologists must not only break with a perspective that seeks to depict native experience and native representation of such experiences, but also pursue a second break by questioning the presuppositions associated with the view of an outside observer. The second break is necessary because outside observers become so preoccupied with interpreting native practices that they are likely to transform the latter's relation to the object of study into the object of inquiry. Even worse, notes Bourdieu (p. 2), is the constitution of "practical activity as an object of observation and analysis, a representation," by first pulling away from action in order to observe it from above and with the benefit of distance, so as to attain a more detached view of the action.

According to Bourdieu (pp. 3–4), the social world can be apprehended by the pursuit of three modes of theoretical knowledge. The first he

terms "phenomenological" or "ethnomethodological," which he views as
the concern with making "explicit the truth of primary experience of the
social world" or its unquestioned familiarity or its "unquestioned
apprehension of the social world" in an unreflective way, such that it
"excludes the question of the conditions of its own possibility.

The second mode of theoretical knowledge is termed "objectivist" in
the sense of a Saussurian theory of meaning that presumes a standardized
or uniform set of coding and decoding operations inherent in the notion
of *langue*. This mode of theoretical knowledge calls into question the
objective truth of primary experience and the conditions associated with
making such experiences possible.

The third mode of theoretical knowledge seeks to examine the
conditions that make experience possible while exploring the limits of
what is deemed objective and the notion of an objectifying perspective
that claims to possess an external procedure for grasping practices. What
is needed, notes Bourdieu, is to understand practices from within the
activity of their accomplishment and their dialectic relationship to the
access afforded by the objective structures that can be attained by this
mode of theoretical knowledge.

Bourdieu seeks to escape from the dualism of subjectivism and
objectivism in the social sciences by proposing theories of practice and
practical knowledge that are embedded in a broader theory. This
comprehensive theory seeks the limits of this third mode of knowledge
by examining theoretical and general social conditions associated with
objective apprehension.

Bourdieu's work can be seen as encompassing both structural and
processual theoretical issues systematically, but his empirical work,
while exceptionally broad in scope, is somewhat more eclectic. For
example, in his early work among the Berbers of Algeria (Bourdieu *et al.*
1963, 1979a) is an ethnographic account of the Kabyle that was to have a
pervasive influence on the way Bourdieu conceptualized and studied
cultural and symbolic power and the kinds of practices associated with
power in general. But he also collaborated in a combined ethnographic
and survey research study (Bourdieu *et al.* 1963) of rural and urban
Algerians that carefully revealed the problems of both kinds of research
in a colonial setting. The sensitivity displayed in these early works nicely
complemented his prior philosophical training.

The unusual combination of ethnographic and survey research in
Algeria (with a team of statisticians) began a long series of empirical
studies that he has been used continually to broaden and deepen his
theoretical interests in cultural and symbolic power and practice and to
increase his sensitivity to problems of epistemology and evidence. The

data include tables derived from the survey and are nicely supplemented by many appendices devoted to interview accounts that sought to display how informants expressed themselves. The thrust of his empirical work, however, seems to be concerned less with assessing the validity of theory by reference to methodological practices during research and the way inferences are drawn from selective descriptions of informants or respondents than with obtaining general empirical support for his important theoretical ideas about power and social stratification.

Subsequent research in France appears to have been heavily influenced by the politics of French intellectual life and the national political scene. For example, the Bourdieu and Passeron book (1977) was originally published in 1970 after the events of 1968. The book can be viewed in part as a reaction to the absence of a theory of culture in Marxism. Thus, in broad terms, it can be said that the reference to an interactional process helped to mitigate the preoccupation with ideology by urging the study of everyday praxis. Bourdieu's preoccupation with process, however, remained structurally motivated.

The careful theoretical arguments and empirical analysis of detailed ethnographic evidence from his study of the Berbers in Algeria and the complicated theoretical analysis of earlier research in *Outline of a Theory of Practice* both refined and extended previous epistemological, conceptual and substantive views. Linking the research analyst's collection, organization, and analysis of data to the epistemological assumptions of Bourdieu's rich theoretical and substantive contributions, however, can be a difficult task. Although he projects an impressive, broadly based theory that includes a clear, promising set of processual foundations to his general theory of practice, the discussions of process do not appear to be integrated with the way in which different types of evidence were obtained across different research projects in Algeria and France. For example, he does not describe the relation between gaining access to sources of information, the research analyst's personal or indirect relationships with informants or respondents, and the way the latter two conditions are part of local circumstances of data collection that can influence the coding of data and the subsequent use of coded aggregate data for theoretical claims. Yet, *Outline* contains references to problems of misinformation and the ways in which informants can and did contradict themselves. Similar problems are reported in *Distinction*. Theoretical and substantive contributions reported in *Distinction* appear to rely on epistemological and methodological issues associated with earlier ethnographic work.

Bourdieu's work can be viewed as two contrasting yet overlapping sets of activities. One set is epistemologically and ethnographically oriented and devotes most of its attention to theoretical and substantive issues that derive from a structural view of practice. Complex topics like kinship, the nature of classificatory systems, honor, and habitus provide the basis for developing a theory of symbolic power that is carried over into empirical and theoretical research in France that deals with symbolic power, cultural capital, and social classification in complex nation-states. The philosophical foundations for addressing the above important ideas are always addressed in considerable detail. Yet his major work, *Outline of a Theory of Practice*, can be seen as a distinctive combination of substance and theory that contrasts with the way in which Bourdieu addresses class relations in *Distinction* and *La Noblesse d'État*. Thus, the work in France does not examine such topics as honor or kinship, and the notion of habitus is no longer embedded in ethnographically examined settings. There is continuity, however, in his use of classificatory systems. They provide a useful, though somewhat abstract, framework for examining class differences and symbolic power.

Bourdieu's structural view presumes an objective social reality that leads to the development of a theory of symbolic power. The origins of symbolic power lie in a necessary period of socialization or durable training or habitus in which the basic principles of an initial culturally arbitrary system of beliefs, values, norms, and practices are inculcated or internalized in order to perpetuate or reproduce the authority and dominance of an essentially arbitrary but dominant power group or class. The dominant power group, therefore, seeks to impose what Bourdieu and Passeron (1977) call a "cultural arbitrary," or symbolic system of meanings, and a projection of legitimacy that seeks to conceal the power relations that are the basis of its force. The book links the notion of power in Marx and Weber to the idea of a symbol system as proposed by Saussure and Lévi-Strauss. The integration of these conceptual frameworks is perhaps epitomized by the "double," or "dual," arbitrariness of culture as power and symbol system. Within the perspective of this earlier view of symbolic power, a view that Bourdieu would surely reject today, there is an interaction that binds pedagogic agent and child to structures of dominance and symbolization.

Something of a paradox emerges in this earlier work by Bourdieu and Passeron with respect to the relation between process and structure. Whereas the notion of structure dominates the conceptual issues at all times, there does not appear to be any clear sense of how process affects structure and vice versa. The recipient of process, therefore, is like an empty black box. This earlier theoretical view remains within the confines of the classical structural tradition, despite the fact that Bourdieu and Passeron are being critical of the classical French structuralist point of view. More recent work, like *Outline* and *Distinction*, avoids the rather mechanistic notion of "inculcation" and instead seems to prefer terms like "incorporation" or "embodiment." Habitus becomes a more central aspect of Bourdieu's theory because it reflects the way in which differently situated actors are related to the dominant culture and the personal assessments of these relations.

The notion of habitus is now more processual-like by its reference to the way the body is displayed and the idea of a life- style that includes a broad range of activities or appearances such as the use of gestures, posturing, speaking, dressing, and eating. The broad, yet specific, senses in which the term "taste" (*goût*) is employed by Bourdieu give him a powerful entry into the ramifications that the habitus can have over the reproduction of a dominant culture in a society. Habitus, therefore, is both an "internalization" and an "incorporation" of culture. What needs to be clarified is how habitus and the idea of social distinction become visible over the course of locally managed, contextualized displays of speaking, dressing, moving one's body, and eating.

The processual view embedded in ethnomethodology has often been characterized as the taken-for-granted practices through which members of a presumed group or society constitute, or create, and coordinate their activities in a locally managed environment. A preoccupation of this perspective has been the situated nature of the way in which ordinary activities are constructed in locally negotiated settings. A paradox of this concern with the constitution and coordination of members' activities is that the social scientist's inquiry into such practices is itself to be viewed as an "achieved", or "constructed", accomplishment or task. Such a view has often produced the criticism that an infinite regress is inevitable. Another way of stating the problem is to note that research analysts must believe in an objective reality in order to initiate their own inquiry even while theoretically stipulating that such activities are themselves practical accomplishments. The empirical conditions whereby inquiry is initiated are often neglected in ethnomethodological studies. Likewise, these problems also are not uncommon in work by symbolic interactionists. For example, fieldwork that involves extensive participant observation and/or elaborate open-ended interviews often does not clarify how gaining and sustaining entry into a group influences the research analyst's field notes, interview questions, inferences, and explanations.

An early concern of ethnomethodology was Parsons's (1951) later structural theory and the reference to internalized norms as an explanation of social action. Parsons's view overlooked the interpretative and judgmental work or cognitive processing and knowledge of language needed on-line during the course of interaction in order for actors to make sense of norms as a practical accomplishment. The role of the mental models of the natives and the research analyst as they sought to assess the rational (for the actor) nature of their own and others' activities on-line was not part of Parsons's theory. In particular, the sequential interaction of actors and their use and comprehension of language and nonverbal aspects of exchanges were not viewed as directly relevant. What was relevant was a meta, or system, level of concern in which idealized prescriptive and proscriptive normative elements were identified by the theorist and attributed to actors.

Although each of the structural and processual perspectives begins with an intact sociocultural world, they call into question different aspects of this world and use different theoretical and empirical strategies. Bourdieu's structural view sees the exercise of symbolic violence or power as being under a cloak of legitimacy and constitutive of sociological knowledge and knowledge of society, particularly if it is possible to conceal the power relations that are the basis of its force, thereby enhancing its own ability to influence its use of symbolic force. What are problematic, however, are the structural and hypothetical processual conditions whereby the projection of legitimately sanctioned symbolic power is brought into existence and perpetuated by primary and secondary agencies of socialization, such as familial and educational systems. The projection of legitimacy that a dominant group seeks to have attributed to these latter two systems masks the way in which a dominant cultural arbitrary contributes to and controls the reproduction of existing power relations. This structural view, as described so far, addresses a theory of symbolic violence or power by examining its production and reproduction in systems that are foundational for the ability of groups, societies, and nation-states to create and sustain not only power relations, but their daily and long-term existence.

The structural view does not address the moment-to-moment or locally managed and practiced activities that sustain the idea of an objective reality necessary for the practical emergence and historical evolution of systems of meaning, talk, and interaction. The stimulus conditions that bring into existence interactional frames of reference that permit on-line decisions and actions that produce and reproduce a cultural arbitrary are not addressed directly: for example, the way in which topics or issues associated with power, honor, and social identity emerge and are identified as "appropriate" or not and discussed, debated, adopted, modified, and implemented in daily life discourse and practices.

The processual view, on the other hand, overlooks the essentially power-laden structural conditions through which pedagogic agencies and agents become central elements in the way that systems of talk and social interaction are learned and are sustained over time. The idea of preserving an objective reality through a system of practical or mundane or commonsense reasoning is always embedded in organizational contexts of power relations. An empirical issue is the extent to which systems of talk and interaction are influenced by the cultural arbitrary of dominant groups. In addition, how do cognitive and linguistic conditions and the scale and dynamics of ethnographic or organizational activities influence the structure of social interaction and talk?

In more abstract terms, the identification of the power relations of a dominant cultural arbitrary presupposes systematic and sanctioned structural and local processes of talk and interaction for recreating everyday social life. On the other hand, what conditions are necessary to examine the structure of local social interaction as a phenomenon in its own right, as intrinsically constituted and reconstituted by mundane reasoning, beliefs, and practices that are essential for preserving the idea of an objectively given world or social reality? Presumably, some kind of system of symbolic power is presupposed and practiced and enforced by daily life participants. Participants do not interact merely to preserve conversational structures and their belief in the idea of an objectively given social reality; they also interact as part of a larger system of social and emotionally charged interpersonal and structural power relations to which they are differentially committed and entangled on a daily or periodic basis. Indeed, the very idea of scientific knowledge about the foundations of structural and processual knowledge is contingent on the negotiated power relations of inquiry.

Structural and processual theories of knowledge tend to under-represent the cognitive and semantic basis for their claims to the meanings that both acknowledge as essential for their respective perspectives. But the cognitive and linguistic theories currently available revolve around an individualized perspective in the sense that cognitive and semantic theories address the way a single mind functions in processing information during problem solving or establishing the meaning of a lexical item or single sentence. The environment remains a residual category. The task of identifying, much less describing, the experiences of participating in surveys or experimentally with those being studied is seldom an explicit part of the structural, processual, and cognitive-linguistic approaches to theories of knowledge. Even when the environment is recognized as relevant, it is underrepresented.

The environments, or natural habitats, of human animals are difficult to describe, because research analysts are inescapably embedded in some or many aspects of the lifeworlds they must invoke as background conditions to the phenomena of explicit systematic concern. The problem exists in all field research, including work in ethnomethodology, symbolic interactionism, and conversation analysis, and perhaps more obviously in the case of experimental, demographic, and survey research where everyday environmental conditions are glossed with a vocabulary that is directly linked to the research analyst's taken-for-granted commonsense knowledge of the same habitat. Research analysts using these latter research methodologies ask subjects or respondents to answer questions about their everyday environments and beliefs, emotions, intentions, goals, and perceptions independently of describing the influence of prior and local ecological settings within which such topics might emerge and be discussed.

SYMBOLIC POWER, HABITUS, AND THEIR ECOLOGICAL VALIDITY

Bourdieu and Passeron (1977) introduce the notion of pedagogic work to account for the way that a pedagogic agency (the family, school, or similarly organized social institution) can reproduce the principles of a cultural arbitrary in a set of recipients. The cultural arbitrary (values, beliefs, norms, practices) refers to those principles that a dominant group or class delegates to a pedagogic authority. Pedagogic action is required to develop long-lasting training consequences, or habitus.

The socialization period alluded to above has long been part of sociological theory but is seldom linked to the kinds of structural symbolic power relations and content identified by Bourdieu. Sociological writings (see Lindesmith *et al.* 1975) about socialization have invariably followed the developmental ideas presented by G. H. Mead, Freud, and Piaget. There is also an extensive anthropological tradition associated with research on culture and personality (including Benedict 1934, 1949; Landy 1959; Mead 1946; Sapir 1949; Whiting and Child 1953; and Whiting 1966) that could be incorporated into the notion of habitus.

Habermas (1987) also has recently addressed this developmental view, primarily by focusing on G. H. Mead and seeking to integrate his work on symbolically mediated interaction and the nature of social action that emerges with roles with Durkheim's collective consciousness as a prelinguistic foundation for communicative action. Durkheim's work, notes Habermas (pp. 45–7), adds conditions that are not adequately attended to in Mead's work. For example, Durkheim provides a basis for "the normative validity of institutions and values," as well as "the sacred roots of the moral authority of social norms." The focus of Habermas's work also has been on universally structured processes rather than locally managed socialization practices and on-line communicative displays.

The identification and measurement of the durability, transferability, and exhaustiveness of a habitus presume criteria or evidence that goes beyond structural data: for example, looking at natural settings and examining interactional instantiations of habitus in terms of family and school exchanges, as reported in Whiting 1966, Cicourel *et al.* 1974, Corsaro 1985, Heath 1983, Mehan 1979, Ochs 1988, Philips 1982, and Schieffelin 1990. The processual studies, however, are less able to identify longitudinal aspects of the socialization process; but they do address speech events that can be useful resources for pinpointing the power relations that Bourdieu has stressed throughout his writings on habitus. The ethnographic studies contain valuable material whose reinterpretation could yield important substantive details on the exercise of power and the child's developmental understanding of adult domination. In the case of Schieffelin's (1990) research, it is not necessary to re-read her data and analysis in order to say it is about power; the topic is evident at all times in her study of language and socialization issuses.

Within the structural tradition outlined by Bourdieu, an inherent system of power relations is presumed to be in place and is to be understood from the perspective of research analysts who are knowledgeable about the workings of their own and similar societies and pedagogic agencies. Research analysts would be expected to make use of the native categories and measures of school achievement and assessment in order to construct measures of the durability, transferability, and exhaustiveness of a habitus and the productivity of pedagogic work.

A central aspect of the notion of symbolic capital and the socialization experiences associated with a habitus is the way symbolic capital is said to impose categories of perception on the viewer such that the act of observing and recognizing symbolic capital transforms the latter into economic or cultural capital. The implied process here is said to be important for reproducing and reinforcing the power structures which define the organization of social space.

A number of conceptual and empirical issues come to mind when we try to assess the extent to which individuals and groups are said to acquire the symbolic capital that imposes on the minds of others a vision of social divisions by invoking some sense of a legitimate social authority. For example, in large-scale societies, there are invariably two or more competing groups seeking to impose their views through private and public lobbying or behind-the-scenes activities. The impact that these competing groups have on what takes place in the school system is not self-evident in terms of what takes place locally in both policy-making bodies and daily teaching and administrative practices.

The idea that objective relations are independent of actual social interaction is valid only when using aggregate data that eliminate the "noisy" conditions of actual exchanges and their reproductive role in recreating and modifying objective structures perceived by members and research analysts. Bourdieu might counter that the power to force objective relations will be exhibited in interaction in ways so as not to appear to be what it in fact is, namely, arbitrary force. The general idea is that force is displayed unconsciously by the agent with power. Agents with power may not be self-conscious about the violence they are able to accomplish. The agent of power who is accomplished at his performance should be genuinely mystified by anyone calling attention to his or her power. Misrecognition, therefore, enables objectivity to become subjectivized by agents of power. Hence, objective structures exist independent of the consciousness of agents. These issues can be resolved only partially by reference to elegant structural conceptual distinctions and the abstract and aggregate sources of data assembled initially by some of the very agents and agencies about whom a study is initiated. Establishing the independent validity of such data remains an empirical problem.

How do research analysts identify differences in the kind of "false consciousness" they associate with displays of power? The general idea is that agents of power can be "mystified" by claims that they are exercising power, or that such agents (for example, parents or schoolteachers) will seek to exempt their use of power by claiming that it is temporary and being used only for the occasion or incident at hand. I find Bourdieu's observations convincing only so long as a rather abstract notion of consciousness is used.

A number of important empirical issues need to be addressed if the viability of his theory of power is to be increased. For example, in more concrete terms, persons interacting in daily life settings do not always remind each other of the other's power or lack of it in direct terms, yet such verbal and nonverbal displays can be explicit on occasion. The empirical issues revolve around a more immediate sense of consciousness and the various ways in which participants of interaction can be said to be unaware of exercising power or seek to convey the idea of not exercising power. What strategies are employed that resist displays of power or that seek to neutralize it? We lack adequate empirical studies of different displays of power (and its perception) irrespective of whether they can be linked to the notion of habitus and its duration in subsequent life settings. We are often dependent on the research analyst's abstract descriptions of power relations because they appear to resonate well with (tacitly understood) personal experiences.

Concepts like habitus and cultural capital are structural notions that presume differentiated social class environments which have and can be described in general and specific terms by virtue of the availability of information from within most societies about the distribution of material resources, a network of positions or observed differences, and the appropriation of rare goods. To refer to such structures or relations as objective, notes Bourdieu, is to claim that they exist independent (of what I presume are the daily life displays) of consciousness by (actual) agents, language (used), (recorded) myths, and (locally observed) educational systems. But this notion of "genetic structuralism" also embraces the social genesis of abstract mental structures of schemes of perception, thought, and action which are constitutive of habitus.

The idea of objective structures remains ambiguous from a processual perspective, because notions like mental structures of schemes of perception, thought, and action of the agents, language, myths, and educational systems associated with the production or reproduction of structure presume levels of processual research not met with in structural theorizing and findings. For example, the ability to acquire and use language necessitates empirical study to establish the universal structures associated with speech events involving two or more persons in locally managed sociocultural settings. The reasoning or thought processes that emerge in childhood and are necessary for attributions of adult communicative competence during speech events, particularly when such events revolve around on-line practical decision making, are foci of research that are neglected by structural theorists. Similar observations can be made about the myths and belief structures attributed to individuals, groups, and societies by structural theorists.

The above processual research issues and the structures they identify and produce are constitutive of, and implicated in, the production of what are termed "objective social structures" – for example, officially recorded or respondent-derived distributions of persons in a society by the use of such cultural categories as age, sex, occupation, income, health, education, religion, status group, political organization, and other domains of institutionalized activities. These objective structures are assumed to be essential for depicting historical development and change. They are also necessarily implicated in the socially organized activities that frame and guide the processes inherent in establishing and sustaining locally managed social interaction. How these structures are implicated in daily life processes is an empirical matter that tends to be neglected by both perspectives.

In the pages that follow, I briefly examine aspects of research that can clarify Bourdieu's notion of habitus by calling attention to empirical issues inherent in a structural theory that also seeks to account for mental structures or schemes of perception, thought, and action said to be constitutive of habitus.

The case of the child's acquisition of commonsense or practical reasoning is at the heart of the conceptual and empirical issues that must be addressed to sustain a link between the structural view and daily life practice. The evolution of the child's commonsense view of the world is constitutive of learning to adapt to the local power and interpersonal relations in which all socialization is embedded.

SOME EMPIRICAL ISSUES

A number of issues emerge about the ability of the research analyst to observe power and the kinds of evidence that can be obtained to affirm or deny its acquisition, use, and loss. Bourdieu provides a convincing structural view of power, which begins with socialization experiences embedded in a dominant cultural arbitrary that perpetuates the existing power relations, endures beyond the habitus, and reveals how power is evident structurally in terms of the appropriation of scarce goods and the distribution of symbolic and cultural capital.

The socialization of children can be viewed as problem solving and decision making while exercising power in actual settings. Bourdieu's notion of habitus can be enhanced by conceptual refinements and empirical studies that make use of routine developmental issues as sources of knowledge about the acquisition of power. Missing from Bourdieu's theory and virtually all developmental theories of language, cognition, and culture is the perspective of the child. But Turiel's (1983) study of the child's understanding of social convention is a useful resource here. We know very little about how children perceive, comprehend, implement, and modify power relations during periods of socialization. The research analyst is to some extent always captive of the adult's vocabulary and background knowledge that is used to identify and describe the existence of sources of power and their implementation.

The achievement of structural power is often contingent on the necessary use of mundane communicative competence, and the latter is essential for sustaining the sense of an objective reality presupposed in the idea of power relations. In more general terms, the acquisition and subsequent implementation of power relations and communicative competence cannot be taken for granted as structurally obvious if we are to understand the way in which power is exercised or sustained throughout local circumstances of social interaction.

The study of the acquisition and use of power by children and adults in actual settings draws upon a member's or native's understanding of a larger organizational, as well as a locally managed, context and sequences of perceived activities or speech events and gestures or movements. The use of structural data forces the research analyst to rely on taken-for-granted native categories used in the manipulation and analysis of materials that is seldom made evident to the reader. The study of local settings requires both ethnographic description and different analytic tools for the analysis of the language and interaction recorded, as well as an understanding of the organizational relations that exist among participants.

Commonsense or practical reasoning is essential to the way humans carry out the business of reconstructing sociocultural relations and institutions. Bourdieu, ethnomethodologists, and their intellectual forebears have devoted a great deal of their work to the study of practical reasoning (Garfinkel 1967, Pollner 1987, Schutz 1945, 1953). Commonsense reasoning has been addressed developmentally by Piaget, among others, and these views are refined and altered continually in recent research. Below, developmental views are presented to illustrate the kind of theorizing and research that can clarify and expand the notion of habitus.

Forguson and Gopnick define a commonsense view of the world as an "interconnected network of implicit beliefs about the world and our relation to it that informs our everyday thought and behavior as adults, and to which we appeal in defending our everyday claims and explaining our own and others' actions" (1988:1). Several familiar notions are described by the authors: for example, the idea of an implicitly presumed common background necessary for interpreting others as rational and who with ourselves are seen as part of a common world. Believing that one has shared basic beliefs with others becomes the basis for interpreting their actions as human behavior.

A commonsense view of the world, note Forguson and Gopnick, refers to the psychological notion that human actions are causally dependent on the role of the actor's epistemic state or knowledge and beliefs about what is or was some state of affairs and what will or would be some state of affairs if such and such prevailed, and, in addition, the state of affairs the actor would for the most part like to obtain.

The commonsense metaphysical view of the world presumes the existence of a single world of objects, events, people, and states of the world that the individual and others experience through perception and thought. The core of this belief system is that this single world exists independent of the way in which the individual and others think about and experience it.

The notion of mind refers to the individual's and others' internal or subjective or imagined or dreamed-about or make-believe objects, events, and states of affairs. The internal perspective contrasts with the view that refers to the external and independent existence of an objective world. The metaphysical view also postulates that the internal view leads to differential states of knowledge vis-à-vis what one person can know about an alleged fact or what others may or may not know.

The two views described by Forguson and Gopnick (1988) imply, but do not address, the sociocultural basis of communicative competence and how the child learns to interact with others in different social settings. For example, how do people report experiences and thoughts about the same objects and events or about similar emotional experiences on different occasions? Little is said about the organization of sociocultural communication necessary for thoughts and experiences to be perceived as the same or similar and as part of a collective enterprise that must be reproduced and reaffirmed continuously. The beliefs involved in the philosophical and psychological views defined by Forguson and Gopnick include the earlier notion of an environment of objects that remains intact when not perceived by an individual or others and the idea that physical action is required to change the world and not simply wanting or wishing it to happen.

The coerciveness or constraining nature of primary and secondary agents of socialization and social control are not central elements in philosophical views of commonsense realism. The latter are concerned primarily with tracing the growth of the child's cognitive and linguistic skills. Nor are socially sanctioned power relations and modes of interaction or the study of locally managed forms of discourse part of the philosophical view except as abstract speech acts. Speech acts are viewed as self-evident aspects of the features of realism that are said to form the background knowledge of things about which we believe and talk (for example, beliefs). The philosophical view proposes abstract interaction between propositions that express beliefs and propositions that express the background knowledge of one's beliefs.

Forguson and Gopnick (1988: 6) cite research that points to a commonsense view of the world among children that is acquired gradually from about 18 months to about 5 years of age, with a key threshold occurring around 4 years of age. The basic aspects of common-sense reasoning include believing in some event or the existence and nature of an object or the mental ability to represent the event or object (first-order representation) and the ability to imagine yourself or others believing in the same event or the same object's existence and nature (second-order representation).

A dramatic change occurs around 18 months (consistent with changes in language acquisition), when the child is able to invent or deduce solutions to difficult problems such as where an object might be located even if it has not been seen before. Forguson and Gopnick explain this as dependent on the ability to reflect on one's own cognitive processes as if simulating courses of action and consequences even without having the requisite experiences of actions or consequences. These processes are closely linked to early use of language. The documentation for the developmental changes noted above and below is not unequivocal with respect to the relative ages at which children are capable of comprehending and performing successively complex cognitve reasoning and tasks (Jean Mandler, personal communication).

Around 4–5 years of age, note Forguson and Gopnick, the child recognizes that both real and unreal objects, events, and states of affairs can be mentally represented. The 4-year-old thus develops a representational model of the mind rather than simply distinguishing between what is real and what is not. Mental states now contain contents that can be satisfied in conditions of an external reality. A meta-cognitive view about representations that can be private in part or attributed to different others emerges, and this process is said to be pretty much complete by 6 years of age, when the child is able to recognize representational diversity and representational change.

Five- and 6-year-olds, note Forguson and Gopnick, find it difficult to deal with aspects of sociocultural reality when they realize that the meaning of rules of a game and language use are not uniform or invariant to interpretation by others. We can extend this observation by noting that the difficulties include playing a game in which knowledge of the rules becomes somewhat problematic and the behavior of the other players can be confusing and disturbing and reflect new power relations. These new power relations parallel earlier experiences at home. But the empirical status of these home experiences is not part of psychological experiments on the acquisition of practical reasoning.

The child's acquisition of commonsense reasoning and beliefs is fundamental for understanding the notion of power relations and the implementation of authority and power in practical settings. The idea of a habitus, therefore, presumes, but does not examine, traditional socialization processes for conceptualizing and studying abstract power relations. The acquisition and use of power from the perspective of the child remains unexamined – for example, when, as noted above, the child comes to realize that the interpretation of social practices is not invariant to particular agents and their ability to exercise symbolic power.

The experiments reported by psychologists take for granted many aspects of the commonsense reasoning that permit experimenters to impose their authority on children. The language and world knowledge used and attributed to the children leave unexamined, but presuppose that children possess a mental model that can accommodate the task and the power relations imposed by the experiment. The experimenter takes for granted the local and world knowledge and the general and local pragmatics of language use needed to trace the ability of 3- to 6-year-old children to report the sources of their beliefs. Implementing the experiment reproduces the commonsense belief in an objective reality and also reproduces the taken-for-granted dominant power relations inherent in the way children are recruited, spoken to, and assessed vis-à-vis their performance.

The design and execution of experiments reaffirm the unexamined use of everyday social organization as a resource for generating new knowledge about children's ability to represent objects, their own thoughts about objects, and others. The research conditions invite the children to be reflexive about their ability to know about sources of information about objects, others, and representations of such conditions. The experiments rely on unexamined aspects of the socially distributed nature of cognitive tasks to produce new knowledge about the child's memory of sources, alternative sources, and memory of experiences about past events as sources of information.

Traditional psychological research on the development of commonsense reasoning is consistent with Piaget in its determination of universal stages of cognitive development, but is not concerned with the role of cognitive and linguistic development in the child's acquisition and use of power relations.

Sociological theory must ask how "universal" or uniform are the principles of habitus within and across sociocultural environments? What kinds of cultural variation do members of a culture or a nation-state identify, impose, and tolerate during socialization? Do variations exist that are congruent with the notion of the progressive acquisition of commonsense reasoning as identified by developmental psychologists? Are there variations by gender and by social class groupings?

An example of how a cultural group attributes practical reasoning to its children in ways that lead to the assignment of tasks and responsibility can be found in the book *Six Cultures* edited by Beatrice Whiting (1966). The chapters by T. and H. Maretzki and by K. and R. Romney on Okinawan and Mixtecan villages, respectively, describe the transition from early to late childhood. As Romney and Romney note (p. 118), "At the age of 5 [or] 6, the child encounters changes in the daily round of activities and increasing demands for participation in the simpler household tasks and the care of younger siblings." Strikingly similar conditions are described by the Maretskis for Okinawa. The

Romneys describe the transition as taking two to three years, but as typically beginning in the fifth year of life. Girls tend to be trained earlier than boys. Variations are linked to the family's labor requirements, including child care in the Okinawan case. What is significant is that parents at this stage attribute "reason" to the child and assume that the child can go beyond imitation and be taught by reasoning and counseling. The general idea is that the child is now capable of understanding his or her place in the family's daily routine and in life generally (Romney and Romney 1966: 119).

The Romneys' description of the child's transition to late childhood and of changes in role relationships and responsibilities is not conceptualized explicitly in terms of power relations. Yet the detailed ethnographic descriptions provided by the authors reveal terms like "constant demands," of learning "compliant behavior," and of an increase in the ratio of punishment to rewards. There is continual reference to an interplay of threats of punishment for noncompliance, nurturance, and rewards. Their ethnographic descriptions and analysis report repeated important differences in the way in which girls and boys are treated. These remarks point to the need to expand the notion of habitus to include not only gender differences in socialization but how such differences are linked to circumstances that can occur within and across cultures and social classes or ethnic groups within larger nation-states.

The Romneys also describe important activities in their Mixtecan village's classroom. These activities underscore the power of the teachers and the minority status of Mexican Indians. The descriptive material provided by the Romneys also permits the reader to make inferences about power relations among elementary school students and once again calls attention to the necessity of expanding the notion of habitus so as to include the everyday experiences within the family, the peer group, and the school as a way of understanding how the child acquires a sense of his or her own power and that of adults and peers, as he or she is assigned and assumes different relationships within and outside the family, peer, and school settings.

The study of language socialization is another way of expanding and documenting what is implied by the notion of habitus. An important aspect of everyday reasoning is the ability to acquire and employ narratives. In the psychological literature, the experimental setting imposes the conditions for a specific kind of narrative that is part of a particular kind of task. The narratives that children produce by themselves, whether at play or when interacting with adults in natural settings, are often different from those produced in experimental settings. Recent work by Elinor Ochs (1988 and under review) on three communicative strategies for speaking to children and work by Bambi Schieffelin (1990) on reciprocity in conversational strategies available to children and adults are especially useful for expanding our understanding of the acquisition of power relations in a habitus. Mothers, notes Ochs, can become "invisible," by making themselves appear as powerless creatures by accommodating to a local setting. Power is of concern to all actors, even if the term is not used explicitly. An empirical issue is how power is exhibited in presumed egalitarian societies.

I have ignored considerable work on language socialization in the family and in school contexts that suggests ways in which the notion of habitus can be reconceptualized and studied empirically. For example, around the world, children for the most part grow up in settings in which there is multiparty discourse, not the two-party discourse often associated with studies of Western middle-class families. In addition, children are often raised in the midst of multiparty discourse in which more than one language and/or dialect is used. Finally, studies of socialization suggest that social class is a gradient, not the categorical property that structural theory and research tends to promote. Differences within social classes can be as important as those attributed to conditions across classes.

A final area which deserves more attention than I can give it here is the child's communicative competence at home and at school. In particular, a large body of literature has accumulated on minority children's performance in different Western countries, by comparison with that of the dominant socioeconomic groups. These studies have examined language use in classroom settings (Cicourel *et al.* 1974, Gumperz and Herasimchuk 1975, McDermott, *et al.* 1978, McDermott and Hood 1981, Mehan 1979, Michaels 1981, Piestrup 1973, Rist 1970, and Sinclair and Coulthard 1975). Other studies report on language use and socialization practices at home, comparing them with the language and culture of the school (see Cicourel and Mehan 1985, Heath 1983, and Philips 1982 for a review of some of the findings and their implication for primary and secondary educational mobility and post-habitus social mobility). The above studies do not address directly Bourdieu's concern with power relations and the reproduction of a dominant group's hegemony, but they do provide considerable data that could be reinterpreted in terms of Bourdieu's general and specific suggestions about symbolic power and cultural capital. An exception to the remark about the lack of empirical work using the concept of cultural capital, however, is the research by Lareau (1989) on two elementary schools in northern California. She notes how middle-income families differ from lower-income families in the way that the families' resources can contribute or become obstacles to facilitating their children's progress in school. The above studies provide a level of conceptual and empirical detail that can supplement and enhance the notion of habitus.

CONCLUSION

I have addressed, in a selective way, a few of the important epistemological, theoretical, and substantive issues that are prominent in the writings of Pierre Bourdieu. In particular, I have focused on the useful notion of habitus as a way of supplementing and extending a small part of his influential ideas. In the process, I have sought also to suggest some of my own ideas about structural and processual theories and the advantages and shortcomings of these later views. For example, theorists have given insufficient attention to empirical and methodological issues and to the ethnographic or organizational or ecological circumstances within which data are gathered or elicited, or the way data have been gathered and/or elicited by official agencies.

Studies of socialization have for the most part ignored Bourdieu's distinctive way of calling attention to how power or forms of dominance are reproduced in settings like the family and the school such that they have lasting effects on future behavior and the way in which dominant groups sustain themselves. Neither, however, have Bourdieu nor most students of socialization, language development, and educational processes examined the local ways in which a habitus reproduces dominant beliefs, values, and norms through the exercise of symbolic power and by bestowing cultural capital; in particular, the way children perceive, acquire, comprehend, and implement power. Bourdieu's notion of habitus, however, provides a powerful conceptual tool for examining domination as everyday practice; but this notion must be cognitively and linguistically documented. For example, the study of language socialization (see Schieffelin 1990) can contribute greatly to an understanding of power at different levels of analysis. The emphasis on process calls attention to the fact that locally managed power relations can be observed in the way in which children as novices interact with adults and teachers as experts. An understanding of local circumstances of displays of power is essential for making inferences about more abstract conceptions of power in complex organizations and as institutionalized activities.

A general problem is the level of abstraction and generality attributed to notions like habitus and social class. Structural conceptions tend to overstate such ideas because of the broad brush strokes employed to paint the overall picture. Processual theories, however, often ignore the institutional and organizational circumstances that can facilitate and constrain the kinds of locally managed speech events and nonverbal interaction that are essential for understanding the reproduction of symbolic power and cultural capital in everyday life settings.

From a processual perspective, unless structural theorists attend to the reproduction of notions like domination and subordination in the locally managed settings where social structure is reconstituted relentlessly at several levels of analysis, it will be difficult to realize important structural theoretical goals. The history of sociology has always strongly endorsed the use of structural data because such materials clearly have the appearance of self-evident objectivity and provide the research analyst with an important way of depicting global aspects of a group, including the distribution of different characteristics in the population. These data provide an important basis for understanding broad historical development and change and for future policy planning. But these "objective structures" do not clarify the emergent processes inherent in the production and reproduction of the structure of daily life reasoning, language use, and practical action. Each level of analysis, however, mutually constrains and facilitates the other's emergence and existence.

The assembly and use of broad sources of research material presuppose different kinds of epistemological assumptions and power relations with respect to how information is elicited or selected for assembly or recording. Research analysts seldom acknowledge the way in which their knowledge about the world and the environments they study interacts with research sources that can influence claims about findings. Users of structural and processual theories and methods tend to view their methods and their products as resources, not topics of study. The availability of data is often contingent on establishing and making use of networks of relationships that are constitutive of power relations.

Processual theorists vary in the extent to which they recognize and report the power relations that facilitate and constrain their access to methods and materials for inferring the structure of conversation, emotions, decision making, and social interaction in locally managed settings. Broad and local institutional and organizational patterns and constraints that shape and facilitate the way participants engage in conversation and in interviews embedded in social interaction remain unexamined resources, not topics of research.

In field research in which either forced-choice questions or open-ended formats are used, the task of obtaining permission to record conversation and record and/or conduct interviews or engage in participant observation often forces informants or respondents or participants to speculate about issues or conditions which they normally do not address when research analysts are not around. Students of social interaction, however, assume that it is difficult for most participants to sustain interaction over extended periods of time and successfully mask their normal patterns of language use and nonverbal and paralinguistic behavior.

Students of process can easily recognize that the use of elicitation procedures always involves parallel efforts by the research analyst and respondent to create frames or models of reference of what each intends and is seeking to convey about different states of affairs. The general issue is what participants during interviews or other interaction bring to the settings such that prior expectations and the local circumstances activate their memories and guide their perception of what to say and do. A similar observation can be made about structural theorists who use secondary sources of information such as reports, memoranda, letters, diaries, or newspapers.

Structural and processual research analysts of human behavior engage in routine behavior that is often not recognized as exercises of power. The taken-for-granted contacts and methods used sustain the belief in an objective reality that is independent of the activities of research personnel. The beliefs and activities of theorists and research analysts are necessary for bringing into existence the frames of reference that guide all inquiry into the nature of knowledge systems.

REFERENCES

Benedict, R. 1934: *Patterns of Culture*. Boston: Houghton, Mifflin.
—— 1949: Continuities and discontinuities in cultural conditionings. In C. Kluckhohn and H. A. Murray (eds), *Personality in Nature, Society, and Culture*, New York: A. A. Knopf, 414–23.
Cicourel, A. V. 1974: *Cognitive Sociology*. New York: Free Press.
—— and Mehan, H. 1985: Universal development, stratifying practices and status attainment. *Research in Social Stratification and Mobility*, 4, 3–27.
—— et al. 1974: *Language Use and School Performance*. New York: Academic Press.
Corsaro, W. 1985: *Friendship and Peer Culture in the Early Years*. Norwood, N.J.: Ablex.
Forguson, L. and Gopnik, A. 1988: The ontogeny of common sense. In J. Astington, D. Olson, and P. Harris (eds), *Developing Theories of Mind*, Cambridge: Cambridge University Press, 226–43.

Garfinkel, H. 1967: *Studies in Ethnomethodology.* Englewood Cliffs, N.J.: Prentice-Hall.

Gumperz, J. and Herasimchuk, E. 1975: The conversational analysis of meaning: a study of classroom interaction. In M. Sanches and B. G. Blount (eds), *Sociocultural Dimensions of Language Use*, New York: Academic Press, 81–115.

Habermas, Jürgen 1987: *The Theory of Communicative Action*, Vol. 2: *Lifeworld and System: a critique of functionalist reason.* Boston: Beacon.

Heath, S. B. 1983: *Ways with Words.* Cambridge: Cambridge University Press.

Landy, D. 1959: *Tropical Childhood: cultural transmission and learning in a rural Puerto Rican village.* New York: Harper and Row.

Lareau, A. 1987: Social class differences in family–school relationships: the importance of cultural capital." *Sociology of Education*, 60, 73–85.

—— 1989: *Home Advantages: social class and parental intervention in elementary education.* London: Falmer Press.

Lindesmith, A. R., Strauss, A. L., and Denzin, Norman K. 1975: *Social Psychology.* Hinsdale, Ill.: Dryden Press.

Maretzki, T. and Maretzki, H. 1966: Taira: an Okinawan village. In B. B. Whiting (ed.), *Six Cultures*, New York: Wiley, 363–539.

McDermott, R. P. and Aron, J. 1978: Pirandello in the classroom. In M. Reynolds (ed.), *The Futures of Education*, Reston, Va.: Council for Exceptional Children, 41–61.

—— Gospodinoff, K., and Aron, J. 1978: Criteria for an ethnographically adequate description of concerted activities and their contexts. *Semiotica*, 24 nos 3–4, 245–75.

—— and Hood 1981: Institutionalized psychology and the ethnography of schooling. In P. Gilmore and A. A. Glatthorn (eds), *Ethnography and Education: children in and out of school*, Washington, D.C.: Center for Applied Linguistics, 232–49.

Mead, M. 1946: Research on primitive children. In L. Carmichael (ed.), *Manual of Child Psychology*, New York: Wiley, 735–80.

Mehan, H. 1979: *Learning Lessons.* Cambridge, Mass.: Harvard University Press.

Michaels, S. 1981: Sharing time: children's narrative style and differential access to literacy. *Language in Society*, 10, 423–42.

Ochs, E. 1988: *Culture and Language Development: language acquisition and language socialization in a Samoan village.* Cambridge and New York: Cambridge University Press.

—— (forthcoming): Indexing gender. Essay to appear in Barbara Miller (ed.), *Sex and Gender Hierarchies*, under review by University of Chicago Press.

Parsons, T. 1951: *The Social System.* Glencoe, Ill.: Free Press.

Philips, S. 1982: *The Invisible Culture: communication in classroom and community on the Warm Springs Indian Reservation.* New York: Longmans.

Piestrup, A. M. 1973: Black Dialect Interferences and Accommodation of Reading Instruction in First Grade. Berkeley: Monographs of the Language-Behavior Research Laboratory, University of California, Berkeley.

Pollner, M. 1987: *Mundane Reason: reality in everyday and sociological discourse.* Cambridge and New York: Cambridge University Press.

Rist, R. C. 1970: Student social class and teacher expectations: the self-fulfilling prophecy in ghetto education. *Harvard Educational Review*, 40, 411–51.

Romney, K. and Romney, R. 1966: The Mixtecans of Juxtlahuaca, Mexico. In B. B. Whiting (ed.), *Six Cultures*, New York: Wiley, 54–691.

Sapir, E. 1949: The emergence of the concept of personality in a study of cultures. In D. G. Mandlebaum (ed.), *Selected Writings of Edward Sapir*, Berkeley: University of California Press, 1949, 590–7.

Schieffelin, B. 1990: *The Give and Take of Everyday Life: language socialization among the Kaluli.* New York: Cambridge University Press.

Schutz, A. 1945: On multiple realities. *Philosophy and Phenomenological Research*, 5, 533–75.

—— 1953: Common-sense and scientific interpretation of human action. *Philosophy and Phenomenological Research*, 14, 1–38.

Sinclair, J. M. and Coulthard, R. M. 1975: *Toward an Analysis of Discourse.* New York: Oxford University Press.

Turiel, E. 1983: *The Development of Social Knowledge: morality and convention.* Cambridge and New York: Cambridge University Press.

Whiting, Beatrice B. 1966: *Six Cultures: studies of child rearing.* New York: Wiley.

Whiting, J. W. M. and Child, I. L. 1953: *Child Training and Personality.* New Haven: Yale University Press.

6

Determination and Contradiction: An Appreciation and Critique of the Work of Pierre Bourdieu on Language and Education

James Collins

INTRODUCTION

The main thrust of Pierre Bourdieu's work is now well established: to rethink the subject–object dichotomies of classical and current social theory. In reworking this dichotomy, Bourdieu problematizes our usual ways of thinking about couplets such as necessity/freedom, structure/practice, determination/contingency. This is true whether we consider language, a dimension of social life that has been subjected to the most powerful structural formulations, or education, an arena of social life in which the idea of individual effort and achievement rests uneasily alongside evidence of constraint and conditioning.

Language and education are linked in Bourdieu's work, embedded in a larger dynamic of material conditioning and symbolic power. Central to his account of that linkage and the larger dynamic are concepts of *capital*, accumulable social-symbolic resources, *field*, the arenas of social life and struggle, and *habitus*, "embodied social structures" that serve as principles organizing practice. These concepts are both exciting and problematic: they seem to provide new ways of relating "objective"

Thanks are due to John Lucy for his written coments; to Loïc Wacquant for generosity with conversation, references, and manuscripts; and to Pierre Bourdieu for a frank and informative post-conference discussion. Adrian Bennett, Jon Church, Wesley Shumar, and Fiona Thompson have been part of an ongoing conversation about many of the issues discussed here. Support for writing and revision came from a National Academy of Education Spencer Fellowship.

social structure and "subjective" human dispositions and actions; yet they are also intricately linked to one another, and the precise articulation often seems to depend on the particularities of case or ethnographic situation. The concepts of capital, field, and habitus have been useful in thinking about the role of language in the reproduction of class positions, and Bourdieu used these concepts to reformulate the "linguistic deficit" question in interesting and radical ways. Thinking about the linkage among these concepts raises questions about the nature and role of agency in Bourdieu's social theory. Pursuing this issue, we will examine the relation Bourdieu postulates between social interaction and social structure and will focus upon the antinomy in Bourdieu's work on language between a social structural determination of verbal interaction and a social creativity found in discursive "classification struggles."

Although this tension between determinism and constructivism is not resolved, either in specific formulations about language or in arguments about the role of language in education, Bourdieu's work stands as both stimulus and challenge to many approaches to language-oriented social and educational research. We will discuss two such approaches, one objectivist and statistical, the other subjectivist and interpretive. They share certain concerns with Bourdieu, are susceptible to constructive critique from the perspective of his research program, and they point to something missing in his program. That "something" is an appreciation of the role of contradiction in social processes and discursive action. A final set of linguistic studies are discussed that provide different perspectives on the linguistics of social contradictions. They reveal the dilemmas and dynamics that underlie processes of domination, reproduction, and determination, suggesting new ways of thinking about agency, the discursive, and the structural.

THE USEFULNESS OF BASIC CONCEPTS: A RADICAL REFORMULATION OF THE "LINGUISTIC DEFICIT" DEBATE

Much of Bourdieu's work concerns the role of educational systems in the reproduction of social and economic relations and institutions. In Bourdieu's account, language figures in education primarily as a code. Much curriculum and pedagogy tacitly presuppose discursive knowledge and dispositions transmitted within class groupings. Critically appropriating the work of Bernstein and Labov, Bourdieu and Passeron (1977) argue that mismatches between the language of home and school are an important cause of educational failure. Conversely, a close fit between the "codes" of primary socialization and those of school is the implicit enabling condition of much educational success. In their analysis, the nature of these codes remains largely unspecified, but language is omnipresent, as media of institutional authority, index of class cleavage, and constraint on pedagogical innovation.

The general features of "class codes" are described by Bourdieu and Passeron in terms of "bourgeois" and "common" parlance. The former is marked by a literary orientation, latinate vocabulary and constructions, and a striving for rare and novel expression, the latter by a situational orientation, nonlearned vocabulary, and a reliance upon shared figures of speech (Bourdieu and Passeron 1977: 116).[1] The former, of course, is much closer to the language expected in educational settings; that is, it contains much more *linguistic capital* in the educational field, in the educational market, where the dominant language is the official, legitimate language.

This is close to the schematic formulations of the early Bernstein (for example, Bernstein 1964) about "restricted" and "elaborated" codes, and it evokes the whole debate about "linguistic deficits." But Bourdieu and Passeron enrich those earlier accounts by differentiating between *linguistic capital* – class-linked traits of speech differentially valued in a specific field or market – and a *linguistic habitus* – a class-linked relation to language. The linguistic habitus of upper-class students, an automatic tendency towards "abstraction, formalism, intellectualism, and euphemistic moderation," serves them well in classroom encounters and essay examinations. The converse habitus of working-class students, a tendency towards "expressionism . . . mov[ing] from particular case to particular case, from illustration to parable, or shun[ning] the bombast of fine words" serves them poorly in classrooms and essays (Bourdieu and Passeron 1977: 116). In both their linguistic capital and their linguistic habitus, one group possesses what the system expects and is able to appropriate what the system offers, in the forms it expects, whereas the other lacks what the system expects and is less able to appropriate what it offers.

The treatment of linguistic difference in terms of capital and habitus, as activated in particular fields, is elaborated in Bourdieu's article "The economics of linguistic exchanges" (1977a). In this article, as in Bourdieu and Passeron's *Reproduction*, linguistic capital is treated as essentially a matter of class dialects; that is, usage is a diacritic of status. Linguistic markets are defined as social domains within which language use is valued; they determine the specific value of that "capital" at a given time and place. A central historical role is given to the state and its educational apparatus in creating a "unified linguistic market" in which a single language becomes the norm for legitimate speech and all other forms of speech become devalued (as dialects or patois, or simply as "foreign" and categorically unintelligible). The history of language standardization provides supporting case studies (see Bloomfield 1933, Williams 1961, Bourdieu 1982a).

Strong influences on linguistic production in a given situation are the objective and subjective tensions induced by intersecting field and habitus effects. Fields are arenas of endeavor, and they vary in terms of the formality, or "objective tension," they induce in a given situation. In official and public settings of various kinds, social expectations are greater (that is, more widely shared, more intensely felt) that legitimate – careful, authoritative, 'standard' – language will be used; hence there is an objective, nonpersonal tension. A counterpart to this nonpersonal tension is the "subjective tension" caused by the linguistic habitus, a class-based relation to language (and especially to the dominant language). A speaker's feelings of competence, of ability to meet the perceived requirements of public, official language, will vary as a function of class experience, with personal tension increasing as distance from the dominant code, and hence presumed incompetence with the dominant language, increases.

The positions formulated in *Reproduction* and "Economics" develop perspectives on the general issue of dominant and dominated modes of conduct and communication. In "Economics" and, more recently, *Ce que parler veut dire* (1982a), Bourdieu emphasizes the historical construction of linguistic dispropriation: that the state and its schooling systems create a unified linguistic market, a standard language that is a dominant metric of linguistic worth, a dominant metric controlled by the dominant classes. Bourdieu and Passeron also emphasize institutional agency, not just mismatched codes. They argue that pedagogic action operates via a ruse of communication, a use of tacit assumptions and highly presupposing discursive forms to select for those who already know what they need to know, who already have what they need to have. They argue that pedagogical authority insures recognition of the legitimacy of school language, but that communication of information and rational discussion and checking of that communication and information constitute at best a minor, nonessential aspect of pedagogical activity. The largely implicit codes of curriculum and teacher talk presuppose a familiarity with legitimate language, but neither curriculum nor instruction renders that language explicit. Instead, receiving or being denied the pedagogic message depends on a match or mismatch of codes.

Bourdieu's work thus considerably advances the inquiry into the relations between social experience, language use, and educational achievement that came to be known as the "linguistic deficit" hypothesis. Formulated in the United States by psychologists and others who were neither social scientists nor linguists (Bereiter and Englemann 1966, Hess 1970, Whiteman and Deutsch 1968), the deficit hypothesis argued that working-class and minority children were linguistically deprived. It located the source of that deprivation in the homes and communities of those children and advocated programs to change their language in order to improve their educational performance. Deficit researchers drew inspiration from the early writings of Bernstein (1964) on class, codes, and educatability (see Edwards 1976 for a full discussion, Collins 1988 for a discussion of linguistic models, class divisions, and cultural-political traditions as they bear upon this debate). As Bernstein's work developed, it presented a nuanced account of the social bases of class-specific forms of language use, emphasizing occupation, family structure, and socialization. Bernstein (1972) argued that class-linked "codes" were tendencies to certain patterns of language use, not fixed deficiencies. Indeed, by the mid–1970s Bernstein was arguing that an important dimension of class-based differences in language use was the situated interpretation of "ground rules" (implicit assumptions) for verbal behavior in school or school-like settings (1974). In work up through this period, however, Bernstein neglected to analyze the institutional dynamics of scholastic linguistic preference.

By contrast, Bourdieu provides a political analysis and critique of language use in a system of schooling that is part of a system of discursive, social, and economic domination. Implicit expectations (ground rules) are neither historical accidents nor politically neutral preferences for the expression and evaluation of knowledge. Working classes and ethnic minorities have devalued linguistic resources because of a historical process of state-driven and school-implemented linguistic standardization, that is, a unification and revaluation of language. Although Bourdieu appreciates the power and social consequences of communicative technologies such as literacy (or print-capitalism we might say, following Anderson's (1983) useful focus on technological means and the political-economic matrix), he critiques claims about the universal rationality and logical capabilities of school-based, bourgeois language. Arguments about the logical superiority, aesthetic refinement, and communicative efficacy of school-based standard language hide a literate-class bias, in which images of text are tied up with notions of truth, and social domination is represented as mental development.

There can be no simple tearing away of the veil of illusion, however; neither programs to correct working-class language nor edifying descriptions of the school's tacit assumptions about language use will suffice to change the fundamental language/education relation. As Bourdieu and Passeron argue, pedagogies that tacitly select the privileged and exclude the underprepared are not regrettable lapses; they are systematic aspects of schooling systems serving class-divided societies.

DETERMINISM VERSUS CONSTRUCTIVISM IN LANGUAGE AND
EDUCATION

Determined language

Discussing what changes in the selective preferences of scholastic communication would require, Bourdieu and Passeron (1977) are pessimistic about the limits of reform of educational "language":

> Maximizing the productivity of pedagogic work would ultimately imply not only recognition of the gap between the linguistic competences of transmitter and receiver but also knowledge of the social conditions of the production and reproduction of that gap, that is, knowledge both of the modes of acquisition of the different class languages and the scholastic mechanisms which consecrate and so help to perpetuate inter-class differences . . . .*[O]nly a school system serving another system of external functions and, correlatively, another state of the balance of powers between the classes, could make such pedagogic action possible.* Bourdieu and Passeron 1977: 127, emphasis added)

That is, it is insufficient to recognize a difference between the language of teachers and that of students (as deficit researchers did). The modes of acquiring class languages must also be understood, and the schooling procedures that value one language and one mode of acquisition and devalue others must be identified and critically analyzed if we are to understand how pedagogic language both inculcates knowledge and imposes domination. Such inquiry and reform face strict limitations from wider social determinants: "[O]nly a school system serving . . . another . . . . balance of powers between the [social] classes could make such . . . action possible." In short, only with a basic transformation in class relations can pedagogy, and in particular the language of pedagogy, be modified. A change from such a pedagogy's typical function of social conservation[2] to a different function of social transformation would require methodical attempts to reach (that is, really teach) those whose backgrounds do not prepare them for the language of schooling.

This determinist position regarding the social matrix of language might be thought to result from the institutional characteristics of education. A similar determinism is found, however, in work devoted specifically to language use. In "The economics of linguistic exchanges" Bourdieu calls for attention to the conditions of appropriate utterance. The conditions of utterance depend on "linguistic production relations," and these in turn devolve into linguistic capital, valued in particular linguistic markets and deployed in particular fields of endeavor, with the linguistic habitus serving as an essential mediating principle between capital and field or market.

This formulation of "relations of linguistic production" in terms of capital, fields, and habitus leads to a frank social determination of discourse:

> We learn that the efficacy of a discourse, its power to convince, depends on the authority of the person who utters it, or, what amounts to the same thing, on his "accent" functioning as an index of authority. *Thus the whole social structure is present in the interaction (and therefore the discourse): the material conditions of existence determine discourse through the linguistic production relations which they make possible and which they structure. For they govern not only the places and times of communication* (determining the chances of meeting and communicating, through the social mechanisms of elimination and selection) *but also the form of the communication*, through the structure of the production relations in which discourse is generated (the distribution of authority between speakers, of the specific competence, etc.). (Bourdieu 1977a: 653 emphasis added)

Bourdieu provides some indications, in the quote and elsewhere, about the "presence" of social structure in discursive-interactional encounters. Social structure determines the times and places of discourse, who is included and who excluded, and the temporal rhythms of statement and response. It also determines the distribution of authority and competence: who speaks (or writes) well and who badly, who with presumed competence and who under suspicion of incompetence. We should note, however, that the general determinants of discourse, that is, the "conditions of linguistic production", derive from a set of interdependent concepts – capital, field, and habitus. Capital, in its various forms (economic, social, cultural, scientific, and so on) is field-dependent. Actions and attributes attain value in specific arenas of endeavor and contestation, in symbolic "markets" and social "fields". Yet fields are constituted by capital, by the attributes necessary to enter into particular endeavors and competitions ("entry costs" in economist jargon), and by the attributes unevenly possessed by those who "play" in a particular field. Habitus is a general disposition to action, a scheme of practice and perception, inculcated early and with longer-term ("trajectory") effects, yet highly specific in its operation in a particular situation. Taken singly or together, these concepts provide exciting breaks with earlier formulations of the relation between structure and action; but they do not lend themselves to precise definition or close empirical assessment, in part because of their very interconnection.

Bourdieu's formulation emphasizes and provides insight into the *pregivenness* of verbal situation, into the already-situatedness of situated encounters. We may still wonder, however, about an *immediate*, determinate relation between social structure and (verbal) interaction. There may be exigencies of face-to-face encounters, whether of individuals or the coordinated cries and responses of massed multitudes, that give an autonomy, an emergence, an *un*pregivenness to the situation, to what Goffman called the "interaction order" (1983). For Goffman the realm of interaction constituted a separate sphere of social practice that was "loosely coupled" with social structure. Nondiscursive social structure impinges through myriad constraints that are not formalized as capital, markets, embodied dispositions, and whatnot, but are rather envisioned as status hierarchies and formal institutional constraints. But the impingement is indirect, not necessarily determinate. How, and whether, social structure will influence interaction is left a more open question, hence the "loose" coupling. There is, in short, an action-in-interaction, an aspect of human agency that emerges from the particularities, not the pregivens, of encounter.

For Bourdieu, however, the actions between agents, or personal intersubjective relations, are not the social. The social is fundamentally defined by fields of relations (Bourdieu 1988b, Wacquant 1989). As part of his critique of subjectivism, he rejects any attempt to "reduce social space to the conjunctural space of interactions" and argues that it is necessary to construct an objective social space, "a structure of objective relations which determines the possible form of interactions" (1984: 244). Analysis must move beyond this objectifying construction, however, in order to avoid "treating social facts as things" and in order to recognize that objective social positions are also "strategic emplacements, fortresses to be defended and captured in a field of struggles" (ibid.). Positions are also subjective perceptions of position.

Constructive language

In Bourdieu's treatment of symbolic struggles we find the strong social determinism of language use counterposed to a creativity of discourse at the group level, in struggles over definition and classification. The enabling condition for this creativity is an indeterminacy between "objective" social structure and "subjective" representation. Objective social structure is that social space defined by the distribution of economic and cultural capital. But an essential aspect of human sociality, of what we can call "culture", is the creation and use of categorical structures, engendering a perception organized into differentiating categories; and this cultural representation never matches actual social structure (1979b, 1984). In this respect Bourdieu is, as he frequently acknowledges, a Durkheimian, for he posits an essential socio-logic, a logic of "how things are" ultimately derivable from material social conditions. He differs from Durkheim (and Mauss) in insisting on an inescapable dialectic of the social space and its representation. Representations are inherently perspectival, views taken from points in the social space, rather than some Archimedean overview. They are closely related to the schemes of perception founded in the habitus, which is itself formed at one "moment" of the social space, but with trajectory effects that outlast the moment in which they were was formed. This gap, lag, or lack of fit between social structure and social representation is an enabling condition, a site for struggles over that representation.

By changing the representation, such struggles can change the social space, for "representations of the real are part of the real." The value of capital, for example, depends in part on the importance given to particular traits comprising different types of capital. The importance assigned to given traits will itself depend on struggles to define, describe, and represent what is real, what is basic. The American academic field is currently engaged in highly publicized struggles over curriculum, the "canon wars". These struggles reflect, among other things, a rivalry between opposed visions of education – for example, as inculcation of unifying, liberal (elite) culture or as practical training for the world of work. The complex misrecognitions and symbolic displacements of "real interests" need not distract us from an essential point: the outcome of this struggle will affect the cultural and economic standing of many academics and students.

The recent wave of "English Only" campaigns in the United States provide illustrations of the political struggles required to create and maintain a unified linguistic market in which only one language is recognized as legitimate and appropriate for discourse in official settings and for official purposes. The campaigns frequently pit older generations of European immigrants, whose assimilation into American society has been based on fierce acceptance of the dominant language (English), against younger generations of Latino and Asian immigrants, who question the realities and costs of assimilation.[3] Phrased in terms of a contested equation English = American, the campaigns raise struggles over definition of political and social acceptability and have numerous consequences for schooling and jobs.

It is in such representation struggles, such classification struggles, that we see the power of discourse, which is the power to impose descriptions and definitions. The struggles are never ending, because representations are always out of sync with the changing objective social structure. Bourdieu phrases the matter as follows when discussing struggles over job classifications, in which the stakes are credentials and renumeration:

> The fate of groups is bound up with the words that designate them . . . [but] the order of words never exactly reproduces the order of things. It is the relative independence of the structure of the system of classifying, classified words . . . in relation to the structure of the distribution of capital, and more precisely, it is the time-lag . . . between changes in jobs, linked to changes in the productive apparatus, and changes in titles, which creates the space for symbolic strategies aimed at exploiting the discrepancies between the nominal and the real . . . (1984: 481)

Arguments about the "credentialing of society" are familiar, and the process is seen in the raising of educational requirements for jobs, in both the corporate and the public sector. Various occupational groups struggle to redefine the world of work: for tests, certificates, and degrees to insure the "professionalism" of their interests, whether it is a health care workers' union seeking to exclude the uncertified or community colleges insisting on Ph.D.'s for teaching positions previously held by those with B.A. and M.A. degrees.

For Bourdieu, however, there are basic constraints on representations and representation struggles, on the autonomy of the subjective moment:

> The individual or collective classification struggles aimed at transforming the categories of perception and appreciation of the social world and, through this, the social world itself, are indeed a forgotten dimension of the class struggle. But one only has to realize that the classificatory schemes which underlie agents' practical relationship to their condition and the representation they have of it are themselves the product of that condition, in order to see the limits of this autonomy. Position in the classification struggle . . . depends on position in the class structure. (1984: 484)

In the canon wars, for example, prescription of the traditional liberal arts curriculum originates in elite universities and disciplines, by those who see it as a civilizing effort necessary for cultural-political stability and progress: for example, Bloom (1987), University of Chicago, and Hirsch (1987), University of Virginia. The traditional liberal curriculum is opposed, in sharpest form, from positions in non-elite institutions and disciplines, by those who see it as an arrogant, exclusionary project, an effort at cultural-political domination masquerading as an essential "cultural core": for example, Giroux and McClaren (1988), members of the education department at Miami University of Ohio and Rose (1989), who is in charge of the Special Freshman Education Program at the University of California at Los Angeles.

The missing contradiction

For Bourdieu, the power of discourse is always the power of groups; it is the ability to mobilize a group, to invest a group with identity and will to act, that constitutes an essential source of the "power of words".[4] These symbolic struggles are always (ultimately) linked to nondiscursive social structure: "Position in the classification struggle . . . depends on position in the class structure." Bourdieu thus provides an important critique of subjectivist attempts to construct the entire social world from members' representations and practices. He rejects the "situationist fallacy" of reducing social space to "a discontinuous series of abstract situations" (1984: 244) and affirms the "relative autonomy of the logic of symbolic representation," while arguing for its ultimate determination by socioeconomic conditions (p. 483). He thus advances our understanding of the dialectic between objective and subjective dimensions of social life.

I would argue, however, that he has erred in the objectivist direction. I will do this by reconsidering the question of discursive interaction and by focusing on what is missing from Bourdieu's dialectic: a sense of *contradiction* (not just conflict) in social relations and social practice.

In Bourdieu's work, discursive interaction seems to have no reality except as a highly constrained, epiphenomenal reflection of social structures. Notions such as capital, habitus, and field provide mediating terms through which social structure determines the time, place, and participants and the codes and competences of discourse. The tight interdependence of Bourdieu's basic concepts is problematic, however: the concept of capital is field-dependent, especially that of social capital; fields are extremely diverse domains of life and struggle, and distributions of capital are importantly constitutive of a field; and the habitus is "embodied" capital, yet the mechanisms of embodiment remain unclear. This interdependence is not necessarily a bad thing. It provides us with an analytic framework for appreciating the relative independence of forms of accumulation, arenas of social endeavor, and schemes of practice and perception, and it reminds us of the ultimate and essential interconnection of accumulation, arena, and scheme. Such interdependence does provoke caution, however. Despite Bourdieu's commitment to mapping large-scale social structure, phrased as mapping the objective space of social positions as a prior analytic move to understanding classification struggles (1984, 1986b), it becomes increasingly evident that to understand the intersection of capital, fields, and habitus, we must have detailed ethnographic information, as well as a healthy respect for the semiotic complexity of classification struggles and face-to-face verbal interaction.

Bourdieu postulates a gap between objective social space and members' representations of that space, a site for symbolic struggles that transform the real by renaming it. We may ask, however, whether there is not a similar gap between interaction and its social structural pregivens, a "loose coupling" in Goffman's terms. If so, we must ask what occurs in this interactional space, beyond a routine repetition of the pregivens.

One thing that occurs is cultural creation of a certain kind. In his classic ethnography of English working-class "counter-school culture," Paul Willis (1977) argues that the cultural and discursive forms through which tough, working-class males subvert pedagogic authority are educationally disabling, hence reproductive, since they limit the young men to the industrial labor of their fathers. Yet, through these forms the young men also simultaneously achieve a penetration of educational ideology, a real, practical critique of the false promises of educational meritocracy. Hence there is a contradiction: the students are simultaneously (self-)disabled and achieve collective insight, in advance of their conforming peers or the liberal staff who would "reach them". In his criticisms of both Bourdieu and Althusser, Willis argues that it is necessary to descend to the level of ethnographic particulars, close descriptions of concrete interactional practice, in order to capture this contradictory moment of grounded, collective critique of oppressive social structures acted out in forms that limit other understandings and perpetuate the actions of – that is, reproduce – those structures. Bourdieu also argues against the meritocratic illusion, a "reproductive struggle . . . in which [dominated classes] are beaten before they start" (1984:168). But for Bourdieu, change in the "tacit acceptance which the dominated classes . . . grant to the dominant goals" occurs only during periods of general – that is, economic – crisis (ibid.). For Willis, however, there is more potential in the contradictory, practical rebellion of working-class "lads", rebellion limited by racism and sexism but nonetheless an ongoing interactional creation and cultural critique, a rejection, not "tacit acceptance," of competitive meritocracy.

Educational systems in capitalist democracies face a basic dilemma: they must profess egalitarian ideals while rationing class privilege. Other commentators have criticized Bourdieu for failing to address this essential contradiction (Schwartz 1977); and in later work Bourdieu (1984) analyzes how the educational apparatus handles this dilemma, by displacing it. But the contradiction does not thereby disappear. Furthermore, social contradictions are found not just in economic crisis, but also in individual consciousness and interactional arrangements.

IMPLICATIONS OF BOURDIEU'S WORK FOR STUDIES OF LANGUAGE AND EDUCATION

This argument can be developed by turning our attention to other approaches to the study of language, social structure, and education. For our purposes here, I will focus on three sets of work: the quantitative sociolinguistic work of William Labov, which represents an objectivist pole of sociolinguistics; the interactional sociolinguistic work of John Gumperz, which represents a subjectivist pole; and a group of studies, including my own, which investigate what might be called the 'linguistics of social contradictions."

Quantitative sociolinguistics

Labov's empirical findings about language figure importantly in Bourdieu's specification of various concepts in various texts (for example, *Reproduction, Distinction*, and "The linguistics of economic exchanges"). The formulation of "linguistic habitus," for example, draws upon Labov's descriptions (1972) of class-specific orientations to prestige (standard) forms of language. The argument that dominated groups *recognize* the norms of dominant language and culture without actually mastering or controlling the abilities to which those norms point receives empirical confirmation in Labov's work. He has shown that speakers shift toward prestige variants as the formality of task and setting increases and, further, that there are class-specific differences in perception of and elicitable allegiance to dominant norms versus actual speech practices (1972).[5]

We may appreciate, as does Bourdieu, the weight of accumulated empirical confirmation of Labov's basic findings about the social stratification of language.[6] Yet, as Bourdieu continually reminds us, when inquiring into the *meaning* of statistical distributions, when asking *why* these distributions should be found, we must remain aware of the effects of particular fields and the shifting states of class relations. In Labov's studies of social stratification and language use, it is precisely the lower middle class, the class which lacks significant economic or cultural capital and is therefore most dependent upon educational credentials for occupational position, that conforms most closely to the prestige norms *in formal contexts*. But the prestige norms to which they conform are precisely the spelling and pronunciation norms, the standard phonological norms, of school-based and school-reinforced language. We face a circularity: conformity to educationally enforced linguistic norms by all groups, but most powerfully by that group which most depends on what the system confers, credentials, for its status in the larger social hierarchy. We have a plausible and interesting account of this circular reinforcement of dependent and independent variables if we attend, as Bourdieu's work suggests we should, to the constrained, but dynamic, role of educational systems in shaping class relations and in distributing language (capital) and relation to language (habitus).

Labov's findings about class and ethnic differences in language use quickly entered into the late 1960s controversy over linguistic "deficit" and "difference". Many had asked whether low educational achievement among working-class and minority students was due to a mismatch between their language and the language expected in the school? Labov developed this question in an interesting way by arguing that it was not a simple structural mismatch between the dialect of home and the literary dialect that led to difficulties with reading and writing ("structural interference"); rather, it was the potent symbolism of language difference, the way in which it was treated in school settings, the way in which it figured in acquiescence or resistance to the school ("functional interference"), that most dramatically affected educational achievement among working-class minorities (Labov 1973).

This hypothesis was confirmed by other studies (for example, Piestrup 1973, Melmed 1971, Gibson and Levin 1975). Given that Bourdieu and Passeron formulate the notion of code very generally and are well aware that a key issue is the *imposition of code*, such findings agree with their position. The "functional interference" hypothesis does suggest, however, that it is important to look at actual patterns of classroom interaction. In a series of articles, I have developed this argument by analyzing the historical dynamics of class-divided standard language literacy, the general institutional dynamic of educational grouping (for example, ability grouping and curriculum tracking), and the way in which they play themselves out in particular, but recurrent and amply documented, processes of classroom interaction (Collins 1986, 1987a, b, 1988, 1989).

Interactional sociolinguistics

Close attention to discursive interaction is not among Bourdieu's emphases; rather it results from attempts to understand the mediation of historical development and social structure by intersubjective communicative action. Such an effort is found in the interpretive sociolinguistics of John Gumperz. In various studies from the 1950s through the 1970s, Gumperz and his collaborators have investigated multilingual situations, examining how language alternation figures in the larger communicative economy, as well as in the situated and systematic minutiae of conversational exchange (Gumperz 1971). Building upon this work, Blom and Gumperz (1972), in particular, showed that while language alternation is partly derivable from power relations, it is also part of an interactional exploration of conversational place, a contextualizing practice that is central to the language-situation dialectic (see Chapter 7 below).

Aspects of Gumperz's research are consonant with Bourdieu's general arguments about language. Gumperz, like Bourdieu, has argued that national languages are (traditional) grammarians' artifacts (see Bourdieu 1977a, 1982a; Gumperz 1982), which have their reality as representations of official language but are typically far removed from the actual organization of practical speech. Like Bourdieu, Gumperz pursues a line of research in which diverse elements are understood as forming systems of relational options as, for example, in his studies of conversational contextualization "The notion of contextualization convention enables us to treat what on the surface look like quite separate phenomena – code and style switching, prosody, phonetic and morphological variation, choice of syntactic or lexical option – under the same heading by showing that they have similar relational signaling functions" (Gumperz 1982: 208).

Gumperz's notion of "situational [code] switching" also conforms to Bourdieu's vision of general linguistic production relations determining discourse, but the linked concept of "metaphorical switching" advances into an area that Bourdieu neglects. Metaphorical code-alternation is not context-deducible, but rather appears to violate public, conventional appropriateness judgments; it more "creates" than is defined by situation. It is of a piece with the everyday, informal organization of communicative conduct that *goes against* formal institutional expectations and prescriptions. Understanding the creative, counternormative potential of everyday communicative practices, of metaphorical switching in this case, requires intensive analysis of verbal interaction before its place in the wider sociocommunicative order can be discerned, let alone understood.[7]

A general argument of Gumperz (1982) is that alternations between languages or dialects often involve a general "us/them" contrast of intimacy versus formality that acquires complex rhetorical implications in given settings or conversational activities. Two of his examples are particularly interesting. One involves Spanish/English code-switching by a Puerto Rican woman telling about personal problems; another involves a black graduate student alternating between standard English and exaggerated Black English when requesting a favor of a professor and then addressing fellow students. In addition to the details of the analyses, which cannot be recapitulated here (see Gumperz 1982: 70–2, 29–37), what is notable in each case is the difficult predicament, the contradictory "consciousness," of each speaker. For the woman this involves the solace yet ultimate degradation of drink, linked to feelings of abandonment by and dependence upon a man; for the student it involves the dependence of the student in the educational hierarchy versus the need to maintain (self-)respect and autonomy. In each case, the alternation (between Spanish and English and between hypercorrect standard English and exaggerated Black English) signals subtle, yet systematic and important, aspects of this dilemma, which is at once existential, social, and communicative. Significantly such cues are not necessarily "understood" by all participants;[8] but they are certainly part of the "functional conflict" between dominant and dominated languages in (and out of) educational settings.

What we have in these cases are intricate but not atypical instances of the construction of a contradictory symbolism of self and tradition in conversational practice. Bourdieu's approach alerts us to the pregiven structuring of situation that Gumperz's analysis elides in favor of an argument about the plurality of interpretations. In different ways, both speakers are situated by race and gender as well as by "setting" (interview with a researcher, a university seminar). That granted, however, it remains the case that a significant range of social contradictions are manifested – expressed, realized, and struggled over – in the realm of face-to-face interaction.

Linguistic dimensions of social contradictions

In a study of language choice and valuation in Barcelona, Woolard (1985) critiques Bourdieu's conception of symbolic domination and shows that it was in the everyday "solidaristic" sphere of familial, peer, and work-related communication that the truly dominant language, Catalan, was maintained and reinforced vis-à-vis its rival, Castilian, the official language of education and government. The linguistic situation in Barcelona revealed a division between "state" and "civil society," a contradictory opposition of linguistic "counter-markets," opposed to state-driven Castilian "unification".⁹ Discussing the Barcelona materials along with other cases of dominated yet resistant ethnic minority and working-class linguistic practices, situated in face-to-face conversational exchange, Woolard argues: "It is . . . critical to understand that these vernacular practices are productive, not merely reproductive, that they arise not from a mere bending to the weight of authority, but are paradoxically a creative response to that authority, mediated by the oppositional value of solidarity" (1985: 745).

Gal (1987) extends Woolard's argument in a study of code-switching and consciousness in various countries of the European periphery. Her analysis attends both to comparative political economy and actual language alternation in conversational settings. The most relevant case for our purposes involves the adolescent children of second- and third-generation Italian "guest workers" in Germany. These youth alternate rapidly between German and Italian, blending the linguistic resources of both in radical ways. Gal argues that while this linguistic practice is decried by officialdom and elders in both Germany and Italy, it is a strategy that permits maximum accessibility and inclusion of newcomers. Unwelcome in the German state and its institutions (such as schools) and separated by a long-term migration from their "native" Sicily, these youths have devised a stigmatized but creative conversational strategy for dealing with the structural ambiguity of their condition.¹⁰

Gee's recent work on discourse and literacy (1989b) provides numerous case studies of the intricate micropolitics of interpretation that underpin the class-based and unexamined judgments about language and human worth that are basic operating procedures for the US educational system.¹¹ Using an argument similar to Bourdieu's about habitus and socialization conflict in education, Gee asserts that the development of mind and social persona through discourse is always a contradiction-ridden experience for dominated groups. In a study of forms of moral reasoning that reveal class-based orientations to (printed) text or (collective) talk, Gee (1989a) analyzes the distribution of referring and anaphoric nouns, moral-evaluative terms, and attributive quotations (text-based versus invented quotes) in the oral accounts of working-class, middle-class, and upper-class high school students. His analysis provides rich characterizations of class-specific linguistic habitus (which he calls "discourse traditions").

Thinking about his analysis of this material in connection with Bourdieu's arguments about language, while conducting a study of regular and remedial college composition courses, I developed an account of an analogous state of affairs: class-based orientations to text or talk (Collins 1990a). Regular composition students – the approximate counterpart of Gee's middle-class "reasoners" – consistently oriented to written text in classroom discussions. Remedial composition students – the approximate counterpart of Gee's working-class "reasoners" – consistently oriented to group talk, rather than text. In the research context, the orientations were clearly reproductive of social class differences in educational achievement. The orientation to text made the task of teaching expository writing easier with the middle-class students. The lessons proceeded in an orderly fashion, with attention to the official task of revising a written paragraph. The orientation to talk made the task of teaching expository writing more difficult with the working-class students. The official lessons were disrupted as students attended to their emerging talk, with the text serving merely as a pretext for strongly evaluative talk about the content of the text, and with little attention to the official task of text revision.

There is more at issue, however, than reproduction tied to linguistic habitus. The "orientation to talk" reveals a contradiction basic to (many) reproductive processes. In the remedial writing classroom, the under-prepared students were simultaneously disrupting the teaching of writing and achieving a collectively voiced and closely argued critique of their educational situation, including a critique of tests and testing situations and a frank debate about supposed meritocracy and the economic value of educational credentials. Their difficult, pedagogically disruptive behavior also included a moment of real, collective insight and critical appraisal, unmatched by their better-prepared counterparts.

CONCLUSION

As is the case with all important thinkers, what matters is not whether we agree with Bourdieu's solutions, but that he raises important questions and does so in ways that compel critical investigation of his arguments, our assumptions, and whatever empirical materials can be brought to bear on the questions at hand. Bourdieu has repeatedly analyzed how schooling reproduces class position despite ideologies of equal opportunity and meritocracy, and he has enriched the terms of debate of the "linguistic deficit" controversy by developing political and historical, as well as sociocultural, critiques of educational systems. The nonreformist position he adopts regarding educational change parallels his determinism regarding language use; yet, in his conception of symbolic struggles, he furthers our understanding of the dialectic of subjective action and objective conditioning.

This dialectic lacks a sense of the primacy of contradiction, however, and we are left with an account of conditioned strategies for action that overrides the conflictual creativity of interaction-based agency. As I read Bourdieu's account of language, whether in discussions of the educational system, treatises on discourse itself, or in analyses of the general material and cultural logic of advanced capitalist societies, the discursive always seems deducible from, reducible to, in a word, determined by something else: class conditions, capital composition, habitus, field effects. There is a truth in this determinist argument, but it is one-sided. We might agree that the configuration of capital, habitus, and field provides general constraints on the discursive or interactive, that it seems to account for objective social space and to provide a systematic account of practice, but it also ultimately depends on such a precise articulation that we are left genuinely puzzled, and troubled, by just how the dialectic of objective possibilities and subjective aspirations unfolds. In rethinking the relations between "structure" and "practice," we need to appreciate the role of contradictions in human affairs. We need to allow for dilemmas and intractable oppositions; for divided consciousness, not just dominated minds; for crisis-ridden divisions in cultural "texts," as well as in economic systems; for creative, discursive agency in conditions prestructured, to be sure, but also fissured in unpredictable and dynamic ways.

NOTES

1 In certain respects this parallels the distinction between "centred" (common) and "coordinate" (bourgeois) semantic/spatial orientations described by Hanks (Chapter 7).
2 Social conservation is perpetuated through "forms of teaching which . . . dispense with expressly teaching the transmission code because they speak

by tacit agreement to a public prepared by insensible familiarization to understand their tacit meanings" (Bourdieu and Passeron 1977: 126).

3 e.g. *New York Times*, 25 Feb. 1989, article on "English Only" legislation in Suffolk county, legislation proposing draconian prescriptions against the use of Spanish.

4 This theme has been developed in a series of essays and case studies (1982a) emphasizing the power of description as definition in political polls and surveys; the power to mobilize ethnic and regional identity around a name, then to submerge that identity around a different name; and analyzing discursive strategies for gaining and maintaining the upper hand in an intellectual field.

5 Bourdieu's habitus concept is more general. It refers to a systematic orientation, pervading all aspects of social and cultural life; the "linguistic habitus" is just one variant of the more basic orientation.

6 These findings have been widely confirmed in urban settings in the United States, England, Latin America, and Western Europe (Hudson 1980; Trudgill 1984).

7 Perhaps some formulation of strategic calculation of profit – here, persuasion – attained from manipulation of context-based expectations would begin to account for the phenomena, as, perhaps, would a close specification of "field." But these "perhaps" point to the matter at hand: the lack of empirical precision and nuance in many of Bourdieu's arguments about language.

8 Or appreciated by all analysts. The Puerto Rican example was a reanalysis by Gumperz of what Labov (1971) had analyzed as idiosyncratic, non-rule-governed variation. Indeed, in the initial chapters of *Discourse Strategies*, Gumperz (1982) raises an important issue: what is the significance or meaning of statistically characterizable patterns of linguistic variation for practical actors engaged in conversation? This, of course, is akin to Bourdieu's concern with the structure of the social space and actor's "practical sense" of that space and their position in it (1977c, 1984). For Gumperz, the practical relevance is that variations feed into typification jugments (stereotypes) of other actors, of situations, and of communicative purposes, whereby conversationalists construct a sense of their current encounter. My point is that this practical sense of self, other, and situation often embeds contradictions, as the two examples discussed in the text suggest.

9 Using a distinction between status hierarchies and solidaristic co-feeling, Woolard argues that sociolinguistic analysis of language use "reveals a significant fissure in the monolith of linguistic hegemony and contradictory forces in the apparently integrated linguistic market" (1985: 744).

10 There are similarities with the often decried and little understood "Spanglish" of New York City Puerto Rican youth.

11 Gee's studies of narrative (e.g. 1989c), together with work by Sarah Michaels (1981) and Frederick Erickson (1984), have shown the underlying logic of those minority and working-class forms of speech that – as Bourdieu and Passeron (1977) briefly mention in characterizing "common parlance" – tend to "move from particular case to particular case."

REFERENCES

Anderson, B. 1983: *Imagined Communities: reflections on the origin and spread of nationalism.* London: Verso.

Bereiter, C. and Englemann, S. 1966: *Teaching Disadvantaged Children in Preschool.* Englewood Cliffs, N. J.: : Prentice-Hall.

Bernstein, B. 1964: Elaborated and restricted codes. In J. Gumperz and D. Hymes (eds), *The Ethnography of Communication. American Anthropologist* Special Publication 66, no. 6 part 2.

—— 1972: A sociolinguistic approach to socialization; with some reference to educatability. In J. Gumperz and D. Hymes (eds), *Directions in Sociolinguistics,* New York: Holt, Rinehart & Winston.

—— 1974: Postscript to *Class, Codes and Control.* New York: Schocken.

Blom, J-P. and Gumperz, J. 1972: Social meaning in linguistic structures: code-switching in Norway. In J. Gumperz and D. Hymes (eds), *Directions in Sociolinguistics,* New York: Holt, Rinehart & Winston.

Bloom, Allan 1987: *The Closing of the American Mind.* New York: Simon & Schuster.

Bloomfield, L. 1933: *Language.* New York: Holt, Rinehart & Winston.

Collins, J. 1986: Ability grouping and differential instruction. In J. Cook-Gumperz (ed.), *The Social Construction of Literacy,* New York and Cambridge: Cambridge University Press.

—— 1987a: Conversation and knowledge in bureaucratic settings. *Discourse Processes,* 10, no. .4, 303–19.

—— 1987b: Using discourse analysis to understand access to knowledge. In D. Bloome (ed.), *Literacy and Schooling,* Norwood, N.J.: Ablex.

—— 1988: Language and class in minority education. *Anthropology and Education Quarterly,* 19, no. 4, 299–326.

—— 1989: Hegemonic practice: literacy and standard language in public education. *Journal of Education,* 171, no. 2, 9–34.

—— 1990a: The literacy 'crisis' at the university: institutional contradiction and linguistic hegemony. Paper presented at invited sessions on 'Language, ideology, and political economy', American Anthropological Association Annual Meetings, Nov. 1989.

—— 1990b: Socialization to text: structure and contradiction in schooled literacy. Submitted for M. Silverstein and G. Urban (eds), *Natural Histories of Discourse,* to be published by Cambridge University Press.

Edwards, A. 1976: *Class, Culture, and Language.* London: Heinemann.

Erickson, F. 1984: Rhetoric, anecdote and rhapsody: coherence strategies in a conversation among Black American adolescents. In D. Tannen (ed.), *Coherence in Spoken and Written Discourse,* Norwood, N. J.: Ablex.

Gal, S. 1987: Codeswitching and consciousness in the European periphery. *American Ethnologist,* 14, 637–54.

—— Gee, J. 1989a: Literacies and "traditions." *Journal of Education,* 171, no. 1, 26–38.

—— 1989b: *Literacy, Discourse, and Linguistics. Journal of Education* Special Issue, 171, no. 1.

—— 1989c: The narrativization of experience in the oral mode. *Journal of Education*, 171, no. 1, 75–96.

Gibson, E. and Levin, H. 1975: *The Psychology of Reading*. Cambridge, Mass.: MIT Press.

Giroux, H. and McClaren, P. 1988: Critical theory, cultural literacy, and the closing of the American mind: a review of Hirsh and Bloom. *Harvard Education Review*, 58, no. 2, 172–94.

Goffman, E. 1983: The interaction order. *American Sociological Review*, 48, 1–17.

Gumperz, J. 1971: *Language in Social Groups*. Stanford, Calif.: Stanford University Press.

—— 1982: *Discourse Strategies*. New York and London: Cambridge University Press.

Hess, R. 1970: Social class and ethnic influences on socialization. In P. Hussen (ed.), *Carmichael's Manual of Child Psychology*, vol. 2. New York: Wiley.

Hirsch, E. D. 1987: *Cultural Literacy*. New York: Houghton Mifflin.

Hudson, R. 1980: *Sociolinguistics*. New York and Cambridge: Cambridge University Press.

Labov, W. 1971: The notion of "system" in Creole languages. In D. Hymes (ed.), *Pidginization and Creolization of Languages*, Cambridge: Cambridge University Press.

—— 1972: *Sociolinguistic Patterns*. Philadelphia: University of Pennsylvania Press.

—— 1973: *Language in the Inner City*. Philadelphia: University of Pennsylvania Press.

Melmed, P. 1971: *Black English Phonology: the question of reading interference*. Monograph no. 1, Language-Behavior Research Laboratory, University of California, Berkeley.

Michaels, S. 1981: "Sharing time": an oral preparation for literacy. *Language in Society*, 10, 423–42.

Piestrup, A. 1973: *Black Dialect Interference and Accommodation of Reading Instruction in First Grade*. Monograph no. 4, Language-Behavior Research Laboratory, University of California, Berkeley.

Rose, M. 1989: *Lives on the Boundaries: the struggles and achievements of America's underprepared*. New York: Basic Books.

Schwartz, D. 1977: Pierre Bourdieu: the cultural transmission of social inequality. *Harvard Education Review*, 47, no. 4, 538–652.

Trudgill, P. 1984: *Sociolinguistics*, 2nd edn. Harmondsworth: Penguin.

Wacquant, L. 1989: Toward a reflexive sociology: a workshop with Pierre Bourdieu. *Sociological Theory*, 7, no. 1, 26–63.

Whiteman, M. and Deutsch, M. 1968: Social disadvantage as related to intellective and language development. In M. Deutsch, I. Katz, and A. Jensen (eds), *Social Class, Race and Psychological Development*, New York: Holt, Rinehart & Winston.

Williams, R. 1961: *The Long Revolution*. London: Chatto and Windus.

Willis, P. 1977: *Learning to Labor*. London: Routledge & Kegan Paul.

Woolard, K. 1985: Language variation and cultural hegemony: towards an integration of sociolinguistic and social theory. *American Ethnologist*, 12, 738–48.

7

Notes on Semantics in Linguistic Practice

William F. Hanks

INTRODUCTION

It is obvious that language plays a basic role in much of social life and that a sociology of practice must include verbal communication among its objects. People construct the social world using language; they deliberately and continually formulate reality through reference, description, and a variety of other speech functions. This capacity of language to objectify an "outer" world is offset by an equally basic capacity to embody the cognitive, affective, and corporeal orientations of agents. To speak is inevitably to situate one's self in the world, to take up a position, to engage with others in a process of production and exchange, to occupy a social space. In its structure and use language is one of the central vehicles of habitus. This is so not only because it provides the means of objectifying and inculcating aspects of social reality apart from itself, although this is a significant function; even more important is the fact that language embodies and routinizes social orientations which are constitutive of habitus. More than just a tool for describing the world, language, no less than perception and bodily mobility, is a means of access to the world. Objects talked about are thereby made available to agents under certain aspects, and the act of speaking itself constitutes a here-now-we in which practice takes place. How do these and other processes of meaning construction that take place through language contribute to social practice more broadly, and how do social facts mold linguistic practices?

For critial comments that I am still trying to come to grips with, and have therefore inadequately integrated into the essay, particular thanks to to John Brenkman, Jan Farlund, Steve Gabel, John Haviland, Ben Lee, Greg Urban, and Michael Warner.

These questions raise a slightly narrower one that I shall explore here in a provisional way. What kind of semantic theory is likely to be the most productive in describing language within a practice framework? "Semantics" here designates the system of meaning that relates grammatical forms and what is literally said when these forms are uttered in context. On the face of it, Bourdieu's insightful critiques of structuralism and functionalist anthropology (1977c, 1988a), and Saussurian-derived linguistics (1982a) call into question most of the standard semantic theories, by subverting their most basic premises. In *Ce que parler veut dire*, for instance, Bourdieu undermines the separation between language and world upon which truth-functional semantics rests. In the *Outline of a Theory of Practice*, he critiques the notion that practice (and hence linguistic practice) is rule-governed, one of the axioms of linguistics. The focus of practice sociology on social conflict, struggle, asymmetry, and difference inevitably calls into question the idea that interactants must all share a single code in order to be able to communicate. This assumption is present in one form or another in nearly all current semantic theories.

Inaugural contradictions notwithstanding, practice theory has so far produced no framework in which to talk in detail about semantics. The notions that linguistic practice takes place within a "market," according to an "economy" of exchange (1982a), that language is a form of symbolic capital (1982a), and that utterances are formed according to the combined constraints of habitus and the social field (1983a, 1985c, 1988a) can all contribute significantly to an understanding of meaning production, but they cannot substitute for a semantic description. Indeed, the analysis of symbolic practice requires a theory of signification that includes the linguistic system in a nonreductive way. In attempting to articulate practice theory with the study of language, therefore, it is important to keep in mind the difference between parts and wholes. Linguistic premises that may be erroneous or fatally flawed when taken as claims about the total phenomenon of language can nevertheless be accurate and even requisite when taken as claims about one or another aspect of language. What is needed is not a sheer denial of objectivist formalism, but instead what Bourdieu (1977c: 3) called the "second break," through which objectivism is granted a limited role in theoretical knowledge. "The critical break with objectivist abstraction . . . has no other aim than to make possible a science of the dialectical relations between objective structures to which the objectivist mode of knowledge gives access and the structured dispositions within which those structures are actualized and which tend to reproduce them." Note in this passage, as in the overall movement of practice theory, that abstract systems are presupposed, although never accorded the privileged status usually given them by their theoretical proponents. The special significance of this for linguistic practice is that it takes account of the overwhelming fact that all human languages have grammars (whether or not one posits a single universal grammar), while challenging us to move beyond this to a genuinely social framework. But how can linguistic and sociological perspectives be reconciled, or at least articulated, without disfiguring each other beyond recognition?

FIVE POINTS OF DIFFERENCE

Like any other study of language, semantic description is inevitably based on certain premises regarding the relative independence, conventional content, and systematicity of linguistic form. Different theoretical frameworks make different assumptions, and it would be misleading at present to speak merely of "semantics" without saying what kind. Yet there are several dimensions on which theoretical frameworks inevitably take a stand, one way or another. One of these is *truth functionality*. Although there is little doubt that properly linguistic meaning includes much more than strictly propositional information, reference and description still contribute crucially to communication. Thus one must at some point come to grips with truth functionality, whether this is accorded the central role of separating sense from nonsense, as in what Kaplan (1979: 385) called "Golden Age Pure Semantics," or whether one takes a more nuanced position. A variety of contemporary theories concur in rejecting the "Golden Age" view in which, to paraphrase Kaplan, each designator has both an intension and an extension, sentences have truth values as extensions and propositions as intensions, and terms have individuals as extensions and individual concepts as intensions. Kaplan's alternative holds that "some or all of the denoting phrases used in an utterance should not be considered part of the content of what is said, but should rather be thought of as contextual factors which help us interpret the actual physical utterance as having a certain content" (1979: 389).[1]

If part of the linguistic form of an expression belongs to context, and content is fixed only in the joining of form with context, then truth and falsity cannot be judged by positing a fixed intensional meaning and checking its correspondence (truth) or noncorrespondence (falsity) to a world of ontologically independent objects. In various contemporary frameworks, the boundaries between language and world have been shifted away from those posited in correspondence theories of truth. Putnam's (1975) critique of the golden age claim that intension determines extension, along with his thesis that meanings are fixed by local standards (themselves established through a "division of linguistic labor" in society) is another case in point. The link of meaning to socially distributed standards is a species of indexicality that has in both cases the effect of relativizing semantic content to context. (This is not to deny significant differences between Kaplan and Putnam on other points.) Thus, even retaining the notion that the central function of language is to formulate propositions whose truth can be evaluated, we come to see propositions as containing variously context-bound elements. Like literal meaning in Searle's (1979) account, truth functionality is sustained, but only relative to a set of assumptions about the world. To borrow Searle's example, it is only because we share assumptions about the nature of objects and gravity that a sentence like "The cat is on the mat" can appear to have such a banal literal meaning, such obvious truth conditions.

Another kind of relativization takes place in what has come to be called "cognitive semantics," itself a relatively heterogeneous collection of approaches (usefully discussed and illustrated in Eco *et al.* (eds) 1988). Common to cognitive approaches is a focus on human understanding of language, as opposed to model-theoretic or purely truth-conditional meaning. That is, rather than merely implementing a semantic system whose properties can be specified *apart from* human psychological processes, cognitive frameworks take as their main object how language-users construct meaning on the basis of a combination of factors. The latter include the relatively abstract linguistic meaning of verbal form, typical patterns of image projection (Lakoff 1987), deferral of reference (Fauconnier 1984), transposition, metaphorical and metonymic extensions from literal sense (Lakoff 1987, Johnson 1987), along with further socially derived local and schematic knowledge (Cicourel 1985, 1986; Encrevé 1988; de Fornel and Encrevé 1983). In these models the meaning systematically associated with linguistic form functions as a set of "instructions" (Ducrot 1984; Fauconnier 1988) on the basis of which the language-user must build an understanding. It is the entire process of understanding, and not just the encoded instructions, that is the object of semantics. The instructions themselves are never sufficient to uniquely determine the understanding a speaker will construct. In other words, the conveyed meaning of an utterance is axiomatically *underspecified* by the linguistic meaning of the forms uttered.[2]

Despite basic differences among them in the role they accord to social and psychological processes, these developments in cognitive semantics and pragmatics concur on the central point that the object of semantic description is situated meaning, which is derived from a combination of the human context and linguistic form.[3] How one defines this context is of course a matter of considerable debate, or at least difference, among theorists. The key point is the active role which these frameworks accord to language-users in the construction of meaning. In view of this, we can call them and any similar frameworks "constructivist." It is likely, in my opinion, that the kind of semantics appropriate for describing linguistic practice is a constructivist one, just as practice is constitutive of social realities more generally.[4] It is also likely that truth-functional meaning as such will play less of a role than it does in other theories, being replaced by a closer study of the processes by which meaning is derived in the first place.

Bourdieu (1982a, ch. 3) observed that, under proper social circumstances, reference and description constitute performative "nominations" in which reality is defined, rather than merely represented. In all such cases, truth functionality can no longer serve as evaluation metric, because the nominating word makes its own truth: "In structuring the perception that social agents have of the social world, nomination contributes to making the structure of this world – all the more deeply, the more widely it is recognized, that is to say, authorized" (p. 99). There are two points here. Given an authorized speaker under authorized circumstances, to describe the world is to define it and therefore to set the terms on which other actors must treat it. But even failing this Austinian version of nomination as felicitous performance, the patterns of reference and description that make up a language import their own perceptual orientations on what they describe and thus help to form reality as it is socially experienced. When we add to this the fact that language is produced, learned, distributed, and exchanged in accord with social factors, then it becomes clear that truth-functional analysis is revealing only within limits. It applies only to the linguistic elements that contribute to propositional content, holding aside much of what goes on in talk, and even here, the truth of an utterance can only be judged relative to a set of assumptions about the world. The question of how speakers understand an utterance and who is authorized to produce it emerge as more important than whether or not it could be claimed to be true. Indeed, to claim that *p*, and make it stick, is an act that always rests on a social foundation. It is therefore erroneous to elevate it to the position of an analytic standard against which all meaning is judged.[5]

There is a family of other concepts alongside truth functionality that inevitably comes into question along with it; these include objectivist realism, formalism, conventionality, and the distinction between type and token. The realism I have in mind fits the description put forth by Devitt and Sterelny (1987: 187): namely, "a metaphysical doctrine with two dimensions. First, it is a doctrine about what exists and second, it is a doctrine about the nature of the existence. Concerning the first, it holds that such physical entities as stones, trees and cats exist ('are real'). Concerning the second, these entities do not depend for their existence or nature on our minds, nor on our awareness, perception or cognizance of them." This definition properly reflects the commitment of realism to the objective and independent existence of physical reality, but it is still incomplete as it stands. It leaves unstated the additional premise that it is the correspondence between language and this outer, objective reality that is most important to semantics. That is, one could readily concede that things exist (any other claim seems gratuitous if not indefensible) while still asserting that purely physical things play a relatively minor role in the semantics of language. The worst fate for realism so described is the possibility that it is trivially accurate but irrelevant to a properly linguistic semantics. It is the social understandings of things, the production of social realities not reducible to their physical correlates, the sociocultural construction of thinghood itself, and of the physical conditions of language that should be integral to semantics.[6] But Devitt and Sterelny would be loathe to accept such a qualified statement because to do so would be to concede that realism is appropriate to part of semantics but not to the whole, to the part treating the conditions of correspondence between linguistic forms paired with literal meanings and a world outside them. Realism in its strong form goes beyond this in asserting its own a priori relevance, refusing any relativization. Thus it is unsurprising that Devitt and Sterelny define reference as "the link between language and reality" (p. 218), explicitly repudiating the notion that it is socially established concepts rather than things that serve as the referents of linguistic expressions.

Perhaps the most debilitating aspect of realism of the sort referred to here is that it arises out of a dichotomous view of the world in which there are minds and there are physically (that is, scientifically) definable things, and the measure of meaning is the degree of fit between the two. It is revealing that Devitt and Sterelny (1987: 188) qualify their position as "common sense realism" rather than "scientific realism," since this epithet accurately reflects the commonsense basis of their view. From a sociological standpoint it is conspicuously naive, however, to project one's common sense to the level of scientific doctrine, obscuring the fact that common sense is a social product par excellence.

In response to realism, practice sociology offers the claim that reality, as agents treat it in everyday practice, consists of a world primarily defined by social agents acting through typified understandings, even when their typifications are utterly without scientific merit (and equally when they are informed by science). It may be that stones would exist even if everyone believed they didn't (Devitt and Sterelny 1987: 187), but it is far from clear whether this fact of existence would have any significance to the description of linguistic practice in such a belief-world. On the other hand, it may be that Santa Claus really doesn't exist; but the advertisers who project his image, who refer to him for the purpose of selling consumer items as gifts during the late fall in North American cities, need worry little about scientific fact. They know that Santa Claus exists, and their accountants can give reasonably empirical measures of the fact. The duality between mind and world that underlies Western common sense realism is one of the first casualties of what we might call "sociological realism." On this view, what is realistic is not the baggage of objectivity, but the recognition that objectivism and realism themselves are historically derived genres of understanding, and that the objective social reality of institutions is undeniable. Whereas Bourdieu (1977c, ch. 1) explored the objective limits of objectivism, a practice approach to language would pass by the realistic limits of realism too.

The premise of formalism is complementary to realism, since it holds that symbolic form (in this case mainly linguistic) is governed by a system of rules strictly independent of other objective reality. There are numerous possible formalisms. The Saussurian thesis of arbitrariness is one of the cornerstones of one variant of formalism, in that it holds that linguistic form is essentially separable from the world of objective reality and that it is governed by autonomous principles proper to it alone. Meaning, insofar as it falls within the purview of linguistics or philosophy at all, is contained within symbolic form. Saussure makes the distinction between the *signifié* of a sign (its intensional sense) and its reference on given occasions. It is the former that provides the object of semantics for Saussure. While we can measure the truth of a proposition only by comparing it to the real conditions of its referents, it is crucial to formalism that the proposition itself be specifiable apart from its reference in a given social context. Notice that the constructivist approaches cited above concur in rejecting this kind of formalism to the extent that they take propositional content to be determined only through the mediation of context or human cognition. This is as much as to say that semantic content is not encoded in the forms, but rather in the combination of form with circumstance of utterance.

But one cannot so quickly dispatch the formalist project as a whole. What does it mean to suggest that meaning is produced, not encoded in form? Does this hold for all meaning, and must all formal systematicity derive from encoded meaning? The two questions are separate, but both can be answered in the negative. Not all semantic meaning can be pinned on form as the *signifié* is pinned on the *signifiant* in a Saussurian paradigm, but so what? Constructivist semantics recognizes this fact, but need not deny that verbal form is systematic because of it. To reject formalism entirely is to deprive oneself of a powerful tool for describing grammatical structure. We come back to the fact that all human languages are grammatically systematic in ways that one would be hard pressed to motivate on extralinguistic functional, cultural, or sociological grounds. The formal regularities of morphosyntactic derivation and inflection, phonological systems, the formal difference between particles, verbs, and nouns in any language that has all three types – these are the sorts of things that it would be fruitless to attempt to describe without any notion of formal grammar: fruitless and, above all, unnecessary, because there is no need for practice sociology to deny the reality of linguistic form. What is necessary is to reappropriate language from formalism, by demonstrating the irreducible role of agents, social fields, markets, the distribution of capital in the form of knowledge and, hence, potential semantic creativity, and the social body. That is, formalism can be encompassed without according it the primacy or constant relevance in which it is usually enshrined.

Another monumental premise of contemporary objectivism is the idea that in order for speakers to communicate with one another they must share the same conventional system of linguistic rules. It is because we know both the meanings and grammatical patterns of English that we can understand the literal sense of an utterance like "The cat is on the mat". As Barwise puts it:

> In general, just what content a statement has depends on more than the sentence used and the circumstances in which it is used. It also depends on the shared conventions *R* of the language community of which it is a part. This is so obvious that it might seem to go without saying, but it is worth making explicit. In working out a semantic theory it is exactly these relations that one is trying to make explicit. (1988: 31)

Barwise goes on to describe the conventions he posits as being constraints, and notes that "A very important property of conventional constraints *R* is that they must be mutual, or shared (Lewis 1969). They must mutually bind all the parties to the convention in order to be successful communications between agents" (Barwise 1988:31).

Although Barwise's framework for semantics is innovative in a number of ways, his commitment to conventionalism is a case of standard convention itself. It follows in the Saussurian logic of arbitrariness that one must know the conventions of *langue* in order to interpret *parole*, as of course Saussure observed. More recently, linguists working in Gricean pragmatics have also posited a level of conventional meaning, of which the grammar is the repository (Grice 1967, 1975; Levinson 1983). It is this conventional core that defines what is literally said in utterances and so provides the basis on which implicatures are computed. Speech act theories derived from Austin (1962) similarly posit conventions of language use, starting with Austin's first felicity condition (alpha 1), which stipulates that there must exist a convention according to which saying such and such has a certain effect. Indeed, it is hard to think of a single linguistic framework that does not posit the conventionality of the system. For how else can a formally autonomous and relatively arbitrary system of language exist except by way of social convention?

The reasoning of which Barwise's statements are an excellent expression has merit; but, more important, it has appeal to common sense. Society is made up of individuals, each with a mind and a different range of private experiences and motivations. It is only because we submit to a common code that we can assume consensus on ground rules, and only by virtue of consensus that communication can take place. Precisely because words are cut loose from natural reality, convention is the necessary socializing factor. If I started making up words in speaking, no one would understand them; my activity would cease to be language in the true sense and would ultimately degenerate into babble. Semantics is the system of the ideal speaker-hearer, the system of conventions that everyone must learn in order to derive propositional content, successfully convey implicatures, and perform felicitous speech acts. At what point in this mass of phenomena one draws the boundary between semantics and pragmatics may vary; but this is a matter of the character of the conventions, not the presence or absence of convention (see Morgan 1978).

The problem with conventionality is not that it fails to capture a significant feature of language, but rather that it serves to obscure other, equally significant features. Once again, it is a case of parts and wholes and common sense elevated to the level of analytic principle. In his early work, Bourdieu (1977c) rightly took to task the vision of society that animates conventionalism, critiquing the legalist idea that society functions by rules and the functionalist idea that consensus is a ubiquitous feature of practice (on the contrary). Indeed, the just so story sketched in the preceding paragraph is so at odds with contemporary social theory as to make it hardly worth arguing against. The problem for one who would study linguistic practice is that linguistics is by tradition locked into conventionalism, and to reject it totally is to undermine grammar. Let us rather, in a very preliminary way, explore some of the limitations of the idea for describing language.

To say that it is shared conventions that make communication possible is to invite the assumption that speakers and addressees must share exactly the same system. There are actually two distinct parts to this: first, the notion that commonality among participants is requisite to successful communication, and second, that what is common is the linguistic system. Despite its appeal for describing certain sorts of communication among small groups of similar actors, the notion of a language community on which it rests is excessively simplified. It ignores, among other things, the facts that rights and abilities to know and use language are socially distributed, and that social groups develop various specialized patterns of usage which may hinder or mystify their exchanges with others but nonetheless do not preclude them. Even a framework such as Bernstein's (1972) elaborated and restricted codes, or Brown and Gilman's (1960) early work on pronoun usage, or Gumperz's (1972, 1982) researches on speech communities and modes of contextualization all point in the direction of differentiation. If Bourdieu is right in positing struggle and competition over symbolic capital, and language is a form of capital, then we should be on the lookout for points of discord, breakdown, conflict, and so forth – not merely as negative cases that prove the rule of convention, but as loci of the production of meaning. The reference to production is significant in this context, since conventionality invites the further assumption that the semantic system is prefabricated in the sense that its existence is logically prior to any occasion of its instantiation. This, of course, serves to hide the significant fact that speakers, like other actors, innovate frequently and use language in ad hoc but highly effective ways.

Finally, to speak of conventionality is to invoke the possibility of its absence, which raises the question: what is the opposite of conventional? That is, if some aspects of language are conventional and others are not, what positive features characterize the latter? In Gricean pragmatics, this question is addressed directly: what is not conventional is natural.[7] In his early paper, Grice (1971) put forth the thesis that the word "meaning" is used in two different ways, denoting two sorts of cases. He called the two cases "natural" and "non-natural" meaning. The former is illustrated by statements such as "Spots mean measles" and "Smoke means fire," the latter by "I meant that remark to reassure you," "A red light means you're supposed to stop," and "The word 'dog' means a kind of canine." The distinction here appears to be between nonnatural cases in which the "meaning" of an object derives from the intentions of some agent (often, the speaker or author) and natural ones in which there are physical, nonintentional, causal links between the object and what it is claimed to "mean." In his later work, Grice developed further the idea of natural meaning and its role in conversational inference. In overly brief outline, Grice holds that conversational interaction is guided by a set of universal rational principles which he summarizes in the Cooperative Principle (P) and its associated maxims. This enjoins speaker-addressees to make their contribution just as is required (accurate, adequate, relevant, and perspicuous). The CP itself, and all situational inferences that are derived by using it, are held to be natural, just as it is natural that rational humans cooperate. What is unnatural is conventional: namely, the arbitrary facts of the language that the interlocutors are using. The two categories are mutually exclusive; that which is natural cannot be conventional (or only trivially, redundantly so), and that which is non-natural is by definition conventional. This dichotomy once again has enormous appeal to a certain kind of common sense and has helped to preserve the notions of conventionality and naturalism in linguistics.

A description of language genuinely informed by practice sociology must reject the Gricean dichotomy while also questioning the embedded premises that social action is guided by rationality and that facts are either natural or conventional in the technical sense of this term. The Gricean framework, as is, is based on a further division between human intentions (the core feature of nonnatural meaning) and natural reality (as it would be in the absence of any human intentionality). Unfortunately, there really is no nontrivial role for society to play in this model, banished as it is by the duality of mind and nature.[8] There is nonetheless at least one aspect of this framework that can contribute significantly to a description of verbal practice: namely, the distinction between features of conversational meaning that somehow inhere in language, because of its own systematicity, and features that inhere somehow in the interaction between linguistic forms and the contexts of utterance in which they happen. Where linguistic semantics can add most to the study of linguistic practice is in relation to the former; whereas anthropology, sociology, and cognitive studies can shed most light on the latter. Grice's approach has the great advantage of focusing attention on the surplus of conversational meaning that is produced in talk and the virtue of recognizing that some of this meaning belongs to language, some to something else.

The final concept I wish to draw attention to is the distinction between types and tokens. Introduced by C. S. Peirce in connection with his classification of signs, this dichotomy is a basic part of linguistics. "Any conventional sign," as Peirce (1955: 102) observed, is not a single object, but a general type which, it has been agreed, shall be significant. . . . Every [conventional] legisign signifies through an instance of its application, which may be termed a Replica of it . . . .[E]very legisign requires sinsigns. . . . Nor would the Replica be significant were it not for the law [convention] which renders it so.

What Peirce calls a "conventional legisign" is a type, and the replicas of the type that occur in individual situations are tokens of it. This division is basic to linguistic analysis because it allows the linguist to abstract from the particulars of a specific utterance in such and such a context in order to examine the formal and functional features of the semiotic type of which the utterance is a token instantiation. (For a clear discussion and further references see Lyons 1977: 1. 13ff.). That is, in order to analyze the syntactic or semantic properties of noun phrases in English, it is necessary to abstract from the particulars of given utterances and construct a general account of the properties that remain constant across instances. A grammar is a system of types plus the processes that operate on these, relating them by combination, permutation, and so forth. How one decides which features are constitutive of a type and what kinds of types are at stake are both technical questions that would require more discussion than can be undertaken here. The important point is that in describing the conventional semantics of a language, we are describing a system of types. Notice further in the above quotation from Peirce that the relation between the two levels is necessary in both directions: there are no types of which there are no tokens (all types must have tokens), and no would-be sign is in fact a recognizable token except insofar as it replicates a type. Without some distinction of this order, it would be impossible to make generalizations regarding recurrent properties of language; nor would it be possible to segment the speech stream into units or to identify securely examples of a word or construction.

The division between types and tokens is overdetermined in linguistic semantics, in the sense that it is motivated by the conventionalist premise that semiotic systems are shared codes and by the formalist premise that symbolic (linguistic) form is guided by autonomous principles proper to it alone. Types are conventional, as Peirce pointed out, and the system of forms constructed by the formalist must include types. Indeed, it is difficult to imagine a semantics of any kind that fails to incorporate something like the type–token distinction.

But this apparently simple concept introduces difficulties of its own, because it subsumes the claim that in speaking, interlocutors are merely reproducing the conventional linguistic system of language. Peirce's term "replica" should be read literally as the claim that the infinite instantiations of a type are just that, repetitions whose individual differentiae are accidental relative to their constant sameness. This relation is part of what justifies the abstraction from tokens in the first place; yet it invites the debilitating assumption that speech, or *parole*, is no more than a degenerate manifestation of a purer, constitutive system. On this view, linguistic practice falls into the epiphenomenal role that Saussure accorded to *parole*. Furthermore, in adopting the notion of types uncritically, one risks losing all focus on temporality, since types, being prefabricated totalized units, logically preexist any instance of their use. *Parole* can have diachrony, but the system of types is a pure synchrony, or perhaps what the Pragueans called a "dynamic synchrony" – changing, but remaining the same. As Jakobson and Tynianov (1985) put it, "the history of a system is in turn a system"; or, we might add (under this view), diachrony itself is guided by a superhistorical system.

What we need, rather, for describing linguistic practice is a limited commitment to types and tokens, just as we need a formalism of more limited proportions. The key issue, as I see it, is to open up the question of how types are produced and to focus on the significant variations among cases along with the social dynamics of what Peirce calls "instantiation." The fact of instantiation cannot be merely axiomatic in practice theory, since to instantiate is to act and therefore to take up position in a field. Similarly, the fact of totalizing practice cannot be definitional but must be achieved by agents and may well be contested. It cannot be the case that interactants need to agree on which types are being instantiated in an encounter in order to communicate, precisely because this question is so often subject to dispute and difference of interpretation. Thus, for all these reasons, only a qualified use of the type–token distinction can be justified for our purposes.

CONCLUSION

My goal in this brief essay has been to suggest some of the pressure points that must be worked through in order to develop a semantics of practice, but I have not yet worked them through. Truth functionality, realism, formalism, conventionality, and the type–token distinction are sufficiently ingrained in the training of linguists and in their working habits as to be part of the disciplinary habitus. Unfortunately, as is often the case with deeply inculcated habits of mind and practice, these ideas serve as much to exclude some topics of inquiry as to include others. I presuppose in these remarks that practice sociology must incorporate elements of linguistics sooner or later, just as a viable linguistic semantics and pragmatics must incorporate insights from sociology. It is inevitable that in such a combination, both the contributing approaches will be altered. It is inadequate merely to deny either the internal systematicity of language or its constant articulation through social contexts. The production of meaning, which I take to be the central object of semantics, cannot be encapsulated in purely conventional systems, nor can it be completely severed from these systems. I think we should work towards a semantics in which meaning is distributed among co-participating agents (as cognition is distributed; see Chapter 5 above), subject to revision by interested actors, and in which attributions and imputations of meaning, which may fall short of the determinacy needed to judge truth and falsity, are seen as important phenomena to be described. At the same time, it is a matter of historical fact that language is used to make reference and description under certain circumstances and that truth is asserted and meaning fixed. We cannot merely reject truth functionality as though, once deprived of its commonsense naturalism, it were to disappear from the social landscape entirely. The kind of break with objectivism envisioned by this essay encompasses it within historically specific circumstances but does not attempt to erase it entirely. Rather than using type-level systems to cut off meaning from the material circumstances of speech and from experiences in which agents live it, a more constructive approach is to explore and question the boundaries of abstract systems. Rather than starting from a conventional literal meaning which one then "contextualizes" through added inferences, the challenge is to see the literal core of language as already permeated by context and subject to reconfiguration and novel production in activity. To be sure, it is easier to state these goals than to realize them.

NOTES

1 Barwise (1988) presents a very similar model which agrees in all relevant ways with Kaplan's: namely, that semantic content is determined by the combination of encoded meaning and circumstance of utterance.
2 Stated in terms of conveyed meaning and linguistic meaning, this claim bears a strong resemblance to the Gricean theory of implicatures, in which "conveyed meaning" is made up of what is literally said (linguistic meaning) plus what is implicated (inferences derived from a combination of what is said and the conversational circumstances under which it is said). The parallel is

valid, but should not obscure important differences. For Grice, what is literally said is a propositional content accurately representable in the metalanguage of symbolic logic. Natural language, in other words, contains a solid logical core of literal propositional meaning, and implicatures are really a pragmatic overlay that can be calculated only by starting from the logical core. What I am suggesting, on the contrary, is that literal meaning itself exists only in the union of linguistic form and the context of its production. It cannot be posited first and then "placed in context," since outside the circumstantial frame of its utterance, the forms have no determinate content to start with. Furthermore, Grice's assumption that natural language works like logic overlooks myriad interactive and cultural dimensions of meaning that must be taken into account in a sociological description of talk.

3 For interesting comparative cases dealing with mathematics and learning as situated practices, see Lave 1988 and Lave and Wenger, in press.

4 This is not to deny the existence of institutions and structures that transcend the local conjuncture of activity, but rather to say that meaning (even literal meaning) is produced and reproduced in linguistic practice, not fixed in a structure that always preexists it.

5 To question truth functionality is by no means new. One of the mainstays of Prague school linguistics (e.g. Jakobson 1960) and the ethnography of speaking (e.g. Hymes 1972, Silverstein 1976) has been the plurality of nonreferential functions in speech. While these traditions have contributed in a major way to the perspective developed here, they share with truth-functional semantics commitments to conventionality, the type–token distinction, and the centrality of rule-governed systems.

6 This is close to the argument that I make in regard to deixis in natural language (Hanks 1990). Much of the literature on deixis is mired in the realist assumption that "here" and "there" are zones of relative proximity to a speaker in physical space. In fact, a careful application of this principle in describing deixis in natural languages yields a wrongheaded and empirically dubious account of how speakers actually use and gloss the forms.

7 There is a strong similarity in Grice's dichotomy to the one put forth by Saussure (1974: 100–1) in presenting his first principle, the arbitrariness of the link between signifier and signified. Noting that there is nothing "inner" or natural in the bond between the two parts of the sign he says, "In effect, all received means of expression in a society depend in principle on a collective habit or, equivalently, on convention."

8 It is obvious that the Gricean framework can be used to interpret actual cases only by assuming a vast amount of social knowledge in order to be able to judge when the CP and its maxims are being followed and when they are being somehow violated, sidestepped, or brought into clash. Sociologists and anthropologists can take heart that the explanation of implicatures requires information of the sort that they typically think about. But this really is a trivial contribution, whose main focus is the application of the model to a corpus of data. The point I wish to underscore is that with respect to the

theory itself, Gricean pragmatics leaves no place for a constitutive social world.

REFERENCES

Austin, J. L. 1962: *How To Do Things with Words*. New York: Oxford University Press. First pub. 1955.

Barwise, J. 1988: On the circumstantial relation between meaning and content. In U. Eco *et al*. (eds), *Meaning and Mental Representations*, Bloomington: Indiana University Press, 23–39.

Bernstein, B. 1972: Social class, language and socialization. In P. P. Giglioli (ed.), *Language and Social Context*, New York: Penguin, 157–78. First pub. 1970.

Brown, R. and Gilman, A. 1972: The pronouns of power and solidarity. In P. P. Giglioli (ed.), *Language and Social Context*, New York: Penguin, 252–82. First pub. 1960.

Cicourel, A. 1985: Text and discourse. *Annual Review of Anthropology*, 14, 159–85.

—— 1986: The reproduction of objective knowledge: common sense reasoning in medical decision making. In G. Böhme and N. Stehr (eds), *The Knowledge Society*, Dordrecht: Reidel, 87–122.

Devitt, M. and Sterelny, K. 1987: *Language and Reality*. Cambridge, Mass.: MIT Press.

Ducrot, O. 1984: *Le Dire et le dit*. Paris: Éditions de Minuit.

Eco, U. *et al*. (eds) 1988: *Meaning and Mental Representation*. Bloomington: Indiana University Press.

Encrevé, P. 1988: C'est Reagan qui a coulé le billet vert: la dérivation généralisée. *Actes de la recherche en sciences sociales*, 71, (no. 2), 109–28.

Fauconnier, G. 1984: *Espaces mentaux: aspects de la construction du sens dans les langues naturelles*. Paris: Éditions de Minuit.

—— 1988: Quantification, roles and domains. In U. Eco *et al*. (eds), *Meaning and Mental Representation*, Bloomington: Indiana University Press, 61–80.

Fornel, M. de, and Encrevé, P. 1983: Le Sens pratique, construction de la référence et structure de l'interaction dans le couple question/réponse. *Actes de la recherche en sciences sociales*, 43, 3–30.

Grice, H. P. 1967: Logic and conversation. Unpublished manuscript, William James Lectures, Harvard University.

—— 1971: Meaning. In D. Steinberg and L. Jakobovits (eds), *Semantics: an interdisciplinary reader in philosophy, linguistics and psychology*, Cambridge: Cambridge University Press, 53–9. First pub. 1957.

—— 1975. Logic and conversation. In P. Cole and J. Morgan (eds), *Syntax and Semantics* Vol. 3: *Speech Acts*, New York: Academic Press, 41–58.

Gumperz, J. 1972: The speech community. In P. P. Giglioli (ed.), *Language and Social Context*, New York: Penguin, 219–31. First pub. 1968.

—— 1982: *Discourse Strategies*. Cambridge: Cambridge University Press.

Hanks, W. F. 1990: *Referential Practice: language and lived space among the Maya*. Chicago: University of Chicago Press.

Hymes, D. 1972: Models of the interaction of language and social life. In J. J. Hymes and J. Gumperz (eds), *Directions in Sociolinguistics*, New York: Holt, Rinehart & Winston, 35–71.

Jakobson, R. 1960: Concluding statement: linguistics and poetics. In T. Sebeok (ed.), *Style in Language*, Cambridge, Mass.: MIT Press, 350–77.

—— and Tynianov, J. 1985: Problems in the study of language and literature. In K. Pomorska and S. Rudy (eds), *Roman Jakobson: verbal art, verbal sign, verbal time*, Minneapolis: University of Minnesota Press, 25–7. First pub. 1928.

Johnson, M. 1987: *The Body in the Mind: the bodily basis of meaning, imagination and reason*. Chicago: University of Chicago Press.

Kaplan, D. 1979: Dthat. In P. A. French *et al.* (eds), *Contemporary Perspectives in the Philosophy of Language*, Minneapolis: University of Minnesota Press, 383–400. First pub. 1978.

Lakoff, G. 1987: *Women, Fire and Dangerous Things: what categories reveal about the mind*. Chicago: University of Chicago Press.

Lave, J. 1988: *Cognition in Practice: mind, mathematics and culture in everyday life*. Cambridge: Cambridge University Press.

—— and Wenger, E. In press: *Situated Learning: legitimate peripheral participation*. Cambridge: Cambridge University Press.

Levinson, S. C. 1983: *Pragmatics*. Cambridge: Cambridge University Press.

Lewis, D. 1969: *Convention: a philosophical study*. Cambridge, Mass.: Harvard University Press.

Lyons, J. 1977: *Semantics*, vols. 1 and 2. Cambridge: Cambridge University Press.

Morgan, J. 1978: Two types of convention in indirect speech acts. In P. Cole (ed.), *Syntax and Semantics* vol. 9: *Pragmatics*, New York: Academic Press, 261–80.

Peirce, C. S. 1955: Logic as semiotic: the theory of signs. In J. Buchler (ed.), *Philosophical Writings of Peirce*, New York: Dover, 98–119.

Putnam, H. 1975: The meaning of meaning. In *Mind, Language and Reality*, Cambridge: Cambridge University Press, 215–71.

Saussure, F. de 1974: *Cours de linguistique générale*, Édition critique préparée par T. de Mauro. Paris: Payot.

Searle, J. 1979: *Expression and Meaning: studies in the theory of speech acts*. Cambridge: Cambridge University Press.

Silverstein, M. 1976. Shifters, verbal categories and cultural description. In K. Basso and H. Selby (eds): *Meaning in Anthropology*, Albuquerque, N. M.: School of American Research, 11–57.

8

Gender and Symbolic Violence: Female Oppression in the Light of Pierre Bourdieu's Theory of Social Practice

Beate Krais

INTRODUCTION

With the concepts of "class" and "gender," sociology addresses two different, fundamental dimensions of social differentiation that entail domination. Whereas class domination has long been a subject of sociological research and, indeed, was one of the social problems that gave rise to sociology as a science, our knowledge about the bases, mechanisms, and consequences of gender differentiation is more recent and more fragmentary. This, it could be argued, is related to the fact that, even in many advanced capitalist societies of Europe, women became free legal subjects with the same rights as male citizens only after the war.[1] And even in those countries where the concept of the free legal subject applies to every adult person and is a constituting part of the social order, one can still find some restrictions for women. This is especially the case for married women, who may be prevented from acting as free legal subjects in the full sense of the concept. But these relics of former social orders, influential as they may be in the everyday life of women, are not what I shall be dealing with here.

The problem of male domination over women as a sociological problem arises when those legal restrictions are, in principle, abolished or, more exactly, when they are no longer accepted as part of the "natural order." In this sense the emergence of a gender problem has to be seen as parallel to the emergence of a class problem. Class became a problem for sociology only when the social agent, whom Marx called the "free wage-laborer," entered the stage of history. Of course, this social agent did not have full civil and political rights from the first days of capitalism; but essentially he was a free person – free to make contracts and free to move from one place to another. Yet it was necessary to explain, through the means of social science, why, under these conditions, domination, in the form of class domination, continued to exist.[2]

In a similar way, gender differentiation continues to exist as a form of domination in modern society. Thus, gender domination will be discussed here not as a universal, ahistorical phenomenon, but in its specific modern form as it is found in advanced capitalist societies. In the social practice of advanced capitalist societies, "female" is also a synonym for "inferior," women's jobs are bad jobs, "female" behavior is "weak" behavior, and "female" activities are of less value than "male" activities. What mechanisms are at work to make gender differentiation function as a dimension of domination, and where in social practice can we observe this type of domination? Why are women excluded from power positions in most social fields? How are "male" and "female" actions, ways of thinking, and judging reproduced in social practice?

Over the last decade, much theoretical debate on the gender problem and its origin has centered around the issues of domestic labor and the female labor capacity,[3] capitalism and patriarchy,[4] and gender and class.[5] Surprising as it may seem, when one observes the often impetuous attacks of feminist theorists against Marx and Marxism, this debate developed mainly in the intellectual neighborhood of Marxism. But there are, of course, common grounds where feminist and Marxist social theory meet. They share a critical perspective in social analyses, that is, a perspective focusing on relations of domination, oppression, and exploitation; a concept of social theory as a necessary condition for emancipation; and the conviction that the (theoretical) solution to the problem in question (gender or class, respectively) has to be searched for in basic social relations.

The feminist debate on social theory has already had important consequences. For example, the oppression of women in modern society can no longer be considered a "secondary" or "trivial contradiction," a "historical relic" of earlier societies. This line of argument has, for decades, been the "classical" point of view in Marxist thinking. Likewise, the debate about domestic labor has brought to light the "forgotten" labor that is done at home, in the "private" sphere, in personal relations, and which takes place through a specific, seemingly "natural" division of labor between women and men. Domestic labor is now seen more and more as a constituent part of modern economy, with the "natural" division of labor between women and men and the "hiding" of domestic labor in the "private" or "personal" sphere being a prerequisite for the actual functioning of modern societies. And the debate on class and gender, as Kreckel (1989) recently mentioned, leads to revising the way in which sociologists normally construct their models of social structure, involving a number of quite practical questions for empirical research – such as whether the individual or the household constitute the unit of analysis, how to measure the social status of housewives, how to deal with cross-class families, and the like. In short, social theory is no longer as it was before.[6]

However, so far no satisfactory answer as to the bases of female oppression in modern society has been found, and the same is true for the "mechanisms" of the reproduction of gender domination. I think there is a consensus in the ongoing feminist debate that the theoretical key – if the idea of a single key to the problem is not an illusion – to the gender problem has not yet been discovered. Therefore, we still have the laborious work of theoretical reasoning, of developing, defending, and rejecting arguments, and of assessing the variety of social realities of women and men through empirical research. Here I propose to assess the problem of gender in terms of the social theory of Pierre Bourdieu; that is, as a social construction and a social relation emphasizing the symbolic order of the world.[7] From the bulk of empirical research and theoretical discussions on the condition of women that has emerged during the last decade, it is clear that the symbolic aspects of social practice are an essential part of the repression of women. A discussion of those aspects in terms of a theory dealing explicitly with cultural constructions should contribute to a better understanding of the gender problem.

SOCIAL STRUCTURE AND MENTAL STRUCTURES

The starting point for Bourdieu's social analysis, resuming the Marx of the *Theses on Feuerbach*, is that the objects of knowledge are constructed and that the principle of this construction is practical activity oriented towards practical functions. But "practice always implies a cognitive operation, a practical operation of construction which sets to work, by reference to practical functions, systems of classification (taxonomies) which organize perception and structure practice" (Bourdieu 1977c: 97). Thus, perception of the world inseparably involves mental actions by which the world is given an order; or, as Bourdieu says, the vision of the world is at the same time a di-vision of the world:

A vision of the world is a division of the world, based on a fundamental principle of division which distributes all the things of the world into two complementary classes. To bring order is to bring division, to divide the universe into opposing entities, those that the primitive speculation of the Pythagoreans presented in the form of "columns of contraries" (*sustoichiai*). The limit produces difference and the different things "by an arbitrary institution", as Leibniz put it, translating the "*ex instituto*" of the Scholastics. This magical act presupposes and produces collective belief, that is, ignorance of its own arbitrariness. . . . *Natura non facit saltus*: it is the magic of institution which, in the natural continuum, the network of biological kinship or the natural world, introduces the break, the division, *nomos*, the frontier which makes the group and its specific customs ("vérité en deçà des Pyrénées, erreur au dela"), the arbitrary necessity (*nomô*) through which the group constitutes itself as such by instituting what unites it and what separates it (1990e: 210).

One of the most powerful and ubiquitous systems of classification in social practice – even in complex societies – is the taxonomy of male/female, and it is this taxonomy through which the division of labor between the genders is assessed, perceived, defined, and structured. On several occasions Bourdieu has used Kabyle society to demonstrate how the division of labor between the genders becomes the foundation of the vision of the world, of the way of understanding the world and mentally structuring it – that is, of a cultural construction (cf. 1977c, 1990e). He describes the Kabyle as a society with virtually no other dimension of differentiation and domination than that of gender; the Kabyle, in Bourdieu's analysis of gender differentiation, serve as an ideal type – in the sense of an extreme case – for the functioning of the male/female taxonomy. The thorough analysis of this case even allows for the decoding of something like a "collective unconscious" haunting the brains of male anthropologists, as well as those of their male readers. Thus, Bourdieu says,

Anthropology . . . becomes instead a particularly powerful form of socio-analysis. By pushing as far as possible the objectification of subjectivity and the subjectification of the objective, it forces one, for example, to discover, in the hyperbolic realization of all male fantasies that is offered by the Kabyle world, the truth of the collective unconscious that also haunts the minds of anthropologists and their readers, male ones at least. The colluding or horrified fascination that this description may arouse should not disguise the fact that the same discriminations which assign women to continuous, humble, invisible tasks are instituted, before our very eyes (increasingly so as one moves down the social hierarchy), both in things and in minds (1990e: 146).

The Kabyle vision of the world is a cultural construction in which the division of labor between the genders is not just one of several axes of social differentiation, but the central axis. The male/female taxonomy serves as the first instrument for the expression of social differences, or, even more generally, to give the world an order – an order not only for the social world but also for what we would call the "natural" world. This instrument is a relational and antagonistic concept: it cuts the world into no more than two parts, but at the same time into opposite and complementary parts. In Kabyle society, even the most basic conditions of human life – that is, the localization of the body in space and time – are understood in terms of the male/female taxonomy.[8] The space inside the house, or the house itself, is organized according to a highly complex, mythically transcended system of male/female dichotomies; in the same way the social definition of space outside the house relies on this system – and there are no definitions of space that are not social. The calendar, relating the lapse of time to human activity over the year, also uses the male/female dichotomy.

I shall not attempt to summarize Bourdieu's fascinating analysis of the highly complex cultural construction that is the division of labor between the genders in the Kabyle; it should be read in detail in the original. One aspect of this construction, however, may be of some importance in the analysis of gender differentiation in other societies, too: this is the "game of twofold objective truth" (1977c: 133) by which order is constructed through the male/female taxonomy and transgressed at the same time. The mental representation of the division of labor between the genders does not just consist of a system of dichotomies, however differentiated this may be. In the division of labor between the genders, as well as in other cases of the division of labor, the contrary is not just separate but is related and complementary. Thus ideas and operations aimed at uniting the contraries or at separating the united contraries – marriage and ploughing, for example – are at least as important as the dichotomies themselves. In the same way, transitional periods, passages, or thresholds between two spaces, where the antagonistic principles confront one another, play their role in social practice. This consideration for the limits and for the legitimate transgression of the limits – and the corresponding rites and ritual actions – is one of the most productive features of Bourdieu's analysis of social practice, and it is particularly convincing when the division of labor between the genders is analyzed.

Magical transgression of the frontier installed by magical logic would not be so imperatively necessary if the contraries to be united were not life itself, and their dissociation a murder, the condition of life . . . . In fact, the union of contraries does not abolish the opposition and, when united, the contraries are still as opposed as ever, but quite differently, manifesting the dual truth of the relationship that unites them, at once antagonistic and complementary. (1990e: 213) [9]

The division of labor between the genders is a social construction and a social structure, but, like every established order, it appears to represent the so-called natural order of the world – not only in Kabyle society, but in modern society, too. This cultural pattern lends itself all the more to naturalization, since it is based, as Bourdieu points out, on the division of sexual labor – in the sexual act and in reproduction – and thus has a biological foundation, unlike other principles of social differentiation (1977c: 92ff.; 1990e: 146ff. and *passim*). What is more, the division of labor between man and woman objectifies itself in a very fundamental sense, as it becomes embodied: the differentiation of male and female shapes the body, the *hexis*, and the habits of the body; guides perception of one's own body and of others' bodies; and determines the agent's relation to his or her body and its sensual perceptions and expressions, and therefore determines identity in a very fundamental, "bodily" sense. The body cannot be thought of if not as "male" or "female." With this bodily point of reference and with its embodiment (in the real sense of the word), the division of labor between the genders is not only as deeply rooted in the social agent as is possible; it also seems to refer to nothing but "nature."

DOMINATION AND THE REPRODUCTION OF THE SPECIES

So far, I have discussed, by referring to Bourdieu's social theory, gender differentiation and the role of the mental (and bodily) representation of the division of labor between the genders in structuring social reality, but not gender domination. To deal with this aspect, Bourdieu's line of reasoning suggests that we can proceed further in the debate on the symbolic reconstruction of the division of labor between the genders. Feminist social theorists have drawn attention to the process of reproduction as the possible clue for domination in the relation between the genders. Some argue for a theory of reproduction, as does, for example, Ursula Beer (1984). Taking a different point of view, Irene Dölling (1989) discusses the problem from the perspective of the

German Democratic Republic, where the class dichotomy had lost much
of its impact on society, but not the gender dichotomy. Another author,
relatively close to Bourdieu's way of reasoning, is Mary O'Brien (1981),
who deals explicitly with the social construction of reproduction. In the
following I rely mainly on an argument advanced by O'Brien.

O'Brien has written a feminist critique of political theory. Theory is
consciousness about human experience, in the double sense that it is a
conscious expression or formulation of human experience and at the
same time organizes experience. But, thus far, she says, political theory
has been consciousness about *male* experience. At what point can *female*
experience be brought into political theory? That is, what is the starting
point for a critique of traditional political theory on the grounds of its
being an ideology of male supremacy? "To the question: Where does
feminist theory start? I answer: within the process of human reproduction. Of that process, sexuality is but a part. I intend to argue that it is not
within sexual relations but within *the total process of human reproduction* that the ideology of male supremacy finds its roots and its
rationales" (O'Brien 1981: 8).

Following Hegel's discussion of the family,[10] O'Brien analyzes the
reproductive process abstracted from the social context, a strategy
inspired by Marx's analysis of the labor process in *Das Kapital* (vol. 1, ch.
5). Stated "in its plain and abstract moments" (as Marx writes when he
analyzes the labor process), the reproductive process for men involves a
problematic experience: the "discovery of physiological paternity is the
discovery *at the same time* of men's inclusion in and exclusion from the
natural reproductive process" (1981: 52). In terms of the theoretical
tradition to which O'Brien owes so much, paternity is primarily an
experience of exclusion or of alienation from the means of reproduction
of the species. To overcome this exclusion, man has invented paternity as
appropriation of the child, a right to the child – and "right" is not a
natural but a political concept, which makes no sense except in a social
context. As a social construction, therefore, paternity demands a support
system, a whole set of social institutions ensuring the rights of the father
to a particular child; it is a concept that allows transcending natural
realities with historical, man-made realities.

Now, the necessarily social construction of paternity does not
necessarily entail male domination. The biological aspects of the
reproductive process by no means determine the whole of that process;
nor do they determine the division of reproductive labor. Maternity, of
course, is also a socially constructed institution, but in a different sense.
In every historical form, the social institution "maternity" rests upon the

female experience of integration with natural process and genetic time, as well as upon the experience of separation – "alienation" in O'Brien's terms – from the child mediated by labor. As O'Brien states, it is maternal labor that "does confirm for women the conception of the child as *her* child" (1981:36), and not, as for men, *acknowledgment* – appropriation of the child by social action based on a complex ensemble of social institutions, laws, and practices. In societies with male domination, be this Kabyle, ancient Greek or contemporary European societies, we find a *symbolic* representation of the reproductive process and a division of sexual labor that impairs and denies women's labor in the reproduction of the species. The most famous expression of the symbolic dispossession of women from their reproductive labor and the corresponding appropriation of this labor by men is the myth of Athena being born out of the head of Zeus. Zeus, afraid that Metis might give birth to a son more powerful than himself, devoured Metis; but whereas the mother was annihilated, the child of Metis and Zeus was not. The child, Athena, was born from the father and she was appropriated by her father in the same way as women experience separation from, and at the same time, relation to the child – by labor.

The denial of women's reproductive labor in reproductive consciousness involves two aspects. The first refers directly to the symbolic representation of biological aspects of reproduction: most of the reproductive labor of women is not seen as labor. Pregnancy, for instance, is perceived as mere waiting; the female part of that aspect of the reproductive process is deprived of any active elements and is defined as being passive. Women are seen simply as receptacles for the male seed, passive vessels, a kind of safe place where the product of male potency may rest for a while and unfold its human potential.[11] Women, on this view, have no productive part in that aspect of human reproduction; they contribute "material," as Aristotle remarks, while men contribute spirit or soul or some human "essence." This view is far from being outmoded or obsolete, as the abortion debate shows. One common argument advanced by opponents of legalized abortion is that a woman should continue her pregnancy and give birth for the only and explicit purpose of producing a child that can be adopted by other people.

The second and more complex aspect of the denial of women's reproductive labor refers to the localization of the reproductive process in the symbolic order of the world, operating within the dichotomies of public/private, nature/reason, nature/society. O'Brien, at the beginning of her critique of political theory as consciousness about male experience, stated that there is no philosophy of birth, no consciousness in political theory of the reproductive process as a *social* fact. The reproductive labor of women is located outside society, outside the public debate on the present and future of society. It belongs, in Plato's terms, to the "first nature" of humanity, mere nature in our understanding. What makes man human is his "second nature," his capacity to transcend his first nature by the activity of reason, and this is seen as a basically male activity. O'Brien discusses Plato's philosophy as playing an important role in the enterprise of symbolically reconstructing the world after the transition from matrilinearity to patrilinearity. Plato, by taking over the reproductive dynamic from gender relations and relocating it in the creative intellectual intercourse between men, constructs continuity – and thus history – as the product of the community of men, a community dedicated to philosophy. This movement from nature towards reason, without any doubt an important step in the history of humanity, goes hand in hand in Plato with the exclusion of women from man-made history. He thus developed a line of thinking that, with variations, became a dominant *topos* in male-dominated societies for thousands of years.

To overcome his exclusion from the means of reproduction of the species, man has invented paternity, a system of social institutions and of relations among men aimed at ensuring the right of the father to a particular child. To establish the primacy of paternity, man used a symbolic representation of the reproductive process in which the reproductive labor of women was denied; the activity of men was separated from and opposed to the female part in the reproductive process – as the activity of reason opposed to nature or as the public opposed to the private, the city to the home. The focus of this opposition of male to female activity has varied in history; thus, for example, the dichotomy between man-made history and nature, the identification of woman with nature, and the subsequent dichotomies between nature and culture and nature and technology have flourished, in the European history of ideas, especially since the romantic period. And, of course, what is seen as "nature" or "private" or "home" is historically variable, too, since it depends on the mode of production and historical circumstances. The home in the Greek *polis*, which comprised productive labor in the form of slave labor, was something very different from the home (or household) in a modern capitalist society, where productive labor is organized by the market – that is, outside the home. Thus, defining the home as the realm of the "private" and of women implies different conditions of life for women in the Greek polis and in contemporary capitalist society. The common feature, however, of these *in concreto* differing realizations of the division of labor between the genders is in a representation of the division of gender labor which, by annihilating the reproductive labor of women, excludes women from the social activities aimed at constructing history, continuity over time.

THE SOCIAL REPRODUCTION OF THE DIVISION OF LABOR
BETWEEN THE GENDERS

The division of labor between the genders rests, following Bourdieu's line of thinking, on a cultural construction that guides all our practices: visions of the world, body experience, perception, and action. This male/female taxonomy, as discussed above, with the characteristic that it denies female labor in the reproductive process, is a powerful operator even in those fields of practice that, following their own ideology of autonomous functioning according to a specific principle, should entirely disregard such cultural constructs: the modern economy and the labor market. But the economy itself, by taking into account the division of labor between the genders and working on the male/female dichotomy as rooted in social practice outside the economic sphere, has an important part to play in the constant reestablishment of the doxic order.

Once women left the house to participate in the value-producing economy, the division of labor between the genders resting on the dichotomy of the public and the private, of the economic sphere and the house, had to be restructured: as limits were transgressed, social arrangements had to be found to make these transgressions legitimate, analogous to the practice Bourdieu describes in the Kabyles. In other words, women's jobs had to be created. And this social arrangement works by a generalization of the central theme in the male/female taxonomy: by devaluing the labor of women. A cherished historical legend tells us that women, when they first entered the labor market, "went into women's jobs," that is, into jobs that were not only badly paid but were (and still are) thought to meet the specific abilities of women: dexterity, linguistic fluency, sociability, flexibility going as far as submissiveness, quickness, accuracy. Angelika Willms-Herget (1985) has shown, for nineteenth-century Germany, that there was no female segment of the labor market, no traditional women's jobs. Women did not create new jobs in the economy just by transforming their domestic tasks into jobs in the market economy. In industry, as well as in the services, the so-called women's jobs were jobs previously done by men: those of clerks, teachers, cooks, tailors, assistants in the "helping occupations."

To be turned into women's jobs, men's jobs had to be transformed: sometimes rather fundamentally, in other cases quite marginally. Margaret Maruani and Chantal Nicole-Drancourt (1989) document a recent case of the social construction of "men's" and "women's" jobs in the transformation of traditional jobs in the French printing industry along the male/female dichotomy. In this instance, the magic word for the construction of the difference is "skill." It is the definition of skill, of who is skilled and who is not, of who is a professional and who is not, that creates the difference between men's and women's jobs. At the *Clavier enchaîné*[12] in 1969, women, together with a new technology, set foot in the realm of a male worker elite: printers, typesetters, proofreaders, and other professionals in the printing industry, whose relatively strong social position was, in the final instance, grounded in the fact that they had succeeded in transforming their skills and competences into a monopoly.

The new equipment was used to break this monopoly. The product produced was no longer lead type but a simple paper strip. The machines were no longer heavy equipment, exuding the smell and dirt of oil and heated metal; they were smaller, soft and smooth, and electronic; the keyboard was more like an electric typewriter. And who, normally, worked with letters, paper, and a keyboard? Women, typists. When the first female typesetters were hired at the *Clavier enchaîné*, the men went on strike for three days. As a result, union and management came to an agreement that fixed a new definition of "skills": women would do the "unskilled" work – that is, type in a continuous flow – whereas men would do the "skilled" work, that is, type with corrections and margin justifications. The traditional skills of printers and typesetters – that is, mastery of grammar, mastery of language in general – continued to be of great importance the definition of "skilled" work in this special case being based on these skills and what was considered "unskilled" work *by definition* not requiring these skills. It was simply denied that the work tasks of the women required skills similar to those of the men; this denial is, as the analysis of the female labor capacity has shown, the "normal" mechanism of devaluing the work done by women. Thus, a new (but unstable) order was founded, an order that got some additional support through the spatial segregation of women and men: the women worked in a separate place (Maruani and Nicole-Drancourt 1989: 34–41).[13] But what is interesting here, of course, is that the *social construction* of the difference can be traced.

As time went by, more changes in printing technology occurred, and more changes in work organization. However, all adjustments and transformations of work organization carefully observed the relevant difference, the line that separated men's and women's jobs. This difference had important consequences: women's salaries were substantially lower; they had larger work loads (380 lines per hour as opposed to 180 lines for men), fewer break times and more social and time control; and they worked in variable shifts (1989: 46ff.). But the difference between "skilled" and "unskilled" work at the *Clavier enchaîné* had almost disappeared, faded to a symbolic relic. In 1983, the spatial separation of men's and women's workplaces had been reduced to a mere curtain; the difference in machinery, a difference of high symbolic value, since it objectified the difference between "skilled" and "unskilled" labor, consisted of a cable connecting the men's keyboards with the central computer, thus establishing a direct link between the men's workplaces and the computer.[14] Women were still said to do the "simple" input without corrections and justifications; nevertheless, they did corrections, as no more than a 5 percent margin of errors was tolerated. During the summer holidays, when the male proofreaders were absent, women did their jobs, after two weeks of training, working – at a much higher speed – on the men's machines. Women were said to have had no vocational training, which meant training at the École du livre ("School of the book," a professional college for the printing occupations) – but they had obtained vocational training at secretarial colleges, learning with modern technology, whereas training at the École du livre apparently was not fully adapted to the ongoing modernization in the printing industry. Moreover, there were men, skilled workers, who had never attended the École du livre (pp. 48–52).

When, in 1983, the curtain was abolished to allow for a new, more integrated work organization at the *Clavier enchaîné*, it became evident that the difference between "skilled" and "unskilled" labor, coinciding with the difference between men's and women's jobs, was virtually nil. Men and women *saw* each other at work; gender inequality, against the background of the women's prior experience in substituting for the men during the summer holidays, became *visible*. The consequence was that *doxa*, as Bourdieu says, the correspondence between the objective order and mental structures, could no longer be maintained. The women went on strike for equal wages and working conditions.[15]

This example is a caricature, of course, with its symbolic cable and curtain. But it is a caricature mainly because the critical view of the authors extricates a social mechanism from doxic experience and exposes it as a mechanism of gender discrimination. Gender discrimination on the labor market, as is shown above, operates by the social recognition or denial of competences and skills. Recognition of skills, as well as the construction of jobs, as the excluding and tying together of work tasks into a bundle, is mediated by power relations – not only between employers and workers, but also between different groups of workers. Thus, mastery of language, which for a long time constituted the core of the printers' and typesetters' highly valued skills, lost its value when it became clear that it could no longer be considered a scarce resource; many women offered the same or higher linguistic competences in direct competition on the labor market. The recognition of mastery of language now became bound to a specific certificate, whereas in the former, exclusively male, world of the printing industry the certificate could well be substituted for by professional experience or other credentials. A second element of male skills now gained importance: the technical competence of men, represented at the *Clavier enchaîné* by the famous cable.

Research on the social impact of new technologies in the labor process has shown that in many cases the implementation of new technologies is used to define jobs differently, which also affects gender-specific labor-market segmentation, as in the case of the printing industry. In the process of restructuring jobs, the definition and recognition of skills always plays an important role, though not the only one, of course. Equal skills of men and women, as defined by the same professional training and certificate, are used in a different way, those of women as a rule in a narrower way, as documented in the research on "women in men's jobs."[16] Correspondingly, further training is often seen by a firm as a means of developing the skills and competences of their male but not their female personnel (Krüger 1988). Thus, a whole set of actions is at work to reestablish the doxic order in the labor market.

HABITUS AND SYMBOLIC VIOLENCE

Domination has many faces: physical violence, coercion, structural violence as operated by the power of economic forces and social institutions, intimidation, and symbolic violence. Bourdieu argues that modes of domination in social formations with objectified relations of appropriation, typically the institutions of a self-regulated market, of bureaucracy, of literacy, and of an educational system, are fundamentally different from those in social formations like ancient Kabylia, which lacked market economic institutions. Whereas societies with objectified social relations (constituting relatively autonomous social fields) tend to assure their own reproduction by their very functioning, a society like that of the Kabyles is obliged to resort to elementary forms of domination; in other words, in such a society "relations of domination are made, unmade, and remade in and by the interactions between persons" (1977c: 184). Now, this analysis of different modes of domination as constructing a historical sequence, closely linked to different stages of social evolution, should not be read as if physical and symbolic violence disappeared in differentiated modern societies with their various objectified social relations. They are still present, but rather as a concomitant of structural domination in face-to-face interaction, sometimes supporting, sometimes compromising a mode of domination that essentially operates by resorting to the "tacit force of circumstances," as Marx put it, and physical violence especially is banned from the normal course of social life, for instance, in power relations inside the firm, in class relationships, in debates in the field of science, and so on.

Every mode of domination, even if it uses physical violence, presupposes a doxic order shared by the dominated and the dominants. For gender domination, this order is represented by the division of labor between the genders. But how does this order, this symbolic representation of a social structure, come to work in the actions of the agents? Bourdieu's answer is: by being incorporated as part of an agent's habitus. History is objectified in two forms, says Bourdieu, one form being objectification in the human organism, history turned into human nature, as habitus, the other being objectification as institutions, works, and social structure. And the real logic of action works by activating these two objectifications of history. It is by habitus that the meaning objectified in institutions is reactivated, that institutions are kept alive, but only by imposing the revisions and transformations that are counterpart and condition of the reactivation: "The *habitus* . . . is what makes it possible to inhabit institutions, to appropriate them practically, and so to keep them in activity, continuously pulling them from the state of dead letters, reviving the sense deposited in them, but at the same time imposing the revisions and transformations that reactivation entails" (1990e: 57).

The concept of habitus refers to an ensemble of schemata of perception, thinking, feeling, evaluating, speaking, and acting that structures all the expressive, verbal, and practical manifestations and utterances of a person. Habitus has to be thought of as a *modus operandi*, a "generative principle of regulated improvisations" (Bourdieu 1977c: 78) (which are called practice), an incorporated structure formed by the objective conditions of its genesis. It is "embodied history, internalized as a second nature," as Bourdieu says, "the active presence of the whole past of which it is the product" (1990e: 56). By contrast with the familiar sociological concept of role, habitus refers to something *incorporated*, *not* to a set of norms or expectations existing independently of and externally to the agent. Likewise, as it is thought to be part of the living organism, thus functioning in the way of living systems, habitus refers to a *generative* principle, *not* to a set of fixed and finite rules.

It has already been mentioned that gender identity is a deeply rooted, bodily anchored dimension of an agent's habitus. It affects the individual in the most "natural" parts of his or her identity, as it concerns his or her body, the vision of the body, the possibilities of sensual perception, of feeling and expressing pleasure and pain. Bourdieu generally stresses the stability of the habitus in its basic features, and this seems fairly reasonable considering Bourdieu's focus on social reproduction and his thinking along the lines of the causality of the probable (1974a), of average conditions. Nevertheless, restructuring some aspects of the habitus seems possible, at least under specific circumstances. Relearning another gender identity, however, appears to be almost impossible, even in extreme cases, such as transsexuals who never had an untroubled gender identity. Professional experts in voice and body training report extreme difficulties in the process of restructuring gender-specific body behavior in transsexuals; in this process, it seems to be easier to "forget" body-related behavior produced by the former identity than to acquire a new *natural-looking hexis* (Hirschauer 1989: 109ff.).

Thus, in the course of the socialization process every agent inevitably acquires a gendered habitus, an identity which has incorporated the existing division of labor between the genders. Two aspects of the acquisition of a gendered habitus are noteworthy here. The first concerns the social construction of male and female identity as antagonistic identities. In this respect, gender identity differs from class identity, both being part of the habitus. Class identity may refer to a complex scale of social differentiation; even if it is based, in societies with a capitalist mode of production, on an antagonistic opposition, conditions of life may be very different inside the two classes defined by the economic antagonism. Gender identity is the product of a labor of differentiation, of *distinction*, a labor that consists of exclusions, simplifications, oppression of ambiguities along the antagonistic concept of male and female. Freud spoke of the child as being "polymorphously perverse" in its sexuality; it is by socialization that this polymorphism or diffuseness is transformed into one of two possible gender identities. The space of the possible – actions, feelings, evaluations, expressive acts, verbal and bodily behavior – is restricted for every individual. "Male" aspects/dispositions in the girl are suppressed, and "female" dimensions in the boy are suppressed – but they are always related. So, for instance, the phrase "Boys do not cry," still a familiar phrase, implicitly has to be completed by "But girls do." And what is female cannot be male, and vice versa. In a way, the process of acquiring gender identity is a constant check of actions, signals, and so forth along a binary code, building up a mode of existence by constantly suppressing the "other" of the two possibilities.

Second, this characteristic of the process of acquiring gender identity – that it is a process of narrowing, of cutting off, of suppressing ambiguities – has the paradoxical result that *both* genders, women and men, are restricted in their potential; and it is in this sense that the dominants are themselves dominated by their domination. Fears of appearing effeminate, hence homosexual – that is, of not being a "real man" – are common among men, and demonstrating "real" male behavior seems to put great strain on them. Remarkable also is the poverty of men whose gender-specific socialization has been very successful, that is, has resulted in a "perfect" male habitus where all female tendencies and dispositions have been successfully suppressed.

The domination of men over women included in the division of labor is, today, a social relation that essentially lacks objectification. One might argue with Hegel that the children – together with the property – who constitute the unity of the family objectify the division of labor between the genders[17] and that the family should thus be seen as the social structure providing the necessary objectified framework for structural domination. But what is called "family" today no longer represents those powerful structures defining basically different rights and roles for women and men in all spheres of social life. Only a few features of the family today are reminiscent of the traditional social institution known under the same name. Most families lack property, an essential aspect of Hegel's concept of the family; also, the period during which children need intensive parental care – the phase in the life cycle where the division of labor between the genders still finds its "natural" or "objective" foundation – has become relatively short in the life of both partners. Thus, in the same process whereby this particular social institution that is the family lost its excessive power in defining and structuring the social condition of women, the family also lost its function of providing the objective framework for a structural mode of domination over women. And if the relation between men and women is to work as a relation of domination, it has to resort to the elementary forms of domination, those that are "made, unmade, and remade in and by the interactions between persons": physical as well as symbolic violence. In this perspective, the use of an archaic mechanism of domination such as physical violence may be seen as nothing more than a corollary of the decomposition of an older doxic order.

But physical violence against women is not in itself the problem of a social theory dealing with the oppression of women; still less may it be seen as a key for theoretical understanding. Physical violence just draws attention to the fact that in the oppression of women elementary modes of domination play an important role and that, therefore, we have to look at the complementary mode of domination, too – namely, at symbolic violence.

In the various social fields outside the family, and probably in the normal course of life inside the family, too, it is symbolic violence that acts upon women to maintain a relation of domination. Symbolic violence is a subtle, euphemized, invisible mode of domination that prevents domination from being recognized as such and, therefore, as misrecognized domination, is socially recognized. It works when subjective structures – the habitus – and objective structures are in accord with each other. In *Language and Symbolic Power*, Bourdieu speaks of the "complicity" of the dominated, which is necessary if symbolic domination is to be realized:

> The distinctiveness of symbolic domination lies precisely in the fact that it assumes, of those who submit to it, an attitude which challenges the usual dichotomy of freedom and constraint. The 'choices' of the habitus . . . are accomplished without consciousness or constraint, by virtue of the dispositions which, although they are unquestionably the product of social determinisms, are also constituted outside the spheres of consciousness and constraint. The propensity to reduce the search for causes to a search for responsibilities makes it impossible to see that *intimidation*, a symbolic violence which is not aware of what it is (to the extent that it implies no *act of intimidation*) can only be exerted on a person predisposed (in his habitus) to feel it, whereas others will ignore it. It is already partly true to say that the cause of the timidity lies in the relation between the situation or the intimidating person (who may deny any intimidating intention) and the person intimidated, or rather, between the social conditions of production of each of them. And little by little, one has to take account thereby of the whole social structure. (1991 b: 51)

"Complicity" implies, then, that the person who is confronted by acts of symbolic violence is disposed to perceive the violence in these acts, to decode the relevant signals, and to understand their veiled social meaning, but without recognizing them consciously as what they are – namely, as words, gestures, movements, and intonations of domination. In other words, she (because it is a "she" in the case concerned here) has to be endowed with a habitus providing her with the *sens pratique* to react and to act correspondingly.

A number of studies in recent years have focused on such symbolic mechanisms in the interaction between men and women, especially in language behavior (Thorne and Henley 1975, Spender 1989, Trömel-Plötz 1983, 1984). The academic world is a good terrain for field research on symbolic violence against women. In university courses, as well as in meetings and conferences, it has been observed that women are regularly overlooked when they wish to make a point; they are interrupted when they speak; male speakers refer to contributions of other male speakers, but not to those of women; if a woman has said something that seems interesting to a male speaker, he refers to this by attributing it to a male participant; nonverbal, reinforcing communication behavior of men is addressed to men, but not to women; and so on. Some years ago, women said that "they felt uncomfortable" in those situations,"as if they did not belong to the community." Today, as those situations have been analyzed, women are more conscious of the violence perpetrated on them in seemingly "neutral" professional interactions and talk about it; but men are often incapable of seeing what they are doing, even when the problem is discussed overtly.

The importance of symbolic aspects in gender domination suggests that a socioanalysis of the social practice and thereby a denaturalization of the division of labor between the genders is a *conditio sine qua non* for the liberation of women. The struggle for the liberation of women thus consists, above all, in an analysis and critique of the perceptions, words, notions, and meaning of acts, the mental representations of the division of labor between the genders. The conditions of the possibility of this struggle have to be seen in the fact that mental structures are not perfectly adjusted to the complex social structure, with the social structure constantly producing problems and contradictions that cannot be solved on the basis of the dispositions of the habitus. But, as a social scientist, I believe that the necessity of this attack on cultural constructions can be theoretically understood only within the context of a theory that relates social structure and mental structure; so the theory of Pierre Bourdieu is of utmost relevance. Theories of the patriarchate or the exploitation of female labor fail to reach this essential point, as they give a much too restricted account of social practice.

NOTES

1 When I speak of "free legal subjects," I am referring not only to constitutional rights, like the right to vote, but also to the right to receive a passport, travel across national borders, have one's own bank account, be

gainfully employed, etc., without needing the formal consent of one's husband or father.

2 Marx has given an answer to this very difficult question by stating the problem of class in terms of the exchange of equivalents resulting in unequal gains (and unequal social conditions), thereby relating the analysis of social structure to the analysis of the basic principles of economic production in "modern" society – that is, in societies with a capitalist mode of production. Marx's answer has not been accepted unanimously in the social sciences, but it remains at the heart of the class debate, just as the problem of class itself remains a troubling feature of our societies.

3 See Seccombe 1973 and the subsequent debate between Coulson *et al.* (1975), Gardiner (1975), and Seccombe (1975). For the German debate and its accent on the female labor capacity, see Kittler 1980, von Werlhof *et al.* 1983, and the debate between Braig and Lentz (1983), Beer (1983), and von Werlhof (1983), as well as Beck-Gernsheim and Ostner 1976, Becker-Schmidt and Knapp 1987, Bennholdt-Thomsen 1983, Frerichs, Morschhäuser, and Steinrücke 1986.

4 Cf. Kuhn and Wolpe (eds.) 1978, Eisenstein (ed.) 1979, Sargent (ed.) 1981, Hamilton and Barrett (eds.) 1986, Walby 1986. For the German debate see Heise 1986 and Ostner 1983.

5 See Crompton and Mann (eds.) 1986 and Phillips (ed.) 1987.

6 A discussion of the impact of the gender debate on British sociology may be found in Maynard 1990.

7 Meanwhile, Bourdieu has published an article dealing explicitly and solely with gender domination, which is written, as the title "La domination masculine" suggests, from a clearly male perspective (Bourdieu 1990c).

8 Compare in detail Bourdieu 1977c: 96–158 and Bourdieu 1990e: 201–70 and the appendix, "The Kabyle House or the World Reversed."

9 The same logic of transgression of limits, of uniting the contraries, that is, of the double game with the ordinary order and the transgression of this order as well as the collective denial of this transgression in ritual acts guides Nicole Loraux's (1989) analysis of the role of the female in masculinity in ancient Greece.

10 She refers mainly to Hegel's fragment "On Love" in his *Early Theological Writings*, as well as to his *System of Ethical Life*.

11 Attwood (1985) has written a famous satyrical novel dealing with this topos.

12 "Enchained keyboard," pseudonym for a French journal used by Maruani and Nicole-Drancourt.

13 The male workers' fight involved two issues: the preservation of their social position by continuing recognition of their skills and an employment guarantee. The authors summarize the agreement of 1969 as follows: "The computer will expel the lead, but keep the men of lead" (Maruani and Nicole-Drancourt 1989: 40).

14 Two typists reported the following about this famous cable:
"We don't have the same keyboard, that's the difference. They have a keyboard which is directly connected to the computer, but we, our machine, . . ."

"...a cable.... They have made a whole system to connect their machines to the computer, to adapt it. So they have a direct entry to the computer we don't have."
"What does it actually allow for?"
"Nothing, in the end nothing."
"It's there to better mark the difference." (Ibid., 47)

15 Just to complete the story: apart from some minor ameliorations, the women were not successful in their fight. And when the strike was over and equality not obtained, men and women at the *Clavier enchaîné* wanted to have their curtain back, and got it (ibid., 52–4).

16 Cf. Müller-Demary, *et al.* 1989, Martius-Spitzy *et al.* 1986, Bednarz-Braun 1983, Stegmann and Kraft 1986.

17 Cf. Hegel 1970: 173: "In substance marriage is a unity, though only a unity of inwardness or disposition; in outward existence, however, the unity is sundered in the two parties. It is only in the children that the unity itself exists externally, objectively, and explicitly as a unity" (trans. T. M. Knox, G. W. F. Hegel, *Philosophy of Right* (London, Oxford, New York: Oxford University Press, 1952), p. 117).

REFERENCES

Atwood, Margaret 1985: *The Handmaid's Tale*. London: Virago.

Beck-Gernsheim, Elisabeth and Ostner, Ilona 1976: Der Gegensatz von Beruf und Hausarbeit als Konstitutionsbedingung weiblichen Arbeitsvermögens. In Ulrich Beck and Michael Brater (eds), *Materialien zu einer subjektbezogenen Theorie der Berufe*: Vol. 2: *Die soziale Konstitution der Berufe*, Frankfurt am Main: Campus, 25–53.

Becker-Schmidt, Regina and Knapp, Gudrun-Axeli 1987: *Geschlechtertrennung–Geschlechterdifferenz. Suchbewegungen sozialen Lernens*. Bonn: Dietz.

Bednarz-Braun, Iris 1983: *Arbeiterinnen in der Elektroindustrie. Zu den Bedingungen von Anlernung und Arbeit an gewerblich-technischen Arbeitsplätzen für Frauen*. Munich: Deutsches Jugendinstitut.

Beer, Ursula 1983: Marx auf die Füße gestellt. Zum theoretischen Entwurf von Claudia von Werlhof. *Probleme des Klassenkampfs*, 13, no. 1, 22–37.

—— 1984: *Theorien geschlechtlicher Arbeitsteilung*. Frankfurt am Main: Campus.

Bennholdt-Thomsen, Veronika 1983: Die Zukunft der Frauenarbeit und die Gewalt gegen Frauen. *Beiträge zur feministischen Theorie und Praxis*, 9–10, 207–22.

Braig, Marianne and Lentz, Carola 1983: Wider die Enthistorisierung der Marxschen Werttheorie. Kritische Anmerkungen zur Kategorie "Subsistenzproduktion." *Probleme des Klassenkampfs*, 13, no. 1, 5–21.

Coulson, Margaret *et al.* 1975: The housewife and her labour under capitalism – a critique. *New Left Review*, 89, 59–71.

Crompton, Rosemary and Mann, Michael (eds) 1986: *Gender and Stratification.* Oxford: Polity.

Daele, Wolfgang van den 1988: Der Fötus als Subjekt und die Autonomie der Frau. Wissenschaftlich-technische Optionen und soziale Kontrollen in der Schwangerschaft. In Uta Gerhardt and Yvonne Schütze (eds), *Frauensituation: Veränderungen in den letzten zwanzig Jahren,* Frankfurt am Main: Suhrkamp, 189–215.

Dölling, Irene 1989: Marxismus und Frauenfrage in der DDR. Bemerkungen zu einer notwendigen Debatte. *Argument,* 31, 709–18.

Eisenstein, Zillah (ed.) 1979: *Capitalist Patriarchy and the Case for Socialist Feminism.* New York: Monthly Review Press.

Frerichs, Petra; Morschhäuser, Martina; and Steinrücke, Margareta 1986: Weibliches Arbeitsvermögen und Politikzugänge von Frauen am Beispiel betrieblicher Interessenvertretung. In Werner Fricke *et al.* (eds), *Jahrbuch Arbeit und Technik in Nordrhein-Westfalen,* Bonn: Neue Gesellschaft, 479–92.

Gardiner, Jean 1975: Women's domestic labour. *New Left Review,* 89, 47–58.

Gensior, Sabine 1988: Teilzeitarbeit und frauenspezifischer Arbeitsmarkt. Zur "Interessenidentität" zwischen Frauen und betrieblicher Personalpolitik. In Ute Gerhard and Jutta Limbach (eds), *Rechtsalltag von Frauen,* Frankfurt am Main: Suhrkamp, 61–75.

Hamilton, Roberta and Barrett, Michèle (eds) 1986: *The Politics of Diversity: feminism, Marxism and nationalism.* London: Verso.

Hegel, Georg Wilhelm Friedrich 1970: *Werke:* Vol. 7: *Grundlinien der Philosophie des Rechts oder Naturrecht und Staatswissenschaft im Grundrisse.* Frankfurt am Main: Suhrkamp. First pub. 1821.

Heise, Hildegard 1986: *Flucht vor der Widersprüchlichkeit: Kapitalistische Produktionsweise und Geschlechterbeziehung.* Frankfurt am Main: Campus.

Hirschauer, Stefan 1989: Die interaktive Konstruktion von Geschlechtszugehörigkeit. *Zeitschrift für Soziologie,* 18, no. 2, 100–18.

Kittler, Gertrude 1980: *Hausarbeit. Zur Geschichte einer "Natur-Ressource."* Munich: Frauenoffensive.

Kreckel, Reinhard 1989: Klasse und Geschlecht. *Leviathan,* 17, no. 3, 305–21.

Krüger, Helga 1988: Qualifizierungsoffensive – Chance für Frauen? *Argument,* 30, 65–75.

—— *et al.* 1987: *Privatsache Kind–Privatsache Beruf. Zur Lebenssituation von Frauen mit kleinen Kindern in unserer Gesellschaft.* Opladen: Leske & Budrich.

Kuhn, Annette and Wolpe, Ann Marie (eds) 1978: *Feminism and Materialism.* London: Routledge.

Loraux, Nicole 1989: *Les Expériences de Tirésias: le féminin et l'homme grec.* Paris: Gallimard.

Martius-Spitzy, Christine; Pelz, Monika; and Wagner, Ina 1986: *Mit technischem Verstand: Facharbeiterinnen in handwerklich-technischen Berufen.* Vienna: Bundesministerium für soziale Verwaltung, Frauenreferat.

Maruani, Margaret and Nicole-Drancourt, Chantal 1989: *Au labeur des dames. Métiers masculins, emplois féminins.* Paris: Syros.

Marx, Karl 1969: *Das Kapital.* In *Marx Engels Werke,* vols. 23–5. Berlin: Dietz Verlag.

Müller-Demary, Petra; Mutz, Kerstin; and Wald, Renate 1989: Junge Frauen in qualifizierten atypischen Berufen. *WSI-Mitteilungen,* 42, no. 1, 46–55.

O'Brien, Mary 1981: *The Politics of Reproduction.* London: Routledge.

Ostner, Ilona 1983: Kapitalismus, Patriarchat und die Konstruktion der Besonderheit "Frau." In Reinhard Kreckel (ed.), *Soziale Ungleichheiten,* Soziale Welt, Sonderband, 2, Göttingen: Schwartz, 277–97.

Phillips, Anne (ed.) 1987: *Feminism and Equality.* New York: New York University Press.

Sargent, Lydia (ed.) 1981: *Women and Revolution: a discussion of the unhappy marriage of Marxism and feminism.* London: Pluto.

Seccombe, Wally 1973: The housewife and her labour under capitalism. *New Left Review,* 83, 3–4.

—— 1975: Domestic labour: Reply to critics. *New Left Review,* 94, 85–96.

Spender, Dale 1989: *Invisible Women: the schooling scandal.* London: Women's Press.

Stegmann, Heinz and Kraft, Hermine 1986: Chancen und Risiken von Mädchen mit einer betrieblichen Berufsausbildung für einen "Männerberuf". *Mitteilungen aus der Arbeitsmarkt- und Berufsforschung,* 19, no. 3, 439–56.

Thorne, Barrie and Henley, Nancy (eds) 1975: *Language and Sex: difference and dominance.* Rowley, Mass.: Newbury House.

Trömel-Plötz, Senta 1983: Frauen und Sprache: Unterschied und Unterdrückung. *Jahrbuch für Internationale Germanistik,* 24, no. 2, 79–97.

—— (ed.) 1984: *Gewalt durch Sprache. Die Vergewaltigung von Frauen in Gesprächen.* Frankfurt am Main: Fischer Taschenbuch Verlag.

Walby, Sylvia 1986: *Patriarchy at Work: patriarchal and capitalist relations in employment 1800–1984.* Cambridge: Polity.

Werlhof, Claudia von 1983: Lohn ist ein "Wert", Leben nicht? Eine Replik auf Ursula Beer. *Probleme des Klassenkampfs,* 13, no. 1, 38–58.

—— et al. 1983: *Frauen, die letzte Kolonie. Zur Hausfrauisierung der Arbeit.* Reinbek bei Hamburg: Rowohlt.

Willms-Herget, Angelika 1985: *Frauenarbeit.* Frankfurt am Main: Campus.

9

Bourdieu, the Cultural Arbitrary, and Television

Nicholas Garnham

The central purpose of this essay is to raise the question of the implications of Bourdieu's theory for the development of a practical political project. In examining this question I will use broadcasting, as a field of cultural practice, and the politics of that field as an example. To what extent, I will be asking, are developments in this central field of contemporary cultural practice congruent with Bourdieu's general analysis of cultural practice? Can one ground an appropriate political response to current developments in broadcasting in the UK and Europe in that analysis?

DOES BOURDIEU'S THEORY HAVE A POLITICS?

At a time when class analysis in particular, and all forms of Marxist and socialist thought and politics in general, are in retreat, at least in Europe, it is important to start by stressing the continuing scientific and political importance of Bourdieu's work. This lies in the following core characteristics: its central focus on the class determination of cultural dispositions and practices, its frontal assault on all idealist explanations of the cultural sphere and of the aesthetic and social values it propagates as autonomous and as in opposition to the material and the economic, and its critique of such idealist explanations as the expression of the class interests of the intelligentsia. It is particularly important to stress this last point at a time when a particularly virulent version of such an ideology – namely, postmodernism – has taken such widespread hold.

That being said, however, I want to argue that the scientific and political efficacy of Bourdieu's project is seriously undercut by a contradiction that lies at its heart. In attempting to play in combination the Marxist and Durkheimian hands, Bourdieu has retained too many of the idealist cards of the latter for comfort. In particular, the Durkheimian notion of the cultural arbitrary lies at the heart of his theoretical schema. This makes it very difficult, if not impossible, for it to exert any purchase on political action and leaves it vulnerable, particularly in the current political climate, to recuperation by the irrationalist, postmodernist variants of late capitalist ideology.

Central to Bourdieu's thought is the notion that the "primary experience of the social world is that of doxa," which is defined as "an adherence to relations of order which, because they structure inseparably both the real world and the thought world, are accepted as self-evident" (Bourdieu 1984: 471). Thus, for Bourdieu, the maintenance and reproduction of the existing social structure of domination is ensured by the following process. Agents internalize social structures in the habitus as cognitive structures or classificatory schema that operate below the level of consciousness and discourse. Primary perception of the social world and the behavior based upon that perception then involves a two-sided process: on the one hand, a process of cognition whereby a reality is constructed within the rules of the internalized classificatory schema, and on the other hand, an act of misrecognition whereby this classificatory schema is seen as necessary and in its utilization implies, in Bourdieu's words, "the most absolute recognition of the social order." Thus, again in Bourdieu's own words, "the conservation of the social order is decisively reinforced by what Durkheim called 'logical conformity', the orchestration of categories of perception of the social world, which, being adjusted to the divisions of the established order (and thereby to the interests of those who dominate it) and common to all minds structured in accordance with those structures, present every appearance of objective necessity" (ibid.).

If this accurately describes the process of cognition, are we not all caught in an ineluctably determined fate? If our classificatory schemas are implicit, unconscious, and arbitrary, what room is there for willed purchase on the social world – in a word, for a political project? This implies either perpetual stasis or the search for the sources of social and political change in areas outside any possibility of human control. It also tends to lead to a response, with which I am sure we are all familiar, to apparent examples of political reform or oppositional discourse as either futile and/or just another devilish example of the infinite manipulative adaptability of the dominant ideology and its agents. This in turn leads on the Left into the constant temptation to accuse those with whom they disagree of "sell-out" and to the accompanying intellectual rigidities.

Examples of heterodox thought are explained not as true or false explanations of concrete external reality and thus as the more or less reliable sources of alternative courses of political action, but as the occupation of a symbolic space made available within the structure of a given symbolic field and defined purely in relation to other occupants of that field. Social action is reduced to a game of musical chairs and implicitly judged as both misguided and futile – the unconsciously adopted mask of self, status group, or class interest. Disputes within the symbolic realm are reduced to squabbles among the survivors of a shipwreck as to which seat in the lifeboat they may occupy rather than about how they might reach land. Within such a schema there is no room for the possibility of social experience producing radically critical alternative world views and political programs with a real purchase on the process of social change.

It seems to me that one cannot reconcile the widespread political mobilization and associated forms of both popular and elite cultural expression involved in either the rise of the labor movement and socialism in the nineteenth century or in the more recent development of the women's movement with "an adherence to relations of order which are accepted as self-evident." The debate about the social role and appropriate forms of organization of the mass media is rendered trivial, if not meaningless, if every variety of symbolic form distributed through those media is defined a priori as reinforcing "the conservation of the social order." Debates concerning the appropriate modes of funding, advertising or license fees, the Fairness Doctrine, the terms of access for political parties and minority groups, cross-ownership, and so on become irrelevant because deprived of any purchase on the distribution of social power.

Now of course Bourdieu himself does not accept the full rigor of his own theory. Otherwise how can one explain his very public involvement in attempts to reform the French educational system and in a recent campaign to defend and reform public service, license fee-financed broadcasting? But the tension between political practice and theory is reflected by an ambivalence within the theoretical writings themselves towards intellectuals and intellectual practice. On the one hand, true to the Saint-Simonian roots of French sociology and in a way similar, ironically, to that of his old combatant Althusser, Bourdieu advocates a form of the politics of the vanguard party in which the sociologist takes on the leading role. Sociologists alone are capable of escaping, by self-reflexively analyzing, the cultural and political trap the theory sets for everyone else. Only they are capable of unmasking the intellectuals, revealing their self-interested practice for what it really is, and thus seeing society as it really is. A familiar trope.

On the other hand, the fundamental anti-intellectualist thrust of Bourdieu's work – the revenge of the rural provincial on Paris – leads to a crude form of workerism. In *Distinction* there is an attempt, perhaps not fully acknowledged, to validate popular culture, find sources of authenticity and popular resistance, and thus a base for opposition to the prevailing social order below the level of discourse. In a Rousseauesque movement it seems that it is the symbolic order itself that is the problem. The danger of such a position is that it can too easily lead politically to support for the most dangerous forms of irrationalist populism, although this is a path down which, I am sure, Bourdieu himself would be unwilling to go. Again, this is at present a widely influential trope.

To illustrate the problems with Bourdieu's position, it is necessary to make a brief and necessarily, therefore, somewhat simplified detour through the history of post-Enlightenment social theory. When the Enlightenment broke the doxa of premodern Europe, it gave us a set of intellectual questions with which we are still grappling and which have defined the traditions of both the social science and the politics created by the effort to solve them.

The Enlightenment linked, in one movement of thought, the process of critique that broke the doxa with the process of human political liberation. Truth and freedom were seen as indissoluble, and the link was reason. Thus social science came into being, offering the possibility of discovering the true laws of human social behavior as a basis for designing a social world fit for free human beings to inhabit, just as the natural sciences offered the possibility of obtaining knowledge about the material world with which to manipulate that material world.

The worm in the bud of this unifying vision, however, was the obstinate refusal of the lion of human interest to lie down with the lamb of human reason. On the one hand, the development of a more global vision made it glaringly apparent that our world was home to a range of viable, but different, social structures and classificatory cultural schemas. On the other, the process of violent and rapid social change ushered in by capitalist development unleashed increasingly violent disagreement as to the desirable direction of social change and the preferred set of social arrangements.

There was, in particular, a divergence between those who stressed the values of stability and continuity and those who stressed the values of progress and change. This division did not map neatly onto the political divisions of Right and Left. Economic liberalism was linked to progress, and there has always been a deeply nostalgic strand in socialist thought.

Certainly the response of the Durkheimian tradition to the problem was to undermine reason as a guiding principle by stressing the arbitrary and thus relative nature of interpretive schema and to place the sociopolitical emphasis on the problem of social cohesion. The Marxist tradition, by contrast, held on to the possibility of rationally guided action and the Enlightenment hope of the construction of a social world congruent with a set of universal human interests. Thus, while the Marxist theory of ideology shares with the Durkheimian tradition a view of the cultural superstructure as both determined by and an expression of a social structure or base, its theory of social change and political action is based on the idea that the working class will escape from ideology and that political action will be motivated by direct rational analysis of its material conditions of existence. Thus the Marxist theory of knowledge, unlike the Durkheimian, requires both the recognition of a real world and the possibility of its cognition in terms of a nonarbitrary and at least potentially universal classificatory schema within which a common set of truth claims can be accepted and values agreed upon. Thus the misrecognition of reality that is ideology in Marxist thought stems from the misapplication of the classificatory schema, not from the structure of the classificatory schema itself.

In addition, the Durkheimian view, adopted in part by Bourdieu, differs crucially from the Marxist view in its handling of the relationship between social contradiction and the realm of cognition and thus of willed social action. Both theories recognize the existence of materially based differences of class interest. But while the Durkheimian tradition stresses the role of a common shared classificatory schema in the achievement of social cohesion and a relatively smooth process of social reproduction, Marxist thought stresses the always fragile nature of social cohesion and the role of social struggle in a fraught process of uneven development and an always problematic process of social reproduction.

For Bourdieu, social contradiction is simply dissolved into a unified classificatory schema that always leads to the misrecognition of social contradiction and thus the reproduction of the given social totality. The acceptance of the cultural arbitrary makes it impossible for the classificatory schema to itself express social contradiction. There may be subsets of classificatory schema within each distinct field. But that field, precisely because it is a field – that is, its structuring principles are, following the general structuralist model derived from Saussurian linguistics, entirely endogenous – cannot represent contradiction. And all the subsidiary classificatory schema are governed by the same central classificatory logic derived from the habitus, a logic that is both always one and unified, and must be if Bourdieu's theory of habitus as the key structuring relay between real world and thought world is to work (Bourdieu 1977c: 77–8, 96–158). This common classificatory logic is always "adjusted to the divisions of the established order (and thereby to the interest of those who dominate it)." It is thus a logic that unconsciously reconciles social contradiction. Thus there is no room in Bourdieu's theory for social contradiction to be expressed as different and contrasting interpretations of reality, and thus for willed social action based upon such interpretations.

Marxism has within it an explanation of purposeful social change, because it presupposes a social structure that is fundamentally contradictory and thus from which alternative and conflictual interpretations of reality can and do arise. And this is the crucial point, that the outcome of the struggle between those alternative visions is not preordained within the already existing social structure; thus the process is not a closed circuit as it appears to be in Bourdieu. In effect, the participants in each of Bourdieu's fields is as governed by an ineluctable invisible hand as any participant in the Smithian free market.

There are two problems here. First, can we specify sociologically mechanisms of social change that might serve as a basis for politics as the willed intervention in that process of change? Second, what role does legitimation, the exercise of symbolic power, play in reproduction of a social system? Marxism has alternative explanations of the process of social change, depending on whether it is in its economically determinist or politically voluntarist mode. On the one hand, change stems from contradictions within the economic structure as such, either a falling rate of profit or the increasing socialization of production or the increasing relative immiserization of the proletariat. On the other hand, change stems from a political mobilization stemming from the grasping of the meaning and potential of those economic changes at the level of ideology and politics. We have to ask what might be the sources of social change within Bourdieu's explanatory schema. It clearly has no problem with the economic determinist explanation. Indeed, insofar as Bourdieu is concerned with the problem of social change at all, a crude base/superstructure model underpins his work. What would remain to be specified is at what point and how changes in the mode of production produce changes in the basic logic of the classificatory schema such as to reproduce a new structure of class interest. The problem, however, is whether we can find any sources for willed social change, and thus for a politics, within Bourdieu's explanatory schema. I do not see any.

The nearest he gets to identifying such a source is in his discussion of the relationship between the process of educational certification and the labor market. He argues broadly that demands for greater economic

democracy were defused by expanding formal education and certification, which disguise real differences in economic power between levels of
the managerial hierarchy and within the division of labor as differences
in level of educational qualification themselves stemming from individual
inborn differences in intellectual capacity. He goes on to argue, however,
that this system came under pressure when the labor market was unable
to deliver suitable jobs to those who were appropriately certificated.
Here he seems to be arguing that a contradiction between the educational
field and the field of material production produced a contradiction that
the classificatory schema was unable to handle, thus producing real
political effects (Bourdieu 1984: 143–68). In his own words, "Everything
suggests that an abrupt slump in objective chances relative to subjective
aspirations is likely to produce a break in the tacit acceptance which the
dominated classes – now abruptly excluded from the race, objectively
and subjectively – previously granted to the dominant goals, and so to
make possible a genuine inversion of values" (p. 168). But in this case the
basic theoretical schema is found wanting, since potential participants in
the job market were able to perceive a disjuncture between the thought
world of certification and the real world of the labor market, on the basis
of which they were prepared, at least provisionally, no longer to adhere
unquestioningly to the prevailing relations of order. Indeed, they were
part of that coalition which voted the socialists into power in France in
1979 after more than two decades of conservative hegemony.

The second problem is that of the relative role played by legitimation,
on the one hand, and by the dull compulsion of economic relations, on
the other, in the maintenance of that structure of social domination we
call capitalism. Bourdieu's work stems from a tradition, most famously
associated with Gramsci, which argues that to explain the stability of
capitalist social relations in terms of the use of overt physical coercion is
incompatible with the empirically observable realities of everyday life
and that therefore the explanation must be sought in the manufacture of
consent. But this is to neglect a more obvious explanation, one which is
strongly supported by work such as that of Michael Mann (1973) and
that of Abercrombie and his colleagues (1980) in the UK. They found
that the subordinate classes were quite well aware of the nature of
domination – that is, no process of misrecognition was taking place and
that they did not share in the belief systems of the dominant ideology.
Indeed, so diverse were people's belief systems that it was hard in any
way to talk of a dominant ideology. They went along with the prevailing
social order solely on the clear-sighted grounds that it was difficult to
change and that the risks associated with such change were simply too
great. This attests to the now well-supported proposition that human

beings are inherently risk-averse for good, rational, and historically supported reasons. In short, we have to take seriously the argument that insofar as there is a common classificatory schema, it does not necessarily lead to support for the social status quo and that the social status quo does not need the support of "logical conformity" to explain its stability. A better explanation of such stability, then, would be the existence of what Gellner has called "generalized bribery" as the society's structuring principle.

Third, how do we validate social change and oppositional politics? The political claims of socialism cannot be divorced, in my view, from some notion of a shared human rationality and associated set of social values. The very idea that domination is in some way illegitimate, which underpins all Bourdieu's work (since otherwise he cannot pose the theoretical and empirical questions as to how domination is legitimated), has to be based on a shared set of ethical values that cannot be reduced to the culturally arbitrary. For if they are so reduced, we have to explain (a) how such an oppositional view can arise and (b) how politics can be anything other than a crude Hobbesian power struggle between interests.

Certainly, in Bourdieu, cultural production tends to be reduced to such a power struggle, with the result that what, for want of a better phrase, I will call "cultural content" disappears. While I would be the last to want to argue that both aesthetic theories and cultural practices are not bound up with, and in important ways determined by, struggles over access to scarce material resources and social status, I would also want to ask whether this is a sufficient explanation. This is not just of theoretical, but also of political importance. Let me take one example related to my own area of interest in the mass media. It is certainly possible to argue that the idea of press freedom has been and is being used to defend both the specific interests of journalists as a professional group and/or the property rights of press proprietors against the interests of subordinate social groups and that it can be so used because the concept is decoupled from considerations of the material realities of press production. Thus free press arguments can and have been used, most famously in the US First Amendment, to argue against any state intervention to alter the structure of media markets and, in particular, media ownership, by equating a free market in the scarce material resources required for the production and distribution of media products with a free market in ideas, thus disguising and protecting the unequal power over the flow of ideas that existing market structures grant to a small minority of the economically powerful. At the same time they have been used, as has the related idea of creative freedom, to bolster the status and autonomy of journalists and media producers as a quasi-professional group, some-times against the managerial claims of the proprietors themselves, and to shield from social questioning a specific set of cultural practices of which the journalists are the mystical guardians – the concept of news values, for instance – practices that give journalists power over the symbolic representation of other social groups. However, to discard the concept and the writings on the theme as merely expressing those ideologies is to cut off oppositional groups from the possibility of using such ideas for their own ends by utilizing the very legitimacy of the concept as the basis for a critique of current press practice and the realization of a more extended concept of press freedom.

Certainly I believe it to be the case that the Left intelligentsia in Britain was extensively disarmed against the neoconservative backlash by its own internalized guilt in relation to a self-propagated view of its values as part of a self-serving bourgeois conspiracy. When the neo-liberal Thatcherites attacked the universities and public service broadcasting on similar lines, these intellectuals were hardly in a strong position to mount an impassioned defense. I will return to this theme in more detail below.

Do we need to complement Bourdieu's analysis of the forms of cultural production and appropriation with a development of the Frankfurt school's cultural analysis, which gives due weight to the oppositional potential of cultural forms and content and to the socially progressive and utopian potential of cultural practice? This is an old debate that relates to my previous discussion of universal values and to the question of whether socialism is building upon and expressing the full potential of bourgeois values or creating something entirely new. Clearly the pertinence one assigns to this question depends on the specific historical conjuncture. In Eastern Europe and the countries of the former Soviet Union this question will be posed differently from the way it might be posed in Western Europe or the United States. Certainly it is my perception that the object for pertinent critique has changed. Bourdieu's work came out of a specific political conjuncture, when the priority was to expose the inadequacies of the social democratic, welfare state compact, to reveal the false prospectus of meritocracy through universal state education and of cultural enfranchisement through state-subsidized cultural programs of a traditional kind. Now the priorities have changed and, in this changed climate, Bourdieu's use of the cultural arbitrary as a central explanatory concept and the vacation of the field of cultural content which results plays into the hands of those who are propagating the total cultural relativism of postmodernism. Such a position makes it difficult, if not impossible, to critique this particular legitimation of the process of commodification, not just of all cultural practices and relations, but of historical memory itself, the increasingly rapid reduction of all human experience to that of the shopping mall and all human social identities to that of membership of targeted and segmented taste publics. I am now showing the prejudices of an unreconstructed bourgeois intellectual out of tune with the times, but if I have to choose between a culture dominated by the dominated fraction of the dominated class in its traditional forms or by the multinational advertising agencies, I am afraid I know which I would choose. However, while I know that a battle or two too many may have been lost, I do not despair utterly of the war.

THE MASS MEDIA

On that note let me turn to one particular instance of contemporary cultural practice: namely, television and the problems it seems to raise for Bourdieu's theory.

It is, I think, significant that there is only one reference to television in the index of *Distinction*. This lack is surprising on a number of counts. First, because of television's sheer centrality as a contemporary cultural practice. It is worth reiterating the figures. In the UK people on average are now watching television for over twenty-seven hours per week in winter and over twenty hours per week in summer. Thus, for a project such as Bourdieu's, which is concerned with the distribution of cultural practices and competences and their relation to the reproduction of the structure of social power, the case of television, the most widely shared and socially pervasive cultural practice (one, moreover, through which increasingly all others are refracted and projected into the very heart of the habitus), can hardly be ignored without making the whole theoretical enterprise vulnerable.

Second, central to Bourdieu's work, especially his work on photography, has been the examination of cultural practices that present the minimum of direct economic barriers to participation, the better to study the less visible barriers erected by the structured distribution of competences and dispositions derived from the habitus. Here again, broadcasting in general, and television in particular, to which there is now virtually universal household access in advanced industrial societies and which, because of its very cheapness at the point of reception, occupies the major portion of the cultural consumption time of the lower socioeconomic groups, represents a key field for the study of the ways in which cultural consumption and appropriation is structured in ways that are not directly material.

Third, Bourdieu's neglect of television is surprising if only because much of the debate around the question of the dominant ideology and its formation and function in contemporary capitalist societies has been conducted within US and UK social science in terms of the mass media in general and television in particular.

Whatever the reasons for it, the absence of an adequate treatment of television does, I think, raise questions for Bourdieu's work. The first relates to patterns of consumption; for what we appear to see with television is a breaking down of the class-specific patterns of consumption that Bourdieu identifies elsewhere. In the UK at least, the link between class and patterns of consumption across all program types is very weak to nonexistent. Contrary to popular myth, as for instance the detailed work of Barwise and Ehrenberg (1988) has shown, there is no evidence that members of the dominant fraction of the dominant class watch demanding, minority, "cultural programs," whereas the popular classes watch less demanding, lowest-common-denominator pap. On the contrary, high-rating programs achieve their high ratings precisely because less heavy viewers (who do come from higher socioeconomic groups) join heavy viewers to watch them (Barwise and Ehrenberg 1988). These observed viewing patterns do not of course mean that within the audience for a given program there may not be significant differences in modes of appropriation structured in ways congruent with Bourdieu's theory. We simply do not know. The point I want to make, however, is that, at least in the UK, we have observed in relation to television a significant breaking down of the class-based distinctions among types of cultural consumption and their related hierarchy of social values. Indeed, there are signs that where such hierarchies survive, they have been turned on their head, so that museums, for instance, are increasingly adopting the values of popular television, and the life-styles and cultural markers of the traditional upper class have been repackaged as the heritage industry.

This collapse of stable cultural categories would be both explained and praised by some as postmodern. But I want to suggest another explanation. In my view we are witnessing a further stage in the development of the cultural industries and the expansion of the commoditization of the cultural sphere. This development presents a serious problem for Bourdieu's approach, because it accentuates the contradiction between the dominant and the dominated fraction of the dominant class. First, once capital moves into cultural production and distribution in a major way (and here it is worth pointing out that the cultural sector in the UK is now more significant economicaly than the motor industry and that film and television constitute the USA's second largest export sector), a divergence develops between the economic and ideological interests of the dominant class, since, as in other social areas, the spread of capitalist relations of production and exchange is corrosive of inherited social distinctions and hierarchies. Increasingly, as basic material needs are satisfied, the use value of commodities becomes cultural, and an unholy alliance develops between intergroup status competition and marketing. Advertising becomes the key cultural field where commodity design and markers of cultural distinction form and reform in a constant dialectical interchange driven by the forces of capital circulation and realization.

Thus the dominant fraction cannot safely leave the cultural field to be shaped by the interstatus group competition between subsets of the dominated fraction, since the reproduction of their economic capital now depends directly upon both the costs of production and the size of the markets for symbolic goods. Moreover, cultural taste publics are increasingly also market segments not just for symbolic goods but for an associated range of material goods. Thus much of the current restructuring that can be observed in advanced capitalist economies of the relationship among cultural institutions, the corporate sector, and the state, as well as the political debates and struggles surrounding them, can be explained in these terms. For the dominant fraction, culture is no longer arbitrary, in the most fundamental sense. They have a direct economic interest in the structure of cultural fields, and members of the dominated fraction have to be brought within the disciplines of capitalist production. This process of proletarianization of the intelligentsia is undercutting the structural separation of the dominated and the dominant fraction and the accompanying process of systematic misrecognition which that separation made possible; it thus strikes at the very heart of Bourdieu's theory.

This process may be more effective in maintaining the social structure of late capitalism than that theorized by Bourdieu, not because it causes the misrecognition of social hierarchy as cultural hierarchy, but because it dissolves cultural hierarchies and by so doing produces the appearance of dissolving social hierarchies. Certainly I think we need to discuss what the relationship might be between this process and the widely recognized breakdown of modes of social solidarity – the decline of political parties, trade unions, associations of all sorts – in favor of an increasingly individualized and fragmented social world of shifting interest and taste groups. We need to ask to what extent this is a process determined by changes in the labor process and by associated changes in the division of labor, as the post-Fordist school would have it, and to what extent it is a relatively autonomous cultural process compatible with a range of capitalist structures of production and rooted in the sphere of consumption itself.

Finally, this links back to the relationship between Bourdieu's scientific and political projects and to the earlier discussion of the dangers of the cultural arbitrary. As I have said, this general process has led to a restructuring of the institutions of cultural production and distribution and thus of the fields that surround them. One form of that restructuring, particularly in Europe, has been a process of so-called deregulation whereby the sphere of broadcasting, previously a domain dominated by state or parastatal national monopolies financed largely by license fees rather than advertising and pursuing politically defined national cultural policies, has been progressively opened up to competitive, advertising-financed, private-sector corporations, often operating on an international scale and responding to the commercial pressures of a global market.

The debate in the UK about television's role in the creation and propagation of the dominant ideology was linked to a political debate about the structure of broadcasting, and in particular about the social function of public service broadcasting in the form of the BBC. At a time when the tradition of public service broadcasting is in crisis all over Western Europe, as part of the wider crisis of the social democratic welfare state and in the face of precisely that spread of cultural commoditization and the development of an advertising-based culture, to which I have pointed, it is worth dwelling for a moment on this issue. In the UK in the 1970s, many on the Left argued that the institutional forms and practices of public service broadcasting – for instance, requirements of objectivity in news reporting and the scheduling of "minority" and "cultural" programming – served precisely as a form of misrecognition that reinforced the BBC's role as the ideological agent of the dominant class. Those holding this view therefore attacked the BBC from the left as elitist, undemocratic, etc. Others, of whom I am one, held to the view that, for all its faults, the fact that the BBC was noncommercial and protected to a significant institutional extent from direct political control represented a real social democratic gain and created at least a bridgehead for the development of a true public sphere and what Raymond Williams called "a common culture." That while it was undoubtedly true that the BBC was controlled in their interest by the dominated fraction, nonetheless the range and relative objectivity of its news and current affairs coverage represented a real and progressive contrast with the capitalist press which could not be reduced to a mere ideological smoke screen. Moreover, in the UK at least, we witnessed a real involvement by the intelligentsia in the creation of forms of truly popular programming that cannot be reduced to notions of patronizing or vulgarizing (Garnham 1990: 115–35, Connell 1983, Gardner 1984). The fact that the BBC has been under continual assault from neo-liberal free marketeers and the political new Right since 1979 seems to me to support this view. It has, however, undoubtedly been the case that much of the British Left, having mounted a critique of the BBC and of the concept of public service broadcasting that was broadly congruent with Bourdieu's analysis, have found themselves disarmed in the face of the new Right's assault.

Two questions are at issue here for our purposes: first, the extent to which certain cultural values and institutional forms of cultural practice can be considered to have some general objective value and progressive political potential, whether or not they may be used in any particular historical conjuncture by a specific social interest group for their own purposes; and second, the extent to which the alliance between economic and cultural capital is necessary to the maintenance of the status quo. In the UK in the 1980s we witnessed an assault across a wide front on the prerogatives of the intelligentsia by the neo-liberal political representatives of economic capital, often in the name of precisely that set of cultural values embodied in mass commercial popular culture. Thus the values endorsed are those carried by advertising and the tabloid press. All questions relating to education and the arts, narrowly defined, are reduced to problems of marketing and its funding, increasingly handed over directly to the advertising industry and private capital. Public service broadcasting and the regulatory structure that sustains it is overtly attacked as the last refuge of elitist cultural workers, who must be forced to serve the people more adequately and efficiently by being opened up to the bracing winds of commercial competition. In the UK the Peacock Committee on Financing the BBC stated, in 1986, that "our own conclusion is that British broadcasting should move towards a sophisticated market system based on consumer sovereignty." In reaching this conclusion, the committee was dismissive of the cultural claims of the intellectual fraction that has traditionally controlled television. "We had some difficulty in obtaining an operational definition from broadcasters of public service broadcasting," they dismissively concluded. With irony they remarked that

> it is entirely understandable that so much attention is paid in the Annual Reports of both the BBC and IBA to the most important professional symbols of success – EMMY and BAFTA awards. It could reasonably be claimed that such awards for all manner of programming skills afford a glow of satisfaction to viewers and listeners who are sensitive to our international cultural reputation. However the award of professional

accolades, which is important in many professions can only be at most an indirect guide to what will promote the interests of those for whom the system is ultimately designed. (Peacock Committee 1986)

In a similar vein, a U.K. Minister of Education recently quite explicitly equated institutions of higher education with manufacturing industry, asking why they too should not lower unit costs and increase quality by increasing output. And this is entirely in line with a consistent strand in public rhetoric. Not only can we not explain this political process, and similar ones in other advanced capitalist economies, within Bourdieu's theoretical schema which requires that the value hierarchies of the cultural fields be "distanced" from those of the economy if the process of misrecognition is to work. The adoption of such a schema disarms us in any political struggle to develop a democratic public sphere in the face of the processes of cultural commodification by forging an alliance between progressive sections of the intelligentsia and other democratic social forces and thus to make cultural critique politically relevant.

REFERENCES

Abercrombie, N. *et al.* 1980: *The Dominant Ideology Thesis.* London: Unwin Hyman.
Barwise, P. and Ehrenberg, A. 1988: *TV and its Audience.* London: Sage.
Connell, I. 1983: Commercial broadcasting and the British Left. *Screen,* 24, no. 6 (London: Society for Education in Film and TV).
Gardner, C. 1984: Populism, relativism and Left strategy. *Screen,* 25, no. 1 (London: Society for Education in Film and TV).
Garnham, N. 1990: *Capitalism and Communication: global culture and the economics of information.* London: Sage.
Mann, M. 1973: *Consciousness and Action among the Western Working Class.* London: Macmillan.
Peacock Committee 1986: Report of the Committee on Financing the BBC. Cmnd. 9824. London: HMSO.

10

Pierre Bourdieu: Cultural Economy and Social Change

Scott Lash

If Pierre Bourdieu presents us with a general sociological theory, it is in his words "a general theory of the economics of practice" (1977c: 183). In such a theory, Bourdieu underscores, economic practice is only one of a whole set of social practices. All of these practices, however, are conceived along the lines of an economic model, and the majority of them are, in fact, symbolic practices. Hence his general sociology of culture is a general theory of the economics of symbolic practice. The aim of this essay is a close examination of Pierre Bourdieu's "cultural economy." What I hope to demonstrate is that this economic heuristic takes major responsibility both for many of the considerable virtues and for the vices of Bourdieu's sociology of culture.

An example of the sort of virtue I refer to is that Bourdieu's general sociology of culture is not only the best, but it is the only game in town. Neither Weber nor Durkheim nor especially Marx gave us even the elements of a general sociology of culture. Durkheim's *conscience collective* encourages the glossing over of crucial social divisions, while Weber's sociology of culture is largely a sociology of religion only. The boom in "culture studies" in the late 1980s, despite its heavily broadcast theoretical pedigree, has not done much better when it comes to a general theory of culture. Adornians, Lacanians, and the followers of Roland Barthes (not to mention those influenced by Peirce and Umberto Eco) have given us a mainly production-side aesthetics. Literary critical disciples of Hans Robert Jauss and the immensely influential Birmingham Centre for Culture Studies have given us a rather one-sided aesthetics and sociology of reception, while the Derridians have ignored both production and reception – indeed, have forgotten the social altogether in their rather obsessive textualism. Even the signal work of Raymond Williams, though rich in social explanation, is placed more accurately in a literary critical tradition. Further, Williams's formulations lack the systematic coherence and analytic incisiveness of properly sociological investigation.

Bourdieu's economy of symbolic practices, in contradistinction, provides the tools for analyses of production, text, and audience in culture studies, as well as for the all-important analysis of the mediating role of the institutions of culture. It can, moreover, provide a basis for the analysis of social and historical change in cultural practices. It is his economic heuristic that gives to this theory both its coherence and its unusual breadth.

The vices have been discussed by other commentators. They are – in a sentence – tendencies towards idealism and elitism and insufficient epistemological and ethical universalism. Some of these criticisms have been overplayed, although I believe there are important measures of validity in each of them. These too, we shall see, follow largely from Bourdieu's economic heuristic.

This said, the first section below will introduce Bourdieu's model of a cultural market. The second section will expand on this in consideration of his related notion of "the field" and will spend some time in scrutiny of artistic, intellectual, cultural, scientific, academic, and political fields. The third section will briefly consider Bourdieu's notion of reflexivity. These initial, brief sections comprise the first half of the chapter. The aim here is to explicate and locate the virtues in Bourdieu's cultural economy. It is also to show how this economic model bears responsibility for the elements of relativism, idealism, and elitism present in his analyses.

Bourdieu has frequently been taken to task for a bias in his work towards social *reproduction*, as opposed to social *change*. In the second half of the chapter I propose to rework the cultural-economic model in the context of social change. I thus suggest a reworking of Bourdieusian reflexivity in the context of the new social movements, of symbolic production in the context of recent shifts towards flexible specialization in the real economy, and of the cultural fields in the context of changes in the structuring of concrete urban space. Once such social change is taken on board the vices – idealism, relativism, and elitism – of Bourdieu's cultural economy are negated, and the model takes on exemplary explanatory importance.

MARKETS

The notion of a "cultural economy" informs Bourdieu's analyses of both traditional and modern societies, traditional societies being understood in the unmediated exchange of gifts, modern societies in terms of exchanges mediated by markets. Bourdieu's work on markets was very concentrated around the early 1970s; the work on fields is more prevalent from the mid–1970s to the present. The markets, while not identical with fields, provide a skeleton framework for the latter.

In the early 1970s Bourdieu was much influenced by Weber's sociology of religion, recasting the latter's model of religious change in the framework of cultural markets. Thus Weber's (bureaucratic) priests and (charismatic) prophets are producers of "symbolic goods" competing for consumers among the "laity" (1987d). In this formulation we already have the three elements of the economy of culture: (1) the supply side, or the producers of cultural goods; (2) the symbolic goods, or products themselves; and (3) the demand side, the consumers of cultural goods. The symbolic goods produced here only have a chance of realizing their value if they have a relation of "elective affinity" to the consumers – that is, to their ideal and material interests. Bourdieu keeps intact the Weberian conceptualization of social change via the struggle between bureaucratic priests and charismatic prophets for the allegiance of the socially stratified masses.

In a benchmark article on painting, Bourdieu (1971d) extends this Weberian paradigm. The prophets are the modernist painters in late nineteenth-century France. The priests are the academic painters. Here Bourdieu also introduces the "*institutions* of culture" as "instances of conservation and consecration." On this count, he notes that the Académie française is similar to Weber's bureaucratic church. Other institutions include museums, newspaper critics, dealers and gallery-owners, and the art colleges. Orthodox painters and avant-garde "heresiarchs" compete to be consecrated by the institutions. Such symbolic markets for artistic goods and their corresponding "fields" do not exist in traditional, "undifferentiated" societies, but only come to exist with differentiation in the process of modernization. Modernization for Bourdieu – and again, Weber's conceptions in "Politics as a vocation," "Science as a vocation" (Wolff 1959) and the methodological articles on the world religions serve as a model – lies in the differentiation and autonomization of fields (Whimster and Lash 1987).

There are two types of such fields. One is the "large-scale field," in which production is for the broader social field. The other is the "delimited field" (*champs restreinte*), in which production is for other producers – that is, the agents and institutions in the field. Thus, in the delimited field the supply side is also, and at the same time, the demand side (Bourdieu 1971d: 54–5). In the art field of late nineteenth-century

Paris, then, in the delimited field, bohemians of the avant-garde made paintings for other bohemian and avant garde painters and for galleries and other art institutions. Such institutions consecrate art through their powers of "nomination" (p. 58). They have the power to "name" schools of art, to impart value to them, and to impose these nominations in an act of "symbolic violence" on the ordinary consumers in the wider social field.

What emerges from the delimited field of production to the social field is not a construction of the artist but a construction of the entire field (Bourdieu 1980a: 264). In this sense the institutions of art do not mediate between production and consumption but are part of the production side itself. What emerges is a cultural product with a value assigned to it (p. 267).

Mediating between the delimited artistic field and the large social field – that is, between the the fields of production and consumption – is the education system (p. 265). Unlike the institutions of art, which help produce cultural objects, the education system produces not cultural objects, but consumers of art to match the cultural products. That is, the education system produces a "habitus," in this case an "art habitus" (Bourdieu 1971d: 114).

Bourdieu's habitus can be understood – to follow the cultural economy model – in terms of a supply, or production, side and a demand, or reception, side. The production side of the habitus produces actions. Bourdieu talks of this production side of the habitus in terms of "dispositions" to action. These dispositions are in Chomsky's sense "competences" and "generative capacities." They operate like a *sens pratique*, in that they orient behavior to ends without that behavior being consciously directed to those ends. (Indeed, Bourdieu's *sens pratique is* arguably the production side of the habitus.) Not perhaps dissimilar to Merleau-Ponty's conception of the body, the production side of Bourdieu's notion of the habitus embodies "intentionality without intention" (see Bourdieu 1987a: 13–14). The consumption, or reception, side of the habitus is reminiscent of Kant's categorial schemata. Thus the reception side is comprised of "schemes," first of "categories of perception and appreciation" along the lines of *The Critique of Pure Reason*'s "transcendental aesthetic" and, second, of principles of classification or of thought along the lines of its "transcendental logic" (see Bourdieu 1987a: 147–66).

Through education, a set of classificatory schema is inculcated in consumers of art. This is on the reception side, and it enables the consumer to "decipher" the work of art. The more developed the art habitus, Bourdieu writes (1968a: 592–3), the more finely one can classify.

If modernization entails the differentiation of an autonomous aesthetic field, then the appreciation of (modern) art that this brings about entails the inculcation of a "differentiated" habitus. The visitor to an art museum who lacks any such training or differentiated habitus uses the classifications with which he or she perceives everyday reality to perceive the work of art (p. 598), hence his or her appreciation of a landscape, perhaps, but dismissal of, say, a Pollock or a Mondrian. In this sense the stuff of the habitus is not what Bourdieu terms "symbolic capital"; nor is it "economic capital," but *cultural* capital. The habitus can be oriented primarily to the accumulation of symbolic capital (honor, prestige) or to the accumulation of economic capital. But the habitus itself, even in undifferentiated tribal societies, is made up of cultural capital or, in the very widest sense of the word, knowledge (including skills). We tend to think of cultural capital in terms of life-chances on labor markets – that is, as on the production side – in which it is comprised not just of knowledge but of rhetorical ability, titles, and academic qualifications. But the family and the education system also enable the accumulation of cultural capital on the *consumption* side – for example, in the just-mentioned ability to appreciate works of art.

The field of artistic production, like other fields, is relatively autonomous from the social field. Note here that Weber's religious field was also only relatively autonomous. Productive interests in the artistic field would find "homologies" with class interests in the social field. Because the popular classes, due to relatively undifferentiated cultural capital, are in most cases effectively excluded from even the large-scale social field of artistic production, the interests that pertain here are those of the two main fractions of the dominant class, the bourgeoisie and the intellectuals. The former tend to have homologies with – that is, be the relevant consumers of (or have an elective affinity with) – the productions of "consecrated artists" (priests), while the intellectuals have homologies with the avant-gardes or *artistes maudits* (Bourdieu 1968a: 600–1).

FIELDS

Just how Bourdieu's fields (and markets) work can be encapsulated in the following statements. The specific and differentiated fields are sites of collective symbolic struggles and individual strategies, the aims of which are to produce valuable cultural goods (or be associated with their production in the case of institutions and marketers). The value of a symbolic good depends upon the value assigned to it by the relevant consumer community. These value judgments are in most fields determined by the amount of symbolic capital accumulated by the producer (or producers). Victory in a symbolic struggle means that one's symbolic goods have been judged to possess more value than those of one's competitors. The fruit of such victory is the right to impose one's symbolic goods on the social field: that is, to exercise symbolic violence on the "consumers" in the social field, and this entails the complicity of those subject to such violence.

How much "relative autonomy"?

The central axis of variation of the fields is their degree of autonomy. Bourdieu is not entirely consistent in his assessment of just what this autonomy is from. At points it is from the dominant classes in the "field of power" (for example, in *Homo Academicus*). At points it is from the entirety of the social field. The degree of such autonomy is neatly captured by Bourdieu via the economic heuristic. The more autonomous a field is, the greater the extent to which production in that field is only for other producers and not for consumers in the social field (or field of power) (1975: 21). Thus the most autonomous of fields is the scientific field. The academic and artistic fields (high culture) occupy rather intermediate positions, autonomy in the former being from the field of power and in the latter from consumers in the social field. Still less autonomous is the legal field. And least autonomous with regard to the social field (all classes in the social field) is the political field.

Struggles and strategies within the fields also have at stake the degree of such autonomy. For example, as the scientific field emerged historically from the religious field, some agents struggled against others for such autonomization (1975: 32–3). In general, "prophets" tend to gain by autonomization, while "priests" stand to lose. Thus the various "secession" movements in the arts (Paris, Berlin, Vienna) struggled for autonomy from the field of power, while those associated with the "academies" struggled against it. Or, in the academic field, the "priests" associated with the École national d'administration, the Sorbonne, L'École des hautes études en sciences politiques, the aggregation and the teaching and reproduction functions, have tended to struggle against autonomization from the field of power. In contrast the "prophets" of L'École des hautes etudes en sciences sociales, the *doctorat du troisième cycle*, and research and cultural production have struggled for autonomy (Bourdieu 1988b: ch. 3).

The scientific field is the paradigm case of autonomy. The more a field is autonomous from the social field and the field of power, the more,

Bourdieu notes, the field speaks the language of science. This is the logic of true and false, instead of the friend or foe logic of the field of power (1986a: 10). Yet the main stake in the scientific field, according to Bourdieu, is not the production of valid statements but the "socially recognized capacity to speak and act legitimately." This is at the same time the power of imposition of the definition of science: that is, the power to draw the limits of the field, to decide who is in and who is out. The stake then is the "monopoly" of "scientific competence" or "authority" (1975: 26ff.), the accumulation of "scientific capital." The latter is less a form of cultural capital of scientific competences than a form of symbolic capital, based on the prestige of the university one went to, the graduate school, one's references, one's membership on prestigious editorial boards, grant committees, and institutes (p. 25). The habitus that would enable this sort of accumulation is not one primarily structured by scientific competence but one attuned to the accumulation of symbolic capital.[1]

The political field is the least autonomous of fields in that it is furthest from the logic of true/false and must speak the friend/foe vernacular. Moreover, the value of political products is largely determined outside the political field (1981b: 13). But even the political market tends to increase its autonomy during modernization – the Michelsian oligarchic mass party was one step in this direction; its recent supersession by politics as presentation through the media is a further step (p. 6). The value, then, of a political product (produced, of course, by the professionals in the field) is dependent on two factors: (1) the symbolic capital of the political agent and his or her party (p. 18) and (2) the extent to which these political symbols, which Bourdieu likens to "signifiers," correspond to the interests and central meanings ("signifieds") of stratified consumers in the social field (p. 8).

These political products are symbolic products or, in some sense, "signifiers" and include "positions, programmes, analyses, commentaries, concepts, and events" produced by the professionals of the field. These political symbols have three functions vis-à-vis their relevant "reception classes" in the social field. They are (1) instruments of perception, (2) instruments of expression, and (3) instruments of mobilization (pp. 5–6). Instruments of mobilization are crucial for class formation. Though, structurally, classes already exist through "objective relations" in the social field, what Bourdieu calls "empirical classes" do not yet exist. Instead, they instead have to be made, formed into working-class parties and trade unions, and this entails the work of professionals from the political field.

Bourdieu's idealism

There is, I think, an uncomfortably substantial measure of idealism in Bourdieu's analyses.

1 Law and politics, which are conventionally seen as coercive (state) apparatuses, are understood by Bourdieu in terms of symbolic power. This rests on a rather narrow conception of what constitutes coercion. In the case of law, for example, Bourdieu says that judges produce symbolic goods in the form of performative utterances. But what about the utterance whereby the judge orders the defendant to spend three years in prison? Does the judge have physically to throw the convicted defendant into jail before he can be said to wield nonsymbolic power?

In the political field Bourdieu does at times speak of material power as "objectified political resources," meaning the police, the army, the administration (1981b:8). It is, however, symbolic power that receives Bourdieu's attention. This is state-guaranteed power to *faire croire*, to impose beliefs. It is the power of "nomination" through "state and official discourses" (p. 13). Bourdieu does say, to his credit, that symbolic struggles concern nonsymbolic (that is, the "objective") relations between social classes (1987a: 150) and that political power is power to "transcribe" and hence to "transform or conserve" the "social world" (1981b:8). Yet this transformation comes about through "nomination" and "prescription" (p. 4), through "classification" and operation on the social world via its "systems of classification."

2 "Symbolic capital" has, I think, the greatest amount of explanatory power of any of Bourdieu's concepts. This is true in his account of primitive societies and of both the supply and demand side of modern societies. The main sense of the *sens pratique* in traditional societies is "honor," which is alternatively called "symbolic capital." Bourdieu says that economic capital plays a homologous role in modern societies (1987a: 131). Yet his treatment of the supply side of the various fields emphasizes, as we saw above, the principle of *symbolic* capital. So does his most extensive treatment of the demand side in *Distinction* (1984).

3 Bourdieu says in a comment on *Distinction* that "objective relations" make up the structure of and hence constitute the "social world." He goes on to say that the structure of objective relations then "presents itself as a symbolic world" (1987a: 158). This looks to be eminently materialist until we consider what he means by these objective relations. Remember, it is not "interactions" that constitute fields, but objective relations, of which interactions are partly an effect. The "economic" relations here are not themselves the structure. What, then,

are these "objective relations" of which Bourdieu speaks? They are not the Marxist and materialist relations between means of production and both capitalist and worker. They are not even Weberian relations of legal rational domination (*Herrschaft*). They are instead "the relations between the positions occupied in the distribution of resources" – that is, of economic, symbolic, and cultural capital. Thus the dominant class has more total capital than the popular classes. And within the dominant class, the bourgeoisie has a higher admixture of economic capital, the intellectuals of cultural capital (p. 152). When classes are spoken of in the latter way, they become determined by "attributional" properties rather than "relational" ones. To the extent that informs Bourdieu's theory, the latter is not materialist like Marxism or "conflict theory," which are based on relational notions of stratification. It comes instead to resemble the attributional hierarchies that characterized the eminently non-materialist functionalist (and consensus) stratification theories of traditional American sociology (see Runciman 1966).

4 What about the place of the real economy? Bourdieu states that "the generating principle of the economic field" is the "system of differences that are constitutive of its structure" (1987a: 126). He notes the importance of symbolic parameters in the behavior of entrepreneurs and argues that the value of economic products themselves is determined by struggles and by the (symbolically conditioned) preference structures of consumers (p. 128). Bourdieu does, however, attempt to account for why economic capital, and no longer symbolic capital, is the dominant principle in modern societies. This is so, he suggests, because in comparison with symbolic capital, for example, economic capital is easy to "transmit" and to "objectify." It possesses "liquidity." In fact, he concludes, "the particular 'power' of economic capital could be because it permits an economy of economic calculation . . . that is, of rational management, of labour and transmission, that it is, in other terms, easier to manage rationally, to calculate and to predict" (p. 131). One could not here be much closer to the Weberian understanding of the economy in terms of rational calculability. Weberian rationalization is (sociologically) idealist, beginning from the religious sphere, and entering the social sphere, including the economy (Schluchter 1987). As it enters a social sphere it only has to find its appropriate class-bearer (*Träger*), its consumption classes, and its prophets and priests.

REFLEXIVITY AND VALIDITY

No pure theory of structure or pure theory of agency can have a notion of reflexivity. Reflexivity assumes a subject, an object, and a medium of reflection. Theories of reflexivity differ to the extent that these three parameters vary.

The reflecting subject can be an individual, a social class, an entire society. If an individual, it can be *inter alia* an intellectual, an artist, a scientist, or a sociologist. The object of reflection can be the norms that structure society or the norms that structure a part of society. It can be symbolic, aesthetic, or ethical. It can be the products of knowledge of, for example, sociology. The medium of reflection is usually either consciousness or language. Hence, for example, in Habermas it is a speech community that reflects through language primarily on social or ethical norms. For Lukács, class subjects reflect through consciousness on the social. In Giddens reflection is largely on social rules.

All these writers hold in common that reflexive action is possible only in modernity. The implication is that the modern actor is capable of formulating and reflecting on his or her means and ends of action, which was impossible in traditional action, structured by unreflective convention. Weber's "ethics of responsibility" (and their subsequent neo-Weberian formulations) also exemplify reflective action, in which the demands of the different life orders (*Lebensordungen*) are weighed and assessed.

Reflexivity can also mean the reflection of the subject on the subject itself, as in Hegel's notion of self-consciousness (*Selbstbewusstsein*). This meaning is also at least implicit in Gouldner's demand for a reflexive sociology, heralded in *The Coming Crisis of Western Sociology*. Bourdieu's sort of reflexivity seems to be rather closer to this type, hence the stated aim of *Homo Academicus* to "classify the classifiers." Reflexivity in this sense refers to the producers of knowledge. In Bourdieu's account these producers are understood most importantly through their habitus and through their individual strategies and collective struggles. They (and their self-reflexivity) inhere in their structural position in three senses: (1) their position in the objective relations of the academic or sociological field, (2) their position and trajectory in the objective relations of the social field, and (3) their position in the struggles between orthodoxy and heterodoxy, which determine the output of structure in the academic/sociological field.

What are the implications of this for notions of truth and validity? Bourdieu says in the preface to *Homo Academicus* that the idea is not to render uncertain, but "to make more secure the foundations of sociological thought." The *modus operandi* here should not be "transcendental reflection" but "classifying the classifiers." He maintains that the "self-reflection of sociology" will lead to anti-relativism and to "scientific profits." He also says (in the Honneth interview) that the way to the "universal" is not through "foundations" but through "reflexive critique" (1987a: 45).

How can we make sense of this? Given the assumptions of self-interest and instrumental action built into Bourdieu's economics of symbolic practice, there are three routes to truth and universalism: (1) through the innovations of "heterodoxy," (2) through cross-control by scientific method, and (3) through the autonomization of the given field. He uses these elements effectively to speak of validity in the aesthetic field. Here he writes that with a succession of avant-gardes taking the place of established avant-gardes there is a certain *epuration* of poetry in which the latter is "reduced" to its own "proper materials" (1987a: 170). This sounds very much like Adorno's "aesthetic rationality." Art that is too much tied to the field of power has little to worry about from avant-gardes. This is also true if "cross-control" is tied to the field of power. Similar prescriptions would hold for sociology's "self-reflexive critique." These would be (1) to examine and criticize the openness of sociology to challenging heterodoxies, (2) to try to insure the autonomization of sociology from the field of power, and (3) to sharpen methods of cross-control. In one case or the other, these are prescriptions for the examination of the producer more than the product. Would not systematic critique of the descriptive utterances of sociology (that is, of sociology's products) be a surer way to truth and the universal?

Also Bourdieu's presuppositions make it seem as if a rational way forward is more or less ruled out in the political field. Autonomous fields, such as science and to a lesser extent art, follow the "logic of true and false" (valid and not valid). But the political field is inscribed with the logic of friend and foe. Here statements are not descriptive utterances but performative. Here, unlike the scientific field, it is no great advantage to be "armed with reason." How does Bourdieu's view of reflexive critique give any hope for a political future?

RECASTING BOURDIEU: THE PROBLEM OF SOCIAL CHANGE

Bourdieu's economic heuristic entails key assumptions of *reproduction* – of his circuits of symbolic and cultural capital and of social classes and class distinctions. It does so in a manner that inhibits the possibility of any strong theory of *social change*. In this section I want to make suggestions for recasting certain aspects of Bourdieu's framework in order to make it capable of accounting significantly for social change. I want first to address the changing nature of reflexivity via the classifications of Bourdieu's habitus; then I shall consider shifts in relations between the cultural economy and the real, material economy.

Aesthetic reflexivity

Sociological theorists, in particular Ulrich Beck (1986) and Anthony Giddens (1990) have recently developed a notion of *reflexive modernization*. This notion can best be developed via Bourdieu's habitus. Reflexive modernization means that increasing modernization will be accompanied by increasing reflexivity – that is, by the increasing ability of agents to reflect on structure. These gains in reflexivity can be usefully subdivided into cognitive, normative, and aesthetic reflexivity.

Cognitive reflexivity entails cognitive judgments. It is instantiated in the sciences and in instrumentally rational action in everyday life. For example, in today's increasingly flexible industrial relations, a much greater level of reflexivity is required by workers on the shop floor. The assembly line production of the old Fordist industrial relations is in the process of being superseded (Boyer (ed.) 1986). Alain Lipietz of the French École de regulation, leading theorist of the transition to post-Fordism, argues that for post-Fordist capital accumulation to be possible, there must be a qualitative change in the "habitus" of the work force (Leborgne and Lipietz 1990). This means that agents must be reflexive in taking into account the very rules and resources of the productive situation itself. The new shop floor relations entail responsibility and higher levels of risk taking for white-collar and skilled blue-collar workers – hence the psychological stress experienced by East German workers, previously not accustomed to risk taking and responsibility at work, now employed in West German, or West German-owned, factories (Beck 1986: 25–34, Giddens 1990: 124–32).

Second, there is "normative reflexivity." Thus Beck (1986: 205–19) speaks of the "paradox of modernization": increasing reflexivity should lead to positive political change; but increasing individuation makes it difficult to organize collectively to bring about such change.

The possible solution to Beck's paradox of modernization is present in the third, aesthetic-expressive type of reflexivity that Habermas, for example, has addressed since his linguistic turn. The model of course is Kant's *Critique of Judgment*. The French edition of Bourdieu's *Distinction* is subtitled *Critique sociale du jugement*. Let us note that Bourdieu here stands in a French tradition of the social-scientization of Kant's philosophic concepts. This includes notably Durkheim and Mauss's "primitive classifications," Durkheim's "elementary forms," and the work of Jean Piaget. But whereas Durkheim and Mauss (1969: 14–15) were quite explicit that their classifications were a critique of the logical categories of Kant's *Critique of Pure Reason*, Bourdieu is clearly taking aim at the categories of Kant's third Critique, that of aesthetic judgment.

Kant's aesthetic judgment was already a correction from the point of view of the particular of the excessive abstraction of cognitive and normative judgment. The sort of judgment that is at issue in Bourdieu's *Distinction* is a further correction of Kant in the direction of the particular. This is true in three ways. First, the object of judgment is particularized in Bourdieu. Instead of a work of art or the "aura" of a distant mountain in the Kantian beautiful or sublime, Bourdieu is speaking of the aesthetics of the very profane everyday objects of consumer societies. Second, the subject of judgment is particularized. In the place of the abstract subject of the Kantian a priori, subjects are socially situated in classes and class fractions. Third, the aim of judgment is shifted from the assessment of the validity of aesthetic objects – in terms of either the beautiful or the sublime – to how aesthetic objects are used by concrete subjects in order to establish invidious social distinctions between them.

Bourdieu's concepts can be used to address Beck's paradox of modernization inasmuch as they suggest that modernization may allow us to become *so* rational that we can reflect upon the conditions of possibility of creation of new collectivities and thereby overcome the problem of individuation.

To classify *à la* Bourdieu – that is, to "nominate" – is not only to create invidious distinctions. It is also, at least in the most meaningful classifications, to constitute a *conscience collective*, to create collective identity. In this context, fr example, Klaus Eder (1988: 274), drawing on Bourdieu, shows how certain classifying practices served to create collective identity in an ecological commune in which he did research. There is a certain symbolic "core" to our judgments of taste – to the clothes we wear, our bodily habitus, our classifying practices – which are constitutive of collectivity. This creates the possibility of new communities that could overcome modernist individuation and make collective political action possible.

This creation of collective identity is reflexive in the sense that members of the new communities are typically quite aware of the symbols central to the creation of the new identities. It is also reflexive in that membership is a matter of *choice* and entails *risk* on the level of identity. Shall I opt for deep ecology? For black cultural nationalism? For radical lesbian feminism? These are identity risks. Traditional *Gemeinschaften* were not chosen. The new ones are present as alternatives. Aesthetic reflexivity is the basis of such post-traditional *Gemeinschaft*.

Cultural and real economies

Bourdieu provides a framework for this sort of notion of aesthetic reflexivity. But why does he not come to the notion himself? Perhaps because of his focus on reproduction rather than social change. In Eder's account (1988: 265) the primacy of aesthetic-expressive statements in contemporary politics of the new social movements is part of a process of social change. The primacy of this sort of discourse, he notes, did not characterize the eighteenth-century bourgeois movement or the earlier twentieth-century working-class movements. Moreover, the delegitimation of abstract political ethics in recent years and the new primacy of a more concrete and particularized ethics, also captured in the Bourdieusian framework, are a consequence of social change.

The same can be said of the relationship of Bourdieu's cultural economy to the real material economy. In this case the real material economy, through social change, is becoming more like Bourdieu's cultural economy. Michael Piore and Charles Sabel (1984) have argued that contemporary, post-Fordist economies have been characterized by the phenomenon of "flexible specialization." This means a shift from the days of Fordist mass production and mass consumption to flexible production and specialized consumption. Sabel and Piore see the shift to flexibility in production as a *response* to specialized, niche-market consumption.

The question then, which Piore and Sabel insufficiently address, is how specialized consumption develops. Bourdieu's *Distinction* provides the beginnings of an answer. Consumption takes place largely via the creation of invidious distinctions between various classes and class fractions, and such distinctions are created, not via the use values but via the symbolic properties of goods. Further the emergence of new class fractions within the professional-managerial classes, as well as the increased internal stratification of the working classes, not to mention the heightened importance of age and gender stratification within and without all classes, will be integral to the shift towards specialized consumption. In sum, the material economy is increasingly driven by the cultural economy in the sphere of consumption.

If consumption is becoming specialized, then shorter production runs of a given item will follow. Thus individuals and firms must shift to more flexible production methods, which also entails a greater role for the cultural in the economic life. That is, production must become more *design*-intensive. Compare, for example, the US and Japanese automobile industries. For a given volume of sales at any one time, the Japanese industry manufactures four times as many different models as the American. Further, the average life of a given model is twice as long in the United States as in Japan (*Economist* 1990: 15, 100). In order to market such specialized products, Japanese industry must produce flexibly. In plain terms, it must *innovate* eight times as quickly as American industry. This design intensivity entails an increasing implication of the scientific field in the economic field, so that real economic production comes increasingly to resemble symbolic production.

What about the literal production of culture itself, in television, film, recording, publishing, and advertising? Under Bourdieu's influence, one might propound the parallel thesis that the economic sphere is coming increasingly to resemble the cultural. There is considerable truth value in this sort of claim. Major companies typically release some 1,000 recordings per year. This means, if we compare with the auto industry, some 1,000 new "models" per year. The lifetime of an American car model is typically some eight billion dollars in sales volume, of a Japanese model some one billion dollars, and of a hit disk some twenty-five *million* (Lash and Urry forthcoming). That is, *ceteris paribus*, the US car industry must innovate each time it achieves eight billion dollars in sales, the Japanese after one billion dollars, and the record company after twenty-five million dollars. Or, *ceteris paribus*, the recording industry must innovate forty times as quickly as the Japanese auto industry and 320 times as quickly as the US car sector.

This means incredibly high levels of design intensivity. In the recording industry such high levels of innovation are necessary that the costs of design, or recording costs, are much higher than those of the actual production – that is, the creation of compact disks or tapes in the company's plants. The main outlay of resources in the recording industry – and this is also true in the other culture industries – is thus for the equivalent of research and development, not for direct production. Other expanding economic sectors, such as software and business and finance services, also provide short batches of very specialized products and hence must be innovation-intensive, design-intensive, and research and development-intensive, just like the culture industries. But the crucial point is that whereas previously the production of culture was trapped in the logic of the commodification of the manufacturing sector, now the increased levels of innovation necessitated for post-Fordist accumulation in manufacturing itself necessitates that it must follow the design-intensive logic of the culture sector.

CONCLUSIONS

The value of Bourdieu's cultural economy can be well assessed, perhaps, by comparison with Althusser's conceptions. Even today Althusserian assumptions about structure and ideology – even if they now come to us through Gramscian and Foucaultian prisms – are a leading current in culture studies. The Althusserians have spoken of "practices" as an effect of the structures; yet they have paid considerable lip service to these practices once constituted. But for concrete description of such "theoretical," "ideological," "political" and "economic" practices the Althusserians have had little time. Bourdieu's cultural economy, by contrast, actually enables the account of empirical practices in the structures (that is, fields). That is, in the latter you do not have some abstract invocation of capitalist class and proletarian practices, but an account of the day-to-day practices of professionals, consumers from the various classes and class fractions, and of concrete collective struggles. In effect Bourdieu's cultural economy gives us a structuralism that simultaneously allows space for and accounts for agency.

The closest that Althusser himself comes to a notion of agency is in the famous "Ideological state apparatuses" article, in which ideology is an imaginary relationship of the subject to his or her real conditions of existence. This statement has been the subject of endless speculation and spilled ink. The problem is that it gives us an "empty" notion of agency. Agency itself is not opened up in any kind of complexity. Jon Elster – coming into contact with the Althusserian ambiance in the Paris of his formative years – developed, partly in reaction to this experience, one of today's most influential sociologies of action. Yet Elster's notion of agency is uncritically instrumentally rational and "decisionistic"; in brief, it is just as empty as Althusserian agency. Bourdieu's cultural economy, by welcome contrast, opens up the notion of agency with the perceptions, classifications, and dispositions of the habitus. On one side the habitus acts as cultural capital enabling the reception of certain types of symbolic goods. On the other side (as dispositions) it acts as cultural capital enabling the production of symbolic goods. Thus Bourdieu's cultural economy also gives us an action theory in which agency itself is "full" and structured.

Yet this very same cultural economy is also responsible for a few things that many of us may not find agreeable. Insofar as it is a cultural economy, it has assumptions of instrumental rationality and an *ad hominem* view of reflexivity that tends to allow insufficient space for the development of rationality in political or intellectual practices. Insofar as it is a cultural economy, it tends to collapse a number of what should perhaps be considered as material or properly economic practices back into the cultural sphere, thereby falling a bit into the trap of sociological idealism. And through its notion of modernization, which assumes the strategic importance of the delimited fields (*champs restreints*) of symbolic production, it gives rise to an uncomfortable measure of elitism.

Once social change is taken on board, Bourdieu's vices become virtues. In the first half of this essay I criticized his notion of reflexivity for its implicit relativism and insufficient regard for rationality. In the second half I corrected this by reworking Bourdieu's notion of aesthetic-expressive reflexivity and arguing that this could provide a basis for a new sort of collectivity, a post-traditional *Gemeinschaft* necessary for collective action and rational social change in the context of today's decentralized politics of the new social movements. This reworking is valid only in the context of the study of social change.

Bourdieu's vice of "idealism" becomes a virtue as cultural economy comes increasingly to provide the driving force of real capital accumulation in today's innovation-intensive, "flexibly specialized" material economies and as practices in the manufacturing sector come increasingly to resemble those in the cultural sectors. Finally, Bourdieu's elitism was based on the autonomy of the cultural field from the social field. But these criticisms also will not be valid in a society in which the elites of the delimited fields are increasingly *becoming* the masses of the social field. Thus the political field no longer acts as an autonomous field in the case of the new social movements. No longer is it possible to contrast a reflexive avant-garde of the "political class" with the masses of new social movement members in the social class. The whole notion of avant-garde, as Alberto Melluci notes (1989: 119ff.), is disparaged by social movements. This is not so much in the sense that everybody now is part of the masses, but that all movement members are themselves part and parcel of reflexive avant-gardes. At the same time, the once-separate political sphere is metamorphosed. Its displacement is not from the state to the public sphere of civil society, but to the de- and re-composing of the most private and intimate of social relationships.

Finally, the autonomous fields and circuits of symbolic capital no longer dictate in an elitist manner to the lived space of the social field. But the cultural fields (and their practitioners) come to constitute the masses now working, retailing, and living in the remolded central areas of the world's cities. It is true that our transformed, gentrified central cities further accentuate already existing inegalitarianism; their built environment is too often in bad taste; they comprise asymmetrical power relations. But these power relations are not exercised from above through elites; rather, this symbolic violence is now immanent in the social field. As elites become masses, symbolic violence is now increasingly exercised from below.

My claim is that the real world has become increasingly like Bourdieu's theoretical world; that Bourdieu is right in terms of how things are, but wrong in *his* implicit claim that they have always been like this. The primacy of reproduction, the pessimism regarding social transformation that pervades Bourdieu's theory, also inhibits adequate reflexivity in the sociologist him or herself. Bourdieu's notion of reflexivity is vastly different from the views of Beck and Giddens discussed above, in its absence of a strong notion of change and its focus on the reflexivity of agents in the delimited, specialist fields and especially of our own reflexivity as sociologists. In both these senses Bourdieu's reflexivity seems to resemble much more that of eth-nomethodologists and sociologists of science.

Let us end by asking ourselves why Bourdieu's work has come to occupy such a central place since the late 1980s? We need not look very far for an answer. Today's situation can be described in terms of the newly perceived importance of consumption in relation to production, the increasing concern with our social formation as a symbol-wielding information society, the increasing cognizance of the massification of the previously elite cultural fields, and the enhanced recognition of the symbolic constitution of individual and collective identity. That is, Bourdieu's work is so central now because the real world has changed to a point at which it has come to agree with Bourdieu's world. And this cannot be said of the work of many other social theorists.

The trouble comes when one considers reflexivity in the very narrow sense of the sociologists of science associated with the "Strong Programme." For these analysts a theory is reflexive to the extent that it can be applied to itself. And it is this sort of reflexivity that is sorely lacking in Bourdieu's theory. That is, without a substantial notion of social change Bourdieu's theory cannot account for its own popularity and its own validity.

I have argued here for the heuristic value of Bourdieu's cultural economy. I have claimed that theoretical statements drawn from this model, which once had doubtful truth value with respect to the real social world, are becoming increasingly true in contemporary circumstances. I must in closing draw the conclusion that Bourdieu's theory has become true. However, without an adequate notion of social change, it cannot achieve sufficient reflexivity to account for why it is true.

NOTES

1 Bourdieu argues, however, that such a state of affairs tends not to impede but to promote "scientific progress." Why? First, because the competition between "priests" with "conservation" strategies and "prophets" with "subversion strategies" for scientific symbolic capital tends to encourage innovation. Second, because the inculcation of scientific cultural capital in the form of scientific method, used in an agents's own selfish interests, helps promote cross-control of result (1975: 32–4). Scientific truth, then, is relegated to the place of an unintended consequence of the instrumental (and not substantive) rationality of agents in the economy of scientific practice.

REFERENCES

Beck, U. 1986: *Risikogesellschaft, Auf dem Weg in eine andere Moderne.* Frankfurt am Main: Suhrkamp.

Boyer, R. (ed.) 1986: *La Flexibilité du travail en Europe.* Paris: Éditions la Découverte.

Durkheim, E. and Mauss, M. 1969: De quelques formes primitives de la classification, contribution a l'étude des représentations collectives. In M. Mauss, *Oeuvres*, Vol. 2: *Représentations collectives et diversité des civilisations*, Paris: Éditions de Minuit, 13–89.

Economist 1990: Apr., pp. 15, 100.

Eder, K. 1988: *Die Vergesellschaftung der Natur.* Frankfurt am Main: Suhrkamp.

Giddens, A. 1990: *The Consequences of Modernity.* Cambridge: Polity.

Gouldner, Alvin W. 1971: *The Coming Crisis of Western Sociology.* New York: Avon.

Lash, S. and Urry, J. (forthcoming): *After Organized Capitalism.* London: Sage.

Leborgne, D. and Lipietz, A. 1990: Fallacies and open issues about post-Fordism. Paper read at conference on Pathways to Industrialization and Regional Development in the 1990s, Lake Arrowhead, UCLA, 14–18 Mar.

Melluci, A. 1989: *Nomads of the Present.* London: Radius.

Piore, M. and Sabel, C. 1984: *The Second Industrial Divide.* New York: Basic Books.

Runciman, W. G. 1966: *Relative Deprivation and Social Justice.* London: Routledge.

Schluchter, W. 1987: Weber's sociology of rationalism and typology of religious rejections of the world. In S. Whimster and S. Lash (eds), *Max Weber, Rationality and Modernity*, London: Allen & Unwin, 92–117.

Whimster, S. and Lash, S. 1987: Introduction to *Max Weber, Rationality and Modernity*, London: Allen & Unwin, 1–34.

Wolff, K. 1959: *From Max Weber.* New York: Oxford University Press.

11

Social Theory as Habitus

Rogers Brubaker

A volume on the social theory of Pierre Bourdieu is not without its incongruities and its risks, not least because it may engender just the sort of "theoretical theory" that Bourdieu has so sharply criticized (1985a: 11). How, in this social setting, can one resist the temptation to "talk about concepts" instead of "making them work" (1979c: 3)?[1]

Bourdieu himself furnishes a clue, suggesting a way in which one can talk about concepts *by* making them work. Characterizing scientific theory as a "modus operandi which directs and organizes . . . scientific practice" (1985a: 12), he invites us, in effect, to substitute a dispositional for a logocentric understanding of theory – to *treat theory as habitus*. I want to follow up this suggestion by discussing Bourdieu's own theory in this way, treating it as a particular sociological habitus. Thinking of theory as habitus permits one to talk about Bourdieu's concepts by applying them reflexively to themselves, to examine his schemes of sociological vision with the aid of those same schemes, and to turn his sociological habitus back on itself in a manner fully consistent with his program for a reflexive sociology.

The first section below argues in general terms for a practical and dispositional, rather than a purely logical and propositional, approach to social theory. The second argues that a theoreticist, logocentric approach is particularly ill suited to Bourdieu's work. The third analyzes Bourdieu's sociological habitus – the core intellectual dispositions that inform and organize his work. The concluding section raises a set of critical questions about the sociological habitus in general and Bourdieu's sociological habitus in particular.

SOCIAL THEORY AND SOCIOLOGICAL HABITUS

What are we talking about when we talk about social or sociological "theory"? This, of course, is a heatedly contested question; for the prestige that attaches to "theoretical" work generates social struggles to impose and institutionalize particular definitions of the sort of work that can legitimately pretend to this dignity. Yet the struggles to define what counts as theory should not obscure the wide agreement among sociologists about what theory is supposed to *do*: namely, to "inform" research.

What is it about theory that enables it to inform research? This is not at all clear from most discussions of sociological or, more generally, scientific theory. These tend to be framed in *logical* terms, characterizing theory as a structure of logical entities (concepts, variables, axioms, propositions, and so forth) possessing certain logical properties (generality, abstractness, precision, and so on) and standing in certain logical relations with one another (consistency, contradiction, implication, and the rest), on which one performs certain logical operations (deduction, generalization, specification, codification, and so on). Such logocentric discussions of theory cannot illuminate the practical directive and generative power that theory is supposed to have. The practical efficacy of theory, I think, is better captured in the *sociological* terms suggested by Bourdieu. As a social practice like others, social research is governed and informed by internalized dispositions, not by codified propositions,[2] by the practical logic of the habitus, not by the theoretical logic set forth in treatises and textbooks.[3]

Every sociological practice, theoretical or empirical, is governed and regulated by a particular sociological habitus, a particular sociological *sens pratique*, a particular "feel for the scientific game" (1989b: 5; cf. Bourdieu and Wacquant 1992: 223). Like any other habitus, the sociological habitus is a "system of lasting, transposable dispositions." Like any other habitus, this system of dispositions "functions . . . as a matrix of perceptions, appreciations, and actions." Like any other habitus, it can engender an infinite variety of practices 'thanks to analogical transfers of schemes' from one task to another (1977c: 82–3). It is the sociological habitus that generates the "regulated improvisation" (p. 79) of sociological perceptions and operations through which one grasps the world as a sociologist. It is the habitus that determines the kinds of problems that are posed, the kinds of explanations that are offered, and the kinds of instruments (conceptual, methodological, statistical) that are employed. More important, the habitus determines the *manner* in which problems are posed, explanations constructed, and instruments employed.

To which it may be objected: isn't this an instance of what Giovanni Sartori calls "conceptual stretching" (1970: 1034)? Doesn't it push the concept of habitus beyond its intended domain of application? Bourdieu himself, after all, treats the habitus as one mode of regulation of practice among others, existing "alongside the explicit norm or the rational calculation" (1987a: 94; cf. 1980c: 89). The distinctiveness of the habitus, as a *particular* mode of the regulation of practice, is that it generates practices in an unconscious, unintentional manner; it is a "modus operandi that is not consciously mastered," a "spontaneity with neither consciousness nor will" (1980c: 95, 94). As such, the habitus has a particularly important regulative role "in societies where few things are codified" (1987a: 94); it is, by implication, less important in rationalized, codified, highly differentiated societies. How, then, can the habitus be said to govern scientific research, with its requisite conscious self-monitoring and rational self-scrutiny? Doesn't Bourdieu himself expound, in *Le Métier de sociologue* (Bourdieu *et al.* 1968), a rationalist philosophy of science founded on the hyper-rationalist, hyper-conscious notion of epistemological vigilance? What place can there be in science for the unconscious, unwilled strategies of the habitus?

This objection rests on a double misunderstanding. In the first place, it rests on a misreading of *Le Métier de sociologue.* Bourdieu would not write this book today, at least not in the same way.[4] Still, the epistemological rationalism expounded in it not something disembodied or free-floating. Scientific rationality does not depend on a hyper-rationalist "pure knowing subject." Logical control and epistemological vigilance are sociologically grounded; they are embedded in institutions and embodied in dispositions. They depend on the institutionalization of certain patterns of criticism (Bourdieu *et al.* 1968: 95, 102–5) and on the internalization of certain habits of thought (p. 16). And these institutionally supported, internalized habits of thought – habits of reflexive self-monitoring, above all – are nothing other than a particular intellectual habitus.

The second misunderstanding concerns the domain of application of the concept of habitus. To treat the habitus as engendering practices in an unconscious and unintentional manner is not to limit its domain of applicability to undifferentiated and unrationalized regions of social space and time.[5] All sorts of specialized practices are regulated by incorporated dispositions. This is most immediately evident in the case of activities requiring trained bodily movements: playing a musical instrument, dancing, athletic activity of any kind,[6] typing, driving, or skilled manual work. But it is no less the case for activities requiring the manipulation of symbols – think of proofreading, writing, or constructing geometric proofs. Persons skilled in any of these activities will not carry them out in a sequence of consciously deliberated and intended moves. To do so would be impossibly inefficient. The proofreader develops an "eye" for errors, the writer an "ear" for rhythm and diction, the geometer a "feel" for proofs.

Nor is it otherwise for the sociologist. One could, indeed, construct a dispositional definition of sociology (as distinguished from a credentialist or a "territorial" definition) by specifying a set of dispositions that structure sociological perception and practice – for instance, the disposition to uncover the mechanisms that are responsible for producing an observed order, to treat as problematic what others would take for granted, to attend to clues that others would miss, to think relationally and comparatively, to perceive structured patterns amidst apparently disorderly variation, and so on. Moreover, it is not only sociological perception that is governed by the ingrained dispositions of the sociological habitus, but even, to a considerable extent, the sort of general and abstract thinking called theorizing.

This is not to say that sociological work is or ought to be governed by the habitus alone. Quite the contrary: the "intentionless invention" of the habitus is and must be complemented, controlled, and corrected by other regulative techniques and mechanisms. This control occurs in and through writing. As an objectified product of the habitus, written (or otherwise recorded) work is amenable to modes of inspection and control that the habitus itself and its nonobjectified products necessarily escape. Writing makes it possible to "return to what one has said," and this in turn makes possible the "confrontation of successive moments of discourse" that is the basis for all "logical control." "Logic is always conquered against chronology. . . . Writing *synchronizes* . . . [and thus] makes it possible to seize in a single glance, that is, simultaneously, the successive moments of practices which were protected against logic by the flow of time" (1987a: 100). Control is further enhanced through publication. Codified, public writing is a particularly effective vehicle of social and logical control. To codify is to institute "explicit normativity," to "transform a practical scheme into a linguistic code," to makes things "simple, clear, communicable" (pp. 98, 100, 101).[7]

Writing thus permits the social and logical control of sociological work. Yet this social and logical control itself has a dispositional, as well as a technical and institutional, base. Writing – in particular, the condensed and codified writing that comprises theories, or what Merton calls "analytical paradigms" – makes logical control possible by permitting the "simultaneous inspection of all terms entering into the analysis" (Merton 1967:70). But the effective exercise of this control will depend on patterns of institutionalized criticism within the scientific field and on dispositions – in particular, what Bourdieu calls the "critical or reflective disposition" (1987a: 27). The social and logical control of the sociological habitus, in other words, must be built into that habitus itself. If reflexivity distinguishes science from other practices, this is in part because it distinguishes the scientific habitus from other habituses. Reflexivity can and should be incorporated into the habitus, in the form of a disposition to monitor its own productions and to grasp its own principles of production.[8] The reflective regulation of the unconscious workings of the habitus, in short, can be inculcated as part of the habitus. Criticism – and the growth of knowledge – has a dispositional, as well as an institutional, anchorage.

READING BOURDIEU: MODES OF APPROPRIATION OF
SOCIOLOGICAL THEORY

What implications does this have for the way in which one reads, or ought to read, the sociological work of Bourdieu? Persons with access to Bourdieu's atelier or his seminar room are structurally disposed to come to terms with that work in a *practical* manner. They are likely, that is, to appropriate his work by appropriating to some extent and in some manner the dispositions that produced it, by undergoing a partial professional resocialization, by acquiring a partly restructured sociological habitus. This practical mode of appropriation corresponds to Bourdieu's pedagogy[9] and propaganda,[10] to his efforts to inculcate and propagate a particular way of sociological thinking, a particular sociological habitus.

But those of us without access to the atelier or the seminar room, confronted with certain published texts, with certain objectified products of his sociological habitus, but not with the mode of work that produced them, are structurally disposed to come to terms with the work in a more *theoretical* manner (in the ordinary, logocentric sense of that term). This holds for my own earlier review of Bourdieu's work (Brubaker 1985). That paper set forth the logical structure and conceptual armamentarium of the systematic meta-theory that, I argued, informed all Bourdieu's work; it showed how these meta-theoretical notions were employed in empirical analyses; and it pointed up some ambiguities in their application. My account was not mistaken in its content, but it was mistaken, I now believe, in its perspective. Its reading of Bourdieu's work, I would now say, was too literal, too logical, too theoretical, too sociologically naive – too respectful, I would almost say, of the texts, endowing them with a dignity and a definitiveness that they were not intended to possess.

Bourdieu's work, it now seems to me, is particularly ill suited to a conceptualist, theoretical, logocentric reading, one that treats it as the bearer of a set of logically interconnected propositions framed in terms of precise, unambiguous concepts. In the first place, the core concepts are not – and are not supposed to be – precise and unambiguous.[11] When I first encountered Bourdieu's work, I collected a dozen or so definitions – or what I took to be definitions – of "habitus" in an attempt to pin down its precise meaning. Only later did I realize that the attempt was not only vain but misdirected, that Bourdieu was not in fact defining[12] but rather was characterizing the concept of habitus in a variety of ways in order to communicate a certain theoretical stance or posture, to designate – and inculcate – a certain sociological disposition, a certain way of looking at the world. The same could be said of the other fundamental concepts: interest, capital, strategy, field, and so forth.

In the second place, Bourdieu's texts are not the products of a pure scientific reason; they are products – and instruments – of particular intellectual strategies and struggles. Hence they must be read in relation to the intellectual fields in and for which they were produced and the intellectual strategies that define Bourdieu's position and trajectory in those fields. The emphases vary considerably from text to text, depending on the particular field or fields in which the text is situated and the structure of those fields at the time the text was written. Reading Bourdieu, then, one must correct for field-specific emphases, biases, even polemics. Bourdieu is quite forthright about this last. Because sociology must routinely contend with false but powerfully entrenched beliefs, it may be necessary to exaggerate or ironize or polemicize in order to "arouse the reader from his doxic slumber" (1987a: 68); it may be necessary to "employ symbolic violence against symbolic violence" in order to "break the circle of belief" (*Actes* 1 [1975]: 3).[13]

A purely theoretical reading of Bourdieu, finally, mistakes the point and purpose of his texts. Their point is not simply to interpret the world; it is to change the world, by changing the way in which we – in the first instance, other social scientists – see it. Since the world is in part a "world of will and representation," since "politics is essentially an affair of words" (1987a: 69), since class struggles increasingly take the form of classification struggles (1984), since the social world is "increasingly inhabited by reified sociology" (1987a: 69), to alter the principles of sociological vision of the social world is to alter that world itself. Bourdieu's texts are not simply an objectified trace of his way of thinking and seeing; they are among the instruments deployed as part of a practical strategy that aims at altering our way of thinking and seeing. Products of his intellectual habitus, they are intended to have an effect on ours. Hence Bourdieu's elaborate attempts to control, through a variety of editorial, syntactical, and rhetorical devices, the manner in which we read. A purely theoretical reading fails to capture this practical, strategic dimension of Bourdieu's writing. It fails to recognize that Bourdieu deploys concepts and propositions not simply in order to state things about the world, but in order to do things to our vision of it; that his texts have – and are intended to have – not only locutionary meaning and illocutionary force but perlocutionary consequences (cf. Austin 1975); that their fundamental aim is to transform our mode of sociological vision. Sociology, Bourdieu notes, is only apparently exoteric: it is in fact an "esoteric science – the initiation is very slow and requires a true conversion of one's whole vision of the world" (1987a: 68). All sociologists, then, are converts, proselytes; and the point of Bourdieu's work is to convert, to proselytize. It is not simply in the classroom or on the lecture circuit but also in and through his published texts that Bourdieu pursues his sociological pedagogy, propaganda, and proselytism, all of which are part of the same practical project of inculcating a set of thinking tools, a manner of grasping the world sociologically.

But there is a more fundamental point, one that is independent of the respects in which Bourdieu's work is ill suited to a theoretical reading. If sociological work is indeed governed by practical dispositions rather than by theoretical logic, then there is no point in a purely theoretical reading of Bourdieu or anyone else. The only sociologically valuable reading of sociological work is a practical reading, one that enables us to appropriate – to make our own and make our own use of – the sociological habitus that produced it. Grasping the logic of a theory cannot help us do sociology or grasp the world sociologically. The only sociologically valuable consumption is productive consumption; and consumption will be productive only if we grasp and appropriate the dispositions that have produced what we are consuming.

Bourdieu himself is explicit on this point. The practice of productive consumption, he notes, is what makes the enterprise of social theory a cumulative one. Referring to the way in which his use of certain key concepts grew out of his critical reading in the sociological tradition, he notes that

> the elaboration and the transmission of effective and fertile methods of thinking have nothing to do with the flow of "ideas" such as one normally imagines it. . . . To understand scientific works, which unlike theoretical texts, call forth practical application and not contemplation, . . . one has to make the way of thinking which is expressed [in such works] function practically à propos a different object, to reactivate it in a new act of production which is as inventive and as original as the initial act. . . . That is why . . . the active appropriation of a mode of scientific thought is as difficult and as rare . . . as its initial elaboration. (1985a: 15–16)

If sociology is to be a cumulative enterprise, despite its relatively uncodified state, it is necessary to "master practically, by incorporating as an habitus" the "thinking tools" available in the sociological tradition (1985a: 16, 12). Exactly the same thing can be said of Bourdieu's own work: the reader should aim to master practically, to incorporate into his or her habitus, the thinking tools that Bourdieu makes available in the form of concepts, propositions, and theories.

It goes without saying – or it ought to go without saying, but probably doesn't, in view of the accusations of "totalitarian" sociology or "intellectual terrorism" to which Bourdieu has been subjected – that the practical appropriation is not an uncritical one. The effort "to actively reproduce the best products of past thinkers by putting into use the instruments of production which they have left behind" necessarily involves both "continuity and rupture" (1985a: 14). Just as Bourdieu is fond of describing his relation with "canonical" theorists in terms of "thinking with a thinker against that thinker,"[14] so too we can and should think with Bourdieu against Bourdieu. But we can do this only by appropriating his sociological dispositions, his thinking tools, making them ours and making our own use of them, testing in practice their practical productivity along with dispositions and thinking tools appropriated from other sources.

BOURDIEU'S SOCIOLOGICAL HABITUS

Granted that sociological work is regulated by practical dispositions, not by codified propositions, and that the best reading (critical reading included) of Bourdieu's work must be a practical, sociologically productive one, how can one best undertake such a practical, productive reading? Confronted with certain texts, certain objectified products of Bourdieu's sociological habitus, how can one go about appropriating the dispositions that informed them? How can one proceed from texts to habitus, from the *opus operatum* to the *modus operandi*?[15]

This can best be done, I want to argue, by reading concepts as that is, by treating the concepts, propositions, and theories set forth in his works not, in the first instance, as bearers of logical properties and objects of logical operations, but as designators of particular intellectual habits or sets of habits. The more general and abstract the concept or proposition, the more important it is to read it in this dispositional manner. All of Bourdieu's "meta-theory" – all general propositions about structures, habitus, practice, capital, field, and so on – must be read in this manner.

General concepts and propositions designate dispositions to see and interpret and construct the social world through certain schemes of appreciation and action. That these are schemes of intellectual action as well as schemes of appreciation is worth underscoring; the sociological habitus includes not only dispositions to see the social world in particular ways, but dispositions to *act intellectually* in particular ways, dispositions to perform certain intellectual operations on the world, to collect and utilize data in particular ways, for example, or to perform particular sorts of thought experiments. Also worth underscoring is that it is not only concepts and propositions, considered individually, that designate dispositions. Even theories in the usual sense – intricate and extended sets of logically interconnected propositions – designate dispositions to perform certain systematically linked sets of scientific operations, as well as institutionalized programs for carrying out such operations. A sociological "theory," then, designates an *internalized and institutionalized* scheme of scientific perceptions and scientific operations. And, on the highest level of generality, Bourdieu's universal theory of practice is best interpreted as a compact, objectified, public designator of his basic intellectual habitus.

Treating concepts and theories as designators of sociological dispositions permits us to move from text to habitus, from Bourdieu's *opus operatum* to his *modus operandi*. Consider, for example, the central concepts of habitus and field. The concept of habitus designates the *disposition to think in dispositional terms*, – the disposition to think of social practices as engendered and regulated by incorporated, generalized, transposable dispositions rather than by rules or norms (as in much structuralist and functionalist social theory) or by conscious intentions, meanings, or calculations (as in much intentionalist social theory, including both phenomenological and rational-action theory).

To understand the sorts of sociological practices that this sociological disposition engenders and regulates, to appraise its value and limitations as a way of thinking, it may be useful to consider the social genesis of the concept of habitus. This is not a matter of conceptual genealogy (1985a: 12), not a matter of identifying conceptual progenitors and more or less distant conceptual cousins; it is a sociological, not a conceptual question. As such, it can be addressed with the help of the very thinking tools whose social genesis we wish to analyze. The concepts of habitus and field can be used to analyze their own sociogenesis.[17]

Like other professional dispositions, acquired relatively late in life, the disposition to think in dispositional terms can be thought of as the joint product of (1) certain prior dispositions and (2) the state and structure of certain intellectual fields. An intellectual or scientific habitus is always overlaid on, without superseding, earlier and more fundamental habituses. Intellectual and scientific dispositions are transformations, not simple successors, of anterior dispositions (cf. 1977c: 86–7). Bourdieu's sociological habitus, including specifically the concept of habitus, the disposition to think in dispositional terms, is a transformation of a prior ethnological, philosophical, and general intellectual habitus. One key disposition, common to Bourdieu's ethnological and general intellectual habitus, is the disposition to see the social world as structured by fundamental binary oppositions, or polarities – dominant and dominated, noble and base, male and female, right and left, inside and outside, and the like – and the corresponding disposition to see the intellectual world as structured by similar bipolar oppositions. Another is the disposition to transcend or overcome these basic structuring oppositions. This disposition finds political expression but also – and this is what concerns me here – intellectual expression. Thus the concept of habitus – or the disposition it designates – is a manner of thinking that enables Bourdieu to transcend a set of basic intellectual oppositions: between structure and action, determinism and freedom, reproduction and transformation, society and individual, and especially, encompassing all of the others, objectivism and subjectivism.

If Bourdieu could plausibly construe the French intellectual field as structured, and social theory as hampered, by such oppositions, this was not only because his penchant for binary oppositions disposed him to such a reading; it was also because the intellectual field was in fact well suited to such a reading. It is not only to Bourdieu's general intellectual dispositions that one must look to explain the development of his sociological habitus; it is also to the synchronization of his formation as a

sociologist with certain states and transformations of the French
intellectual field.

Born in 1930, Bourdieu came of intellectual age when phenomenology
and existentialism, dominant in the immediate postwar years, were being
challenged by structuralism, Sartre by Lévi-Strauss, the unconditional
and unconditioned freedom of the subject by the unconscious determinism of the structure.[18] It is scarcely surprising that Bourdieu,
generalizing from this confrontation in the French intellectual field and
its analogs elsewhere, should interpret them as instances of a fundamental, pervasive opposition between subjectivism and objectivism.

Although Bourdieu adopted the critical posture of the "structuralist
generation" vis-à-vis existentialism, phenomenology, "humanism," and
"political moralism" (1987a: 14), and although his early ethnographic
studies were those of a "happy structuralist" (1980c: 22), he became
disenchanted with the faddish success of structuralism and increasingly
critical of its "realism of the structure" and its correlative exclusion of
active, inventive agents from social explanation. In this context, the
notion of habitus could designate a posture of critical distance vis-à-vis
then triumphant structuralist thought *and* vis-à-vis the subjectivist
thought that structuralism had successfully challenged (1985a: 13; 1987a:
passim; 1980c: preface).[19]

Like the concept of habitus, the concept and theory of fields designate
a set of dispositions that regulate the sociological analysis of "modern,"
highly differentiated societies. These include (1) the disposition to seek
out as units of analysis neither total "societies" nor single institutions or
practices but "relatively autonomous social microcosms" governed by
"specific logics" (Wacquant 1989: 39, cf. Bourdieu 1987a: 91); (2) the
disposition to think "topologically," that is, to construct particular social
"spaces" (by defining their most important "dimensions") and to situate
the objects of study within those constructed spaces (1980b: 113–20); (3)
the disposition to think systematically, characterizing positions in such
constructed spaces not intrinsically, but in relation to the space of
possible positions and the distribution of actual occupied positions
(Bourdieu and Wacquant 1992: 224–35; Bourdieu 1988e: 153–8); (4) the
disposition to think comparatively, attending to structural properties and
relational patterns common to all fields but also to the specificities of
particular fields;[20] (5) the disposition to see all practices (particularly
those claiming to be disinterested) as *interested* practices, oriented (not
necessarily consciously) toward the accumulation, legitimation, per-
petuation, and reproduction of particular forms of power or "capital";
and (6) the disposition to grasp the *specific logic* (the *Eigengesetzlichkeit*,
in Weberian terms) of particular fields by specifying the field-specific

stakes, – the particular forms of interest, capital, or power, the pursuit of which constitutes the fundamental dynamic of all fields.

This sociological disposition set, like that designated by the concept of habitus, developed through the transformation and extension of anterior dispositions – above all, in this case, the quintessentially structuralist disposition to think in relational rather than substantialist terms.[21] If Bourdieu developed the dispositions designated by the concept of habitus in reaction to structuralist objectivism, he developed the dispositions designated by the concept of field by applying structuralist "relationalism."

The dispositional restructuring, the reorganization of intellectual habitus, that was involved in the gradual working out of field theory occurred in the context of a particular intellectual field – the field defined by the study of culture. Here again, Bourdieu's polarized vision of the intellectual world, his disposition to see it as fractured by fundamental binary oppositions, helped engender conceptual innovation. The study of culture, on Bourdieu's reading, was hampered by the opposition between "internal interpretation" and "external explication," between a "formalism born of the theorizing of an art which achieved a high degree of autonomy and a reductionism intent on directly relating artistic forms to social forms" (1985a: 16). Working out his own position through a sort of intellectual triangulation, defining his own perspective in critical opposition to two mutually exclusive one-sided alternatives, Bourdieu sought to grasp the social and "economic" dimension of cultural practices in a nonreductionist manner, to grasp the autonomous values, the *Eigengesetzlichkeit* of particular fields without sliding into idealism or internalist formalism.

QUESTIONS AND CRITICISMS

The reading of Bourdieu proposed here, which focusses on (and draws on) the sociological habitus that animates, generates, and regulates his work, suggests a number of questions and criticisms. Many of these cluster around five themes that I would like to explore in conclusion.

Homogeneity of habitus and collective sociological practice

For two decades, Bourdieu has sought to establish and institutionalize a collective sociological practice based on a shared habitus.[22] This institutionalization – crystallizing around the Centre de sociologie européene, Bourdieu's research seminar at the École des hautes études, and the journal *Actes de la recherche en sciences sociales* – has generated a great deal of research governed by sociological dispositions that bear a strong family resemblance, as Wittgenstein says, to those of Bourdieu himself.[23]

The "collective practice of the same modus operandi," Bourdieu notes, is "common in the more advanced sciences" (1985a: 12). And it is clear that it can enhance the productivity and cumulativity of sociological research. Yet is there not a correlative danger of epistemological closure? Bourdieu's own account of the economies and efficiencies made possible by shared habitus suggests that there is:

> The homogeneity of habitus is what . . . causes practices and works to be immediately intelligible and foreseeable, and hence taken for granted. [This permits one ordinarily to dispense] with close analysis of the nuances of another's practice and tacit or explicit inquiry ("What do you mean?") into his intentions. Automatic and impersonal, . . . ordinary practices lend themselves to an understanding no less automatic and impersonal. (1977c: 80)

This account, to be sure, pertains to the habitus in general. Yet it applies, I think, to the sociological habitus as well. Bourdieu himself warns of the "epistemological isolation induced by institutional compartmentalization" and of the "restricted exchange" within a "mutual admiration society" that may result. "While restricted exchange is well suited to the community of implicit presuppositions [that is, to a shared habitus], generalized exchange requires the multiplication and diversification of types of communication and in this way favors making explicit epistemological postulates" (Bourdieu *et al*. 1968: 104).

A shared habitus, then, is epistemologically ambivalent. It fosters cumulative research and enhances intellectual productivity, permitting one to apply conceptual instruments without reinventing them. Yet its products find confirmation and validation only too readily within the circle of sharers. Habituses are never entirely shared, of course. And this inevitably imperfect overlap is all to the good. Without shared dispositions, science as a social institution would be unthinkable. Yet effective criticism depends, I think, on a certain *heterogeneity* of habitus.

How can one best manage the tension between the sociological productivity and cumulativity on the one hand and the epistemological slackness or closure on the other that the taken-for-grantedness and automaticity of mutual understanding may produce among persons endowed with similar sociological dispositions? How can one combine the efficiencies and economies of restricted exchange (that is, exchange among persons with similar habituses) and the critical benefits of generalized, cross-habitus exchange? And, as a teacher, how can one inculcate sociological dispositions that have proved fruitful in one's own research along with the meta-disposition to appropriate such first-order dispositions in a critical manner?

Reflective and unreflective moments

The habitus governs practice in a subconscious, unreflective manner. The "practical mastery" of the schemes of perception and thought constitutive of the habitus "in no way implies symbolic mastery – i.e., conscious recognition and verbal expression of the procedures practically applied" (1977c: 88). Practical mastery may even be incompatible with conscious symbolic mastery: self-consciousness can inhibit or even destroy the practical efficacy of the habitus.

Yet conscious control and reflective self-monitoring are essential to the scientific enterprise. Such control, it was suggested above, must be both institutionalized and internalized. Institutionalized control depends on (limited) heterogeneity of habitus, on communication among persons whose sociological dispositions are sufficiently different to require conscious explication and self-conscious self-questioning (yet sufficiently similar to make communication possible). On what does internalized control depend?

The scientific habitus, it was suggested above, differs from other habituses in its reflexivity, in including a disposition to monitor its own productions and to grasp and make explicit its own principles of production. Yet it is not clear just what is involved practically in such a disposition. In what sense can we speak of an unconscious disposition towards conscious self-scrutiny, an unreflective disposition to reflect? How can scientists do what other agents cannot: consciously master their habitus without interfering with its workings – indeed, in a way that enhances its workings? We need a more fine-grained analysis of the scientific and in particular the sociological habitus – not simply an analysis of its objectifying posture, which Bourdieu has already undertaken, but an analysis of its capacity for self-monitoring and conscious self-mastery, for making the unconscious conscious. Having thoroughly "objectified the objectifiers," Bourdieu might now usefully "subjectify the objectifiers." He might analyze in greater detail the practical workings of the sociological habitus, focusing on the relation between reflective and unreflective moments.

The stratified habitus

The habitus is the "past which survives in the present," the "immanent law . . . laid down in each agent by his earliest upbringing." Although modified by subsequent experience, it is "dominated by the earliest experiences. The habitus acquired in the family underlies the structuring of school experiences, . . . and the habitus transformed by schooling, itself diversified, in turn underlies the structuring of all subsequent experiences" (1977c: 82, 81, 87).

The sociological habitus, then, is a tertiary or higher-order habitus, overlaid on, transforming without superseding, a primary familial and a secondary scholastic habitus. (In Bourdieu's case, the sociological habitus is overlaid on intervening philosophical and ethnological habituses as well.) One becomes a sociologist through a resocialization in which one's anterior intellectual dispositions are restructured but not erased.

Given the weight of familial and scholastic socialization and their persistence in the form of incorporated dispositions, what are the possibilities – and the limits – of the professional resocialization required for the making of sociologists? How are particular primary and secondary dispositions transformed and turned, for better or worse, to sociological use? What particular inflections do they lend to sociological vision? What sorts of school- inculcated dispositions survive in the sociological habitus? To what extent can one trace differences in sociological style back to differences in school-inculcated habitus? We need a *stratified* account of the sociological habitus, an account of the overlaying of professional on earlier habituses, an account, in particular, of the way in which anterior dispositions survive, even if in altered form, and continue to regulate professional practice.

Bourdieu's own sociological habitus owes many of its distinctive inflections to his prior scholastic, philosophical, and ethnological formation, and he has himself suggested in passing the importance of his temperament, his basic intellectual sympathies and antipathies, for his sociological formation (1987a: 37). Yet this mode of sociological self-analysis could be carried further. To what extent, for example, does Bourdieu's own sociological style reflect specific characteristics of French schooling, whose durable impress on French thought Bourdieu analyzed in his early article "Systems of education and systems of thought" (1971e)? To what extent does it reflect the intellectual training

Bourdieu received at "that great lay seminary," that "national school for the upper intelligentsia," the École normale supérieure? Sociological self-analysis, Bourdieu's own perspective would imply, requires the critical analysis of one's own sociological habitus, in particular the carry-overs from earlier habituses.

False antinomies

So central to Bourdieu's work is his assault on the "false antinomies" that structure social theory and sociological practice – his habit of identifying "epistemological couples," criticizing them as "false alternatives" and "transcending" them with his own theory – that this operation has become a sort of intellectual trademark. A rapid and unsystematic foray yielded the following examples of oppositions to be overcome: structure and history, reproduction and transformation, statics and dynamics, nomothetic and ideographic, micro and macro, structure and action, individual and society, sociology and ethnology, research and theory, determinism and liberty, conscious and unconscious, symbolic and material, culture and economy, teleology and mechanical causality, and, above all, subjectivism and objectivism, characterized in the opening sentence of *Le Sens pratique* as "the most fundamental and costly of all the oppositions which artificially divide social science." Bourdieu's entire work aims to "transcend the antagonism which sets these two modes of knowledge against each other and at the same time to preserve the insights gained by each position" (1980c: 43).

It is doubtless a major merit – perhaps the major merit – of Bourdieu's sociological habitus that it equips him to capture in a remarkably rich and subtle manner the "intrinsically dual" nature of social life, at once objective and subjective, external and internal, material and symbolic, patterned yet improvised, constrained yet (conditionally) free, and to integrate these dimensions or moments in his sociological accounts. Yet I am less convinced by Bourdieu's polarized readings of the field of social theory, by the intellectual triangulation through which he invariably characterizes and locates his own "constructivist structuralism." Applicable to every domain of sociological study and always involving the identification and criticism of equally one-sided objectivist and subjectivist approaches to a problem, this intellectual triangulation calls to mind the intellectual technique described by Lévi-Strauss in *Tristes tropiques* (in a passage quoted approvingly by Bourdieu himself as an "admirable ethnological description of the intellectual and linguistic patterns [that is, the intellectual habitus] transmitted – implicitly rather than explicitly – by French education"):

I began to learn how any problem, whether grave or trivial, can be resolved. The method never varies. First you establish the traditional "two views" of the question. You then put forward a commonsense justification of the one, only to refute it by the other. Finally you send them both packing by the use of a third interpretation, in which both the others are shown to be equally unsatisfactory. Certain verbal manoeuvers enable you . . . to line up the traditional "antitheses" as complementary aspects of a single reality: form and substance, content and container, appearance and reality, essence and existence, continuity and discontinuity. (Quoted in 1971e: 189)

To which might be added: subjective and objective. Does some such school-inculcated habit of thought survive, in sublimated form, among the dispositions that comprise Bourdieu's sociological habitus? And might it not engender, on occasion, rather strained and artificial readings of the sociological field, readings too exclusively governed by the idea of a fundamental opposition between subjectivism and objectivism? Might not such polarized readings exemplify the very sort of false antinomy that Bourdieu aims to transcend? Doubtless there are instances of hyper-subjectivist or hyper-objectivist social thought. But isn't a reading of social theory that gravitates too closely around the subjectivism–objectivism pole bound to be a procrustean one? To think of social thought as fundamentally structured by the subjectivism–objectivism tension may be sociologically productive: it may help engender useful sociological dispositions, thinking tools well suited to capturing objective and subjective moments in social life. But might not this useful and productive principle of sociological thinking be less useful as a principle of sociological reading?[24]

Systematicity and messiness

The schemes of perception, apprehension, and thought that Bourdieu internalized in the course of his philosophical and ethnological formation predispose him towards highly integrated, systematic sociological accounts, structured around correspondences, symmetries, homologies, fundamental oppositions, and "elementary forms." I do not mean to suggest that Bourdieu's schemes of sociological vision make no place for tension, conflict, dissonance, or transformation. Of course they do. But they dispose him to see tension and conflict in systematic terms, as structured by a small number of fundamental oppositions.

Bourdieu's intellectual habitus may incline him to read the social world, or at least some relatively messy social worlds, in too systematic a manner. Wittgenstein remarks somewhere that "mere description is so difficult because one believes that one needs to fill out the facts in order to understand them. It is as if one saw a screen with scattered colour-patches and said: the way they are here, they are unintelligible; they only make sense when one completes them into a shape. – Whereas I want to say: Here *is* the whole. (If you complete it, you falsify it.)" Now I am not advocating a hyper-empiricist descriptive sociology, dependent on the uncritical use of the "prenotions" of everyday life (Bourdieu *et al.* 1968: 27–9). Yet the bias towards systematicity that is, I think, built into Bourdieu's intellectual habitus does raise a cluster of related questions.

Do social worlds differ in their "messiness," and consequently in their suitability for systematic readings? Might certain schemes of thought and apprehension, well suited to bringing out the immanent systematicity of certain sorts of social worlds, be less well suited to others? Concretely: how well suited is Bourdieu's sociological habitus to the study of contemporary American society? Is it better suited, in some respects, to the study of French society? Or is it equally applicable to both? Bourdieu presents his social theory as a "universal anthropology" (1989b: 4). Yet is it in fact entirely domain-indifferent?

To raise these questions is not to invoke some postmodern fantasy of fluid and unstructured social space. Of course there are systematic oppositions among practices and dispositions in contemporary America as elsewhere. Yet Bourdieu himself acknowledges a specific and distinctive fluidity about American society, an "indeterminacy . . . in the relation between practices and positions" that accounts for the peculiar "intensity of symbolic strategies" of the sort anatomized by Goffman (Bourdieu 1987a: 159). I would like to hear more from Bourdieu on this and other cross-national differences and their implications for his sociological habitus. Bourdieu's style of sociological work is intrinsically comparative; but so far he has devoted much more attention to cross-field than to cross-national comparisons. It is to be hoped that the latter will receive more attention in the years to come.

NOTES

1 References are given in this chapter only for direct quotations, not for concepts borrowed from Bourdieu, since the whole chapter, which analyzes Bourdieu's work in terms drawn from that work, is an exercise in borrowing or appropriation. A series of conversations with Loïc Wacquant enabled me to try out, clarify, and extend the perspective adopted here.

Rogers Brubaker

2 This is not to say that there is no point in codification (see below). But
codified bodies of propositions are not, in the first instance, what governs or
informs research.
3 This point of view, long implicit in Bourdieu's work, has only recently
received the beginnings of an explicit elaboration (Bourdieu 1985a;
Bourdieu and Wacquant 1992, part 3. To the best of my knowledge, the
perspective has yet to be developed in detail, despite the rich indications in
these works.

Bourdieu's earlier discussions of theory and theorizing (especially Bourdieu *et al.* 1968 and Bourdieu 1968b) are much more theoreticist. The article
on structuralism, for instance, sets forth the "theory of sociological
knowledge," comprising "the system of principles and rules governing the
production of all [scientifically grounded] sociological propositions."
Sociological work, it argues, "is scientific only to the extent that it makes use
of the epistemological and logical principles of the theory of social
knowledge, that is, of sociological meta-science,' which, in view of the 'unity
of meta-science," are simply the "principles upon which all science, including
the science of man, is founded" (1968b: 681–2).

The philosophy of science outlined in this article is one to which Bourdieu
probably still subscribes. And the manner of sociological thinking it
recommends – emphasizing the need to think relationally – is one that
Bourdieu continues to advocate. Yet Bourdieu's manner of thinking and
talking about sociology has changed considerably: it has become less
theoreticist, more practical, more sociological. He talks less of "epistemological and logical principles," and more of sociological dispositions. Bourdieu's
account of sociological practice has become more consistent, more sociological over the years; sociological practice is increasingly treated as one practice
among others, governed largely by the sociological habitus. If, in *Le Métier
de sociologue*, principles are fundamental, while the sociological habitus is
treated as "the internalization of the principles of the theory of sociological
knowledge" (Bourdieu *et al.* 1968: 16), today it is the sociological habitus that
is fundamental, while theoretical principles are treated as one of its highly
specialized and objectified products.
4 He characterized the book in a recent interview as a "didactic, almost
scholastic book" (Bourdieu and Wacquant 1989: 5).
5 Bourdieu has underscored this point in a recent interview that merits
quotation at length, since, to the best of my knowledge, he has not made the
point so explicitly and emphatically elsewhere:

> The theory of the habitus imposes itself with particular evidence in cases of
> societies where the work of codification of practices has not gone very
> far. . . . But it also applies to highly differentiated societies. All of the
> relatively autonomous social worlds that I call fields – artistic field,
> scientific field, philosophical field, etc. – require of those who are
> engaged in them . . . a practical mastery of the laws of functioning of

this social world, a sense of the game, that is to say a habitus acquired by prior socialization or by the socialization that is exercised in the field itself. The most highly specialized fields, those most profoundly permeated by the requirements of scientific and technical reason, like the economic field or even the scientific field, presuppose and call forth quasi-bodily dispositions . . . a practical mastery of the tacit laws governing the field, a mastery of the categories of perception and appreciation that permit one to apprehend important problems, and so on. Various operations of the daily routine of science have as their principle the scientific habitus, about which one could say what Marx said about customary law: that it is obeyed by a sort of "instinct almost as blind and unconscious as that which produces certain movements of our bodies." (1989b: 4–6)

6 In "Program for a sociology of sport" (1988e) Bourdieu notes the scientific promise of the sociology of sport: "The problems raised by the teaching of bodily practices seem to me to comprise a number of theoretical questions of utmost importance, insofar as the social sciences endeavor to construct theories of actions that are for the most part generated at a subconscious level, and are learned by means of a silent, practical communication, from body to body as one might say" (p. 160).

7 The remarks just quoted are drawn not from an analysis of science but from a general discussion of codification. Their bearing on social and logical control in science reinforces the general point, central to Bourdieu's work and to this essay, that the sociological analysis of sociological practice, including theoretical practice, does not require special categories. Which is not to say that theoretical practice, or scientific practice in general, is not a distinctive sort of practice. It is, but its very distinctiveness can be captured in terms of categories applicable to all practice.

8 In the terms of Bachélard's "exponential" psychology, an extract from which Bourdieu includes in *Le Métier de sociologue* (Bourdieu *et al.* 1968: 117–20), we could distinguish habitus$_1$ from habitus$_2$, such that habitus$_2$ is a set of dispositions to regulate the products of habitus$_1$.

9 For the best statement of this pedagogy, see Bourdieu and Wacquant 1992: 221–4, the written version of Bourdieu's introductory remarks to his seminar at the École des hautes études en sciences sociales in October 1987 (my translation is from the original):

One can acquire the fundamental principles of a practice – and scientific practice is no exception – only by practicing it at the side of a sort of guide or trainer, who assures and reassures, who sets an example and makes corrections by specifying, in a particular situation, precepts directly applicable to a particular case. . . . The teaching of a *métier* . . . requires a pedagogy quite different from that required for the teaching of a body of knowledge. As one can easily see in societies without writing or schools (but this remains true in societies with schools and even in these schools), numerous modes of thought and action – and often the most vital – are transmitted from practice to practice, through practical modes of transmission, based on direct and lasting contact between the one who learns and the one who teaches ("do as I do"). . . . A very large part of the *métier* of the scientist is acquired through thoroughly practical modes of acquisition. . . . The sociologist who seeks to transmit a scientific habitus is more like a highly skilled sports trainer than a professor. . . . He talks little in terms of principles and general precepts. . . . He proceeds via practical indications, very similar in this respect to the trainer who mimes a movement ("in your place, I would do this") or by "corrections" made to practices as they are being undertaken, and conceived in a practical spirit ("I wouldn't ask that question, at least not in that form").

10 "Propaganda" in the technical, nonpejorative sense of the word. The effort to propagate and institutionalize a particular way of sociological thinking, to establish "the collective practice of the same modus operandi" (1985a: 12), is central to Bourdieu's scientific project. (See pp. 223 ff. below.)

11 For both "scientific and political reasons," Bourdieu goes so far as to explicitly repudiate the ideals of clarity and common sense (*bon sens*) (1987a: 67).

12 As Bourdieu put it in a recent interview with Loïc Wacquant, "I do not like definitions much" (Bourdieu and Wacquant 1989: 5).

13 Hence the rhetorical exploitation of oxymoron as in "symbolic violence," "cultural capital," etc.

14 I have often recalled, particularly with respect to my relation with Max Weber, that one can think with a thinker against that thinker. For example, I constructed the notion of field simultaneously *against* Weber and *with* Weber, by reflecting on his analysis of the relations between priest, prophet, and magician. . . . One can think with Marx against Marx or with Durkheim against Durkheim and also, of course, with Marx and Durkheim against Weber" (1987a: 63–4).

15 The point, of course, is not to talk about dispositions but to appropriate them, to master them practically. Yet to focus our talk on dispositions, instead of on theory, increases the chance of mastering them practically, especially since we can talk about Bourdieu's sociological habitus by appropriating parts of that habitus: we can use his concepts of habitus and field to talk about the dispositions that make up his sociological habitus.

16 The function of concepts, Bourdieu himself remarks, is "to designate, in stenographic manner, within the research procedure, a theoretical stance, a principle of methodological choices, negative as well as positive" (1985a: 12).

17 Thus Bourdieu notes that his initial formulations of the concept of habitus "were the product not of a theoretical calculation . . . but of a practical strategy of a scientific habitus, a kind of 'feel' for the game which does not need to calculate in order to find its direction and place" (1985a: 14; cf. 1987a: 29–30).

18 See the long preface to *Le Sens pratique* (1980c) and "Fieldwork in philosophy," in *Choses dites* (1987a).

19 Bourdieu tends to locate himself in intellectual space through a characteristic sort of intellectual triangulation, almost always representing his position as equidistant from two other mutually exclusive intellectual positions.

20 Thus Bourdieu suggests that all fields (e.g. the academic field, the artistic field, the economic field, even the encompassing, higher-order "field of power") have the same "chiastic" structure, based on the cross-cutting of economic and cultural principles of domination (1989c:383). Yet each field also has its distinctive logic, its specific stakes.

21 The "essential novelty" of structuralism was to "introduce into the social sciences the structural method, or, more simply, the relational way of thinking that, breaking with the substantialist way of thinking, leads one to characterize every element by the relations that unite it to the other elements in a system, and from which each element gets its meaning and its function" (1980c: 11). For an extended account, see "Structuralism and the theory of sociological knowledge" (1968b).

22 The collective dimension of Bourdieu's own work has been insufficiently remarked. It is a striking fact that, of Bourdieu's first ten books, all but the very first, a slim textbook on Algeria, were written in collaboration with one or more co-authors.

23 Loïc Wacquant has compiled a useful list of works drawing on Bourdieu's theory and published in *Actes de la recherche en sciences sociales*. See Appendix 2 to Bourdieu and Wacquant 1992.

24 To contrast, e.g., the "idealized and naively irenic vision" of Merton with the "reductionist and naively cynical vision" of the exponents of the Strong Program in the sociology of science, as Bourdieu has done in a recent article, is to give a rather reductionist reading of the field of the sociology of science. It may be an intellectually productive reading; it may encourage Bourdieu to develop intellectual tools for capturing the intrinsic duality of science as a social activity. Yet it is simply not the case that Merton "omits to raise the question of the relation between, on the one hand, the ideal values proclaimed by the 'scientific community' . . . and the norms which it professes . . . and, on the other hand, the social structure of the scientific universe, the mechanisms which tend to assure 'control' and communication, evaluation and reward, recruitment and training" (1990a: 298). The point of Merton's work in the sociology of science, it seems to me, is precisely to pose this question: Bourdieu has in fact given a rather good resumé of the central tendency of Merton's sociology of science.

REFERENCES

Austin, J. L. 1975: *How to Do Things with Words*, 2nd edn. Cambridge, Mass.: Harvard University Press.
Brubaker, Rogers 1985: Rethinking classical theory : the sociological vision of Pierre Bourdieu. *Theory and Society*, 14, 745–75.

Merton, Robert K. 1967: *On Theoretical Sociology*. New York: Free Press.

Sartori, Giovanni 1970: Concept misinformation in comparative politics. *American Political Science Review* 64, no. 4 (Dec.), 1033–53.

Wacquant, Loïc 1989: Toward a reflexive sociology: a workshop with Pierre Bourdieu. *Sociological Theory*, 7, 26–63.

12

Bourdieu in America: Notes on the Transatlantic Importation of Social Theory

Loïc J. D. Wacquant

If it is true that "the meaning of a work (artistic, literary, philosophical, etc.) changes automatically with each change in the field within which it is situated for the spectator or reader" (Bourdieu 1983a: 313), then proper understanding of any given author calls for a double work of elucidation: of his or her ideas and of the intellectual universes in which these come to circulate. It requires that we decode the author's mental space – that is, the categories and postulates that undergird his or her way of thinking and substantive theories – and also that we attain some knowledge of the scholarly space in which his or her writings become inserted.

This twofold hermeneutic is particularly necessary in the case of the international export of social theory. The transatlantic journey of the work of Pierre Bourdieu is a good case in point. I have attempted elsewhere to explicate the internal economy and intellectual roots of Bourdieu's work (Wacquant 1992), arguing that it is best understood as a *generative anthropology of power with special emphasis on its symbolic dimension* – that is, on the mechanisms that mask and help perpetuate domination by misrepresenting it, to those who wield it no less than to those who bear it. This enterprise is advanced by means of a generalized method (a limited set of concepts, problems, and analytical procedures for solving them and for comparing and linking solutions) that Bourdieu applies to a variety of objects across an unusually wide range of empirical

I would like to thank David Stark, William Rogers Brubaker, Craig Calhoun, Randall Collins, Paul DiMaggio, David Laitin, and Don Levine for their critical comments and suggestions on an earlier version of this chapter, as well as the participants in the conference whose collective and individual reactions provided an excellent test *in vivo* for some of the propositions it puts forth and for which I alone bear responsibility.

domains. The distinctiveness of this method resides in its relational and reflexive character. Neither individualistic nor holistic, Bourdieu's theoretical approach proceeds from a thoroughgoing *relationalism* which grasps both objective and subjective reality in the form of mutually interpenetrating systems of relations. All three of his core theoretical notions – habitus, capital, and field – are designed to capture the fundamentally recursive and relational nature of social life. Together, they enable Bourdieu to break out of the two homological antinomies of "micro" and "macro" levels of analysis and structure versus agency that presently polarize much social theorizing and to embark on a grounded search for the immanent logic of social action. Bourdieu's relationalism also lies behind his insistence that social analysts turn the instruments of their science back on themselves in a continual effort to uncover everything that their point of view on social reality owes to their place in it, including the place they occupy in the specific order of the intellectual microcosm. *Epistemic reflexivity* – the inclusion, at the heart of a theory of society and knowledge, of a theory of intellectual practice and of its inherent limitations – is for Bourdieu a *sine qua non* of the sociological method, for it alone allows us to construct scientific objects that do not suffer from the intellectualist bias which defines the scholarly gaze.

In this chapter, I want to complement the explication of the conceptual and theoretical architecture of Bourdieu's work further advanced in this volume by critically surveying its reception in America and (secondarily) Great Britain.[1] My purpose is not to "certify" readings that mirror Bourdieu's own self-understanding of his thought and to castigate this or that author for exegetical mistakes but, rather, to pinpoint the structural causes of the recurrent misinterpretations that his writings have encountered in the course of their transfer across the Atlantic (and the Channel). These causes, I argue, have little to do with the personal intentions and inclinations, likes and dislikes, of particular interpreters. For they are *inscribed in the logic of "foreign trade" in ideas*. They express for the most part the necessary interferences and disjunctures between the objective position (and therefore meaning) of the imported work in its native intellectual space and the position (and correlative vision and interpretive strategies) of its consumers in the receiving academic space. Which is to say that the names of critics and exegetes of Bourdieu mentioned in the following refer not to the empirical individuals who bear them but to the "epistemic individuals" who stand for so many objective points in the field of Anglo-American social science from which Bourdieu has been perceived and appropriated.[2]

This analysis is thus meant as a contribution to the sociology of intellectual relations between France and the United States, in the –

perhaps immodest – hope of helping to move them beyond what one scholar once called the twin attitudes of "blind adulation" and "Yankee yahooism." Beyond the particular case at hand, then, it raises the broader issue of the social roots of the distortions induced by the circulation of social theory across the boundaries of national fields of social scientific inquiry and of what could be done to neutralize or minimize them.

BLURRED VISIONS

Though widely read and cited across the gamut of social science disciplines, especially since the mid–1980s, and despite the voluminous and rapidly accumulating stock of secondary analyses (see Wacquant 1989: 59–60), Bourdieu's work continues to befuddle many of his Anglo-American readers. Three points may serve to document the confused and contradictory perception of which it is the object: the question of Bourdieu's theoretical affiliation, the furor surrounding his style, and puzzlement at the concept of habitus.

Harker *et al.* (1990: 213) have pointed out that Bourdieu "has been authoritatively placed in all the major theoretical traditions": Marxist (even of the Althusserian variety), Weberian, Durkheimian, and structuralist, to which one could add Gramscian, Nietzschean, and poststructuralist.[3] Closer to us, various commentators have detected a kinship or convergences between Bourdieu's views and those of Lévi-Strauss, Geertz, Goffman, Giddens, E. P. Thompson, Basil Bernstein, Raymond Williams, Luhmann, Habermas, Foucault, Derrida, and Searle – a mixed bag, to say the least. Yet others have opposed Bourdieu to many of these same authors! Philippe Van Parijs (1981) judges his theory highly compatible with methodological individualism, while Raymond Boudon (1986), the principal exponent of methodological individualism in France, can find no term strong enough to excoriate what he paints as Bourdieu's crude "holism." Perhaps the most unexpected interpretation, considering his rationalistic and universalistic epistemology and the indifference bordering on scorn that he has manifested toward this intellectual current, is that which associates Bourdieu's work with "postmodernism" and relativism.[4]

Responses to Bourdieu's writing style have been no less diverse. The most frequent reaction among his American and (especially) British readers has been one of bafflement, frustration, and dismay, sometimes giving way to vociferous indignation – one of them went so far as as to vituperate Bourdieu for his "incapacity" to write.[5] Yet, at the same time, German commentators have compared him to literary figures such as

Honoré de Balzac and Thomas Bernhardt. Alain Caillé (1987: 10), one of Bourdieu's most stubborn French critics, registers "no complaint about this style whose Proustian touch is not devoid of charm." Neither does Stanley Hoffman (1986: 48), for whom "Bourdieu writes as a kind of twentieth-century La Bruyère."[6] Which of these judgments is most accurate or most defensible is irrelevant here: what matters is that they are hardly reconcilable.

Bourdieu's pivotal concept of habitus is intended as an answer to – or a way of circumnavigating – the vexing dilemma of structure and agency, and, not surprisingly, readers differ widely in their appraisal of its meaning and function. Steinrücke (1989), Brubaker (1985: 758), and Miller and Branson (1987: 218), *inter alia*, see it as a mediating concept that portrays the agent as "a constant improviser in an ambiguous and partially understood environment." Rasmussen (1981: 276) goes further and asserts that "habitus is a universalizing mediation dialectically conceived which not only generates a realm of objective possibilities but also the subjects who act in it." And Eagleton (1991: 156) describes its workings as a creative, "open-ended system" which "permits ceaseless innovation," rather than as a rigid blueprint. Not so, interject Aronowitz and Giroux (1985: 83), for whom the concept serves to mask "mechanistic notions of power and domination and [an] overly determined view of human agency." Hoffman (1986: 47) agrees with them in finding that habitus robs individuals of their last parcel of freedom, as does Joppke (1986: 62), for whom the concept seemingly "guarantees social reproduction and dips the social world into the dreary light of an endless recurrence."[7]

FRAGMENTED READINGS

These conflicting reactions may be explained by the fact that the importation of Bourdieu's work in to America, and to a comparable extent in Great Britain,[8] has proceeded via fragmented and piecemeal appropriations that have hidden from view the systematic nature and main thrust of his endeavor. Indeed, Bourdieu's reception is eerily reminiscent of that of Durkheim before him, as characterized by Bellah (1973, p. liv): his "worldwide influence" has been "a story of partial misunderstanding, of appropriation of what was perceived as important in one place or another without any necessary recognition of the function of what was appropriated in the total structure of his work."

Thus, to take a few instances of such splintered readings, specialists of education quote profusely *Reproduction in Education, Society and*

Culture (Bourdieu and Passeron (1977)[9] and have subjected the theory of pedagogical authority put forth there to intense scrutiny (for example, Bredo and Feinberg 1979, Gorder 1980, Apple 1982, Lakomski 1984). But rarely do they connect its structural thesis to the conception of action, expounded in *Outline of a Theory of Practice* (Bourdieu 1977c), that underlies it. Nor do they tie it in to Bourdieu's prolific research on the social genesis and efficacy of systems of classification and meaning in educational institutions.[10] This has had the effect of retarding an adequate understanding of this staple in the sociology of education that Bourdieu's so-called reproduction theory has become. The otherwise excellent ethnography of leveled aspirations among working-class youth in an American public housing project, *Ain't No Makin' It* (MacLeod 1987), exemplifies how partial exposure to Bourdieu's writings can lead to systematic misconstrual of his thought.

Jay MacLeod's critique of Bourdieu is based almost entirely on the abstract theoretical propositions articulated in the first part of *Reproduction*, supplemented by a handful of secondary analyses by American commentators.[11] This narrow selection leads him to attribute to Bourdieu exactly the type of mechanistic, objectivist structuralism that he discarded and self-consciously set out to overcome in the mid-sixties (Bourdieu *et al.* 1965b: 17–23; Bourdieu 1968b, 1972: 155–200, 1973c). By overlooking the varied empirical research in which Bourdieu addresses the very issues he is grappling with (namely, why and how agents occupying similar positions in social space come to develop different, even opposite, systems of expectations and aspirations; under what conditions such aspirations result from the internalization of objective chances; how misrecognition induces the dominated to perceive their social fate as ineluctable and to accept their exclusion as legitimate),[12] MacLeod (1987: 14) offers a truncated snapshot of Bourdieu that entrenches the deterministic misconstrual of his work – as when he asserts that this word is a "radical critique of a situation that is essentially immutable." Having drastically misrendered it, the author of *Ain't No Makin' It* finds it necessary to "reinvent" Bourdieu's theory of habitus in an attempt to overcome the duality of structure and agency and the dead end of structural causation that he himself has projected onto Bourdieu. The "theoretical deepening" of the concept he proposes (MacLeod 1987: 139–48) retraces, in a rudimentary fashion, some of the steps taken before him by Bourdieu, and the new theoretical function he assigns to a revised theory of habitus – mediating between structure and practice – is exactly what Bourdieu's foremost motive was in reactivating this old Aristotelian-Thomist notion in the mid-sixties (Bourdieu 1967a, 1984, 1985a). For example, MacLeod (1987: 138 and 128) argues that the system of dispositions acquired by agents is shaped by their gender, family, educational, and occupational histories, as well as by their peer associations and residence, and that the limited social mobility allowed by liberal democracies serves to legitimate inequality. Both these propositions are refined by Bourdieu throughout his work.[13] The final irony, then, is that far from refuting Bourdieu's "reproduction theory" as he maintains, MacLeod's ethnography strongly supports it.[14]

If sociologists of education rarely extend themselves beyond isolated interpretations of *Reproduction* to include Bourdieu's empirical and anthropological undertakings, conversely, anthropologists refer liberally to *Outline of a Theory of Practice* (Bourdieu 1977c,) which has acquired the status of a classic in their field (Coenen 1989), to Bourdieu's rich ethnographies of Algerian peasants and urban workers (Bourdieu 1964, 1965, 1973a, 1979a; Bourdieu and Sayad 1964), but typically overlook his more sociological forays into school inequality, intellectuals, politics, class relations, and the economy of cultural goods in advanced society (for example, Ortner 1984), so many studies that buttress, qualify, and amplify his anthropological arguments. The consequence in this case has been both to truncate the empirical underpinnings of Bourdieu's rethinking of the nature and limits of anthropological knowledge and to obscure the rationale behind his importation of materialist critique into the realm of culture (Bourdieu 1986c, 1988c).

Even recent discussions of *Distinction*, a *summa* of research-cum-theorizing in which Bourdieu (1984) weaves together many of the topics and themes that exercised him and his research team over the preceding fifteen years, only rarely break out of this tunnel vision. With the exception of that of Brubaker (1985), all the major extended reviews of the book (Douglas 1981, Dal Lago 1985, Hoffman 1986, Berger 1986, Garnham 1986, Zolberg 1986, Wilson 1988) fail to mention *Outline* or its companion volume *The Logic of Practice* (Bourdieu 1990e, orig. 1980), in which Bourdieu draws out the general anthropological conclusions of his research on class, culture, and politics in contemporary France and links them to his earlier investigations of rituals, beliefs, and strategies in Kabylia and Bearn.[15]

THE EYE OF THE BEHOLDER:
STRUCTURE OF THE FIELD OF RECEPTION

The reasons for such partial and fractured understandings of a strongly unified scientific corpus that forthrightly questions premature specialization and empirical balkanization are of two kinds. Some are situated on the side of production – if only the fact that Bourdieu nowhere provides a systematic statement of his theories or a general analytic map of how his various research projects fit together.[16] Others stand on the side of consumption, and it is to these that I now turn. Granting that "the meaning and function of a foreign work is determined as much by the field of destination as by the field of origin" (Bourdieu 1990b: 1), the main obstacle to a more synthetic appropriation of Bourdieu in America may have been that he tends to be judged through the very categories of thought that his theories aim at transcending. For, as Brubaker (1985: 771) remarks, "the reception of Bourdieu's work has largely been determined by the same 'false frontiers' and 'artificial divisions' that his work has repeatedly challenged."

These divisions are at once objective and subjective. In the realm of objectivity, they take the form of more or less porous disciplinary divides, theoretical niches, methodological specialties, and academic networks and turfs. One major difference between the sending and the receiving intellectual universes in this respect is that the borders between sociology, anthropology, history, and philosophy are notably more difficult to cross in the United States. For a variety of reasons (including the legacy of the incomplete institutionalization of sociology under Durkheim, the synthetic ambition and role of the *Annales* school, the expansion of the École des hautes Études en sciences sociales after World War II, the dominance of the figure of the "philosopher-king" over the intellectual scene until the 1960s, broken only by the revolutionary onslaught of structuralism), sociology is less isolated from its sister disciplines in France.[17] The objective divisions of the field of US social science are particularly tenacious because, like those of any field, they also exist in the minds of its participants as schemata of academic perception and appreciation inculcated through graduate training and durable immersion in the specific universe. And it is these schemata which shape the assimilation of foreign intellectual products. Thus the first move of American scholars is often to try to read Bourdieu's sociology into the dualistic alternatives – micro/macro, agency/structure, interpretive/positivist, structuralist/individualist, normative/rational, function/conflict, and so forth – that structure their national disciplinary space (see Rhoads 1991 for a discussion of these dualities), however ill suited these alternatives might be to apprehending the conceptual economy of Bourdieu's sociology.

Following the same logic, interpreters often locate Bourdieu in one empirical subspecialty and limit their exegesis to that portion of his research which falls within its purview, ignoring the extensions, revisions, and corrections he may have made when tackling similar processes and mechanisms in a different social setting. For instance, the issue of the "interested" nature of social action is explored not only in *Distinction* but also in Bourdieu's analysis of the fields of literature, religion, and law, in his papers on fertility and marriage strategies, and in his economic sociology of Algeria.[18] Likewise, the concept of habitus is elaborated not simply with respect to class, but in its gendered dimension and in the context of precapitalist society as well (Bourdieu 1977d, 1990c, 1977c). And the role of belief and the body in the functioning of social institutions is examined in Bourdieu's inquiry into the contests of honor among the Kabyles, in his study of the selection and indoctrination of students of French elite graduate schools, and in his essay on "Male domination"; it also stands at the base of his interest in objects apparently as distant as high fashion and sport.[19] Given Bourdieu's trademark proclivity to pursue the same analytic issue *across* empirical domains, then, any decoding that does not similarly trespass over frontiers between them is liable to yield only a fragmentary understanding of his views. Readings that similarly seek to "retranslate" his thought into home-grown theoretical idioms – for instance, as a combination of Blau and Giddens, with a touch of Goffman and Collins, as one author proposed – rather than endeavor first to understand it in its own terms (as is done with other major European social theorists), cannot but further split Bourdieu's work into a patchwork of seemingly unrelated and excessively dispersed inquiries.

It is interesting to speculate at this juncture why the works of Habermas and Foucault, which, on face value, are just as alien as Bourdieu's to American categories of sociological understanding, have not suffered from the same urge to read them into national traditions and preconstructions. Perhaps the fact that Habermas and Foucault advertise themselves as philosophers (or philosopher-sociologist in one case and philosopher-historian in the other), whereas Bourdieu squarely takes up the mantle of sociology, has given them a warrant for legitimate "otherness" and shielded them to a degree from such ethnocentric reduction.[20] Another reason for their differential treatment may be that, by contrast with Habermas's for instance, Bourdieu's work is thick and precise in empirical content and can thus fall prey to both theoretical *and* empirical retranslation. Besides, Habermas and Foucault can be more easily brushed aside by the sociological establishment and therefore left to stand on their own terms, for precisely the same reason: unlike Bourdieu, they do not directly challenge positivist sociologists on their own turf and with their own weapons. Further, Habermas's efforts since *The Theory of Communicative Action* must seem less alien, since they directly engage American strands of social thought (Peirce, Mead, and

Parsons among others); and Germany has long been more attuned to the concerns and trends of American sociology than France, as attested by the newfound popularity of neo-Parsonian "Grand Theory" (as C. Wright Mills called it) east of the Rhine River. Finally, there is the substance of their respective theories as it applies to academics; Bourdieu's sociology contains a disenchanting questioning of the symbolic power of intellectuals that sits uneasily with Habermas's and Foucault's comparatively more prophetic stances.[21]

This intellectual ethnocentrism – the propensity to refract Bourdieu through the prism of native sociological lenses – is of course in no way specifically American (or British), no more than it is applied uniquely to the importation of Bourdieu. *All academic fields tend to be ethnocentric* in this sense. The case of the United States, however, is special in that this urge is encouraged by the worldwide hegemonic status of American social science, which makes it less attentive and open to foreign intellectual currents than foreigners are, by necessity, to American ones.[22] This has not been allayed by the erratic and lagged flow of translations, which has disrupted the actual sequence of Bourdieu's investigations and kept a number of his key writings out of reach of an Anglo-American audience. Practical exigencies of translation have caused a confusing compression of the chronology of Bourdieu's *oeuvre* (aggravated by the author's habit of endlessly reworking his materials and of publishing only after years of delay), sometimes even to a reversal for English-language readers.[23]

Yet another obstacle to an adequate understanding of Bourdieu's enterprise is the fact that its *collective* nature clashes with the American representation of the French "patron" and his "circle" (Clark 1973, Lemert 1986). While it is true that French sociology has long been dominated by a small number of prominent leaders of research teams – the quartet of Bourdieu, Touraine, Boudon, and Crozier being the more readily identified by native producers (Ansart 1990, Touraine 1988) and American consumers alike[24] – it is organizationally and intellectually much more diverse and differentiated – indeed, fragmented (some would even say anomic) – than such a "view from afar" implies (see Mendras and Verret (eds) 1988; Ansart 1990: 20 and 317–22; Wieviorka 1988: 55). Again, for obvious structural reasons, distant observers are inclined to exaggerate the unity and cohesion of the French sociological field and the concerns of its members for journalistic visibility and public fame (as with Lemert's hydra-like *tout Paris*). The uncontrolled projection onto the French intellectual universe of quasi-concepts born of the foreign reader's relation to it can obscure its actual functioning.[25] In the case at hand they have had the effect of hiding the numerous institutional and cognitive parallels that exist between Bourdieu's "workshop" and the Durkheimian school (Wacquant 1987: 86). Another unfortunate result of this is that the voluminous corpus of empirical studies published in the journal founded in 1975 by Bourdieu, *Actes de la recherche en sciences sociales*, is rarely consulted by British and American scholars. And the ongoing work by his colleagues, associates, and students at the Center for European Sociology in Paris is still little known outside France (Broady and Persson 1989).[26]

PECULIARITIES OF THE FRENCH?

There is additionally, among some importers and consumers of foreign social theory, a tendency to attribute the complexities of Bourdieu's work to the specificity of the Parisian intellectual scene and to dismiss them as mere "peculiarities of the French." The inclination to relegate a foreign thinker to his national universe and to depict the latter as a closed, self-referential realm of discourse[27] leads in this case to serious misreading. Thus when Lamont and Lareau (1988: 158) write that "Bourdieu's model could have been influenced by his context of elaboration, i.e., the small and relatively culturally unified Parisian scene," they miss the fact that Bourdieu is uncommonly internationalist in intellectual background, outlook, and practice.[28] His early training was mainly in German philosophy and American and British cultural anthropology, and the theoretical space within which his project acquires its place and its meaning is decidedly transnational (Bourdieu 1979b). *Actes de la recherche en sciences sociales* publishes more foreign authors than any other French social science journal save the *Annales*. The series "Le sens commun" edited by Bourdieu at Éditions de Minuit has published as many foreign authors as it has French. The Center for European Sociology has, since its inception, entertained regular exchanges with foreign researchers.[29] Finally, Bourdieu has taught since 1964 at the Écoles des hautes études en sciences sociales, easily one of the most internationally oriented institutions of social research in the world (Mazon 1988).

The Anglophone reception of Bourdieu has also been hampered by the overall lack of familiarity of American social scientists with the Continental strands of social theory and philosophy which form the backdrop to his endeavor. Many of these intellectual traditions, such as transcendental and existential phenomenology and the rationalist epistemology of Bachelard, do not partake of the "horizon of expectations" (Jauss 1982) of mainstream sociology in the United States or Great

Britain. For example, the writings of Merleau-Ponty and of Maurice Halbwachs, which contribute important background themes and conceptual materials to Bourdieu, are relatively unfamiliar in these countries. Halbwachs's work was far better known in the 1930s (he taught for a quarter at the University of Chicago in 1930, entertained amicable relations with the leading exponents of human ecology, and published several major papers on urban change and ethnic relations in America) than it is now.[30] As for Merleau-Ponty, he has suffered both from the hermetic separation that exists in American universities between philosophy and sociology and from the importation of Husserl via Schutz and the subsequent development of phenomenological sociology at the hands of Peter Berger and Harold Garfinkel (Ostrow 1990).

This, of course, is also true of other major European strands of social theory, including structuralism, Foucault, and Habermas, as Wuthnow *et al.* (1984: 7) note. However, a grasp of the nexus of antagonistic and competing positions within and against which Bourdieu developed his own stance is particularly crucial because Bourdieu is an unusually self-conscious writer who reflects incessantly and intensely upon the intellectual and social determinants that bear on his enterprise. Indeed, much of his thinking was formatively shaped by an intellectual reaction *against* two of the major intellectual movements of his youth: on the one side, the positivist model of social science promulgated by the international dominance of American sociology and imported into France by the first generation of America-trained social scientists in the fifties and sixties (most prominently Stoetzel, Boudon, and Crozier);[31] and, on the other, the "literary-philosophical" tradition that held sway over the French intellectual universe of the 1950s (Merquior 1985, Boschetti 1988, Bourdieu 1989a). A good many key traits of Bourdieu's sociology remain elusive so long as one lacks a precise picture of the streams of thought that influenced him, whether positively or *a contrario*. Among them, a central role must be granted to the opposition between Sartrean phenomenology and Lévi-Straussian structuralism, which Bourdieu regarded, very early on, as the embodiment of the fundamental option between objectivist structuralism and subjectivist social phenomenology; the subtle yet profound influence of Husserl and Heidegger (Bourdieu came close to becoming a Heideggerian philosopher in the late 1950s), as well as of the epistemological and political stances of Merleau-Ponty; the desire to undercut the claims of both structural Marxism and philosophies of the subject; the mediation of Mauss and Halbwachs and the historicist philosophy of science advocated by Bachelard and Canguilhem; and the writings of Cassirer, Saussure, Benveniste, Schutz, and Wittgenstein. It is important to note also what germane traditions of thought Bourdieu drew relatively little upon (the Frankfurt school) or ignored almost entirely (most prominently Gramsci, whom he admits to having read very late)[32] and to identify the images of the intellectual that formed the "regulative idea" of his vocation. Two elements of this idea are the ambivalent rejection of the "total intellectual" (to use the notion coined by Bourdieu in a tribute to Sartre, who epitomized it) and a deeply political opposition to both the "soft humanism" of Christian phenomenologists and the epistemocratic attitude inscribed in the structuralist conception of practice and knowledge.[33]

Unfamiliarity with the intellectual backdrop to Bourdieu's research has been compounded by the fact that recent imports of French social and cultural theory in Great Britain and the United States – Derrida's deconstructionism, Lyotard's attack on "grand narratives," and Baudrillardian semiotics being the main ones (Denzin 1986, Kellner 1990) – stand at a considerable distance from him on matters of epistemology, methodology, and substance. Yet superficial thematic and stylistic similarities between them have led many to enroll Bourdieu among the vanguard of postmodernist theory. The diffusion of "poststructuralism" and the raging fad of "postmodernism" (Dews 1987, Rose 1991, Rosenau 1991) which, much like structural Marxism in France in the 1960s, has now invaded virtually all but the most orthodox journals and proved a boon to publishers, have enshrouded Bourdieu in theoretical currents that he has combatted since their emergence in the sixties,[34] confusing his continued commitment to scientific knowledge, albeit of a postpositivist kind, and his stubborn defense of the role of reason in history (see Bourdieu 1989c, conclusion; Bourdieu and Wacquant 1992: 47–58).

All these factors, internal (deriving from characteristics of the work and of its semantic and organizational context of production) and external (rooted in properties of the receiving social science field and in its hegemonic position in international intellectual relations), have interacted to make it difficult for Anglo-American scholars to get a full grasp of the overall structure and meaning of Bourdieu's sociology. Only a comparative analysis of its reception in other countries or of the importation of other foreign theorists into the same academic universe could sort what is peculiarly American (or British) about the case at hand from what it owes to the general logic of the export of social theory. This chapter suggests, however, that the effects of the latter are underestimated only at considerable cost to all parties.[35] It is clear that *the structures of national intellectual fields act as crucial mediations in the foreign trade of theories*: that of the exporting country formatively shapes the contents and makeup of the product; that of the receiving country acts in a manner of a prism that selects and refracts external stimuli according to its own configuration. The moral of the story is that intellectual products such as social theories should, whenever possible, be exported with as much of their native "context" as possible (if in miniature in the form of a select intellectual self-accounting, preface to foreign readers, and so on), and imported with full awareness of the distortions induced by the mediating interests of, affinities with, and biases built into the objective relations between producer, intermediary, and consumer.

Let us return in closing to the question of the difficulty of Bourdieu's prose. There is no denying that the density of his argumentation and the conceptual idiolect he has devised to break with commonsense understandings embedded in ordinary language (including the ordinary language of conventional social science, with its notions directly borrowed from, or contaminated by, exoteric discourse: actor, role, system, culture, profession, "underclass," and so forth) has not facilitated his entry into Anglo-American social science.[36] The fact that "Bourdieu's style serves a precise theoretical purpose," as Lemert (1990: 301) rightly insists, has not done much to make the nested and convoluted configuration of his sentences – constructed, precisely, to convey the essentially relational and recursive nature of social processes – more palatable to his readers.

Yet, one cannot but wonder whether incessant complaints about Bourdieu's style and terminology are not a symptom of a deeper and different problem, since other "difficult" writers – Habermas, Foucault, or even Weber come to mind – do not elicit the same level of protestation as the author of *Distinction*.[37] Could it be that, instead of a concern with form itself, these criticisms express anxiety at the social gaze that this form conveys? Could the onerousness of reading Bourdieu stem from our uneasiness at seeing our social selves stripped bare, from a vital reluctance to embrace a mode of analysis that makes us squirm as it throws us "back in the game" and cuts through the mist of our enchanted relation to the social world, and in particular to our own condition as intellectuals – that is, bearers of cultural capital and thus wielders of a dominated form of domination that scarcely wants to recognize itself as such? Caro (1981: 2) perceptively expresses this possibility when he writes:

Pierre Bourdieu puts each of us in the presence of an objectivation of our being that rarely fails to arouse in us a number of reticences. He most often presents us with an image of ourselves that contradicts preexisting representations, which generally are all the more comforting as they are more ideological. An academic has only to read certain pages on the university to convince him- or herself of the difficulty of approaching the works of Bourdieu and his colleagues with serenity and in the spirit of a pure scientific engagement. It is not an exaggeration to state that such texts invite us to a kind of "socio-analysis" whose reflexive moment is in many respects as painful as the work demanded by a psycho-analysis.[38]

NOTES

1 It is tempting to develop an analysis of Bourdieu as a strategic resource in the field of American social science and to use him as an "analyzer" to reveal its divisions, tensions and force lines (as Pollak (1988a) does with Weber for French sociology). This, however, would require tracking the prior influence of American social science on Bourdieu (both as a selective trove of theories, findings, and methods and as a – mainly negative – model of scientific practice) and the objective postwar relationships of American sociology with Continental social and cultural theory more broadly, something which stands well beyond the scope of this essay.

2 The important distinction between empirical and epistemic (or constructed) individual is elaborated in *Homo Academicus* (Bourdieu 1988b: 21–35).

3 Bourdieu's alleged Marxism has been both deplored and praised: Ferry and Renult (1990) denounce his work as a "trivial" and "simple window-dressing of Marxism," a "distinguished variant of vulgar Marxism." Frank (1980: 256) lauds *Outline of a Theory of Practice* for "accomplish[ing] the practice of a more scientific Marxism," and Rasmussen (1981: 276) for "construct[ing] a theory in the tradition of the Early Marx," while Rosenau (1991: 106) regrets Bourdieu's alleged "ideological commitment to the metanarrative of Marxism." None of them takes time to remark that Bourdieu has also been attacked by Marxists (e.g. Bidet 1979, Rancière 1984) or to address Bourdieu's explicit critique of, and increasing distancing from, central tenets of Marxism (e.g., Bourdieu 1972 and 1987f). Competing versions of the Weberian reading are defended by Lash (1990), Winkler (1989), and Gartman (1991); yet Collins (1981) and Karabel and Halsey (eds) (1977) deny that Bourdieu is a true conflict theorist in the Weberian mold. A Gramscian affinity is suggested by Hall (1977), Lichterman (1989), and Harker *et al.* (eds) (1990: 107), but disputed by Giroux (1983). Ansart (1991: 31 and *passim*), DiMaggio (1979), and Acciaiolo (1981) insist that Bourdieu is essentially a latter-day Durkheimian, while Wuthnow (1989: 520) surprisingly affirms that his "orientation can in no way be linked to Durkheim."

4 Thus Alexander (1990: 536) counts Bourdieu, along with Derrida and Foucault, among the "poststructuralist" advocates of "arbitrary relativism." For Lemert (1988: 795), as for Lash (1990), Harker *et al.* (eds) (1990), and Rabinow (1985), Bourdieu "qualifies as a postmodernist," if a reluctant or

unwitting one. This position is rejected by Rosenau (1991) in her review of the relations between post-modernism and the social sciences, though she simultaneously maintains that Bourdieu "employed Derrida's epistemology, concepts and vocabulary" in *Distinction*. Easily the most frivolous such attribution is Jenkins's (1989: 641), for whom *Homo Academicus* "boils down to a postmodern re-reading of Talcott Parsons"(!).

5 Jenkins (1989: 643) rails for pages against Bourdieu's "awful, cement-mixer style" and complains that *Homo Academicus* "is written in a language so obscurantist, so dense and so ugly that the effort of reading the damned thing will probably . . . heavily outweigh any final benefit." Reviews of Bourdieu's books typically devote disproportionate space to the difficulties of his style.

6 In a national radio program on Bourdieu broadcast in June of 1990 by France Culture (Casanova 1990), theater actor Podalides likened his writings to those of Courteline, Labiche, and Brecht (a theatrical adaptation of *The Inheritors* was staged in 1968). Asked why he chose to publish Bourdieu, the director of Éditions de Minuit (the press which has published nearly all Bourdieu's books and which has been a European powerhouse of literary innovation – it has revealed Samuel Beckett, the *nouveau roman*, and Nobel laureate Claude Simon among others) answered that he did so because he admired him first and foremost as a writer. Even an unsympathetic critic like Stamm (1983: 318) concedes that most of *Distinction* and *Le Sens pratique* are "written in a precise, vigorous manner and without affectation."

7 For a further review of the contradictory readings of the notion of habitus and an effort to clear them up, see Bourdieu and Wacquant (1992: 132, esp. 85).

8 See Robbins 1988 for a recapitulation of the English reception of Bourdieu. Since its initial publication in *Sociological Theory* (Wacquant 1989: 26–32), a bibliometric study of the American reception of Bourdieu by Broady and Persson (1989) has corroborated my analysis. using the "Social Scisearch" database compiled by the Social Science Citation Index to construct indicators of patterns of citation and cocitation, they show in particular that American sociologists have been slow to incorporate Bourdieu relative to anthropologists and educationalists, and that they have largely ignored the empirical basis of his sociology, as well as the research published by his collaborators and students.

9 The International Scientific Institute (which produces the Social Science Citation Index) proclaimed the book a "Citation Classic" in 1989 (see Bourdieu's reflections on this in his preface to the 1990 paperback reedition). Bourdieu's essay on "Cultural reproduction and social reproduction" (Bourdieu 1973b), although revisited and revised numerous times since its original publication in 1971, is also frequently referred to as representative of his sociology of education, if not of his whole sociology. In their state-of-the-art review of "The Sociology of Education" for Smelser's *Handbook of Sociology*, e.g., Bidwell and Friedkin (1988) cite both this article and *Reproduction*, missing two decades of publications on the topic by Bourdieu

and his associates at the Center for European Sociology, especially Monique de Saint Martin, Gabrielle Balazs, Jean-Pierre Faguer, Jean-Michel Chapoulie, Louis Pinto, Victor Karady, Christophe Charle, and François Bonvin. Much of this research has appeared in the issues of *Actes de la recherche en sciences sociales* on "The Academic Institution" (Nov. 1979), "Elite Schools and Popular Schools" (Sept. 1981), "Academic Classification and Social Classification" (June 1982), "Education and Philosophy" (June 1983), "Powers of the School" (Sept. and Nov. 1987), and "Education and Societies" (Mar. 1991).

10 e.g. Bourdieu *et al.* 1965b; Bourdieu and de Saint Martin 1974; Bourdieu 1967b, 1974b, 1981a, 1989c, part 1.

11 MacLeod (1987: 11, my emphasis) refers to Bourdieu as "a prominent French *reproduction theorist*" (as do Robinson and Garnier (1985) and Connell (1983: 151), who also puts Althusser and Henri Lefebvre in that category) and makes no mention of the vast corpus of empirical research produced by Bourdieu and his collaborators on this topic. When he discusses the substance of Bourdieu's own concepts or propositions, MacLeod repeatedly quotes not from Bourdieu's writings but positions attributed to him by two of his critics, David Swartz (on determinism in the circular relationship between struture and practice, p. 14) and Henri Giroux (on school legitimation, p. 12; on the definition of habitus, p. 138). This leads him to offer an assessment of Bourdieu that features as crucial omissions and shortcomings what have been the very core and strengths of the latter's sociology: "Bourdieu underestimates the achievement ideology's capacity to mystify structural constraints and encourage high aspirations" and ignores "the cultural level of analysis" (McLeod 1987: 151). Compare this with the systematic critique of meritocratic ideology put forth in Bourdieu and Passeron's (1979) *The Inheritors* (a book considered by many to have been the Bible of the student movement in May 1968) and with Bourdieu's elaboration of the concepts of misrecognition and symbolic power (e.g. Bourdieu 1979b and 1991b).

12 See, on French students, Bourdieu 1973b, 1974b, 1989c, esp. 142–62 and 225–64 and Bourdieu and Passeron 1979; on the dialectic of objective chances and subjective hopes among Algerian proletarians, Bourdieu *et al.* (1963, Bourdieu 1973a and 1979a), and among buyers of single-family homes, Bourdieu and de Saint Martin 1990; on class strategies of reconversion, Bourdieu and Boltanski 1977, and the theoretical discussion in Bourdieu 1974a. These issues are also tackled empirically in *Actes de la recherche en sciences sociales* in articles by Balazs (1983), Mauger and Fossé-Poliak (1983), Pialoux (1979), Pudal (1988), and Zarca (1979).

13 See esp. Bourdieu and Passeron 1977 and 1979 and Bourdieu 1974a and 1984, esp. 101–14, 167–75.

14 "The circular relationship Bourdieu posits between objective opportunities and subjective hopes is incompatible with the findings of this book" (MacLeod 1987: 138). Bourdieu never posited such a relation: he states very

explicitly in "Class future and the causality of the probable" (Bourdieu 1974a) that circularity is but one particular instance of possible relations, actualized only to the extent that there exists a good fit between the structures of the habitus and those of the outside world. *Algeria 1960* (Bourdieu 1979a) offers an in-depth analysis of the social genesis and consequences of the discordance between the hopes and desires of recently urbanized members of the subproletariate of Algiers and the objective positions and opportunities assigned to them by the colonial capitalist economy (see Bourdieu 1980b, 1988c, 1990e, and Harker 1984 for a further refutation of the "circularity" thesis). In fact, is it hard to think of anyone who would agree more with the main conclusion of *Ain't No Makin' It* that "social reproduction is a complex process" (MacLeod 1987: 161) than Bourdieu, who has devoted a quarter of a century of tireless research to documenting and penetrating this complexity (see Bourdieu 1989 for a summation).

15 Another area in which Bourdieu has exerted influence, but again only through a selective filtering process, is the social analysis of aesthetics. For example, though clearly influenced by and sympathetic to Bourdieu, Zolberg's (1990) thorough review of the state of the sociology of the arts cites his studies of photography and museum attendance but leaves out his key articles on artistic perception, Manet, Flaubert, and the historical genesis of the "pure gaze" of modern aesthetics (Bourdieu 1968a, 1971a, 1983a, 1987c, 1988a).

16 Bourdieu and Wacquant 1992 is designed to fill this gap.

17 On each of these factors, see Karady 1982, Bourdé and Martin 1983, Mazon 1988, Poster 1975 and Boschetti 1988, and Eribon (1991), respectively. One should add the fact that French sociologists of Bourdieu's generation received their university education not in sociology – the *Licence de sociologie*, the French equivalent of the B.A., was established only in 1958 – but in philosophy or history.

18 See Bourdieu 1985b, 1971b, 1977b; Bourdieu and Darbel 1966; Bourdieu et al. 1963; and Bourdieu 1973a and 1979a, respectively.

19 See, respectively, Bourdieu 1965, 1981a, 1989c, 1990c, 1980b: 196–206, 1987a: 203–16, 1991c.

20 Merquior (1985) has suggested that the academic success of Foucault was in good part a product of his affiliation to the mixed genre of "litero-philosophy."

21 For a sketch of other contrasts and similarities between Habermas and Bourdieu, see Ingram 1982, Inglis 1979, and Chapter 4 above.

22 To be more precise, American intellectual myopia functions in a fashion opposite to that of smaller national sociologies, such as Scandinavian or Dutch sociology (Heilbron 1988); for whereas the latter cannot ignore American Social Science and can even be blinded by it to the point where they cannot see themselves, U. S. Sociology typically experiences difficulty seeing others due to its propensity to project itself everywhere it looks.

252   *Loïc J. D. Wacquant*

23 Two examples: the English version of the 1964 monograph *The Inheritors* came out in English two years after the 1970 book *Reproduction* which was based upon it. The pivotal volume *Le Métier de sociologue*, in which Bourdieu and his associates lay out the tenets of the revised "applied rationalism" that supplies the epistemological foundations of his theoretical enterprise, has become available in English translation only in 1991 (Bourdieu *et al*. 1991a; original French edition 1968). As a result, readers not versed in the thought of Bachelard and of the French school of the history of science (notably Koyré and Canguilhem) are left in the dark about the critical-historicist theory of knowledge that underlies Bourdieu's sociology (this is confirmed by Broady and Persson's (1989) bibliometric analysis). Up until the late 1980s, only seven of Bourdieu's books were available in English, compared to eleven in German. This linguistic roadblock is now being removed: all of Bourdieu's books are in the process of being translated, due largely to the tireless efforts of John Thompson and Polity Press, along with Stanford University Press.

24 Though, in the case of the latter, largely because of the language barrier: few other French sociologists are accessible in English translation.

25 An overly integrated vision of the structure of the French intellectual field is at times compounded with a reflectionist theory postulating that the ideas of French theorists somehow directly mirror their proximate academic environment. Lamont and Wuthnow (1990: 305, 309) fall victim to this mechanistic reduction when they write that if Bourdieu puts forth a "representation of power as arbitrary, of the social system as unfair, and of power relations as ubiquitous, expressed not only through coercion, but through omnipresent zero-sum relations," it must be because the French sociological profession is organized into rigid factions, lacking funds and capacity for normative control, and because its "journals are often controlled by cliques." Collapsing social-scientific thinking into its assumed organizational substructure, they assert that Bourdieu's "analysis of the intellectual field, where positions are defined relationally . . . is a *direct reflection* of the small intricate circles in which Parisian researchers have to operate" (my emphasis). Again, as with Clark (1973), a highly idealized and ideological vision of the American academic field – as a *normalized* space of fair, competitive resources and exchanges – serves as implicit counterpart and normative standard by which to judge another national intellectual field. And, as with Lemert (1986), the integration of the French intellectual field is wrongly attributed to its physical concentration in Paris rather than to the effects of the intense homogenizing intellectual (re)socialization operated by elite schools such as the École normale supérieure.

26 Among these and other writings more or less directly influenced by Bourdieu, one should cite at minimum, from the pen of current and former members of the Center for European Sociology, Boltanski 1969, 1987, de Saint Martin 1971, Grignon 1971, Suaud 1978, Maresca 1983, Muel-Dreyfus 1983, Pinto 1987, Moulin 1987, Castel 1988, Charle 1987, 1990, Combessie

1989, Pollak 1988b, Fabiani 1989, Champagne 1990, and Sayad 1991. Other books include Verdés-Leroux 1978, 1983, Cam 1981, Pociello 1981, Caro 1982, Gamboni 1989, Bozon 1984, Isambert 1984, Viala 1985, Zarca 1987, Marin 1988, Sabour 1988, Boschetti 1988, Pincon 1987, Pincon and Pincon-Rendu 1989, Chartier 1988a, Le Witta 1989, and Kauppi 1991. For a selection of articles from *Actes de la recherche en sciences sociales* that draw upon, apply, or extend Bourdieu's scheme to a variety of empirical objects and sites, see Appendix 2 in Bourdieu and Wacquant 1992: 265–8.

More generally, in France, the influence of Bourdieu can be felt throughout the social sciences. In political science, e.g., the notion of field is increasingly used by the "sociologistic politologists" (Favre 1988: 240–3). For a sample of works by the latter, see Bon and Schemeil 1980, Dobry 1986, Gaxie 1990, Lacroix 1981, and Pudal 1989; see also the articles in two recent issues of *Actes de la recherche en sciences sociales* on the theme "Thinking the Political" (Mar. and June 1988). Historian Aymard (1988: 229) credits the work of Bourdieu, alongside that of Foucault and Elias, with "hav[ing] revolutionized both sociology *and* history" by "forcing them to rethink their relation to the reality they claim to study and describe." Chartier (1988b: 92–3) suggests the importance of the notion of practice in cultural history. Rébérioux (1988: 97–8) notes that Bourdieu's notion of dominated classes has "enriched and modernized the history of the working class," as well as helped the *rapprochement* of social and cultural history. Two other indicators of Bourdieu's intellectual presence are the diffusion of his sociology among the general literate public in France (*Distinction* is reported to have sold upwards of 100,000 copies, and the reader compiled by Accardo and Corcuff (1986) some 30,000 copies) and his impact on official bureaucratic classifications (the coding schemata used by INSEE, the French National Bureau of Statistics, which carries out most of the large-scale survey research done in the country, including the census, were revised in 1982 better to approximate the theory of social space put forth in *Distinction*).

27 Lemert (1986: 690) paints French sociology as a self-contained, idiosyncratic, if not quixotic, intellectual formation that "does not export well" because the "weight of tradition" and the pressuring "gaze of Paris' immensely literate public" compel social scientists to try constantly to be "original, inventive, unique," presumably at the expense of serious (i.e. American-style) scholarship. Thus "the French who do sociology are frequently so beholden to their own culture that they cannot make their ideas accessible to the wider sociological community."

28 Lamont and Lareau (1988) go on to compare this "Parisian scene" with the "larger, highly regionally diversified society of the United States," as if there was a one-to-one correspondence between the type of society and the structure of the intellectual field – a good example of what Bourdieu (1988a) calls the "short-circuit fallacy."

29 Foreign authors published in "Le sens commun" include Panofsky, Bakhtin, Adorno and Marcuse, Cassirer, Bateson, Sapir, Radcliffe-Brown, S. F. Nadel

and Jack Goody, Ulf Hannerz, Basil Bernstein and William Labov, Goffman, John Blacking, Anna Boschetti, Richard Hoggart, Luis Prieto, Peter Szondi, Albert Hirschman, and Joseph Schumpeter. The Center for European Sociology has close relations with research institutes in Brazil, Scandinavia, Japan, Hungary, Romania, Belgium, the Netherlands, and the USA. Numerous foreign scholars and students also come annually to Paris to work with Bourdieu.

30 Lewis Coser's edited volume of writings by Halbwachs (1992) for the Heritage of Sociology series of the University of Chicago Press will hopefully help to correct this.

31 Bourdieu was the only notable French sociologist of his generation conspicuously *not* to attend Lazarsfeld's famous seminars at the Sorbonne in the sixties. A meeting between them followed at Aron's behest, during which they discussed Bourdieu and Darbel's mathematical model of attendance at the art museums of Europe.

32 Bourdieu (1987a: 39). For an account by Bourdieu of the transformation of the French intellectual field in the postwar era and of his situation and trajectory within it, see Bourdieu and Passeron 1967 and Bourdieu 1979b, 1986c, 1987a, 1987e, 1990e, preface; 1989a. A lively portrait of the intellectual atmosphere and battles of those decades is drawn by Eribon 1991; see also Lévi-Strauss and Eribon 1991, Boschetti 1988, and Pinto 1987.

33 Bourdieu (1987a: 31) admits that many of his theoretical choices were guided by a "gut-level rejection of the ethical posture implied by structuralist anthropology, of the haughty and distant relation it established between the scientist and his object, namely ordinary people." This twin set of attitudes was no doubt exacerbated by Bourdieu's firsthand experience of the constraints and ambiguities of the role of the intellectual in the dramatic circumstances of the Algerian war. In his first book, *The Algerians*, written under the harrowing circumstances of this brutal armed conflict, Bourdieu refers to the policy of agrarian reform carried out by colonial authorities as an immense "social vivisection."

34 See Bourdieu's (1984: 569, 494–500) remarks on Baudrillard and Derrida, respectively, and his analysis of the "-logy effect" which is at the root of the appeal of much fashionable French cultural theory of the day (Bourdieu 1987a). Bourdieu and Passeron's (1963) critique of the "sociologists of mutations" and "massmediology" in the early sixties (led by Edgar Morin and Pierre Fougeyrollas) would apply *mutatis mutandis* to much of the Baudrillardian and postmodern writings of today.

35 The transatlantic mutation of Foucault demonstrates this even better than that of Bourdieu. The Foucault constructed by American scholars (particularly those attracted by his theories and politics, because they made him a powerful ally in their campaign to disseminate epistemological relativism and the critique of "science" in the name of the "subject," a reborn humanism, poetics, difference, etc.) is virtually a different author from the French (or European) Foucault revealed by Eribon's (1991) intellectual biography. The

latter is perhaps the best documentation to date of how powerful the distortions induced by uncontrolled international intellectual export can be.

36 In France, the distillation of Bourdieu into textbook material has been assisted by the primer and reader of Accardo (1983) and Accardo and Corcuff (eds) (1986). Champagne *et al.* (1989) have written an excellent systematic introduction to sociology following Bourdieu's teachings, that is, emphasizing rupture with commonsensical notions ("spontaneous sociology"), the multiplicity of methods, the deconstruction of social problems and scientific construction of the object. *Le Métier de sociologue* (Bourdieu *et al.* 1968) has long been a staple in the sociological education of undergraduates.

37 One could well say of Bourdieu's style what Gerth and Wright Mills (eds) (1946, p. vi) said of Weber's:

> It is obvious that this school of writing is not what it is because of the inability of its practitioners to write well. They simply follow an altogether different style. They use parentheses, qualifying clauses, inversions and complex rhythmic devices in their polyphonous sentences. Ideas are synchronized rather than serialized. At their best, they erect a grammatical artifice in which mental balconies and watch towers, as well as bridges and recesses, decorate the main structure. Their sentences are gothic castles.

A worthwhile discussion of Bourdieu's contribution to problematizing writing in the social sciences can be found in Perrot and de la Soudrière 1988.

38 For a vivid illustration of this "socio-analytic" process, see Sayad's (1991, esp. ch. 2, 5, and 7) work on Algerian immigrants and Yvette Delsaut's (1989a, 1989b) ethno(auto)biography of working-class culture in a French mining town.

REFERENCES

Accardo, Alain 1983: *Initiation à la sociologie de l'illusionnisme social: lire Bourdieu.* Bordeaux: Éditions Le Mascaret.

——— and Corcuff, Philippe (eds) 1986: *La sociologie de Pierre Bourdieu: textes choisis et commentés.* Bordeaux: Éditions Le Mascaret.

Acciaiolo, Gregory L. 1981: 'Knowing what you are doing: Pierre Bourdieu's "Outline of a Theory of Practice." *Canberra Anthropology*, 4 no. 1 (Apr.), 23–51.

Alexander, Jeffrey C. 1990: Beyond the epistemological dilemma: general theory in a postpositivist mode." *Sociological Forum*, 5, no. 4 (Dec.): 531–44.

Ansart, Pierre 1990: *Les Sociologies contemporaines.* Paris: Éditions du Seuil.

Apple, Michael 1982: *Education and Power.* Boston and London: ARK Paperbacks.

Aronowitz, Stanley and Giroux, Henri 1985: *Education under Siege: the Conservative, liberal, and radical debate over schooling.* London: Routledge and Kegan Paul.

Aymard, Maurice 1988: Sociologie et histoire. In Henri Mendras et Michel Verret (eds), *Les Champs de la sociologie française,* Paris: Armand Colin, 221–32.

Balazs, Gabrielle 1983: Les facteurs et les formes de l'expérience du chomage. *Actes de la recherche en sciences sociales,* 50, 69–83.

Bellah, Robert N. 1973: Introduction to Emile Durkheim, *On Morality and Society,* Chicago: University of Chicago Press, pp. ix–lv.

Berger, Bennett 1986: 'Taste and domination. *American Journal of Sociology,* 91, No. 6 (May), 1445–53.

Bidet, Jacques 1979: Questions to Pierre Bourdieu. *Critique of Anthropology,* 13–14 (Summer), 203–8.

Bidwell, Charles E. and E. Noah Friedkin, 1988: 'The sociology of education. In Neil J. Smelser (ed.), *The Handbook of Sociology,* Newbury Park: Sage, 449–71.

Boltanski, Luc 1969: *Prime éducation et morale de classe.* Paris and The Hague: Mouton.

——1987: *The Making of a Class: "cadres" in French society.* Cambridge: Cambridge University Press. First pub. 1982.

Bon, Francois and Schemeil, Yves 1980: La rationalisation de l'inconduite: comprendre le statut du politique chez Pierre Bourdieu. *Revue française de sociologie,* 30, no. 6, 1198–1230.

Boschetti, Anna 1988: *The Intellectual Enterprise: Sartre and "les temps modernes".* Evanston, Ill.: Northwestern University Press. First pub. 1985.

Boudon, Raymond 1986: *De l'idéologie: l'origine des idées reçues.* Paris: Fayard.

Bourdé, Guy and Martin, Hervé 1983: *Les écoles historiques.* Paris: Éditions du Seuil/Points.

Bozon, Michel 1984: *Vie quotidienne et rapports sociaux dans une petite ville de province: la mise en scène des différences.* Lyon: Presses Universitaires de Lyon.

Bredo, E. and Feinberg, W. 1979: Meaning, power, and pedagogy. *Journal of Curriculum Studies,* 11, no. 4, 315–32.

Broady, Donald and Persson, Olle 1989: Bourdieu i USA: Bibliometriska noteringar. *Sociologisk Forskning* (Stockholm), 26, no. 4, 54–73.

Brubaker, Rogers 1985: Rethinking classical sociology: the sociological vision of Pierre Bourdieu. *Theory and Society,* 14, No. 6 (Nov.), 745–75.

Caillé, Alain 1987: *Critique de Bourdieu.* Lausanne: Université de Lausanne, Institut d'anthropologie et de sociologie, "Cours, séminaires et travaux," no. 8.

Cam, Pierre 1981: *Les prud'hommes, juges ou arbitres? Les fonctions sociales de la justice du travail.* Paris: Presses de la Fondation nationale des sciences politiques.

Caro, Jean-Yves 1981: La sociologie de Pierre Bourdieu et du Centre de Sociologie Européenne. Appendix to *Le Champ de l'économie en France.* Paris, thesis for the Doctorat d'État, University of Paris.

—— 1982: *Les Économistes distingués*. Paris: Presses de la Foundation nationale des sciences politiques.

Casanova, Pascale 1990: Au bon plaisir de Pierre Bourdieu. Radio program broadcast on France Culture, 23 June 1990.

Castel, Robert 1988: *The Regulation of Madness*. Berkeley: University of California Press. First pub. 1976.

Champagne, Patrick 1990: *Faire l'opinion. le nouvel espace politique*. Paris: Éditions de Minuit ("Le sens commun").

—— Lenoir, Rémi; Merllié Dominique, and Pinto, Louis 1989: *Introduction à la pratique sociologique*. Paris: Dunod.

Charle, Christophe 1987: *Les Élites de la République, 1880–1900*. Paris: Fayard.

—— 1990: *Naissance des "intellectuels," 1880–1900*. Paris: Editions de Minuit ("Le sens commun").

Chartier, Roger 1988a: *Cultural History: between practices and representations*. Cambridge: Polity. Ithaca, N.Y.: Cornell University Press.

—— 1988b. L'histoire culturelle. In *L'Histoire en France*, Paris: Éditions La Découverte, 90–4.

Clark, Terry N. 1973: *Prophets and Patrons*. Cambridge, Mass.: Harvard University Press.

Coenen Harry 1989: Praxeologie en strukturatietheorie preliminaire opmerkingen bij een vergelijking. *Antropologische Verkenningen* 8–2 (Summer), 8–17.

Collins, Randall 1981: Cultural capitalism and symbolic violence. In *Sociology since Mid-Century: essays in theory cumulation*, New York: Academic Press, 173–82.

Combessie, Jean-Claude 1989: *Au sud de Despeñaperros: pour une économie politique du travail*. Paris: Éditions de la Maison des Sciences de l'Homme.

Connell, R. W. 1983: the black box of habit on the wings of history: reflections on the theory of reproduction. In *Which Way is Up? Essays on sex, class, and culture*, London: George Allen & Unwin, 140–61.

Dal Lago, Alessandro 1985: Il sociologo non temperato. *Rassegna Italiana di Sociologia*, 26, no. 1 (Jan.–Mar.), 79–89.

Delsaut, Yvette 1988a: Carnets de socioanalyse I: l'inforgetable. *Actes de la recherche en sciences sociales*, 74, 83–8.

—— 1989b: Carnets de socioanalyse II: une photo de classe. *Actes de la recherche en sciences sociales*, 75. 83–96.

Denzin, Norman K. 1986: Postmodern social theory. *Sociological Theory*, 4, no. 2 (Spring), 194–204.

Dews, Peter 1987: *Logics of Disintegration: post-structuralist thought and the claims of critical theory*. London: Verso.

DiMaggio, Paul 1979: Review essay on Pierre Bourdieu. *American Journal of Sociology*, 84, no. 6 (May): 1460–74.

Dobry, Michel 1986: *Sociologie des crises politiques*. Paris: Presses de la Fondation nationale des sciences politiques.

Douglas, Mary 1981: Good taste: review of Pierre Bourdieu, "La distinction." *Times Literary Supplement*, Feb. 13, 163–9.

Eagleton, Terry 1991: From Adorno to Bourdieu. In *Ideology: An introduction*, London: Verso, 125–58.

Eribon, Didier 1991: *Michel Foucault*. Cambridge, Mass.: Harvard University Press. First pub. 1989.

Fabiani, Jean-Louis 1989: *Les Philosophes de la République*. Paris: Éditions de Minuit ("Le sens commun").

Favre, Pierre 1988: Sociologie et science politique. In Mendras et Verret (eds) 1988, 233–44.

Ferry, Luc and Renault, Alain 1990: French Marxism (Pierre Bourdieu). In *French Philosophy of the Sixties: an essay on anti-humanism*, Amherst: University of Massachussetts Press, 153–84. First pub. 1986.

Frank, Arthur 1980: Review of *Outline of a Theory of Practice*. *Contemporary Sociology*, 9, no. 2 (Mar.), 256–7.

Gamboni, Dario 1989. *La Plume et le pinceau: Odilon Redon et la littérature*. Paris: Éditions de Minuit.

Garnham, Nicholas 1986: Extended review: Bourdieu's "Distinction." *Sociological Review*, 34, no. 2 (May), 423–33.

Gartman, David 1991: Culture as class symbolization or mass reification? A critique of Bourdieu's *Distinction*. *American Journal of Sociology*, 27, no. 2 (Sept.), 421–47.

Gaxie, Daniel 1990: Au-delà des apparences . . ., Sur quelques problèmes de mesure des opinions. *Actes de la recherche en sciences sociales*, 81-2: 97–113.

—— and Lehingue, P. 1984: *Enjeux municipaux*. Paris: Presses Universitaires de France.

Gerth, Hans and Wright Mills, C. (eds) 1946: *From Max Weber: essays in sociology*. New York: Oxford University Press.

Giroux, Henri A. 1983: *Theory and Resistance in Education: a pedagogy for the opposition*. New York: Bergin and Garvey.

Gorder, K. L. 1980: Understanding school knowledge: a critical appraisal of Basil Bernstein and Pierre Bourdieu. *Educational Theory*, 30, no. 4, 335–46.

Grignon, Claude 1971: *L'Ordre des choses: les fonctions sociales de l'enseignement technique*. Paris: Éditions de Minuit ("Le sens commun").

Halbwachs, Maurice 1992: *On Collective Memory*. Edited and with an introduction by Lewis Coser. Chicago: University of Chicago Press.

Hall, Stuart 1977: The hinterland of science: ideology and the "Sociology of knowledge." In Center for Contemporary Cultural Studies (ed.), *On Ideology*, London: Hutchinson, 9–32.

Harker, Richard K. 1984: On reproduction, habitus and education. *British Journal of Sociology of Education*, 5, no. 2 (June), 117–27.

——, Mahar, Cheleen and Wilkes, Chris (eds) 1990: *An Introduction to the Work of Pierre Bourdieu: the practice of theory*. London: Macmillan.

Heilbron, Johann 1988: Particularités et particularismes de la sociologie aux Pays-Bas. *Actes de la recherche en sciences sociales*, 74; 76–81.

Hoffman, Stanley 1986: Monsieur Taste. *New York Review of Books*, 33, no. 6 (Apr.), 45–8.

Inglis, R. 1979: Good and bad habitus: Bourdieu, Habermas and the condition of England. *Sociological Review*, 27,–no. 2, 353–69.

Ingram, D. 1982: The possibility of communication ethic reconsidered: Habermas, Gadamer and Bourdieu on discourse. *Man and World*, 15, 149–61.

Isambert, Francois-André 1984: *Le Sens du sacré: fête et religion populaire*. Paris: Éditions de Minuit ("Le sens commun").

Jauss, Hans Robert 1982: *Toward an Aesthetic of Reception*. Minneapolis: University of Minnesota Press.

Jenkins, Richard. 1989. "Language, symbolic power, and communication: Bourdieu's "Homo academicus." *Sociology*, 23, no. 4 (Nov.), 639–45.

Joppke, Christian 1986: The cultural dimension of class formation and class struggle: on the social theory of Pierre Bourdieu. *Berkeley Journal of Sociology*, 31, 53–78.

Karabel, Jerry and Halsey, A. H. (eds) 1977: *Power and Ideology in Education*. New York: Oxford University Press.

Karady, Victor 1982: The prehistory of present-day French sociology 1917–1957. In Charles C. Lemert (ed.), *French Sociology*: rupture and renewal, Columbia University Press, 33–47.

Kauppi, Niilo 1991: *Tel Quel: la constitution sociale d'une avant-garde*. Helsinki: The Finnish Society of Sciences and Letters ("Societas Scientiarum Fennica").

Kellner, Douglas 1990: The postmodern turn: positions, problems, and prospects. In George Ritzer (ed.), *Frontiers of Social Theory: the new synthesis*, New York: Columbia University Press, 255–86.

Lacroix, Bernard 1981: *Durkheim et le politique*. Paris: Presses de la Fondation nationale des sciences politiques.

Lakomski, G. 1984: On agency and structure: Pierre Bourdieu and J. C. Passeron's theory of symbolic violence. *Curriculum Inquiry*, 14, no. 2, 151–63.

Lamont, Michèle and Lareau, Annette P. 1988: Cultural capital: allusions, gaps, and glissandos in recent theoretical developments. *Sociological Theory*, 6, no. 2 (Fall), 153–68.

—— and Wuthnow, Robert 1990: Betwixt and between: recent cultural sociology in Europe and the United States. In George Ritzer (ed.), *Frontiers of Social Theory: the new synthesis*, New York: Columbia University Press, 287–315.

Lash, Scott 1990: Modernization and postmodernization in the work of Pierre Bourdieu. In *Sociology of Postmodernism*, London: Routledge, 237–65.

Lemert, Charles C. 1981: Literary politics and the "Champ" of French sociology. *Theory and Society*, 10, no. 5 (Sept.), 645–69.

—— 1986: French sociology: after the "patrons," what? *Contemporary Sociology*, 15, no. 5 (Sept.), 689–92.

—— 1988: Future of the sixties generation and social theory. *Theory and Society*, 17, No. 5, 789–807.

—— 1990: The habits of intellectuals: response to Ringer. *Theory and Society*, 19, no. 3 (June), 295–310.

Lévi-Strauss, Claude and Eribon, 1991: *Conversations with Claude Lévi-Strauss*. Chicago: University of Chicago Press. First pub. 1988.

Le Witta, Béatrix 1989: *Ni vue ni connue: approche ethnographique de la culture bourgeoise*. Paris: Éditions de la Maison des Sciences de l'Homme.

Lichterman, Paul 1989: Revisiting a Gramscian dilemma: problems and possibilities in Bourdieu's analysis of culture and politics. Paper presented at the Annual Meetings of the American Sociological Association, San Francisco.

MacLeod, Jay 1987: *Ain't No Makin' It: leveled aspirations in a low-income neighborhood*. Boulder, Colo.: Westview Press.

Maresca, Sylvain 1983: *Les Dirigeants paysans*. Paris: Éditions de Minuit ("Le sens commun").

Marin, Louis 1988: *Portrait of the King*. Minneapolis: University of Minnesota Press. First pub. 1981.

Mauger, Gérard and Fossé-Poliak, Claude 1983: Les loubards. *Actes de la recherche en sciences sociales*, 50, 49–67.

Mazon, Brigitte 1988: *Aux origines de l'École des hautes études en sciences sociales: le rôle du mécénat américain*. Paris: Éditions du Cerf.

Mendras, Henri and Verret, Michel (eds.). 1988: *Les Champs de la sociologie française*. Paris: Armand Colin.

Merquior, J. G. 1985: *Foucault*. Berkeley: University of California Press.

Miller, Don and Branson, Jan 1987: Pierre Bourdieu: culture and praxis. In Diane J. Austin-Broos (ed.), *Creating Culture: profiles in the study of culture*. Sydney: Allen & Unwin, 210–25.

Moulin, Raymonde 1987: *The French Art Market: a sociological perspective*. New Brunswick, N. J.: Rutgers University Press. First pub. 1965.

Muel-Dreyfus, Francine 1983: *Le Métier d'educateur: les instituteurs de 1900, les éducateurs spécialisés de 1968*. Paris: Éditions de Minuit ("Le sens commun").

Ortner, Sherry 1984: theory in anthropology since the 1960s. *Comparative Studies in Society and History*, 26, 126–66.

Ostrow, James M. 1990: *Social Sensitivity: an analysis of experience and habit*. Albany: State University of New York Press.

Perrot, Martyne and Soudrière, Martin de la 1988: Le masque ou la plume? Les enjeux de l'écriture en sciences sociales. *Informations sur les sciences sociales*, 27, no. 3 (Sept.), 439–60.

Pialoux, Michel 1979: Jeunes sans avenir et marché du travail temporaire. *Actes de la recherche en sciences sociales*, 26–7, 19–47.

Pinçon, Michel 1987: *Désarrois ouvriers*. Paris: L'Harmattan.

—— and Pinçon-Rendu, Monique 1989: *Dans les beaux quartiers*. Paris: Éditions du Seuil.

Pinto, Louis 1984: *L'Intelligence en action: le nouvel observateur*. Paris: Anne-Marie Métailié.

—— 1987: *Les Philosophes entre le lycée et l'avant-garde: les métamorphoses de la philosophie dans la France d'aujourd'hui*. Paris: L'Harmattan.

Pociello, Christian 1981: *Le Rugby ou la guerre des styles*. Paris: Anne-Marie Métailié.

Pollak, Michael 1988a: La place de Max Weber dans le champ intellectuel français. *Droit et société*, 9, 189–201.

—— 1988b: *Les Homosexuels et le SIDA: sociologie d'une épidémie*. Paris: Anne-Marie Métailié.

Poster, Mark 1975: *Existential Marxism in Postwar France: from Sartre to Althusser*. Princeton: Princeton University Press.

Pudal, Bernard 1988: Les dirigeants communistes. Du "fils du peuple" à "l'instituteur des masses." *Actes de la recherche en sciences sociales*, 71–2, 46–70.

—— 1989: *Prendre parti: pour une sociologie historique du PCF*. Paris: Presses de la Fondation nationale des sciences politiques.

Rabinow, Paul, 1985: Discourse and power: on the limits of ethnographic texts. *Dialectical Anthropology*, 10, 1–14.

Rancière, Jacques 1984: L'éthique de la sociologie. In *L'empire du sociologue*. Collectif "Révoltes Logiques" (ed.), Paris: Éditions La Découverte, 13–36.

Rasmussen, David 1981: Praxis and social theory. *Human Studies*, 4, no. 3 (July–Sept.), 273–8.

Rébérioux, Madeleine 1988: L'histoire sociale. In *L'Histoire en France*, Paris: Éditions La Découverte, 95–9.

Rhoads, John 1991: *Critical Issues in Social Theory*. University Park, Penn.: Pennsylvania State University Press.

Robbins, Derek 1988: Bourdieu in England. Unpublished typescript, School for Independent Study, North-East London Polytechnic.

Robinson, Robert V. and Garnier, Maurice A. 1985: Class reproduction among men and women in France: reproduction theory on its home ground." *American Journal of Sociology*, 91–2 (Sept.), 250–80.

Rose, Margaret A. 1991: *The Post-Modern and the Post-Industrial*. Cambridge: Cambridge University Press.

Rosenau, Pauline Marie 1991: *Post-Modernism and the Social Sciences: insights, inroads and intrusions*. Princeton, N. J.: Princeton University Press.

Sabour, M'hammed 1988: *Homo academicus arabicus*. Joensuu, Finland: University of Joensuu Publications in Social Sciences, no. 11.

Saint Martin, Monique de 1971: *Les Fonctions sociales de l'enseignement scientifique*. Paris and The Hague: Mouton.

Sayad, Abdelmalek 1991: *L'Immigration, ou les paradoxes de l'altérité*. Brussels: De Boeck Université.

Stamm, Anne 1983: La pensée symbolique: analyses, nostalgies et méfiances d'aujourd'hui. *L'Année sociologique*, 44, 217–29.

Steinrücke, Margareta 1989: Notiz zum Begriff der Habitus bei Bourdieu. *Das Argument*, 30, no. 1 (Jan.–Feb.), 92–5.

Suaud, Charles 1978: *La Vocation. conversion et reconversion des prêtres ruraux*. Paris: Éditions de Minuit ("Le sens commun").

Touraine, Alain 1988: Les écoles sociologiques. In *La Sociologie en France*, Paris: Éditions La Découverte, 26–41.

Van Parijs, Philippe 1981: Sociology as general economics. *European Journal of Sociology*, 22, no. 2, 299–324.

Verdès-Leroux, Jeannine 1978: *Le Travail social*. Paris: Éditions de Minuit ("Le sens commun").

—— 1983: *Au service du Parti: le Parti Communiste, les intellectuels et la culture (1944–1956)*. Paris: Minuit/Seuil.

Viala, Alain 1985: *Naissance de l'écrivain: sociologie de la littérature à l'âge classique*. Paris: Éditions de Minuit ("Le sens commun").

Wacquant, Loïc J. D. 1987: Symbolic violence and the making of the French agriculturalist: an inquiry into Pierre Bourdieu's sociology. *Australian and New Zealand Journal of Sociology*, 23, no. 1 (Mar.), 65–88.

—— 1989: Toward a reflexive sociology: a workshop with Pierre Bourdieu. *Sociological Theory*, 7, no. 1 (Spring), 26–63.

—— 1992: Toward a social praxeology: the structure and logic of Bourdieu's sociology. In Pierre Bourdieu and Loïc J.D. Wacquant, *An Invitation to Reflexive Sociology*, Chicago and Cambridge: The University of Chicago Press; Cambridge: Polity.

Wieviorka, Michel 1988: Les principes. In *La Sociologie en France*, Paris: Éditions La Découverte, 46–56.

Wilson, Elizabeth 1988: Picasso and pâté de foie gras: Pierre Bourdieu's sociology of culture. *Diacritics*, 18, no. 2. (Summer), 47–60.

Winkler, Joachim 1989: "Monsieur le Professeur!" Anmerkungen zur Soziologie Pierre Bourdieus. *Sociologia Internationalis*, 27, no. 1, 5–18.

Wuthnow, Robert 1989: *Communities of Discourse: ideology and social structure in the Reformation, the Enlightenment, and European socialism*. Cambridge, Mass.: Harvard University Press.

—— Hunter, James Davidson; Bergesen, Albert; and Kurzweil, Edith 1984: *Cultural Analysis*. Boston: Routledge and Kegan Paul.

Zarca, Bernard 1979: Artisanat et trajectoires sociales. *Actes de la recherche en sciences sociales*, 29, 3–26.

——1987: *Les Artisans, gens de métier, gens de parole*. Paris: L'Harmattan.

Zolberg, Vera 1986: Taste as a social weapon. *Contemporary Sociology*, 15, no. 4 (July) 511–15.

—— 1990: *Constructing a Sociology of the Arts*. Cambridge: Cambridge University Press.

Concluding Remarks: For a Sociogenetic Understanding of Intellectual Works

Pierre Bourdieu

In order to avoid giving too personal a turn to these concluding remarks or indulging in some form of narcissistic complacency, I would like, rather than taking up each point of disagreement one by one, to try to unearth the factors that seem to me to constitute their roots.

MISUNDERSTANDINGS RELATED TO THE INTERNATIONAL CIRCULATION OF IDEAS

There is first the logic of the international circulation of ideas, together with all the structural misunderstandings resulting from it. Texts, as we know, circulate without their contexts, that is, without the benefit of being accompanied by everything they owe to the social space within which they have been produced or, more precisely, to the space of possibilities (in this case, scientific) in relation to which they constructed themselves. It follows that the categories of perception and interpretation that readers apply to them, being themselves linked to a field of production subject to different traditions, have every chance of being more or less inadequate. There are cases, such as that of Heidegger's reception in France or, even closer at hand, that of "postmodernism," where it is the circulation itself that produces the whole reality of a cultural phenomenon through the accumulation of misunderstandings it generates, without either an object or a subject. Thus arises a huge collective artifact, transcendent to those who believe they are participating in its production and its reception and of whom it would be hard to say whether they are mystifiers or mystifieds, cynics or innocents. To prevent the cultural disjunctures due to the gap between different historical traditions from introducing misunderstanding at the very heart of even the most benevolent and welcoming communication, I believe it is necessary that all researchers concerned about the progress of their respective scientific fields ask of the sociology of science weapons against the social mechanisms capable of introducing distortions into scientific exchanges. In such matters, the implementation of the principle of *reflexivity* is one of the most efficient ways to put into practice the internationalism that science presupposes and promotes.

I would like to avoid at all costs taking up the role, quite unpleasant, objectively and subjectively, of critic of my critics. But I must, nevertheless, object to some of the reproaches that have been directed at me and which, moreover, rely on two opposing principles. Some of my readers "synchronize," in a way, different moments of my work (no doubt aided in this by the time lags and overlaps caused by discrepancies between the publication dates in the original language and translation). They thus uncover apparent contradictions that would vanish if they replaced each of the theses or hypotheses in question back in the movement, or even better, in the progress of my work; if, more precisely, they strove to reproduce the evolution (or the chain) of thought that led me to change progressively without for that ever effecting a resounding "self-critique" (I think here of the progress leading from the substantialist concept of class to the relational notion of class position, which was a crucial turning point, and thence to the notion of social space.)[1] Others, on the contrary, divide my work into fragments, atomize it, or, if one prefers, "postmodernize" it, in a way that ends up effecting a demolition similar to that achieved by the former treatment. In both cases, what is ignored, wittingly or not, is, first, the question of the mode of intellectual production that undergirds my research. Apprehending and comprehending this mode is the condition of an adequate reading, which weds itself, in a way, to the very movement of this research. There is also the question of the epistemological and social conditions under which (that is, at the same time, with which and against which) the intellectual project whose product is the work in question was elaborated. The *sociogenetic point of view* that, in my opinion, one must adopt towards any "creation of the mind" (whether it be Flaubert, Manet, or Heidegger), I am obviously inclined to expect of those who deal with my work – without ignoring the risks that it implies, particularly that of relativization.

MODUS OPERANDI: THE CASE OF THE STUDY OF MUSEUM
ATTENDANCE

I believe that, to avoid the risk of completely misunderstanding the purpose of my work, one must reposition oneself in the epistemological tradition that guides its *modus operandi*, that is, the mode of scientific production of which it is the product, namely, that which, breaking with common sense, makes the construction of the object the crucial moment of scientific research and refuses to dissociate the theoretical from the empirical, the analysis of the particular case conceived as a "particular case of the possible," in Bachelard's phrase, from the search for the invariant. I would like to show this in connection with the book entitled *The Love of Art*,[2] which of all my works is no doubt the one that most conforms to the positivist canon (even Paul Lazarsfeld appreciated it); but I could just as well have chosen any of my other works. Reading this book as a simple, self-contained description of the composition of the European museum-going public at a certain point in time or even as an attempt to propose a model of the frequency of visits to these shrines devoted to the conservation and exhibition of works of art (it does contain a mathematical model that accounts for the increase in and morphology of the museum-going public, at least up to this day) is to apply to it the very categories it strives to transcend, the principles of division it intends to abolish. It is to reduce the *real* object of research (which does not always allow itself to be apprehended on the basis of a single investigation and therefore of a single book) to the *apparent* object as a certain tradition, which for the sake of simplicity I will call positivist, defines it.[3]

It was necessary to break both with theoreticism and with nearsighted empiricism in order to raise, à propos a single, directly observable but theoretically constructed case, the question of the genesis and structure of aesthetic disposition and competence. The real purpose of my investigation of museum attendance was therefore to found a "sociology of artistic perception" (to recall the title of an article that I had published a few years before) on the basis of the empirical materials that sociological methods allowed me to produce, but that could have been obtained just as well by means of an historical study such as that done a few years later by art historian Michael Baxandall.[4] I had started to outline such a research during my stay at Princeton in the 1970s, and it is probable that the study I contemplated then (apart from the fact that it would have appeared infinitely more "chic" than the mildly vulgar dissection of the competencies and preferences of museum-goers) would have better brought out the historicity of the categories of perception, naively held to be universal and eternal, that we apply to a work of art; or, if one prefers, it would have made more apparent the social conditions of possibility of this *historical transcendental* that we call "taste" (that is, the unthought foundation of "pure" theories of art, whose paradigm is Kant's aesthetics). But it is also probable – vulgarity sometimes has its own virtues – that, due to the neutralization associated with historical distancing and cultural canonization, it would not have had the same impact as a *social (and political) rupture*. Uncovering the determining factors – economic and social – of the distribution of artistic dispositions and competencies, which the charismatic ideology of the "eye" demanded be reducible to a distribution of natural "gifts," forces us to recognize that the disinterested play of sensibility, the pure exercise of the faculty of feeling, in short, the use of the sensibility that Kant calls transcendental has definite historical and social conditions of possibility: aesthetic pleasure, this pleasure which "should be able to be felt by every man," is the privilege of those who have access to the conditions (that is to say, the social positions) in which the "pure" and "disinterested" disposition is able to constitute itself durably.[5]

But this study had something more at stake, at the same time more important and more invisible – all the more invisible since the then dominant norms of the scientistic positivism that Paul Lazarsfeld was working to impose everywhere in Europe at the time forced me to keep it hidden. I made mine the Cartesian formula *larvatus prodeo* for fear that the confession of such a theoretical – indeed, quasi-"philosophical" – ambition might ruin the scientific respectability that the rigor of the methodology and the power of the proposed mathematical model could avail me. I wanted, à propos the particular case of artistic perception, to try to clarify the specific logic of the "sensible" or practical knowledge (whose analysis I was pursuing, more or less simultaneously, with a very different empirical object: namely, Kabyle ritual). Alexandre Baumgarten used the term *gnoseologia inferior* to designate this theory of aesthetic perception as *perceptio confusa* and as a special form of knowledge which, although its logic is not that which rules the things of logic, also has its *logos*. In short, to found an adequate theory of artistic perception as a practical implementation of quasi-corporeal schemata that operate below the level of the concept (although they may be condensed in pairs of adjectives), it was necessary to break with the intellectualist conception that – even in the iconological tradition initiated by Panofsky, and especially in the semiological tradition then at its acme – tended to conceive the perception of a work of art as an act of decipherment, a *reading*, by an illusion typical of the *lector* (clergyman or professor – Trans.) spontaneously inclined to what Austin called the "scholastic bias."[6] It was necessary to found a science of aesthetic knowledge, a particular and privileged case of practical knowledge, as the science of the obscure and the confused, which is itself neither obscure nor confused. It was necessary, in other words, to create a theory of practice *as practice*, that is to say, as an activity premised on cognitive operations involving a mode of knowledge that is not that of theory, logic, or concept, without for all that being (as is often claimed by those who feel its specificity) a kind of mystical communion or ineffable participation.

This is without doubt the least finished aspect of my research program as far as *The Love of Art* is concerned. This is readily understandable if one has in mind all the obstacles, especially the social obstacles, which forbade me to transfer to the domain of art and artistic perception, the form *par excellence* of cultured practice, what I had been able to establish about the logic of practice after a detailed analysis (which kept me busy for several years) of the ritual practices of Kabyle peasants. (I must briefly mention here that by purely and simply disregarding in its entirety the chapter entitled "The demon of analogy," in which I demonstrate as thoroughly as possible the necessity of going beyond a structural analysis of the mythical-ritual system of the Kabyle in order to give a complete account of the specific logic of ritual practice, my commentators deprive themselves of both the empirical basis and the theoretical refinements of the analysis that I proposed.[7] They thus give themselves every opportunity to reduce these to a few simple or simplistic propositions, thereby made available for "theoretical" comparison with other "theories.") The analysis I have developed since, in the research I have conducted on the taxonomies in use in academic judgments, on critical discourse on art, or on political thought, have allowed me more precisely to describe the working of practical knowledge, of which aesthetic knowledge is but a specific case, and the social genesis of the classificatory schemata that are the basis of our preferences in the most diverse realms of existence.

I believe one would discover a similar discrepancy between apparent object and real object in my work on education, which extends into my ongoing research on the State. The analysis of social mechanisms that insure the differential elimination from the educational system of children from different social origins (as a result of the logic of the transmission of cultural capital) led to the discovery of the crucial role that the school system plays in the reproduction of the social order, not the only through the allocation of academic credentials commensurable (*grosso modo*) with inherited cultural capital, but also through the inculcation of mental structures and of dispositions (especially linguistic and cultural) universally recognized as legitimate within the boundaries of a (national) territory and adjusted to social structures. This fit between subjective structures and the objective structures that they help to produce is what creates the symbolic power wielded by the academic institution and, through it, by the institution which holds a monopoly over legitimate *symbolic* violence – namely, the State. The specific power of nominating (to positions or occupations, in particular) that belongs to the State functioning as a kind of central bank for symbolic capital resides, to an ever increasing degree, in the specific power of certification belonging to the academic institution and symbolized by academic titles – the true title of nobility in contemporary societies.

SOCIAL CONDITIONS OF PRODUCTION

Before considering other points of disagreement, which are, in my view, also based initially on a misunderstanding of my *modus operandi*, I would like very briefly to bring up the social conditions of the production and functioning of this *modus operandi*. By sketching out this sort of intellectual autobiography, I do not believe I am surrendering to some form of narcissism: on the contrary, by trying to act as an *informant* on the social conditions of the formation of my thought, I would like to serve as an example of and an encouragement to self-socioanalysis.

Even though I am not able to carry out this analysis in full here, I would like to sketch its main lines in bold strokes. First of all, my thought developed in relation to a particular field, both a national field, which has undergone continual transformation itself, and a worldwide field. As early as the 1960s, I proposed an analysis of the context in which my "intellectual project" took root.[8] I must say that this analysis has since been corroborated by empirical investigations and also, if one accepts such validation, by the subsequent history of the field. As a matter of fact, the pendular movement that the article described, which has led us from the anti-individualistic philosophy of the Durkheimians to a philosophy of the subject practised by phenomenologists and existentialists (Sartre, in particular) and later, in the 1960s, to a "philosophy without subject," as Ricoeur, defender of Christian personalism, characterized "structuralism," has moved once again towards a philosophy of the subject in the 1980s, with various strands of rational action theory and "methodological individualism," as well as the ideologues (including some historians, such as François Furet, and a few minor sociologists) who celebrate in the media the "return of the individual" and clamor for the "end of the thought of '68" – that is to say, of Marxism and structuralism conveniently conflated in the same irrevocable condemnation.

If I was able, in a way which seems to me to be rather "exact," to objectivize the field that I had just entered, it was undoubtedly because the highly improbable social trajectory that had led me from a remote village in a remote region of southwestern France to what was then the apex of the French educational system predisposed me to a particularly sharpened and critical intuition of the intellectual field.[9] More precisely, the anti-intellectualism inscribed in my dispositions of "class defector" (*transfuge*) disappointed by the reality of an intellectual universe idealized from afar, contributed to my breaking with the intellectual doxa and, if I may borrow a famous formula of Mao's, twisting the stick in the other direction (for example, by denouncing the conservative functions of a so-called liberating school) or, more precisely, to my realizing the fictitious character of the mundane oppositions that divided the intellectual field as, for example, with the opposition I evoked earlier between a philosophy of the subject and a philosophy "without subject," between the "humanism" of existentialism and the anti-humanism of structuralism, or, more precisely, between a radical subjectivism, incarnated by Jean-Paul Sartre, and a no less radical objectivism, represented by Lévi-Strauss, Foucault (with his provocative statements on the "death of man") and Althusser (who joyfully sacrificed the agents by reducing them to playing the mere role of "bearers" of the structure).

I think, without being able to prove it, that my propensity to anti-intellectualism, by progressively converting itself into a systematic will to bracket intellectual doxa – that is to say, the presuppositions that intellectuals accept as part of the background of their activity – was at the root of a series of more or less profound ruptures bound to shock, sometimes very profoundly, intellectuals. I am thinking in particular of the denunciation of populism, in all its forms, which often led (even in this very forum, to my great dismay) to my being denounced as a pessimist, or even as a conservative; or of the *making conspicuous* of practices testifying to the existence, in all categories of the dominated, of a certain form of submission (which is clearly not exclusive of a certain form of resistance) through which they contribute, to some degree, to their own domination. (I knew what I was exposing myself to at the very moment when I was writing the paragraph in *Distinction* devoted to "popular culture" as a properly intellectual myth, but I did so in spite of everything, because I felt that one day someone had to risk facing the disgrace incurred by those who violate the unwritten laws of their group in order to shed some truth on a very essential point.[10]) And I continue to believe that as much as, if not more than, conservatism, campus radicalism remains one of the main obstacles to the genuine breaks that social science must make with properly intellectual doxa, insofar as it allows certain intellectuals to give the appearance of radical critique to the most comfortable submission to intellectual conformity and, thereby, to a particularly well-hidden form of conservatism. (I could take as an illustration here certain falsely radical questionings of ethnographic writing which in fact do little more than parrot the thematic of the old philosophical critique of the social sciences.) Part of my innermost conviction in this matter is no doubt due to the fact that a good number of those who, in the name of Marxism, criticized my conservatism in the 1960s (accusing me then of being a Durkheimian, a Weberian, and so forth) have in the meantime joined the camp of conservatism and accuse me today of being a Marxist.

Among the illusions with which one has to break in order to help cure social science of its infantile disorders, there is also obviously the individual and/or collective narcissism that incites intellectuals to think of themselves as capable of thinking the world as a totality and that survives, in a more or less euphemized form, in social philosophies, in grand historical narratives, and so on. This criticism of the representation that intellectuals have of their own function and mission in history (I am thinking in particular of the myth of the "organic intellectual") and the discovery of the place they in fact occupy in social space – that of dominated among the dominant – were among the necessary conditions for an analysis of the powers derived from the possession of cultural capital – that is, the powers wielded by "professionals" and, more generally, by the State nobility (as well as what had been called the "new class" in the context of Soviet-style societies).[11] All these breaks, which are often ill received and, in any case, rarely carried out since they imply so many wounds inflicted on intellectual narcissism, have always seemed to me to be a prerequisite for a true knowledge of the social world.

THEORETICAL READINGS

Another major cause of misunderstanding is arguably the fact that, as a rule, non-French interpreters of my work, both anthropological and sociological, have offered a reading of it limited to its purely theoretical dimension. This has often led them to ignore its properly empirical dimension, as well as the contribution that my research brings to our knowledge of French society and, *mutatis mutandis,* of all modern societies. This ignorance, paradoxically, does not preclude a number of my critics from accusing me of limiting myself solely to the French case. In fact, as I have said hundreds of times, I have always been immersed in empirical research projects, and the theoretical instruments I was able to produce in the course of these endeavors were intended not for theoretical commentary and exegesis, but to be put to use in new research, be it mine or that of others. It is this *comprehension through use* that is most rarely granted to me, especially abroad – although more and more often I receive works that, instead of endlessly repeating commentaries and somewhat monotonous criticisms on habitus or some other concept of my making, are making use of a *modus operandi* closely related to mine. And I can only agree with Rogers Brubaker's analysis according to which what I aim to produce and transmit above all is a scientific habitus, a system of dispositions necessary to the constitution of the craft of the sociologist in its universality. The book entitled *The Craft of Sociology*[12] is a somewhat theoreticist version, owing to the effort made in it to clarify the basic principles of the scientific practice of the social sciences, of the teaching I give in practice, for pages upon pages, in all of my books in which I report on my research or in my research seminars. And, as I have also often said, the main function of certain fundamental concepts, such as those of habitus and field, and of the theoretical elaborations to which I submit them is to bring to the level of conscious awareness the dispositions that define "the sociological eye," to raise them to the order of a *method*, though I would not want the distinction between habitus and method to be used to create a new dualism: for if habitus, or craft (*métier*), becomes method through awareness, method turns into habitus, or craft, only through repeated and situated application.

If you will allow me an image true to the spirit of my theory of practice (and thus of scientific practice), I blame most of my readers for having considered as theoretical treatises, meant solely to be read or commented upon, works that, like gymnastics handbooks, were intended for exercise, or even better, for being put into practice; that is, as books that put forth so many programs for work, observation, and experimentation. This way of conceiving scientific work (absolutely irreducible to the kind of pure "theoretical work" that has come back into fashion this past decade in American social science and in all the countries still strongly dominated by it) was in perfect agreement with the conviction – which, from the very beginning, inspired my research strategies – that one cannot grasp the most profound logic of the social world unless one becomes immersed in the specificity of an empirical reality, historically situated and dated, but only in order to construct it as an instance (*cas de figure*) in a finite universe of possible configurations. Concretely, this means that an analysis of the social space of France around 1970 is *comparative history that takes as its object the present or comparative anthropology that applies itself to a particular cultural area*: in both cases, it is a question of grasping the *invariant*, the structure, behind each of the variations observed. (For example, I have never stopped transferring to my reasearch on French society – and not only in my early work on the peasantry of the Béarn region – the problems and concepts elaborated in regard to the Kabyles of Algeria, as with the concept of symbolic capital, originally designed to account for the logic of honor.)

This invariant does not show itself at first sight, especially if the gaze cast upon it is that of the lover of exoticism – that is, of *picturesque differences*. Armed with a knowledge of the structures and mechanisms that escape, although for different reasons, from indigenous and foreign notice alike, such as the principles of construction of social space or the mechanisms of reproduction of that space common to all societies (or to a subset of societies), the researcher, at once more modest and more ambitious than the curiosity-lover, proposes a constructed model that aims at *universal validity*.[13]

When I am accused of limiting myself to the specificity of the French case, it is because a realistic or substantivist reading is given to analyses that aim to be structural or, even better, relational (I refer here to the opposition established by Ernst Cassirer between "substantive concepts" and "functional or relational concepts"). A substantivist or realistic reading stops at practices (for example, playing golf) or consumptions (for example, Chinese cuisine) that the model attempts to account for and conceives the correspondence between social positions, or classes thought of as substantial entities, and tastes or practices as a mechanical, direct relation. Thus, on this naive reading, one is entitled to see a refutation of the model in the fact that – to give perhaps too facile an example for the sake of clarity – American intellectuals affect to like French cuisine, whereas French intellectuals prefer to patronize Chinese or Japanese restaurants; or even in the fact that luxury boutiques in Tokyo or on Fifth Avenue often have French names, whereas their counterparts in Paris's Faubourg Saint Honoré flaunt English names, such as "hairdresser."

The substantivist mode of thinking, which is that of common sense (as well as of racism, even when euphemized under the guise of a blindly ethnocentric sociology) and which tends to consider the activities or preferences of definite individuals or groups in a definite society at a definite point in time as substantial properties inscribed once and for all in a sort of *essence*, leads to the same mistakes in the case of comparison not across different societies but across time in the same society. Thus some will be able to see a refutation of the model put forth in *Distinction* – whose diagram presenting the correspondence between the space of constructed classes and the space of practices gives a vivid and synoptic representation – in the fact that, for instance, tennis and even golf are not as exclusively associated with dominant positions today as they once were; or in the fact that noble sports, such as horseback riding and fencing, are no longer the exclusive monopoly of the nobility, as they were at their inception. (The same can be said, in Japan, of the martial arts.) A practice initially considered noble may be abandoned by the nobility when, as is most often the case, it is taken up by a growing fraction of the bourgeoisie and petite bourgeoisie and maybe the popular classes – this is true of boxing in France, of which late nineteenth-century aristocrats were fervent practitioners. Conversely, an initially popular practice may be taken up for a time by the nobility. In short, one must be careful not to transform into necessary traits intrinsic to a particular group (the nobility or the samurais or factory workers or white-collar employees) the characteristics that they acquire at a given time due to the *position* they occupy in a determinate social space and in a determinate state of the *supply* of possible goods and practices. At every moment and in every society we are faced with a set of social positions bound through a relation of homology to a set of activities (playing golf or the piano) and goods (a vacation home or a masterpiece painting) that can themselves be characterized only relationally.

AN HISTORICIST ONTOLOGY

Another cause of misunderstanding lies in the tradition at once intellectualist and utilitarian (exemplified today by rational action theory) that is taken for granted – or adopted by default – by a good many social science researchers. This is why I might be tempted to accept the interpretation put forth by Hubert Dreyfus and Paul Rabinow, if only because it has the virtue of recording the fact (in my eyes essential) that I intend to break with the philosophy of action which haunts the unconscious of most sociologists. I would not, however, speak of an ontology, unless one is ready to accept the (truly oxymoronic) notion of an *historicist ontology*. As I demonstrated in an old article entitled "The dead seizes the living,"[14] being – that is to say, history – exists in the embodied state as habitus and in the objectified state as fields. Habitus being linked to the field within which it functions (and within which, as is most often the case, it was formed) by a relationship of ontological complicity, the action of the "practical sense" amounts to an immediate encounter of history with itself, through which time is engendered. The relation between habitus and the field through and for which it is created is an unmediated, infraconscious, practical relation of *illusio*, of investment, of interest in the game, which implies a sense of the game and a sense (with the twofold meaning of orientation, direction, and signification) of the history of the game; in short, a practical anticipation or inclination not to be mistaken for a conscious project or a calculated scheme. This investment, realized only in the relation between habitus and field, is the specific libido, the socially constituted and fashioned principle of every action. Both habitus and field (and also the specific form of capital produced and reproduced in this field) are the site of a sort of *conatus*, of a tendency to perpetuate themselves in their being, to reproduce themselves in that which constitutes their existence and their identity (for instance, in the case of the bourgeois habitus, the system of differences and distances constitutive of distinction). This I hold against a finalist, utilitarian vision of action which is sometimes attributed to me. It is not true to say that everything that people do or say is aimed at maximizing their social profit; but one may say that they do it to perpetuate or to augment their social being.[15]

In order to insure a modicum of coherence to my comments, I have taken up only the points of contention that seemed to me to be liable to clarification on the basis of the explanatory principles I stated at the outset. I have obviously ignored all the points of agreement, as well as all the numerous analyses, comments, and criticisms that have enlightened me on my own work and provided me with the powerful and efficacious tools I need to push further still the effort of reflexivity which seems to me to be the fundamental condition for the progress of scientificity in the social sciences.

Translated by Nicole Kaplan, Craig Calhoun, and Leah Florence

NOTES

1 See Bourdieu 1987f, 1985c.
2 Bourdieu *et al.* 1991b; first published in French, 1966.
3 See Judith Balfe, Déjà vu, all over again? *Contemporary Sociology* (March 1992, 152–53), for a paradigmatic instance. The same demonstration would apply, *mutatis mutandis*, to some of my other works that are liable to be misread in a monographic mode, such as *Homo Academicus* (1988b) or *La noblesse d'État* (1989c).
4 Bourdieu, 1968a; Michael Baxandall, *Painting and Experience in Fifteenth-Century Italy* (Oxford: Oxford University Press, 1972).

5 Bourdieu 1987c.
6 Bourdieu, 1990f.
7 Bourdieu, 1990e; first pub. in French, 1980.
8 Bourdieu and Passeron 1967.
9 Bourdieu 1989a.
10 Bourdieu, 1984; first pub. in French, 1979.
11 Bourdieu 1989c.
12 Bourdieu *et al.* 1991a; first pub. in French, 1968. Bourdieu and Wacquant 1992, part 3.
13 Bourdieu 1991d.
14 Bourdieu 1980d.
15 Bourdieu and Wacquant, 1992: 97–101, 115–40, and esp. 127–31.

Bourdieu Bibliography

Writings by Pierre Bourdieu are listed separately in this bibliography. We hope that this will make it easier to find references to his sources as well as make the references to individual chapters less cumbersome. The bibliography contains only works cited in the present volume. A fuller bibliography has been edited by Yvette Delsaut (*Bibliographie des travaux de Pierre Bourdieu, 1958–1988*, Paris, Centre de Sociologie Européenne du Collège de France, 1988, 39 pp., mimeo); a shortened version of this appears as an appendix to Bourdieu's *In Other Words* (Cambridge: Polity; 1990, 199–218).

WRITINGS BY PIERRE BOURDIEU

1964: The attitude of the Algerian peasant toward time. In Jesse Pitt-Rivers (ed.), *Mediterranean Countrymen*, Paris and The Hague: Mouton, 55–72.

1965: The sentiment of honour in Kabyle society. In J. G. Peristiany (ed.), *Honour and Shame: the values of Mediterranean society*, London: Weidenfeld and Nicholson, 191–241.

1966: Champ intellectuel et projet créateur. *Les Temps modernes*, Nov., 865–906.

1967a: Postface to Erwin Panofsky, *Architecture gothique et pensée scolastique*, trans. Pierre Bourdieu, Paris: Éditions de Minuit, 136–67.

1967b: Systems of education and systems of thought. *Social Science Information*, 14, no. 3, 338–58.

1968a: Outline of a sociological theory of art perception. *International Social Science Journal*, 10 (Winter), 589–612.

1968b: Structuralism and theory of sociological knowledge. *Social Research*, 35, no. 4 (Winter), 681–706.

1971a: Disposition esthétique et compétence artistique. *Les Temps modernes*, 295 (Feb.), 1345–78.

1971b: Genèse et structure du champ religieux. *Revue française de sociologie*, 12, no. 3 (July–Sept.), 294–334. Trans. as 1991a.

1971c: Intellectual field and creative project. Michael F. D. Young (ed.), *Knowledge and Control: new directions for the sociology of education*, London: Collier–Macmillan, 161–88. First pub. 1966.

1971d: Le marché des biens symboliques. *Année sociologique*, 22, 49–126.

1971e: Systems of education and systems of thought. In Michael F. D. Young (ed.), *Knowledge and Control*, London: Collier–Macmillan.

1972: *Esquisse d'une théorie de la pratique, précédé de trois études d'ethnologie kabyle*. Geneva: Droz.

1973a: The Algerian subproletariate. In I. W. Zartman (ed.), *Man, State, and Society in the Contemporary Maghrib*, London: Pall Mall Press, 83–9. First pub. 1962.

1973b: Cultural reproduction and social reproduction. In Richard Brown (ed.), *Knowledge, Education, and Cultural Change*, London: Tavistock, 71–112. First pub. 1971.

1973c: The three forms of theoretical knowledge. *Social Science Information*, 12, 53–80.

1974a: Avenir de classe et causalité du probable. *Revue française de sociologie*, 15, no. 1 (Jan.–Mar.), 3–42.

1974b: The school as a conservative force: scholastic and cultural inequalities. In John Eggleston (ed.), *Contemporary Research in the Sociology of Education*, London: Methuen, 32–46. First pub. 1966.

1975: The specificity of the scientific field and the social conditions of the progress of reason, trans. R. Nice. *Social Science Information*, 14, no. 6 (Dec.), 19–47.

1977a: The economy of linguistic exchanges. *Social Science Information*, 16, no. 6, 645–68.

1977b: Marriage strategies as strategies of social reproduction. In R. Foster and O. Ranum (eds.), *Family and Society: selections from the Annales*, Baltimore: Johns Hopkins University Press, 117–44. First pub. 1972.

1977c: *Outline of a Theory of Practice*, trans. R. Nice. Cambridge: Cambridge University Press. First pub. 1972.

1977d: Remarques provisoires sur la perception sociale du corps. *Actes de la recherche en sciences sociales*, 14, 51–54.

1979a: *Algeria 1960*, trans. R. Nice. Cambridge: Cambridge University Press.

1979b: Symbolic power. *Critique of Anthropology*, 13–14 (Summer), 77–85. First pub. 1977. Repr. in 1991b.

1979c: Les trois états du capital culturel. *Actes de la recherche en sciences sociales*, 30, 3–6.

1980a: The production of belief: contribution to an economy of symbolic goods. *Media, Culture and Society*, 2, no. 3 (July), 261–93.

1980b: *Questions de sociologie*. Paris: Éditions de Minuit.

1980c: *Le Sens pratique*: Paris. Éditions de Minuit. Trans as 1990e.

1980d: Le mort saisit le vif. Les relations entre l'histoire incorporée et l'histoire réifiée. *Actes de la recherche en sciences sociales*, 32–3, 3–14.

1981a: Épreuve scolaire et consécration sociale. Les classes préparatoires aux grandes écoles. *Actes de la recherche en sciences sociales*, 39 (Sept.), 3–70.

1981b: La représentation politique. Élements pour une théorie du champ politique. *Actes de la recherche en sciences sociales*, 37 (Feb.–Mar.), 3–24. Trans. in Bourdieu 1991b.

1982a: *Ce que parler veut dire: L'économie des échanges linguistiques*. Paris: Arthème Fayard.

1982b: *Leçon sur la leçon*. Paris: Éditions de Minuit. Trans. as "A Lecture on the Lecture" in Bourdieu 1990d.

1983a: The field of cultural production, or the economic world reversed. *Poetics*, 12 (Nov.), 311–56.

1983b: The philosophical establishment. In Alan Montefiore (ed.), *Philosophy in France Today*, Cambridge: Cambridge University Press, 1–8.

1984: *Distinction: a social critique of the judgment of taste*. Cambridge, Mass.: Harvard University Press; London: Routledge and Kegan Paul. First pub. 1979.

1985a: The genesis of the concepts of "habitus" and "field." *Sociocriticism*, 2, no. 2, 11–24.

1985b: The market of symbolic goods. *Poetics*, 14 (Apr.), 13–44. First pub. 1971.

1985c: Social space and the genesis of groups. *Social Science Information*, 24, no. 2, 195–220. Repr. in Bourdieu 1991b.

1986a: La force du droit. Éléments pour une sociologie du champ juridique. *Actes de la recherche en sciences sociales*, 64, 3–19. Trans. as 1987b.

1986b: The forms of capital. In John G. Richardson (ed.), *Handbook of Theory and Research for the Sociology of Education*, New York: Greenwood, 241–58. First pub. 1983.

1986c: From rules to strategies. *Cultural Anthropology*, 1, no. 1 (Feb.), 110–20. First pub. 1985.

1987a: *Choses dites*. Paris: Éditions de Minuit. Trans. as 1990d.

1987b: The force of law: toward a sociology of the juridical field. *Hastings Journal of Law*, 38, 209–48. First pub. 1986.

1987c: The historical genesis of a pure aesthetics. *Journal of Aesthetics and Art Criticism*, special issue on "Analytic Aesthetics", ed. Richard Schusterman, 201–10. Repr. in *The Field of Cultural Production: essays on art and literature*, ed. Randal Johnson. Cambridge: Polity, 1993.

1987d: Legitimation and structured interests in Weber's sociology of religion. In Sam Whimster and Scott Lash (eds.), *Max Weber, Rationality, and Modernity*, London: Allen and Unwin, 119–36.

1987e: Scientific field and scientific thought. Comparative Study of Social Transformation, Working Paper, University of Michigan, Ann Arbor, mimeo.

1987f: What makes a social class? On the theoretical and practical existence of groups. *Berkeley Journal of Sociology*, 32, 1–18.

1988a: Flaubert's point of view. *Critical Inquiry*, 14 (Spring), 539–62. Repr. in P. Desan, P. P. Ferguson and W. Griswold (eds.), *Literature and Social Practice*, Chicago: University of Chicago Press, 211–34.

1988b: *Homo Academicus*. Cambridge: Polity; Stanford: Stanford University Press. First pub. 1984.

1988c: On interest and the relative autonomy of symbolic power. *Working Papers and Proceedings of the Center for Psychosocial Studies*, no. 20. Chicago: Center for Psychosocial Studies. Repr. in 1990d.

1988d: *L'ontologie politique de Martin Heidegger*. Paris: Éditions de Minuit.

Trans. as *The Political Ontology of Martin Heidegger*. Cambridge: Polity; Stanford: Stanford University Press, 1991.

1988e: Program for a sociology of sport. *Sociology of Sport Journal*, 5, no. 2 (June), 153–61. First pub. 1987.

1988f: Vive la crise! For heterodoxy in social science. *Theory and Society*, 17, no. 5 (Sept.), 773–88.

1989a: Aspirant philosophe. Un point de vue sur le champ universitaire dans les années 50. In *Les Enjeux philosophiques des années 50*, Paris: Éditions du Centre Pompidou, 15–24.

1989b: Entretien sur la pratique, le temps et l'histoire. Interview with Tetsuji Yamamoto, unpublished manuscript.

1989c: *La noblesse d'État: grands corps et grandes Écoles*, Paris: Éditions de Minuit.

1990a: *Animadversiones in Mertonem*. In Jon Clark, Celia Modgil, and Sohan Modgil (eds.), *Robert K. Merton: Consensus and Controversy*, London: Falmer, 297–301.

1990b: Les conditions sociales de la circulation des idées. *Romanistische Zeitschrift für Literaturgeschichte*, 14, nos. 1–2, 1–10.

1990c: La domination masculine. *Actes de la recherche en sciences sociales*, 84, 2–31.

1990d: *In Other Words: essays toward a reflexive sociology*, trans. M. Adamson. Cambridge: Polity; Stanford: Stanford University Press. First pub. 1987.

1990e: *The Logic of Practice*, trans. R. Nice. Cambridge: Polity; Stanford: Stanford University Press. First pub. 1980.

1990f: The scholastic point of view. *Cultural Anthropology*, 5, no. 4 (Nov.), 380–91.

1991a: Genesis and structure of the religious field, *Comparative Social Research*, 13, 1–43. First pub. 1971.

1991b: *Language and Symbolic Power*, ed. with an introduction by John B. Thompson. Cambridge: Polity; Cambridge, Mass.: Harvard University Press.

1991c: Sport and social class. In Chandra Mukerji and Michael Schudson (eds), *Rethinking Popular Culture*, Berkeley: University of California Press, 367–73. First pub. 1978.

1991d: Social space and symbolic space: introduction to a Japanese reading of *Distinction*. *Poetics Today*, 12, no. 4, 627–38.

WRITINGS BY BOURDIEU AND CO-AUTHORS

Bourdieu and Boltanski, Luc 1977: Changes in social structure and changes in the demand for education. In *Contemporary Europe: social structures and cultural patterns*, Scott Giner and Margaret Scotford-Archer (eds.), London: Routledge and Kegan Paul, 197–227. First pub. 1973.

—— and Darbel, Alain 1966: La fin d'un malthusianisme. In Darras (ed.), *Le Partage des bénéfices, expansion et inégalités en France*, Paris: Éditions de Minuit, 135–54.

—— and Passeron, Jean-Claude 1963: Sociologues des mythologies et mythologies de sociologues. *Les Temps modernes*, 211 (Dec.), 998–1021.

—— and ——, 1967: Sociology and philosophy in France since 1945: death and resurrection of a philosophy without subject. *Social Research*, 34, no. 1 (Spring), 162–212.

—— and ——, 1977: *Reproduction in Education, Society and Culture*. London: Sage. Paperback edn. with new preface, 1990. First pub. 1970.

—— and —— 1979: *The Inheritors: French students and their relation to culture*. Chicago: University of Chicago Press. First pub. 1964.

—— and Saint Martin, Monique de 1974: Scholastic excellence and the values of the educational system. In John Eggleston (ed.), *Contemporary Research in the Sociology of Education*, London: Methuen, 338–71. First pub. 1970.

—— and —— 1990: Le sens de la propriété. La genèse sociale des systèmes de préférences. *Actes de la recherche en sciences sociales*, 81–2, 52–64.

—— and Sayad, Abdelmalek 1964: *Le Déracinement: la crise de l'agriculture traditionnelle en Algérie*. Paris: Éditions de Minuit.

—— and Wacquant, Loïc J. D. 1989: For a socioanalysis of intellectuals: on *Homo Academicus. Berkeley Journal of Sociology*, 34, 1–29.

—— and —— 1992: *An Invitation to Reflexive Sociology*. Chicago: University of Chicago Press; Cambridge: Polity.

—— and Darbel, Alain; Rivet, Jean-Pierre; and Seibel, Claude 1963: *Travail et travailleurs en Algérie*. Paris and The Hague: Mouton.

—— and Boltanski, Luc; Castel, Robert; and Chamboredon, Jean-Claude 1965a: *Un art moyen. Essai sur les usages sociaux de la photographie*. Paris: Éditions de Minuit. Trans. as *Photography: a middle-brow art*. Cambridge: Polity; Stanford: Stanford University Press, 1990.

—— and Passeron, Jean-Claude and Saint Martin, Monique de 1965b: *Rapport pédagogique et communication*. Paris and The Hague: Mouton. Trans. as *Academic Discourse: Linguistic Misunderstanding and Professorial Power*. Cambridge: Polity, 1992.

—— and Darbel, Alain, and Schnapper, Dominique 1966: *L'amour d'art. Les musées d'art européens et leur public*. Paris: Éditions de Minuit. Trans. as Bourdieu *et al.* 1991b.

—— and Chamboredon, Jean-Claude, and Passeron, Jean-Claude 1968: *Le Métier de sociologue*. Paris and The Hague: Mouton. Trans. as Bourdieu *et al.* 1991a.

—— and ——, and —— 1991a: *The Craft of Sociology: epistemological preliminaries*, ed. with a preface by B. Krais, trans. R. Nice. New York and Berlin: Aldine de Gruyter. First pub. 1968.

—— and Darbel, Alain, and Schnapper, Dominique 1991b: *The Love of Art: European Art Museums and Their Public*, trans. C. Beattie and N. Merriman. Cambridge: Polity; Stanford: Stanford University Press.

Index of Names

General Index